Bibliographical Essays

A TRIBUTE
TO
WILBERFORCE EAMES

Essay Index Reprint Series

BOOKS FOR LIBRARIES PRESS, INC.

FREEPORT, NEW YORK

First published 1924
Reprinted 1967

The Clerk of Breukelyn

A Clerk ther is of Breukelyn also,
Who unto historye went long ago.
He woot not if his fare be breed or cake,
So is he not right fat, I undertake.
Books been not oonly at his beddes heed,
But whyls thei piled bene upon his bedde,
And al his flores so thik thei heep and hide
That oon to crosse moste like an Yndian glide;
And al his bookes been of historyes
And viages and westerne colonyes.
Amonges them ful manye bene, I gesse,
That bere his name writ in theyr prefaces,
And manye a thank therto thise auctours leye
For that he plukt them out of errours weye.
And when he sekes his bookes atte night
With pen in honde his glosses to endite,
Then mote ye see, if ointed be youre eyn,
A gostly felawshipe aboute him schyn,
And all regarding him with frendly mein
As one to whom thei depe endetted bene,
Kepynge on lyf the light they lit of olde,
Their memorie that mennes hertes holde.
So Ptolemie unrolls his mappe-monde,
Columbus by him hath a globe in honde,
Where Raleigh draweth his Virginian lands;
With open Yndian Bible Eliot stands;
The New Town Psalmist lines his halting laies;
The Catechist his lampe of truthe displaies;
Last, Sabin by the Styx's gloomie tide
Implores him his unburied bones to hide
That he may crosse the fatal streme and dwelle
With Bibliographers in asphodel.
And yet our Clerk he loveth out-of-dore,

And wil not ryde but walketh evermore;
But derest holdeth he above al choises
The pley of children and theyr murye voyses,
And they aloon may lette him to scoleye.
God bless him and his bookes eke, I seye,
And kepe him long in hele and soules pees
That felawshipe and lerning may encrese!

Harry Lyman Koopman

Brown University Library
26 May, 1924

A LETTER OF EXPLANATION

MY DEAR DR. EAMES,

THREE of us sat at dinner last autumn, talking of the future of bibliography in America. Representatives of three generations were present — one has a reputation, such as it is, already made; another is recognized by those who are watching closely, but full achievement is in the future of early manhood; the third is newly entered in our field. We proposed various plans for coöperative effort to advance the interests of our chosen art and craft, and we discussed many ways and means and subjects. Then one said, "But the thing to do first of all is to make our homage to Wilberforce Eames."

This volume is the outcome of that conference. We did not stop to enquire when you will complete some decade of life or of service, for the years make no visible impression on you or on your work — it is only your influence that passing time affects. This grows steadily greater and more widely recognized. We wanted to do this and to do it at once, so that the field might be cleared with this as a permanent record of the appreciation of your personal influence, the influence which makes it possible to expect much of Bibliography in this country.

Those who have written these papers are not a carefully chosen few, but are rather those who found it possible to comply with the request for a contribution at once. Many others would have added their share at another time when pre-engagements were less imperative. The volume stands as it is, a record of representative work now being done. As such we offer it to you, as evidence of our affection and our respect, our common obligation to you for unlimited personal assistance, for unfailing inspiration, for unequalled standards, for *unwearied devotion to the ideals which make your life so perfect a model of scholarship. We all hope long to sit at your feet and call you Master.*

We ask you to accept this volume as our pledge of loyalty, from a band of your devoted disciples, on whose behalf this is written by

Yours most truly,

GEORGE PARKER WINSHIP

June, 1924

HONORARY DEGREES

Master of Arts
Harvard University, June 25, 1896

WILBERFORCE EAMES — Learned bibliographer, especially in Americana; studious of the subject-division of all knowledge, and of the means of keeping accessible multiplying stores of knowledge.

Doctor of Laws
University of Michigan, June 16, 1924

WILBERFORCE EAMES, of the New York Public Library, an authority in the literature dealing with the early history of America. Widely recognized and honored by his colleagues for his devotion to exacting standards of scholarship, for his notable contributions to learning, and for his profound influence in directing and inspiring research, he deserves, in eminent degree, this tribute to his distinction.

Doctor of Letters
Brown University, June 18, 1924

WILBERFORCE EAMES, of the New York Public Library, formerly Librarian of the Lenox Library, erudite scholar in realms of bibliography, whose accurate knowledge of rare books has enriched our generation and shown us the meaning of the ancient scripture, "Speak to the past and it shall teach thee."

Not the least pleasant experience in connection with the publishing of this book of homage was found in reading the letters of appreciation of Wilberforce Eames which accompanied the subscriptions. It is impossible to quote from these at length, but the following extract from the letter of a friend and associate of Mr. Eames, may be taken as expressing the feelings of the whole body of those who subscribed to the book.

"In making my contribution for the Wilberforce Eames memorial book, I am conscious of performing an act of real pleasure. That is due, of course, to the intimate friendship we had for many years. Wilberforce Eames is essentially a man of simplicity and sincerity. The things that men brag about in each other are usually not these, but rather wealth-getting, power, and self advertising. Mr. Eames has none of these. Eleven months of the year we work out our bibliographical problems in the most kindly coöperation; and he likes to check up his problems and discoveries with Mr. Elliott, Dr. Black, and myself. This is always done in the spirit of joyousness. Then in the Adirondacks, Mrs. Nichols and I have found him the most wholesome of companions over many, many miles of forest trails, struggling against storms in the open, and in the silent charm of the evening fireplace at camp. The world talks much of greatness, and is apt to heed those who publish the most. Those who know Mr. Eames intimately and have helped to solve many of the problems he has worked upon, have different ideas upon the subject of greatness.

Yours very truly,

L. Nelson Nichols"

LIST OF SUBSCRIBERS

The following names were received in response to a confidential announcement issued early in May, 1924, which was signed by George Parker Winship, Belle DaCosta Greene, Abraham S. W. Rosenbach, Victor Hugo Paltsits, Randolph Greenfield Adams, Lawrence Counselman Wroth.

The names of those whose contributions made the publication of this tribute possible are marked with an asterisk.

RANDOLPH G. ADAMS, William L. Clements Library.

ELMER ADLER, New York City.

ALDINE BOOK COMPANY (per HERMAN GOLD), Brooklyn.

FRANK ALTSCHUL, New York City.

AMERICAN ANTIQUARIAN SOCIETY, Worcester.

EDWIN H. ANDERSON, New York Public Library.

CLEMENT W. ANDREWS, John Crerar Library, Chicago.

FRANCIS R. APPLETON, New York City.

GEORGE A. ARMOUR, Princeton, New Jersey.

JOHN ASHURST, The Free Library of Philadelphia.

EDWARD E. AYER,* Chicago.

ALBERT C. BATES, Connecticut Historical Society.

MABEL F. BARNES, Harvard College Library.

HENRIETTA C. BARTLETT, New York City.

W. GEDNEY BEATTY, New York City.

WILLIAM BEER, Howard Memorial Library, New Orleans.

CHARLES FRANCIS DORR BELDEN, Boston Public Library.

W. E. BENJAMIN, New York City.

WILLIAM WARNER BISHOP, University of Michigan Library.

GEORGE W. BLACK, New York Public Library.

BOSTON PUBLIC LIBRARY.

R. R. BOWKER, New York City.

MORGAN B. BRAINARD, Hartford, Connecticut.

THE BRICK ROW BOOK SHOP, New York City.

CLARENCE S. BRIGHAM, American Antiquarian Society.

CLARA P. BRIGGS, Harvard College Library.

BRADFORD BRINTON, New York City.

BRITISH MUSEUM, Department of Printed Books, London.

BROOKLYN PUBLIC LIBRARY.

HENRY J. BROWN, London.

JOHN CARTER BROWN LIBRARY.

JOHN NICHOLAS BROWN, Providence.

BROWN UNIVERSITY LIBRARY.

WALTER L. BROWN, Buffalo Public Library.

HENRY L. BULLEN, Typographic Library, Jersey City.

CARL L. CANNON, New York Public Library.

FRANK CARNEY, Harvard College Library.

CHESTER M. CATE, Henry E. Huntington Library.

HOWARD M. CHAPIN, Rhode Island Historical Society.

CHICAGO PUBLIC LIBRARY.

JAMES BENNETT CHILDS, John Crerar Library, Chicago.

CLIFFORD B. CLAPP, Henry E. Huntington Library.

WILLIAM L. CLEMENTS, Bay City, Michigan.

WILLIAM L. CLEMENTS LIBRARY, Ann Arbor, Michigan.

CLEVELAND PUBLIC LIBRARY.

CLUB OF ODD VOLUMES, Boston.

GEORGE WATSON COLE, Henry E. Huntington Library.

ALLEN COLLIER, Cincinnati.

FRANKLIN CONKLIN, JR., Newark, New Jersey.

CONVERSE MEMORIAL LIBRARY, Amherst College.

MAUDE E. C. COVELL, Barrington, R. I.

ROBERT ERNEST COWAN, San Francisco.

FREDERICK COYKENDALL, New York City.

VERNER W. CRANE, Brown University.

ERNEST CROUS, Berlin.

DARTMOUTH COLLEGE LIBRARY.

HIRAM E. DEATS, Flemington, N. J.

HENRY F. DEPUY, Maryland.

ROBERT H. DODD, New York City.

JAMES F. DRAKE, New York City.

DREXEL INSTITUTE LIBRARY, Philadelphia.

DUNSTER HOUSE BOOKSHOP, Cambridge, Mass.

EDWARD EBERSTADT, New York City.

GEORGE SIMPSON EDDY, New York City.

JOHN HENRY EDMONDS, Massachusetts State Archives.

FREDERICK W. FAXON, Boston.

OTTO FLEISCHNER, Brighton, Mass.

WORTHINGTON C. FORD, Massachusetts Historical Society.

WILLIAM E. FOSTER, Providence Public Library.

GEORGE S. GODARD, Connecticut State Library, Hartford.
CHARLES E. GOODSPEED, Boston.
GRAND RAPIDS PUBLIC LIBRARY.
RUTH S. GRANNISS, Grolier Club, New York City.
DOROTHY HENDERSON GRAY, John Carter Brown Library.
BELLE DACOSTA GREENE, Pierpont Morgan Library.
THE GROLIER CLUB, New York City.
CHARLES H. HAMILL, Chicago.
JOHN W. HANCOCK, Roanoke, Virginia.
LATHROP C. HARPER,* New York City.
MARION V. HARRISON, Montclair, N. J.
MAX HARZOF, New York City.
ADELAIDE R. HASSE, Washington, D. C.
CHARLES F. HEARTMAN, Metuchen, N. J.
STAN. V. HENKELS, Philadelphia.
SAMUEL HENSHAW, Cambridge, Mass.
KARL W. HIERSEMANN, Leipzig.
FRANK P. HILL, Brooklyn Public Library.
THOMAS J. HOLMES, Cleveland.
HENRY S. HOWE, Boston.
JOHN HOWELL, San Francisco.
LUCIUS L. HUBBARD, Houghton, Michigan.
HENRY E. HUNTINGTON, San Gabriel, California.
CHARLES L. HUTCHINSON, Chicago.
JOHNS HOPKINS UNIVERSITY LIBRARY.
HERSCHEL V. JONES, Minneapolis.
MATT B. JONES, Boston.
RUDOLF JUCHHOFF, Berlin.
GRENVILLE KANE,* New York City.
LOUIS C. KARPINSKI, University of Michigan.
CARL T. KELLER, Boston.
WILLIAM G. KELSO, JR., Brooklyn.
MITCHELL KENNERLEY, New York City.
HENRY W. KENT, Metropolitan Museum.
ANDREW KEOGH, Yale University Library.
GEORGE L. KITTREDGE, Harvard University.
THEODORE L. KOCH, Northwestern University Library.
HARRY LYMAN KOOPMAN, Brown University Library.
GEORGE F. KUNZ, New York City.
WILLIAM COOLIDGE LANE, Harvard College Library.

MARSHALL C. LEFFERTS, New York City.

NICOLAS LEON, City of Mexico.

ALICE H. LERCH, New York Public Library.

H. C. LEVIS, London.

LIBRARY OF CONGRESS, Washington, D. C.

WALDO LINCOLN, Worcester, Mass.

MRS. ARTHUR LITCHFIELD, New York City.

FLORA V. LIVINGSTON, Harry Elkins Widener Library.

I. FERRIS LOCKWOOD, New York Public Library.

GERHARD R. LOMER, McGill University Library.

ARTHUR LORD, Boston.

MILTON E. LORD, Harvard University Library.

LOS ANGELES PUBLIC LIBRARY.

HARRY MILLER LYDENBERG, New York Public Library.

CHARLES W. McALPIN, New York City.

J. C. McCOY,* Grasse, France.

LEONARD L. MACKALL, Savannah, Georgia.

ALFRED B. MACLAY, New York City.

DOUGLAS C. McMURTRIE, New York City.

CHARLES MARTEL, Library of Congress.

ALEXANDER MARX, Jewish Theological Seminary, New York.

WILLIAM S. MASON, Evanston, Illinois.

MASSACHUSETTS HISTORICAL SOCIETY.

WILLIAM GWYNN MATHER, Cleveland.

ALBERT MATTHEWS, Boston.

JOSÉ TORIBIO MEDINA, Santiago de Chile.

CHARLES E. MERRILL, Jr., New York City.

PERCIVAL MERRITT,* Boston.

G. MICHELMORE, London.

MINNEAPOLIS ATHENAEUM.

MINNESOTA HISTORICAL SOCIETY, St. Paul.

JOHN PIERPONT MORGAN,* New York City.

PIERPONT MORGAN LIBRARY, New York City.

NOAH F. MORRISON, Elizabeth, New Jersey.

JOHN HENRY NASH, San Francisco.

NEWARK PUBLIC LIBRARY.

NEWBERRY LIBRARY, Chicago.

DANIEL H. NEWHALL, New York City.

A. EDWARD NEWTON, Philadelphia.

NEW YORK HISTORICAL SOCIETY.

New York Public Library.
New York Public Library School.
New York State Library, Albany.
Charles L. Nichols, Worcester.
L. Nelson Nichols, New York Public Library.
Martinus Nijhoff, The Hague, Holland.
Ernest Dressel North, New York City.
Stephen H. Olin, Rhinebeck, New York.
John Clyde Oswald, New York City.
Victor Hugo Paltsits, New York Public Library.
Francis H. Parsons, Library of Congress.
Peabody Institute Library, Baltimore.
Harold Pierce, Philadelphia.
Arthur Pforzheimer, New York City.
Carl H. Pforzheimer, New York City.
George A. Plimpton, New York City.
Henry R. Plomer, London.
Alfred W. Pollard, London.
Princeton University Library.
Providence Athenaeum.
Providence Public Library.
Bernard Quaritch, Ltd., London.
Paul North Rice, New York Public Library.
Ernest Cushing Richardson, Princeton University Library.
Gertrude E. Robson, John Carter Brown Library.
Azariah Smith Root, Oberlin College Library.
A. S. W. Rosenbach,* Philadelphia.
Harold G. Rugg, Hanover, N. H.
Joseph F. Sabin, New York City.
St. Louis Public Library.
George H. Sargent, Warner, N. H.
John H. Scheide, Titusville, Pennsylvania.
Edward W. Sheldon,* New York City.
William Green Shillaber, Boston.
Thorvald Solberg, Library of Congress.
Rebecca P. Steere, Providence.
John B. Stetson,* Jr., Philadelphia.
Henry N. Stevens, London.
Margaret Bingham Stillwell, Annmary Brown Memorial.
I. N. Phelps Stokes,* New York City.

EDWARD L. STONE, Roanoke, Virginia.

WILBUR M. STONE, New York City.

THOMAS W. STREETER,* New York City.

HENRY C. STRIPPEL, New York Public Library.

GERTRUDE M. SULLIVAN, Harvard College Library.

ARTHUR SWANN, American Art Association, New York City.

HENRY F. TAPLEY, Boston.

LEWIS M. THOMPSON, New York City.

ADA THURSTON, New York City.

MILDRED M. TUCKER, Harvard College Library.

EDWARD TURNBULL, Walpole Galleries, New York City.

CHARLES E. TUTTLE, Rutland, Vermont.

JULIUS H. TUTTLE, Massachusetts Historical Society.

TYPOGRAPHIC LIBRARY AND MUSEUM, Jersey City.

UNIVERSITETS-BIBLIOTEK, Uppsala, Sweden.

UNIVERSITY OF CALIFORNIA LIBRARY.

UNIVERSITY OF ILLINOIS LIBRARY.

UNIVERSITY OF NEBRASKA LIBRARY.

GEORGE B. UTLEY, The Newberry Library, Chicago.

WILFRED M. VOYNICH, New York City.

HENRY R. WAGNER,* Berkeley, California.

M. HANNAH WAIT, Harvard College Library.

MILTON S. WALDMAN, London.

ALEXANDER J. WALL, New York Historical Society.

FRANK WALTERS, New York City.

BEATRICE BECKER WARDE, Typographical Museum, Jersey City.

OSCAR WEGELIN, New York City.

LEMUEL A. WELLES, New York City.

GABRIEL WELLS,* New York City.

WESLEYAN UNIVERSITY LIBRARY.

WILLIAM A. WHITE, New York City.

JAMES B. WILBUR,* Manchester, Vermont.

GEORGE PARKER WINSHIP, Harry Elkins Widener Library.

GRENVILLE LINDELL WINTHROP, Lenox, Mass.

JOHN WOODBURY, Boston.

JOHN M. WOOLSEY, New York City.

WORCESTER PUBLIC LIBRARY.

LAWRENCE C. WROTH, John Carter Brown Library.

CONTENTS

TABLE OF CONTENTS

BIBLIOGRAPHICAL ESSAYS

WILBERFORCE EAMES

A BIO–BIBLIOGRAPHICAL NARRATIVE

By VICTOR HUGO PALTSITS

*Chief of the American History Division and Keeper of Manuscripts in the
New York Public Library*

THE paternal great-grandfather of Wilberforce Eames
was Jacob Eames, born in Wilmington, Massachusetts,
on March 10, 1755. Wilmington, some fifteen miles north of
Boston, was a section of Woburn which had been set off in
1730. When Jacob was a mere child his father was engaged in
the last intercolonial war, from which he did not return. He
was left in these tender years to the care of his mother, Mrs.
Abigail (Buck) Eames. Before he had attained his majority,
Jacob marched to Lexington and participated in that battle of
the American Revolution. From Wilmington he went to Chester, New Hampshire, and in 1784 removed to Belfast, Maine,
settling on one of the lots in what is now Searsport, which he
cleared for his farm. After some years he sold this farm and
settled on a farm at the Narrows, or Upper Bridge, where he
built a large two-story house that was still standing more than
a century later. It was here, in 1801, that he was one of the in-
corporators of "The Belfast Bridge Company," which built a
toll-bridge across the Narrows on the Passagassawakeag River,
about a mile from the river's mouth. In 1804, he pushed farther north to Swanville, there clearing his third farm. Here he
continued to live until he died, on November 7, 1851, aged
nearly ninety-seven years. His life was noted for its remarkable energy and industry; even in his later years he kept himself employed. At the time of his death there were living of his
descendants eleven of his fifteen children, seventy-one grand-
children, one hundred and nineteen great-grandchildren, and

two great-great-grandchildren, a total of two hundred and three living souls. He had been married three times, first to Jenny McKeen, who died on February 28, 1792. By this union he had seven children, the fourth of whom was John, born at Belfast, Maine, on July 16, 1786, who died at Jackson on September 13, 1839. John married Sarah, called Sally, daughter of Samuel and Sarah [1] Matthews, of Prospect, who had been born at Castine, on January 17, 1790,[2] and died at Jackson in 1856. There were seven children of this union, the third of whom was Nelson, father of Wilberforce.

Nelson Eames was born at Jackson, in the northern part of Waldo County, Maine, on March 21, 1821, and died at Brooklyn, New York, on January 1, 1902. He married Phoebe Harriet Crane,[3] of Orange, New Jersey, born on February 28, 1822, and died at Brooklyn, New York, on March 2, 1892. Besides Wilberforce, they had a second son, Edward Clarendon, born on September 28, 1858, who died on August 27, 1867. Nelson Eames, having reached his majority in 1842, taught school at Prospect, Maine, for two months, and then spent a month on a visit to Cambridge, Massachusetts. From May to November, 1843, he continued his education at Belfast, expect-

1. Mrs. Matthews, born at Groton, Mass., in 1769, died at Searsport, Maine, in 1851, was a daughter of Oliver and Sarah Parker, and on her mother's side was related to the Worcesters. Her father was many years a judge of the court of common pleas for Hancock County, Maine. — A Mother in Israel, sermon by Stephen Thurston (Boston, 1853).

2. This record is confirmed by the original sampler made by her, still in the possession of Wilberforce Eames. Besides the alphabet and a few numbers, it reads thus: "Sally Matthews is my Name and English is my Nation, Prospect is my dwelling place and Christ is my Salvation. Sally M. B. the Year 1790 January the 17."

3. Her oldest brother, Aaron Crane, was a noted maker of clocks that ran a year without rewinding. A specimen of his handiwork, still a going clock, is owned by the New York Historical Society, to which Mr. Wilberforce Eames presented an original daguerreotype portrait of his uncle. This portrait shows him with one of his clocks at his side. Mr. Eames also had a grand-uncle on his father's side, Jacob Eames, who graduated from Boston University, studied law at Belfast, Maine, and died at Boston.

ing thereafter to teach there, but did not secure the appointment. He remained at home for a year, and in December, 1844, went to Islesboro, on Long Island, in Penobscot Bay, where he kept school two months. From April to July, 1845, he worked on a farm at Danvers, Massachusetts, and then, from 1845 till 1846, he taught school at Jackson, Maine, working on the home farm the latter summer, and that autumn he went to Hartford, Connecticut. From the close of 1847 to 1848 he taught at Belfast, and then visited Asa Matthews, an uncle, at Newport, Maine. Thereafter he went to study at Hampden and visited Bangor Seminary. At Stillwater, Maine, he kept school for a part of 1848–1849, and for some months after that studied and spent some time at Bangor, Portland, and Gorham. In October, 1849, he began to teach at Scarboro, Maine, but in January, 1850, removed to Secaucus, New Jersey, where he taught in a school for two years, afterwards teaching in other places in New Jersey until his removal to Brooklyn, New York, at the beginning of the Civil War.

Wilberforce Eames was born in Newark, New Jersey, on October 12, 1855. When he was six years of age his parents left New Jersey and settled in Brooklyn, New York, where he has ever since resided. His home environment was of the simple yet sturdy New England type which his ancestors had cultivated — untouched by levity, concerned with the more enduring aspirations, and "enriched with virtue's rights." The writer's remembrance of both parents in the sanctuary of this home-circle is still vivid after the lapse of many years. We have seen that his father had been a country schoolmaster in Maine and New Jersey. It was therefore a natural act when Wilberforce, as a mere child, was given one of Marcius Willson's series of primers and readers, from which he learned how to read. He first went with his brother to a private school in Brooklyn at the age of nine years; none the less he had already learned to read, up to Willson's 'Third Reader.' To this series of readers he says he was indebted for his introduction to the gentle art of reading and for his original interest in books. In the Brooklyn private school he continued for a short time; but in 1867 or 1868 attended the public school of the East New York neighborhood, and after that always worked.

Those were not days of night schools. Minors commonly left school at an early age to "go to work," and there were no available educational facilities for them. Moreover, hours of labor were not short and weekly half-holidays were unknown. It required mettle and initiative in a lad to keep aglow a thirst for knowledge. For a while after 1868, Mr. Eames performed at a boy's job in his neighborhood. During the first half of the year 1870 he learned the art of printing in the office of the *East New York Sentinel*, a weekly newspaper of his neighborhood, which was issued on Saturday mornings. The whole plant consisted of the owner, his daughter — a mere child — and the lad Wilberforce Eames. The printing was done on a Franklin hand-press. He set type, handled the ink-roller during the printing, cleaned type and press, redistributed type, in short, performed all kinds of jobs there.

It was in this period that Mr. Eames had borrowed some books from his East New York neighbors. Among these books were Rollin's 'Ancient History,' Gibbon's 'Roman Empire,' and Hume's 'England'; and from these, as well as such books as the 'Edinburgh Encyclopædia,' in sixteen octavo volumes, and histories of continental Europe and of England, he made for himself an historical chronology. He then became more interested in Egypt and went with his mother on a special trip to Manhattan to buy a copy of Herodotus, in 1868 or 1869, at the then well-known bookstore of William Gowans, who, when he died in 1870, left a stock of nearly 300,000 volumes. Mr. Eames had done all this before he attained his fifteenth year, and then, in this same year, 1870, he had entered the employ of the post-office.

He served as a post-office clerk, although actually hired as a mail-carrier, in the East New York district, from 1870 to 1873. Most of his time was spent at the stamp-window, but he also took the mail-bag from East New York to the Brooklyn post-office. It was while waiting for the return mail-bag to be made up, that he would go out and visit a neighboring bookstore, which was about a block distant from the Brooklyn post-office, and in these moments he looked over and got acquainted with the books and also made the acquaintance of this bookseller, by whom he was three years later employed as a clerk on his own application for the job. It was a supreme ambition which sought to know and sell books instead of postage stamps, to meet face to face the patrons of a bookstore in the heart of the city of Brooklyn, instead of looking at the faces of postage stamps and of the patrons of a post-office.

This bookstore was the only one in Brooklyn that had a large stock, then about twenty thousand volumes. It was owned by Edward R. Gillespie and located on Myrtle Avenue. Among this stock was a set of the 'Universal History,' in sixty-five volumes, published in the eighteenth century. From it Mr. Eames copied largely by hand, with the bookseller's permission; and finally, at great sacrifice to himself, out of his negligible means, he bought the whole set for thirty-five dollars on instalments, and was filled with unbounded joy. This set the writer remembers very well, because he was privileged to borrow volumes from Mr. Eames more than thirty years ago.

It was in 1873 that Mr. Eames became a clerk in the Gillespie bookstore, where he remained until 1879. About 1874, he had the good fortune to meet there Thomas W. Field, compiler of the 'Indian Bibliography,' a work published in the previous year, which was also the year in which Field had been appointed superintendent of public schools in Brooklyn. Mr. Eames purchased a copy of Field's 'Bibliography,' and with it began his interest in the American Indians and Americana.

Now he occasionally bought items in these classes. Gillespie kept open shop until nine o'clock at night, and his place was a rendezvous for bibliophiles, and for booksellers of Manhattan and elsewhere, whose shops closed at a more reasonable hour. From listening to the bibliophilic conversations of these men about their hobbies, Mr. Eames was infected with many new interests in the realm of books and learning. Among them was E. W. Nash, at one time a clerk in Gowans's great bookstore on Nassau Street, Manhattan, who had gone into business on his own account. It was Nash who had sold Mr. Eames the copy of Herodotus already referred to. From Nash's stock now he secured his earliest accessions of books on the American Indians, and a little later, from E. P. Boon, also of Manhattan, he bought many pamphlets on the Indians. Another frequenter of the Gillespie shop was George P. Philes, in his day among the best of American bibliographers, and editor of the *Philobiblon*. Another was Daniel G. Treadwell, from whom Mr. Eames absorbed an interest in oriental books.

From Gillespie he went, in 1879, to N. Tibbals and Sons, at 37 Park Row, Manhattan, with whom he remained until about 1881. The Tibbals house specialized in theological books and also handled a general book stock. Here Mr. Eames learned the general business in new books and acquired a knowledge of the new lists of publishers. He also went around to the publishers to get in the new stock for his employers. Another feature of his work with the Tibbals firm was to attend for them the book auctions at George A. Leavitt and Co's and Bangs's, both in New York City. For his firm he also went to the Sing Sing and the Asbury Park Methodist Episcopal camp-meetings, where he set up and conducted a bookstand in the open air or in a tent. At this stand he also sold the daily newspapers during the period of the camp-meetings. The counter of his improvised stand was cleaned up of its stock at night and served him as a bed until readorned with the wares in the morning.

His recollections of these camp-meetings form a singularly entertaining story. It was while at these meetings that Mr. Eames met two interesting persons, one being Louis Klopsch, editor of the *Christian Herald*, for whom he took in subscriptions; the other was Alfred William Dennett, the well-known founder of that then unique chain of restaurants in New York City, famous for its "surpassing coffee" and for the framed Bible verses which decorated the walls of his establishments. Dennett was also the founder of rescue missions for men. He attended the camp-meetings, and, a sectarian book which he wished to have circulated having been published, it was sold for him at the book-stand.

Mr. Eames first met at Tibbals's, about 1880, the late James Constantine Pilling, who was then engaged in preparing a card-catalogue of North American Indian linguistics "for the use of the members of the Bureau of Ethnology" at Washington, a work which saw print in 1885 as 'Proof-Sheets of a Bibliography of the Languages of the North American Indians,' a ponderous volume of more than a thousand pages, issued in one hundred copies only, principally for the use of collaborators. From their first meeting they were firm friends, and Mr. Eames was Pilling's chief co-laborer in his various bibliographical undertakings. In the 'Proof-Sheets' Pilling said: "Almost from the beginning of the type-setting the catalogue has had the benefit of his aid and advice. His thorough knowledge of the class of books treated, his interest in the subject itself, his fine library, rich in bibliographic authorities, his scrupulous care and accuracy with the minutiæ which compose so large a part of a work like this, and his judgment in matters of arrangement, have all rendered his coöperation invaluable. The frequent mention of his name throughout shows but imperfectly the extent of my obligations to him." This obligation grew as Pilling's monographs on the Algonquian, Iroquoian, and other linguistic families were being prepared, toward which Mr.

Eames contributed whole sections, indeed many of the best
and most difficult to study, such as Eliot, Lykins, Mather,
Mayhew, Meeker, Pierson, Quinney, Rawson, Sergeant, and
Simerwell, to name only a few of them. Mr. Eames worked in-
dustriously on the proofs as if they were solely his own works
that were passing through the press. It was while some of
the later monographs were being printed that Pilling made
occasional visits to New York, spending days at a time with
Mr. Eames in conferences. It was then that the writer first
met Pilling and glimpsed somewhat of the great professional
unity that existed between these two scholars.

After leaving the Tibbals house, Mr. Eames was employed,
for a year or so, by Henry Miller, first at his bookstore on
Nassau Street, and then in Fourteenth Street, Manhattan. He
then was in the employ of Charles L. Woodward, still remembered by some of to-day as one of the quaintest and most interesting second-hand booksellers of the city of New York during
the nineteenth century. His shop was at 78 Nassau Street.
Here, as he had done in the other bookstores, Mr. Eames
enlarged his acquaintance with bookmen. He remained with
Woodward until urged, in 1885, by Dr. George Henry Moore,
the head of the Lenox Library, to be his personal assistant.

The sale of the library of Dr. Edmund Bailey O'Callaghan,
by Bangs and Co., of New York City, was held in December,
1882. The catalogue had been compiled by E. W. Nash, the
bookseller heretofore mentioned. It was through arrangements made with Nash that Mr. Eames bought at this sale, for
$104, Item 235, the John Carter Brown Catalogue, compiled
by John Russell Bartlett. It was one of only fifty sets of four
volumes printed, and the first complete set that had ever been
offered for sale. Here he also secured Item 851, a copy of the
1685 edition of John Eliot's Indian Bible in the Natick dialect,
for $140. These two purchases, amounting to $244, and to
him a millionaire's purchase, were made at extraordinary

sacrifices. He was obliged to sell most of his Indian books and pamphlets, as well as much more from his forming library, in order to capture the aforesaid two prizes. But these sacrifices proved to be a great gain to American bibliography. The purchase of the Brown catalogue started his interest, systematically, in Americana, and soon led him to buy a set of Joseph Sabin's ' Dictionary of Books relating to America.' At Woodward's shop he had met Joseph F. Sabin. The father—Joseph Sabin — had died, and the publication of the 'Dictionary' had been suspended. Mr. Eames soon developed in his mind an idea for the continuation of the work, which he broached to the younger Sabin. He proposed to continue Sabin's 'Dictionary' as a labor of love and for the experience it would afford him. This arrangement was made and continued for all time. He took up the work at "Pennsylvania" and brought it through the press to "Smith." The work was suspended in 1892, when Mr. Eames's duties at the Lenox Library, increased after Dr. Moore's death, precluded his giving the attention to it which the difficult subject of Captain John Smith's publications imposed. His only tangible reward for his hours of labor and sacrifices, always intentional and acceptable on his part, was the receipt of a set of the page-proofs of the parts he edited, which he added to the rest of his set, formerly purchased by him. He resumed, with assistants, the editing of the remaining copy of the 'Dictionary' in 1906, by favor of a grant for clerical aid given by the Carnegie Institution of Washington. Only now (1924) does the resumption of printing seem to be assured through the coöperation of the American Library Association, Mr. R. R. Bowker, owner of the *Library Journal* and the *Publishers' Weekly*, Mr. Joseph F. Sabin and his heirs, and other patrons. In this matter Mr. Eames stands now, as he has always stood, in the interest of American bibliography, as a willing sacrifice for the good of others.

Mr. Eames remained at the Lenox Library as Dr. Moore's personal associate from 1885 to the close of 1887. In the new environment he was afforded an opportunity of contact with the fine Americana, incunabula, and other rare books which Mr. James Lenox, the founder of the Lenox Library, had brought together during a life-time of careful collecting. The Lenox Library had been opened for the first time to a limited public in 1877. The transfer of books and art objects had been accomplished and an inventory in common copy-books had been made by Mr. Lenox's hand, generally with a lead pencil. One of Mr. Eames's tasks was to transcribe and arrange these and other inventories in a form for printing as 'Lenox Library Short-Title Lists,' issued only for official use. The first ten lists were completed in November, 1887, within a period of about four weeks. It was in this period before 1888, that Mr. Eames made for the Lenox Library a catalogue of the Félix Astoin Collection, numbering about five thousand volumes of French books, comprising reference works, bibliographies, history, art, and particularly belles-lettres of nineteenth-century French writers. Betimes he also continued his bibliographical studies and the preparation of "copy" for Sabin's 'Dictionary.'

On January 1, 1888, Mr. Eames began his official relations as a member of the staff of the Lenox Library, the same day on which the writer's employment by the Library started in a humbler capacity. Dr. Moore was the Superintendent of the Library, and Dr. Samuel Austin Allibone, the well-known literary lexicographer, was then the Librarian. Mr. Eames continued in the new relations the kind of work upon which he had been engaged whilst under private contract with Dr. Moore. When Dr. Allibone retired on April 30, 1888, there was no regular service of readers. Occasionally a scholar came to use a rare work. There were some rare books exhibited in showcases. Such visitors as came to the Library viewed the book exhibitions and the art galleries. The building was open on weekdays, except Mondays, from ten A.M. till four or five P.M., and was closed during the three summer months. The number of visitors during the year 1888 was only 8,263.

In May, 1888, Mr. Eames transferred his location from a closed room of the second story to the only "reading room" on the main floor. There was no systematic shelf-classification, and no finding-system existed for the books. A prodigious memory had to be invoked. In 1889, the printed short-title check-lists were cut up and pasted into four scrapbooks in one alphabet, and served temporarily as an incomplete finding-list on a fixed-location system.[1] The preparation of this scrap-book catalogue by Mr. Eames was the first serious move to make at least partially available a library in a chaotic condition. In the year 1888, the Lenox Library received by legacy of Joseph W. Drexel his extraordinary musical library, which was removed from the Drexel mansion by Mr. Eames and the writer, was tentatively classified, and made available by means of a short-title catalogue printed in 1889. The principal part of the library of Evert Augustus Duyckinck was similarly removed from the Duyckinck house on Clinton Place in 1890, and a short-title catalogue was made of that library directly from the books. The Lenox Library now began to be a place to which persons came for reading and research — not alone a museum of exhibits.

Dr. Moore died on May 5, 1892. On October 7, Mr. Eames was appointed by the trustees to be the assistant librarian, the appointment being retroactive to May 1. He was in fact in charge of the Library after Dr. Moore's death. This was the year of the Columbus quadricentennial, and Mr. Eames made in commemoration an extensive Columbus exhibition, in which was shown for the first time in America the unique

1. For an account of the Lenox Library from its incorporation in 1870, until its consolidation in the New York Public Library in 1895, see H. M. Lydenberg, History of the New York Public Library (New York, 1923), pp. 95–128, and the annual reports of the Lenox Library for the entire period.

Spanish folio edition of the Columbus letter of 1493, then just purchased by the trustees. On this occasion the Duke of Veragua, heir to the titles of the discoverer, visited the Lenox Library and was shown about by Mr. Eames. This year was marked by the addition of the Robert L. Stuart collection, the most valuable accession since the founder's original gift. The care of all these fell upon Mr. Eames's shoulders. In 1893, the trustees purchased the library of George Bancroft, the historian, and so the Lenox Library was materially changed in content in the five years of Mr. Eames's official relations.

On June 2, 1893, Mr. Eames was elected by the trustees Librarian of the Lenox Library. With this title he continued until the consolidation of the Lenox Library as one of the three foundations of the New York Public Library in 1895, from which time, until the collections were absorbed in the new central building, in 1911, he continued in charge of the Lenox Building with the rather unusual title of "Lenox Librarian" — a designation which has a European counterpart in "Bodley's Librarian." As librarian he wrote the annual reports for 1893 and 1894, and they were widely noted in the press and among bookmen. They were different from previous reports and also outstanding in comparison with librarians' reports of that time in the United States. They are up-to-date to-day and can be read with profit, because in them is seen the unerring hand guided by an exact mind.

These years 1893 and 1894 were also record years with respect to notable accessions. The George Bancroft library has already been mentioned. Mr. Eames's report of 1893 analyzed its content. In this year many additions were made of American colonial, province, and State laws, and legislative journals, printed before 1800. The series of Jesuit *Relations* of New France was completed. Most unusual Americana were added, and the Wendell Prime Collection of 'Don Quixote' and other works by Cervantes was received. The Lenox Library had been closed from May 14, 1892, until February 22, 1893, for extensive alterations and repairs and to install the Stuart Collection of books, paintings, and other art objects. A new era had begun. There were now facilities for readers. In 1894 a subject-catalogue was begun. Exhibitions were extended. Classification and book location were set in motion. Some 45,000 numbers of American newspapers were purchased and reported on by Mr. Eames. From the George H. Moore, George Livermore, and other notable libraries dispersed were purchased unusual book rarities and manuscripts. As librarian, Mr. Eames edited for the Lenox Library its hand-books, and particularly a facsimile of the illustrated letter of Columbus on the discovery of America. After consolidation of the Lenox Library in the New York Public Library, he carried out plans devised by Dr. John Shaw Billings for a monthly *Bulletin*, begun in 1897, of which he was the original editor, and to which he still occasionally contributes.

In the new central building of the New York Public Library Mr. Eames was "Chief of the American History Division" from May, 1911, until the end of the year 1915, when he relinquished his administrative relations, continuing, however, since January 1, 1916, as the "Bibliographer" of the Library, a concentrated relationship in bibliographical specialization pleasing to himself, serviceable to scholars, and of incalculable value to the Library.

During all these years as a librarian and bibliographer he has been a Mecca for persons hungry for exact information. From his mountain of knowledge, precious ore has gone out in an abundant correspondence. With an abandon of generosity he has given away the results of his own investigations, to be used by others. His facts have been their help to reward; his advice has been their hope. He has done these things happily and modestly among men.

It is not possible to retrace nearly half a century and name the small army of Mr. Eames's correspondents with whom he exchanged information on bibliography and other matters of scholarship. Mention has already been made of some, notably James Constantine Pilling. In this period of forty years ago we find Mr. Eames making other contacts with persons whose names are unforgettable in American bibliophilism. From 1893 until his death at the end of 1894, a professional correspondence existed with Señor Joaquin Garcia Icazbalceta, the Mexican bibliographer and scholar. When Mr. Eames became Librarian of the Lenox Library in 1893, Icazbalceta sent him an autographed photograph and congratulations. Mr. Eames purchased advance sheets of the 'Bibliografía Mexicana,' and aided this bibliographer in procuring descriptions for that work, sending to him also clues to items he would otherwise have missed. A correspondence with Dr. John Russell Bartlett was begun in 1882, ending only with Bartlett's death in 1886. Dr. Bartlett gave high praise to Mr. Eames's monographic studies. That on the John Eliot Bible he said was "clear and concise"; the Ptolemy was "all that is to be said, and will prove very useful to students of geography," and in a New Year's letter of 1886, he characterized the monograph on the 'Bay Psalm Book' as "excellent and thorough," adding: "Your work is well done and leaves nothing more to be said regarding the work." In January, 1885, Dr. Bartlett gave John Nicholas Brown a letter of introduction to Mr. Eames, and in a personal letter explained his object thus: "My young friend Mr. John N. Brown, son of the late John Carter Brown, will be in New York a few days. Thinking that book collectors & bibliographers should know each other I have given him a letter of introduction to you. Mr. B—— is the present owner of his father's books." From February, 1885, to March, 1898, Mr. Brown and Mr. Eames exchanged many letters on bibliographical subjects. Mr. Brown willingly gave Mr. Eames detailed information with respect to editions of Ptolemy, Raleigh, Captain John Smith, and other works in his library, for inclusion in Sabin's 'Dictionary.' As an example of Mr. Brown's high regard for Mr. Eames's work, we quote from a letter of April 23, 1886: "Allow me to express the hope that when you come to Ramusio and the various editions of the Vespucius letters you will give the world as minute and accurate descriptions of them as you have of the Ptolemies and the Bay Psalm Books. The bibliographical world owes you a debt of gratitude for the information you have given it in regard to these important series of books." Again, in a letter of January 29, 1887, Mr. Brown offered some ideas respecting future sections of Sabin's 'Dictionary,' and added, apologetically: "I have only noted what has especially occurred to me and hope you understand that this letter proceeds solely from an interest in you and the great work you are so admirably compiling."

When, about the middle of the eighties of the nineteenth century, Mr. Eames began the editing of Sabin's ' Dictionary,' he found a willing coöperator in Paul Leicester Ford, then only approaching his majority. A close professional friendship began at this time which lasted until Ford's death nearly twenty years later. Ford's last work was dedicated to his friend, and his last day's work in research was spent at the Lenox Library Building. He was, during many years, interested in Parson Mason L. Weems. On February 7, 1886, he wrote to Mr. Eames: "I have unearthed 42 editions of Mr. Weems' *Lies* of Washington and there are yet very long gaps in my list which remain unfilled." The last afternoon of his life, in May, 1902, Ford spent at work at the Lenox Library on this subject. The next morning a tragedy had cut short his useful life. The Ford family in the earlier years lived at 97 Clark Street, Brooklyn, and here Mr. Eames made occasional visits to the large Ford library, and also dined at times at this hospitable board.

Beginning in 1890, Mr. Eames engaged for a number of years in correspondence with the late Henry Harrisse, eminent Americanist, bibliographer, and historical geographer. It is interesting to note the friendliness of Harrisse in his letters to Mr. Eames, because at the time Harrisse harbored a deep resentment in general toward American scholars. In his letter of January 23, 1890, Harrisse said he had learned that Mr. Eames was "present editor" of Sabin, a fact he had "suspected from the improvements so noticeable of late." Thanking Mr. Eames, on May 19, 1893, for references that were made by him in the second edition of the reprint of the Latin Columbus letter, of which a copy had been sent to him, Harrisse adds: "It is about the first time an American speaks of the B. A. V., to my knowledge, with common decency." It was in a letter of June 18, 1900, that Harrisse informed Mr. Eames why an article on Dieppe maps, a critique of a work by the British geographer Charles Henry Coote, had been "greatly toned down," namely, because he had heard of the illness of Coote; and Harrisse added: "Not that I had any particular reason for showing myself lenient; for he never let pass a chance to harp on my works or self, although I had never attacked him. Yet the Lord knows if I had good grounds to give him fits. It was a mere question of humanity on my part. On the other hand, I court criticisms, provided they are honest and based upon facts — for that is about the only chance I have or may have to correct the errors I commit. With this condition, critics may peg away as long as they please." When Harrisse, in 1908, learned of the death of Professor Edward Gaylord Bourne, of Yale University, he asked Mr. Eames for an obituary notice, and said: "It is a great loss for the United States. So far as my knowledge of American historians of the present day extends, I know of none who equalled him in sound erudition, with a certain tinge of originality." In this correspondence Harrisse did not hesitate to reveal himself.

In April, 1893, upon recommendation of Dr. Samuel A. Green, Librarian of the Massachusetts Historical Society and a former mayor of Boston, Mr. Eames was elected a member of the American Antiquarian Society, of which he was, in April, 1924, the thirteenth ranking resident member. In 1896, Harvard University bestowed upon him the honorary degree of Master of Arts, also upon the recommendation of Dr. Green, an Overseer of the University, who had a penchant for seeking out men who did things, irrespective of other considerations, and putting them on the way to merited recognition. It was in 1904 that the eminent French scholar and sinologist, Henri Cordier, came to the United States to attend the Eighth International Geographical Congress, and paid a visit to the geographical and cartographical exhibition which Mr. Eames had set up at the Lenox Library as coördinate with the International Congress. The writer, recognizing the name of Cordier on a reader's ticket, offered to introduce him to Mr. Eames, remarking at the moment that Mr. Eames had a remarkable personal library of Chinese and Japanese books. The introduction was made, and the next day Mr. Eames took M. Cordier to his home to see the collections. This spontaneous contact proved to be a mutually pleasing event. Some months later, in 1905, Mr. Eames had a surprise. Opening a roll mailed from France, he found he had been elected, on recommendation of Cordier, an Honorary Officer of the Academie d'Instruction Publique des Beaux Arts et des Cults of the French Republic. Perhaps no other American librarian has had bestowed upon him two high honorary degrees in a single week, as was done to him this year, 1924. On June 16, the University of Michigan gave him the degree of LL.D., and on June 18, Brown University honored him with that of Litt.D.

Mr. Eames has had membership in many learned societies, among them the Hakluyt Society, the Bibliographical Society of England, the Society of Biblical Archæology, the

Palestine Exploration and Egyptian Exploration Funds, the American Historical Association, the American Oriental Society, and the American Library Association. Because of his changing interests, some have been discontinued. He is a member of the Bibliographical Society of America, of which he was a founder, and its first librarian from 1905 to June, 1909. He has been a corresponding member of the Colonial Society of Massachusetts since 1898, and of the Massachusetts Historical Society since 1907; a life member of the New York Historical Society since 1906; president of the New York Library Club for the term of 1900–1901, and vice-president for two terms from 1897 to 1899. He is a Fellow of the American Academy of Arts and Sciences, and in 1923 was elected an honorary member of the Grolier Club.

It remains to mention four works which were dedicated to Mr. Eames. On April 30, 1902, there was published, in two volumes, 'The Journals of Hugh Gaine, Printer. Edited by Paul Leicester Ford,' dedicated to him in these words: "These volumes I dedicate to Wilberforce Eames as a slight recognition of his scholarship and in grateful acknowledgment of my debt to it." The first copy that came into Mr. Ford's hands he personally presented to Mr. Eames at the Lenox Library, without saying anything about the dedication. A little while later on the same day, after Mr. Ford had left the Library, Mr. Eames, who had been meanwhile busy, let me see the volumes. Turning over the leaves I observed the dedication and remarked about it, and Mr. Eames was as much abashed as a gentle maiden when surprised by a lover's gift. He had not noticed the dedication when first looking over the volumes in the presence of Mr. Ford. Only a few days later, on May 8, Mr. Ford met his tragic death — a shock to all his friends, but to none more than to Mr. Eames. It was just a year after the dedication of the Gaine volumes that the writer dedicated to Mr. Eames 'A Bibliography of the Separate & Collected Works

of Philip Freneau Together with an Account of His Newspapers,' printed at the University Press of Cambridge in 1903,
as follows: "To Wilberforce Eames, A.M., an oracle in all
that touches the domain of bibliography, I dedicate this work
in loving regard of many years' daily association." In 1905,
Mr. Robert F. Roden dedicated to him the volume on 'The
Cambridge Press, 1638–1692,' in these words: "Dedicated to
Wilberforce Eames Bibliographer and Librarian in grateful
recognition of numerous bibliographical courtesies and kind-
nesses." 'The Spanish Southwest 1542–1794 An Annotated
Bibliography By Henry R. Wagner. Berkeley, California.
1924' appeared as this essay was at the printer's. Its dedication reads: "To Wilberforce Eames, the dean of American
Bibliographers, this work is respectfully dedicated as a mark
of respect and a token of affectionate regard." Perhaps hundreds of authors or editors have paid Mr. Eames tribute or
acknowledged his aid in their printed publications.

No narrative concerning Mr. Eames would be complete
without some idea of the variety and extent of his private
library. We have seen how his interests in books were developed, and what kind of sacrifices he made to possess himself
of the books he coveted. In the formation of his library he
often subjected it to the weeding-out process. He was particular as to the editions and the condition of his books. He
often replaced poor copies by better exemplars, and spent
many hours in cleaning his books, leaf by leaf, especially books
that were discolored by London smoke. Naturally, he sold off,
or gave away, books from his library as the rejected items accumulated. In the year 1904 his library numbered about
twenty thousand volumes. No other private library in the
United States was then so fine and replete in the variety of
subjects he possessed. In this period his health was not very
good. He had suffered much from insomnia and had under-
gone, though with little trouble, an operation for appendicitis.

The hospital incarceration he considered then the longest vacation period he had ever had. During the two weeks of his convalescence in the hospital he must have dispatched a ton of books and periodicals [1] that had lain in the Lenox Library, awaiting the time to be taken to his Brooklyn home, to be looked over, for Mr. Eames does not merely collect books — he knows their insides. Only a few days after Mr. Eames returned to the Lenox Library Building, the late Thomas Allibone Janvier, the American litterateur, entered the Library and asked the writer if Mr. Eames was present. Then followed this colloquy: "He is back again since a few days." "Has he been on a vacation?" "No, he has had an operation for appendicitis." "How does he feel now?" "He is doing very nicely and has a good appetite." "Well," said Janvier, "I am very sorry to learn that he has lost his Appendix but most happy to know that he still retains his Title and Table of Contents."

Mr. Eames realized that he would have to alter his method of living. His sedentary life had taken toll. Some weeks spent under the tutelage of Muldoon at his Westchester resort taught Mr. Eames the value of exercise and recreation. For some years he has taken exercise in long early morning walks, and otherwise has changed his habits. Now he enjoys the best of health. After about six hours of sound slumber he rises between five and six in the morning, and is not fatigued at nightfall. Among the changes he deemed advisable was the reduction of his library. Five parts were sold by The Anderson Auction Company, New York City, between May, 1905, and April, 1907, and these sales required ten days. The Americana sold in May, 1905, consisted of 1,287 numbers; Part II, sold in March, 1906, had 2,607 numbers on the history, literature, etc., of Great Britain and Ireland; Part III, sold in November,

---

1. The tonnage may be an error, attributable to the writer, whose remembrance of hand conveyance from the Lenox Library to the Brooklyn hospital, attended with muscular rebellion, may be pardonable.

1906, embraced 3,735 numbers on the history, literature, languages and races of Europe; Part IV, sold in December, 1906, contained 1,372 numbers, namely, the book-arts and the general library, including bibliography, printing, the early presses, paper-making, bookbinding, etc.; and Part V, sold in April, 1907, with 1,413 numbers, consisted of the history, literature, language, etc., of Western, Central, and Northern Asia, and Egypt. These sales did not embrace his large collections on China, Japan, Korea, India, and Farther India, nor his interesting collection of Africana, nor his extraordinary American Indian books. Nearly all American Indian linguistics that were not in the New York Public Library he gave to that institution. Among these were items of great rarity and market value. Many of his books of Indian captivities, histories, etc., were transferred to the New York Public Library, always at actual cost, and here again were many items that had risen greatly in value since Mr. Eames had bought them. Between January, 1910, and September, 1916, these transfers from his American Indian collection by gift or at cost-price sale, numbered 3940 volumes. There were also, on seven days between April, 1910, and April, 1913, sales from the remainder of his American Indian collection. These sales were conducted by The Anderson Auction Company, and there were 2,500 lots sold. Yet this did not exhaust his American Indian collection. The final disposition of the rest of this class has just been made, in 1924, and the books, etc., filled about ten packing cases. Mr. Eames also gave to the New York Public Library over three hundred volumes of African linguistics in 1909, out of about one thousand volumes he possessed relating to one hundred and fifty languages and dialects of Africa; the rest were sold *en bloc* to the Library of Congress. His general African library, apart from linguistics, was sold in part to the New York Public Library, and the remainder was dispersed in a miscellaneous sale at auction. The Japanese collection, 330 lots, was sold to the Case Memorial Library, Hartford, Connecticut, in 1909. And to that Library he sold, in the same year, his general Chinese collection, including Korea, consisting of 1,153 lots. The remaining half of his Chinese collection, consisting mostly of the Chinese classics, original texts, and commentaries thereupon, largely exemplars from the library of the noted Professor James Legge, he sold to the New York Public Library. His very rich collection on India and Farther India embraced 2,112 lots, and was sold to the Newberry Library in 1907.

Mr. Eames retained many bibliographical "tools" and has added to this class. In the latter part of 1916 he began the formation of a collection of American Imprints in the region of the United States. On this he now concentrated his attention with avidity, and at the end of the year 1923 it embraced 12,468 pieces, mostly pamphlets. These he studied with respect to the origins of the printing press in all parts of the Nation. This collection he has recently sold privately.

Works and Contributions

In 1882 Mr. Eames edited a comparative edition of the authorized and revised versions of the New Testament. From 1885 to 1892, he edited six volumes (vols. 15–20) of Joseph Sabin's 'Dictionary of Books relating to America,' and some parts have been issued as separate monographs, which are listed hereafter. Mention has been made elsewhere of his contributions to the American Indian bibliographies of the late James Constantine Pilling. The following list is intended as a catalogue, rather than as a bibliography, of his printed monographs and other contributions. Studies that remain in manuscript, with one exception, are not included. If garnered and put together, they would make a considerable addition to the printed record, and it is to be hoped that Mr. Eames will be able to bring much more out into the light.

A List of Editions of the Bay Psalm Book, or New England Version of the Psalms. New York: MDCCCLXXXV. 8vo, pp. 14.　(1)
　Twenty-five copies reprinted from Sabin, Vol. xvi.

A List of Editions of Ptolemy's Geography, 1475–1730. New York: MDCCCLXXXVI. 8vo, title and pp. 45.　(2)
　Fifty copies reprinted from Sabin, Vol. xvi.

A Bibliography of Sir Walter Raleigh. New York: MDCCCLXXXVI. 8vo, pp. 35.　(3)
　Thirty-four copies reprinted from Sabin, Vol. xvi.

A List of Editions of the Margarita Philosophica, 1503–1599. New York: MDCCCLXXXVI. 8vo, title and 8 leaves.　(4)
　Eight copies prepared from proof-sheets of Sabin, Vol. xvi, with a separately printed title-page. Three or four copies were also reissued by means of photography.

Illinois and Miami Vocabulary and Lord's Prayer. [Contributed by Wilberforce Eames from the original manuscript in the Lenox Library. Prepared for Dr. John Gilmary Shea. New York, 1891.] 8vo, pp. 9.　(5)
　It appeared in the *U. S. Catholic Historical Magazine*, Vol. iii (New York, 1890), pp. 278–286, from which about 50 copies were issued separately for private distribution.

Bibliographic Notes on Eliot's Indian Bible and his other Translations and Works in the Indian Language of Massachusetts. Extract from a 'Bibliography of the Algonquian Languages.' Washington: Government Printing Office, 1890. Roy. 8vo, title and pp. 58. 21 plates.　(6)

Two hundred and fifty copies reprinted from Pilling's 'Algonquian Languages,' pp. 127–184, while that work, issued in 1891, was going through the press.

The Letter of Columbus on the Discovery of America. A Facsimile of the Pictorial Edition, with a Complete Reprint of the Oldest Four Editions in Latin. Printed by Order of the Trustees of the Lenox Library. New York: MDCCCXCII. 8vo, pp. xiii, (20), 61.   (7)

Two hundred and fifty copies were printed on handmade paper in octavo, for the use of the trustees; and a small-paper edition was printed for sale. A second edition of the latter [pp. xi, (20), 13], with a new preface, omitting the text of the four editions in Latin, was printed in 1893.

Contributions to a Catalogue of The Lenox Library. No. VIII. The Roman Indexes of Prohibited and Expurgated Books. New York: Printed [sic] for the Trustees, MDCCCXCV.   (8)

Mr. Eames prepared this manuscript, which was made in the main in 1888 or 1889. It was intended to print it in 1895, but that purpose was not carried out. There are 389 editions described. The unpublished "copy" is in the New York Public Library.

Early New England Catechisms. A Bibliographical Account of some Catechisms published before the year 1800, for use in New England. Read, in part, Before the American Antiquarian Society, at its Annual Meeting in Worcester, October 21, 1897. Worcester, Mass. Press of Charles Hamilton, 311 Main Street, 1898. 8vo, pp. 111.   (9)

Two hundred copies reprinted from the *Proceedings of the American Antiquarian Society*, New Series, Vol. XII.

The Bay Psalm Book. Being a Facsimile Reprint of the First Edition Printed by Stephen Daye At Cambridge, in New England in 1640. With an Introduction by Wilberforce Eames. New York . . . 1903. 12mo, pp. xvii, (1), and facsimile of the original work.   (10)

The edition was 975 copies on deckle-edge laid paper and 25 copies on Japan paper. The introduction is on pp. v–xvii.

Three Centuries of English Booktrade Bibliography. An Essay on the Beginnings of Booktrade Bibliography since the Introduction of Printing and in England since 1595. By A. Growoll . . . Also a List of the Catalogues, &c., published for the English Booktrade from 1595–1902, by Wilberforce Eames of The Lenox Library, New York. New York: Published for The Dibdin Club . . . 1903. 8vo, pp. xv, 195, (1), one colophon leaf. Illustrated.   (11)

The edition was 550 copies. The list of catalogues by Mr. Eames fills pp. 99–173.

List of Maps of the World in the New York Public Library, exhibited in the Lenox Branch on the Occasion of the Visit of Members of the Eighth International Geographical Congress, 13–15 September, 1904.   (12)

In *Bulletin* of the New York Public Library, Vol. VIII, no. 9 (September, 1904), pp. 411–422; also issued separately as a hand-list in 16mo.

John Eliot. The Logic Primer. Reprinted from the Unique Original of
1672. With Introduction by Wilberforce Eames. Cleveland . . . 1904.
Square 16mo, pp. 94. One facsimile.   (13)
　　Edition 150 copies. The introduction is on pp. 5–13.

The Humble Request of His Majesties Loyall Subjects. The Governour
and the Company late gone for New England to the Rest of their Brethren
in and of the Church of England for the obtaining of their Prayers and the
Removall of Suspitions and Misconstructions of their Intentions. New
Edition in Facsimile of the Rare Original of 1630 with a Bibliographical
note by Wilberforce Eames (Librarian, Lenox Library, New York City)
and with an Historical Introduction by John L. Ewell (Howard University,
Washington, D. C.). Washington . . . 1905. Small 4to, pp. 4, one leaf,
5–12, two blank leaves, half title, and facsimile consisting of title and
10 pp.   (14)
　　One hundred copies "printed for sale." Mr. Eames's "Bibliographical
　　Note" is on pp. [3]–4.

A Narrative of the Captivity of Mrs. Johnson. Reprinted from the Third
Edition, published at Windsor, Vermont, 1814, with all Corrections and
Additions . . . Springfield, Massachusetts MCMVII. 16mo, pp. xiii, (1),
194. One facsimile.   (15)
　　Edition "limited to 350 numbered copies, of which the first 50 copies
　　(Nos 1 to 50) are on Van Gelder handmade paper, and the remaining
　　300 copies (Nos. 51 to 350) are on Alexandria all-rag paper." Mr.
　　Eames contributed the bibliography of editions of this captivity, de-
　　scribing the editions of Walpole, N. H., 1796; of Windsor, Vt., 1807 and
　　1814; of New York, 1841; of Concord, 1822 and 1831; of Boston, 1870,
　　etc., on pp. vii–viii.

The Redeemed Captive Returning to Zion or the Captivity and Deliverance of Rev. John Williams of Deerfield. Reprinted from the Sixth Edition. . . Springfield, Massachusetts MCMVIII. 16mo, pp. xxiv, 212. One
facsimile.   (16)
　　Edition "526 copies on Mittineague paper, 26 of which are Large Paper
　　copies." Mr. Eames contributed the bibliography of editions of this
　　captivity for 1707–1899, on pp. [xiii]–xxiv.

John Eliot and the Indians, 1652–1657. Being Letters Addressed to Rev.
Jonathan Hanmer of Barnstaple, England. Reproduced from the Original
Manuscripts in the possession of Theodore N. Vail. Edited by Wilberforce
Eames. New York: MCMXV. 4to, 31 folios and 22 illustrations.   (17)

Description of a Wood Engraving illustrating the South American Indians
(1505). By Wilberforce Eames. New York, 1920. Oblong folio, title,
facsimile, text pp. (4) in double columns.   (18)
　　This edition was printed by The New York Public Library for official
　　use for the Spencer Collection, and five additional copies were also
　　struck off and were bound in cloth. These and a set of the printing-office

proofs are all that exist in this form. However, it was reprinted with the facsimile of the woodcut in the *Bulletin* of the Library for September, 1922, and was reissued separately in October in an edition of 300 copies.

History of the Press in Western New-York. From the Beginning to the Middle of the Nineteenth Century. By Frederick Follett. With a Preface By Wilberforce Eames. With Facsimile . . . New York, 1920. 8vo, pp. xv, (1), 65,(1), imprint leaf, verso blank.   (19)

Heartman's Historical Series Number 34, the edition consisting of "91 Copies Printed on Handmade Paper. Also Eleven Japan Paper Copies." The preface of Mr. Eames covers pp. v–vii.

AIDS TO THE IDENTIFICATION OF AMERICAN IMPRINTS

By ALICE HOLLISTER LERCH

Of the New York Public Library

A FEW years ago a visiting bibliographer was heard to announce conclusively that Americana collecting ceased, for want of material, about 1878. Regardless of argument or evidence, this statement serves to illustrate the difference in point of view between the two main classes of Americana — namely, the European accounts of discovery and settlement, and the issues of the press in the New World.

In the United States as in no older country the history of printing is a chronicle of the Nation and its people, starting with their prophetic 'Oath of a Freeman' and continuing with their controversies concerning their God and their King, their rights and their taxes. America, to Americans, extends beyond the narrow colonial sea coast, beyond the early forest clearings of the thirteen original states; and as settlements pushed westward the printing-press followed the axe and the covered wagon, and new records appeared and as quickly vanished through the exigencies of pioneer life. The emigrant's guide kindled the camp-fire once the end of the journey was in sight; as always, newspapers had short lives, and as new laws replaced the first, copies of the old were deemed worthless. So adequately has the first group, as a whole, been bibliographically described that a new item is immediately recognized as such and noted as "not in" Harrisse, Sabin, Church, or John Carter Brown. But in spite of changes in the market of this class of early Americana, in spite of the fact that its season is said to have closed in 1878, it is by no means a bibliographically dead or finished subject. Variant issues and different editions come to us for identification and comparison, and undated editions and those without place of publication or name of printer are yet with us.

The need and importance of a complete history of American printing is keenly felt by the bibliographer, but for those whose interests have never led this way we quote the master-printer of Worcester,[1] who wrote: "[It] is more interesting to us than any other nation. We are able to convey to posterity a correct account of the manner in which we have grown up to be an independent people, and can delineate the progress of the useful and polite arts among us, with a degree of certainty which cannot be attained by the natives of the Old World, in respect to themselves."

Perhaps if Sabin's 'Dictionary' had not grounded on the shoals of Smith, following the collapse of Americana collecting, even the bibliography of Americana would have been considered, by some, a finished subject. But when Thevet's 'Les Singvlaritez de La France Antarctiqve,' Anvers, 1558, in original vellum binding bearing the crescents of Diane de Poitiers, could no longer be found in Nassau Street, nor its description compressed to a four-line entry in a sales catalogue; when the great collections and museums were irrevocably acquiring the rarities, and small collectors were lamenting their lost opportunities, there began a persistent search for unknown as well as for additional copies of known works which not only resulted in the formation of several notable collections and the discovery of heretofore unlisted, and listed but lost, Americana, but also led to the knowledge of additional editions and variant issues. Existing collections received closer scrutiny and comparison, and the second group, the local Americana, long overshadowed by its brilliant predecessor, began to receive attention from both collectors and bibliographers. Usually the

1. Isaiah Thomas, The History of Printing in America. Worcester, 1810. Vol. 1, p. 10.

character of the beginning of the earliest of these collections dominated their continuance — and resulted in the highly specialized collections now available for investigation along definite lines of study.

The first attempt at a history of printing had been made, a few general bibliographies and lists had been issued, and Sabin had begun "A painfull work . . . I'll assure you, and more than difficult, wherein what toyle hath been taken, as no man thinketh so no man believeth, but he hath made the triall," [2] when, in 1872, Henry Stevens of Vermont wrote that "Bibliography is fast becoming an exact science, and not a whit too soon. It is high time to separate it from mere catalogue making. It is becoming a necessity to both the scholar *and* the collector."

He explains that "Photo-Bibliography, or a new application of Photography to Bibliography . . . is not intended to supersede, but rather to supplement, improve, systematize, and elevate the present method of cataloguing our libraries and museums, public and private." [3] He tells of his proposed use of photograms, reduced photographs on catalogue cards, and even proposes the plan for a central bureau for files of negatives. He pleads for "tidy, exact, compact, and comprehensive" descriptions. We wish his plea might be broadcast to the amateur bibliographer with an additional word for accurate collations. The ingenuity of the Stevens idea savors of its Yankee origin, but expense and difficulty in the production of numbers of photographs made its use prohibitive at that time.

It was almost fifty years later, when invention had produced a cheap and rapid process of reproduction, that there appeared in 'The Papers of the Bibliographical Society of America' [4] a

2. Anthony à Wood, Preface to the History of Oxford. *Cf.* Sabin, A Dictionary of Books Relating to America, from its Discovery to the Present Time. New York, 1868–1892. Vol. I, title-page.

3. Henry Stevens of Vermont, Photobibliography. A Word on Catalogues and How to Make Them (in his Bibliotheca Geographica and Historica. London, 1872, pt. I, pp. 9–10).   4. Vol. xv, pt. I, 1921.

series of articles on the use of photostat reproductions, including our present application of the Henry Stevens idea of using photographs as bibliographical tools. These papers, however, did not cover the use of the photostat in connection with the study or identification of American imprints as developed by Mr. Wilberforce Eames of the New York Public Library. Mr. Eames there told only of his interest in the use of the photostat as a means of distributing copies of unique or rare works, and of pioneer work, at his own expense, with the camera and later with the photostat in reproducing copies of rarities for the Reserve Collection of that library. It nevertheless is due to his knowledge and foresight and to the friendly and generous coöperation of his friends and the "trade" that this collection has been further enriched by reproductions of entire works of great rarity, which he has personally examined and had reproduced during their brief stay in New York. This is the same bibliographical foresight that once led Mr. Eames, during his administration of the Lenox Library, to expend the principal instead of the income of a book fund for a notable collection offered for sale at prices he was confident would later be far beyond a public-library allowance — books each of which to-day would cost the entire amount expended.

Mr. Eames has, moreover, gone further in the use of photostat reproductions, employing them as type specimens in his study both of fifteenth-century Americana and of the history of American printing, in connection with his personal imprint collection and the Imprint Catalogue. Photostat copies acquired because of the rarity of the original work may become the nucleus of a type collection formed by systematic additions of all early issues of a single press, or the issues of all the presses in a given locality. These reproductions, forming an historical record, serve also as practical specimens for comparative type study. Collection of these specimens frequently entails search of documents or records to prove the sometime existence of a reputed or suspected work, and frequently the printed original is found laid away in unidentified or unrecognized seclusion.

An example of the use of photostat reproductions is furnished by the work of Mr. Eames in connection with his study of the printing of William Bradford, first printer of New York. Beginning with Bradford's Philadelphia printing, titles including the Keith and other Quaker pamphlets, the debatable Fletcher proclamation of "the 29th day of April, 1693," official proclamations, decrees, laws, and miscellaneous books printed at New York have been assembled. The originals, located in the Public Record Office, the British Museum, and in libraries and private collections of this country, have been copied and identified, and usually the place, printer, and date supplied. Other works, previously assigned to Bradford, have been identified as the printing of Reynier Jansen of Philadelphia. With a representative collection sufficiently large for purposes of comparison, a book may be traced to source in spite of there being no title-page or more obvious clue to a printer than a noticeably individual upper-case letter.

With a famous Printer to the King, — staid, respected, even honored, — some results at least would be ultimately certain. But the identification of an anonymous work, "Printed for the Author in 1789," must be reserved as a bibliographer's plaything, and for vacations, for, with only a date for a scent across the fields of printing in thirteen states, the chase is apt to be prolonged by many obstacles. Here, it is only when theories begin to develop into certainties that the photostat again becomes almost indispensable in accumulating evidence to present the case. Reproductions of newspapers make typographical identification possible, and copies of records and manuscripts help complete the story of a soldier of fortune turned printer.

Granted that these are unusual cases, there yet remains to be considered the large number of ordinary seventeenth- and eighteenth-century works not yet fully identified in the general or special bibliographies — those with one or two of the three necessary imprint factors wanting, usually printer's name or date. For such, English printing has its official Stationers' *Registers*, dictionaries of booksellers and printers, and works on the printing and book trade. But in this country there is no official record of printing until the enactment of the first Federal copyright law, 31 May, 1790.[5] "This law required the registration of the titles of copyright productions in the office of the clerk of the district court of the state in which the author lived, which provision as to the recording of the title remained unchanged until the enactment of the statute approved July 8, 1870." [6]

At best, these first copyright records furnish only the name of the author and his residence when entering the copyright. Hence our need for records for ready reference to printers, the period covered by their work and the output of their presses. This need has been partially met by the Imprint Catalogues of the Library of Congress, as planned by Mr. Charles Martel, and by that of the Reserve Room of the New York Public Library, begun under the direction of Mr. Eames at the Lenox Library before 1896. These catalogues entail a minimum of expense and work quite out of proportion to their service to both staff and readers. They may be limited to cover only the American interest, or indefinitely expanded to a complete printing record of a collection — depending upon the character and extent of a collection or the needs of a library.

Three main groups, place, printer, and date, are advisable, and may be formed by using extra copies of catalogue cards, where cards are printed by a library, or by copies of existing cards. To these may be added titles from other libraries, especially those printing their own cards, cuttings from sales cata-

5. Under Article I, Section 8, of the Constitution.
6. Report of the Librarian of Congress . . . 1901, pp. 278–279.

logues, and miscellaneous references. The very practical uses these files serve are: (1) titles of examples of printers' work, (2) dates of the establishment of local presses, (3) output of local presses, (4) lists of printers, and (5) location of copies.

Reluctant to lose sight of two small volumes with unusual imprints, Mr. Eames purchased them and thus, in 1916, began the formation of his personal collection of American Imprints. In seven years it was discontinued, not for lack of interest, nor for lack of material, for "it could have gone on forever," he says, but "after all the wall space was covered, and all the floor space was covered, there was no place to put more books." In seven years it numbered 13,000 volumes. With his characteristic generosity, Mr. Eames has always been ready to consult this collection for the benefit of others. This Imprint Collection, his Printers' List, and the Imprint Catalogue have together been used as bibliographical tools, one supplementing the other, and used in connection with Sabin and Evans.

Although the value of the general bibliographies of Americana is thoroughly appreciated by those who benefit by the labor expended upon them, the need is felt to-day for bibliographies on special subjects rather than for further attempts at general works. With increased facilities for creditable work it is hoped that even the standard of Harrisse [7] may be more nearly approached. The standard: "Whether we consider Bibliography as an indispensable means to explore the sources of literature and of the historical sciences, or as the competent guide which leads conscientious critics to the knowledge of the subjects they are called upon to discuss, it is evident that its sphere of influence may be greatly extended. There is no reason why the bibliographer should limit his efforts to a faithful transcription of titles, coupled with minute collations. He may, without trespassing upon the province of Belles-Lettres, give

7. Henry Harrisse, Bibliotheca Americana Vetustissima, New York, 1866, pp. viii, ix.

the history of the book, enumerate its contents, ascertain its precise place in the chronology of literature, state the references which mark its influence in the preparation of other works, quote the opinions expressed by competent critics, divulge its author or editor when published anonymously, and, if it be devoid of imprint, discover the date at which, and the place where, it was printed, and by what printer. He must, furthermore, describe the typographical peculiarities of the book, the changes they inaugurate, and their bearing upon the history of the art of printing. Nor should he neglect to group around each title the data which may enable critics to correct errors and to elucidate every point in controversy."

THE ROYAL PRIMER

By PERCIVAL MERRITT

Of Boston, Massachusetts

'T HE Royal Primer: Or, an Easy and Pleasant Guide
to the Art of Reading,' has suffered sufficiently through
confusion with its better-known and more distinguished predecessor and probable prototype, the New England Primer, so as
almost to lose its own identity and individuality. In the examination of catalogues and indexes it will frequently be found
listed simply under the general heading of Primers, or even under and in conjunction with the New England Primer. It has
without doubt a generic similarity, as one spelling-book or one
Reader may resemble another.[1] Yet while but for the New
England Primer the Royal Primer might never have come into
existence, its conception, general plan, and execution give it a
distinct personality of its own.

It may fairly be said that it represents the more liberal Anglican standpoint as contrasted with the rigid Puritanical background of the New England Primer. In due course of time it
reacted on the latter and to some extent humanized it, but
apparently the New England Primer had no reaction whatso-
ever on the Royal Primer. The late Paul Leicester Ford, in
his bibliography of the New England Primer wrote: "About
1790 a very marked change was made by printers taking some
mundane rhymes from an English publication entitled the
'Royal Primer' describing various animals, with pictures of
them. From this source were also taken a 'Description of a
Good Boy,' a 'Description of a Bad Boy,' and poems on 'The
Good Girl' and 'The Naughty Girl.' Their insertion marked

---

1. No attempt will be made to trace the origin of the eighteenth-century primer
back to the English primer of the time of Henry VIII or to the early English school-
books, since it is beyond the scope of this sketch.

the beginning of the end, for no longer salvation was promised
to the good, and unending fire to the bad, but 'pert Miss Prat-
a-pace' was to have none of the 'Oranges, Apples, Cakes, or
Nuts' promised to 'pretty Miss Prudence,' and the naughty
urchin was only threatened with beggary, while the good boy
was promised 'credit and reputation.'" [2]

It can be shown, I believe, that this change came about earlier than stated by Mr. Ford. For instance, the Bostonian Society possesses a copy of: 'The New England Primer enlarged:
Or, an easy and pleasant Guide to the Art of Reading. Adorn'd
with Cuts. To which are added, The Assembly of Divines and
Mr. Cotton's Catechism. Boston: Printed by T. and J. Fleet,
at the Bible and Heart in Cornhill.' It is undated, but on the
first page is written: "Ambrose Dunton His Book 1781." This
copy contains verses, cuts, pictures of animals, a secular alphabet, etc., taken directly from the Royal Primer and added to
the regular features of the New England Primer, such as the
Adam's Fall Alphabet, the John Rogers cut and verses, the
Shorter Catechism, and Cotton's Spiritual Milk for American
Babes. Mr. Ford also stated that "The change, nevertheless,
proved popular, alas, and quite a number of editions between
1790 and 1800 contain more or less of these worldly additions." [3]

Mr. Charles F. Heartman apparently considered the Royal
Primer simply as the New England Primer under another
name when he wrote: "From Portsmouth to Philadelphia
there was probably not one printer that did not issue a number

2. Ford. The New England Primer, New York, 1897, p. 47. The statement of
Mr. Ford, so far as it relates to the Description of a Good Boy and a Bad Boy, and
the poems on the Good Girl and Naughty Girl, is questioned with some hesitation,
since it is not possible to know what his authorities may have been. It must be said,
however, that in none of the English and American Royal Primers of the eighteenth
century which have been examined are any such verses to be found. But they do
appear in The New England Primer Improved, printed by Thomas Kirk, Brooklyn,
1811. The descriptive lines 'To a Good Girl,' and 'To a Naughty Girl' had appeared at least as early as 1784 in a Carnan publication, 'The Fairing; or, a Golden
Toy for Children.' This little book was reprinted by Isaiah Thomas in 1788.

3. Idem, p. 48.

of Primers during the eighteenth century. Some occasionally changed the title to 'Royal Primer,' 'Franklin Primer,' 'Family Primer,' 'Boston Primer,' 'New York Primer,' 'American Primer,' 'Columbian Primer,' 'New Primer,' or some such title, none of which achieved any popularity." [4]

Now as a matter of fact the Royal Primer made its first appearance among the earlier publications of that indefatigable purveyor of books for children, John Newbery of London. The year of its publication cannot be exactly determined at the present time, but it was not earlier than 1744, after he had removed from Reading to London and opened a warehouse at the Bible and Crown near Devereux Court, without Temple Bar, with a branch at the Royal Exchange, nor later than 1750, when the first advertisement of the Royal Primer is found in the public press in this country. In 1745 Newbery combined both branches and removed to the Bible and Sun in St. Paul's Churchyard where most of his famous publications were issued, and where he remained until his death in 1767. [5] Newbery's biographer, Charles Welsh, implies, although his statement is not very clear, that: 'The Royal Battledore; or First Book for Children' was publicly advertised in 1745. [5a] The Royal Primer evidently followed the Royal Battledore in due course of time. An advertisement of the Battledore in 1750 is accompanied by the statement: "[After which the next proper Book for Children is] The Royal Primer," which seems to establish the publication period of the Primer as between 1745 and 1750. [6]

4. Heartman. The New England Primer Issued Prior to 1830, p. xvii.
5. Welsh. A Bookseller of the Last Century, Being some Account of the Life of John Newbery, and of the Books he published, with a Notice of the later Newberys. Printed for Griffith, Farrar, Okeden & Welsh, successors to Newbery & Harris, at the sign of the Bible and Sun, West Corner of St. Paul's Churchyard, London, and E. P. Dutton & Co., New York, MDCCCLXXXV, pp. 19, 20.   5a. Idem, pp. 186, 187.
6. A careful search has been made at the British Museum through files of the London Evening Post and the General Advertiser from January to November, 1750, and of the London Evening Post for the years 1744 to 1749 inclusive, without locating any advertisement of the publication of the Royal Primer.

What was Newbery's intent and desire in his long series of children's books can best be shown by quoting what are probably his own words in the preface to the long list of "Books published for the Instruction and Amusement of Children," annexed to one of his little books: 'The Newtonian System of Philosophy Adapted to the Capacities of Young Gentlemen and Ladies, and familiarized and made entertaining by Objects with which they are intimately acquainted: Being The Substance of Six Lectures read to the Lilliputian Society. By Tom Telescope, A.M. And collected and methodized for the Benefit of the Youth of these Kingdoms, By their old Friend Mr. Newbery, in St. Paul's Church Yard. London, Printed for J. Newbery, at the Bible and Sun, in St. Paul's Church Yard. 1761.'

This list comprised twenty titles of "Books published for the Instruction and Amusement of Children," in which the Royal Battledore and Royal Primer are numbers three and four, and seventeen titles of books "For the Instruction and Amusement of Young Gentlemen and Ladies."

The preface reads: "To the Parents, Guardians, and Governesses of Great Britain and Ireland. At a time when all complain of the Depravity of Human Nature, and the corrupt Principles of Mankind, any Design that is calculated to remove the Evils, and inforce a contrary Conduct, will undoubtedly deserve the Attention and Encouragement of the Publick. It has been said, and said wisely, that the only way to remedy these Evils, is to begin with the rising Generation, and to take the Mind in its infant State, when it is uncorrupted and susceptible of any Impression; To represent their duties and future Interest in a Manner that shall seem rather intended to amuse than instruct, to excite their Attention with Images and Pictures that are familiar and pleasing; To warm their Affections with such little Histories as are capable of giving them Delight, and of impressing on their tender Minds proper Sentiments of Religion, Justice, Honour, and Virtue.

'When infant Reason grows apace, it calls
'For the kind Hand of an assiduous Care:
'Delightful Task! To rear the tender Thought,
'To teach the young Idea how to shoot,
'To pour the fresh Instruction o'er the Mind,
'To breathe th'inspiring Spirit, to implant,
'The generous Purpose in the glowing Breast.'

Thompson.

"How far Mr. Newbery's little Books may tend to forward this good Work, may be, in some measure, seen by what are already published, and, it is presumed, will more evidently appear by others which are now in the Press." [7]

Now his intent, as indicated in this preface, is well manifested in the execution of the Royal Primer, which shows all the Newbery characteristics. It is true that Charles Welsh notes a reference to the Primer from the account book of Benjamin Collins of Salisbury, the associate of Newbery in the publication of this and many other books, in which he spoke of it as "My own scheme." [8] Whether this was so or not cannot be determined. Collins might have suggested the general idea, but the style and execution are so thoroughly characteristic of John Newbery that the statement need not be regarded as withdrawing the credit from him.

It has been said above that the Royal Primer reflects the Anglican background as contrasted with the Puritan. The Ten Commandments and the Lord's Prayer are taken from the Book of Common Prayer and not from the King James Bible. The scripture lessons are drawn from the Psalms and Proverbs. The "Second Lesson of Words of one Syllable" is composed of parts of the *Venite* and other psalms adapted to the limitations of a single syllable. The *Jubilate* and third collect of Morning Prayer are taken almost verbatim from the Prayer Book. In

7. Newtonian System of Philosophy, London, 1761, pp. 126, 127.
8. Bookseller of the Last Century, p. 302. Collins also referred to the Royal Battledore as "My own invention." (Id. p. 172).

only one instance is the version of the King James Bible employed — in a shortened form of the Fifty-first Psalm. But the most marked difference between the two primers from a theological standpoint is the fact that the youthful readers of the Royal Primer are promised, as the result of the practice of virtue, a mundane and not a celestial reward.

And this is quite characteristic of the Newbery juvenile books in general. Readers of the famous Newbery nursery classic, the 'History of Little Goody Twoshoes,' will remember that Mistress Margery, after her various tribulations and trials, entered into a comfortable earthly mansion instead of a heavenly one. While at the very moment of her marriage to Sir Charles, her brother Tom, who had gone to sea as a boy and had now returned with a large fortune, dashed up to the church in a post-chaise, halting the wedding ceremony until he assured himself that a proper settlement had been made on his sister.

So in the Royal Primer under the heading of "The Rewards of Virtue," we find this little history: "Miss Goodchild had the Advantage of such Instructions in her Youth, that she could reason justly on the Obligations of Virtue, and on the Being, Providence and Perfections of God; whom she admir'd, lov'd, and reverenc'd, from a Conviction of his infinite Excellencies; and to whom, every Morning and Night, she offer'd up her Prayers for Protection, and for advancement in useful Knowledge, and good Dispositions, the chief Object of her Pursuit! Her Pappa and Mamma soon died; and she had no other Portion left but her undissembled Piety, a decent Modesty, which shewed itself in her Actions, an innocent Simplicity, and a Heart full of Goodness. These raised her Friends; they admired her, they loved her, they strove to make her happy. A Gentleman of Understanding and Virtue became sensible of her Merit, and marry'd her. 'T was the Business of their Lives to make each other happy; and as their Fortune was large, she was enabled to gratify the generous Dispositions of her Heart, in relieving the distrest honest Man; and using the Power her Riches gave her, in promoting the substantial Benefit of all about her." 9

Newbery's system of philosophy with regard to the reasons and rewards for youthful study is set forth in two verses which appear on the frontispiece to the Royal Primer. The page is headed "A good Boy and Girl at their Books," and above and below a cut intended to represent a boy and girl at study in a library, are the following lines:

> He who ne'er learns his A, B, C,
> Forever will a Blockhead be.
> But he who to his Books inclin'd,
> Will soon a golden Treasure find.

> Children like tender Oziers take the Bow
> And as they first are fashion'd always grow
> For what we learn in Youth, to that alone,
> In age we are by second Nature prone.

The first set of these verses had already been used in 1745 in the Royal Battledore, in a slightly different form but with an equally material reward as the prize for youthful studies:

> He that ne'er learns his A B C
> Forever will a Blockhead be.
> But he that learns these Letters fair,
> Shall have a Coach to take the Air.10

Referring to these verses Mr. Ford wrote: "Worst of all was the insertion of a short poem which should have made the true

9. Royal Primer, pp. 67, 68.
10. Reproduced in A. W. Tuer's History of the Horn Book, ii, 234.

Puritan turn in his grave, for instead of teaching that letters were to be learned, that the Bible might be read, and that the figures were to be acquired for the purpose of finding chapter and verse in that work, it said 'He who ne'er learns his A.B.C. etc.'" [11] The first couplet of the second set of verses, "Children, like tender Oziers, take the bow," had also been employed as early as 1744, when it appeared in an advertisement of the Little Pretty Pocket Book in the *Penny Morning Post* of June 18, 1744.[12] Thus it will be seen that, at the very beginning of his career as a publisher of juvenile books, Newbery had proclaimed the standards which he consistently maintained thereafter.

The Royal Primer begins with the customary alphabet in Roman and Italic letters, and the syllabaries, but the vocabulary is made up of words of a varying number of letters instead of syllables. Here the closest similarity to the New England Primer ceases. Two complete alphabets are given, one in verse beginning "A Stands for Apple and Awl," the other a pictorial one, "a Apple, b Ball," etc., with rather crude cuts intended to represent the objects employed. The Scripture Catechism is a brief one, simply intended to explain to the children many of the "principal Persons contained in the Scriptures." The Old Testament portion contains a characteristic Newbery touch in his method of combining instruction and advertisement of his own wares. Thus: "Q. *Who was* David? A. The man after God's own Heart, who was raised from a Shepherd to a King.*" The purpose of the asterisk is shown in a foot note at the bottom of the page: "*See his life in the *Royal Psalter*." Following a hymn by Dr. Watts, "My God who mak'st the Sun to know His proper Hour to rise," etc., in about the middle of the book comes its most essential characteristic — a series of cuts of some twelve animals, birds, and insects, each followed by a

11. Ford. The New England Primer, 1897, p. 47.
12. Bookseller of the Last Century, p. 107.

couplet, or couplets of verse, with a moral lesson in prose attached. The description of the parrot is brief and sufficiently indicative of the whole series:

> The *Parrot* prates he knows not what
> For all he says is got by rote.

The *Par-rot* is a chat-ter-ing Bird; he talks a great deal, yet knows not what he says, and is there-fore not un-like some sil-ly Boys who prate with-out think-ing and learn their Les-son with-out look-ing at their Book.

Then follow cuts and descriptions of the Creation, Adam and Eve, Noah's Ark, the Tower of Babel, Solomon's Temple, the Nativity and Passion, and the Death and Ascension of Christ. Next come cuts of St. Paul's Cathedral, the Rewards of Virtue, a little Boy and Girl at Prayers, a little Boy and Girl asking a Blessing of their Parents, and a little Boy and Girl bestowing Charity. The Primer ends with the Lord's Prayer, prayers for Morning and Evening, and Grace before and after Meat.

Small wonder that, when the opportunity came to the American child, as it did in 1750, the humanity, interest, and diversity of the Royal Primer, as contrasted with the austerities of the New England Primer, must have made a strong appeal to normal and healthy-minded children, embryonic Cotton Mathers excepted. A rapturous change from John Rogers and his poetical advice to his children, the Westminster Catechism infelicitously described as "Shorter," the Spiritual Milk for American Babes, which at times must have turned sour in many little stomachs, and the Dialogue between Christ, Youth and the Devil with its gruesome "Conclusion":

> Thus end the days of woful youth,
> Who won't obey nor mind the truth;
> Nor hearken to what preachers say,
> But do their parents disobey.
> They in their Youth go down to hell,
> Under eternal wrath to dwell.
> Many don't live out half their days,
> For cleaving unto sinful ways.

It is not surprising that, when the Royal Primer was transplanted to this country, it first took root in the more genial soil, from a theological standpoint, of Philadelphia. Miss Rosalie V. Halsey made the discovery that a long list of Newbery publications was advertised in the *Pennsylvania Gazette* of November 15, 1750.[13] and reproduced the advertisement in her delightful book, 'Forgotten Books of the American Nursery,' Boston, 1911.[14] Miss Halsey drew the deduction from the advertisement that "the omission of the customary announcement of special books as 'to be had of the Printer hereof,' points to Newbery's enterprise in seeking a wider market for his wares, and Franklin's business ability in securing the advertisement, as it is not repeated in the 'Journal.'" [15] The list comprises five titles, including the Royal Battledore and the Royal Primer. The first book on the list is: 'A Museum for young Gentlemen and Ladies: Or, A private Tutor for little Masters and Misses,' which had recently been advertised for sale in London in the *General Evening Post*, July 26, 1750.[16] Each of the first two titles is followed by an imprint giving the names of the several publishers. The last three titles are followed at the end of the advertisement by the general imprint: "London: Printed and Sold by J. Newberry, in St. Paul's Church-Yard; J. Hodges on the Bridge; and B. Collins, Bookseller, on the New Canal in Salisbury. By whom good Allowance is made to all Shopkeepers, School-Masters, &c. who buy Quantities to sell again." It was doubtless due to this fact that Miss Halsey concluded that the advertisement was merely "an announcement that John Newbery had for 'Sale to Schoolmasters, Shopkeepers, &c, who buy in quantities to sell again,'" the various books advertised.[17] But an examination of the *Pennsylvania Gazette* itself reveals in an interesting way the fallibility even of photographic reproductions, for it there

13. Page 2/2.   14. Page 60.   15. Page 61.
16. Bookseller of the Last Century, p. 274.
17. Forgotten Books of the American Nursery, p. 60.

appears that the advertisement is actually headed: "*Lately Published in* London, (*Price One Shilling neatly bound,*)" which heading does not appear in the reproduction.

The conclusion then would seem rather to be that Franklin and Hall, (or more probably David Hall himself, since Franklin by this time had given up bookselling),[18] had imported the books on their own account, or had accepted them on consignment, and placed them on sale in Philadelphia. Franklin's custom appears to have been to have his orders for books in London filled through his friend and correspondent, William Strahan, and there is no indication in his published writings or letters that he ever had any direct dealings with Newbery. He may have had some acquaintance with John Newbery, for in a letter to Strahan, under date of November 27, 1755, he wrote: "My respects to Mr. Newbery, of whom you give so amiable a character."[19]

This conclusion is fairly well corroborated by the fact that in the issue of the *Pennsylvania Gazette* of December 11, 1750, there appeared again the list of Newbery publications, as part of an advertisement reading: "Just published, and to be sold by the Printers hereof (Price 3*s.6d.*) Anti-Paedo-Rantism Defended: . . . Lately published at New-York, and to be sold at the Post-Office Philadelphia (Price 1*s.* 6*d.*) A New Memorandum-Book: . . . Lately published at Antigua, and to be sold at the Post-Office, Philadelphia (Price 2*s.*)Medulla Medicinae Universae: . . . Lately Published in London, (Price One Shilling, neatly bound.) A Museum for Young Gentlemen and Ladies: . . ."[20] Then the advertisement of the Newbery

18. Franklin had written Cadwallader Colden, under date of September 29, 1748, of his "having put my printing-house under the care of my partner, David Hall, absolutely left off bookselling, and removed to a more quiet part of the town. . . ." (The Writings of Benjamin Franklin, A. H. Smyth, editor, 1905, ii, 362).

19. Idem, iii, 304.

20. Page 2/2–3. This advertisement was repeated in the issues of December 25, 1750 (p. 4/1), and January 1, 1750–51 (p. 4/3).

publications runs on exactly as in the issue of the *Gazette* of November 15.

Apparently the Newbery books met with favor and a ready sale in Philadelphia, for the *Pennsylvania Gazette* of June 13, 1751, contained an advertisement headed: "Just imported in the Wandsworth, Capt. Smith, and to be sold by David Hall, At the Post-Office, the following Books, viz. . . . ." A long list of books follows under the separate headings of Folios, Quartos, Octavos, and "Twelves." Among the list of the "Twelves" are found the 'Museum for young gentlemen and ladies, pretty Book for Children, Royal Primmers, and Battledores. . . .' [21] The *Gazette* of December 10, 1751, contained a somewhat similar advertisement headed: "Just imported in the last two ships from London, and to be sold by David Hall, At the Post-Office." While this advertisement did not mention Primers specifically, it contained a "parcel of small histories, and useful and entertaining books for children. . . .[22] In the *Gazette* of May 17, 1753, Hall was still advertising that he had for sale spelling-books and "Primmers." [23] His presumable success with them evidently attracted the attention of other book-sellers, for in the *Gazette* of July 18, 1754, Tench Francis Jr. advertised as "Just imported from London," and to be sold by him, a long list of books including "little children's books, lilleputian magazine, doz. royal primers, doz. battledores. . . ." [24]

But to Philadelphia the credit is due, not only of first offering the Royal Primer for sale in this country, but also of publishing the first American edition of it, which was issued by the Quaker bookseller, James Chattin, with the date of 1753 on the title-page. Of this edition only one copy is known to exist, in the private collection of Dr. A. S. W. Rosenbach of Philadelphia. Sabin,[25] Evans,[26] and Hildeburn [27] cite a 'Royal Primer

21. Page 2/2–3. Repeated June 20, 1751, pp. 3/1–2.   22. Page 2/1–2.
23. Page 3/1.   24. Page 2/3.   25. xviii, 70.   26. iii, 7114.
27. The issues of the Press in Pennsylvania, 1685–1784, i, p. 281.

improved' as 'The Second Edition, Philadelphia: James Chattin, 1753, 18mo.' No copy is located or collation given, and it would seem as if the entry might have been derived from some catalogue or advertisement, that none of the bibliographers had had the opportunity of examining it, and that one had followed the other in recording it.

The imprint of the Rosenbach copy reads: '[Cut of Royal Arms] The Royal Primer Improved: Being an easy and pleasant Guide To The Art of Reading. Philadelphia: Printed and Sold by James Chattin, in *Church-Alley*. 1753.' On the fly-leaf is written the name of the original owner with the date of 1754. Curiously enough this first American reprint of the Royal Primer differs more widely from the Newbery publication than any of the other eighteenth-century American editions which have been located and examined, and which in general follow the Newbery Primer very closely. The cut of a "Good Boy and Girl at their Study" is accompanied by a totally different set of verses, six lines in all, beginning "Attend ye sprightly Youth, ye Modest Fair. . . ." The customary "A Apple" alphabet in verse, and the alphabet with illustrative cuts are not employed. The syllabaries, words composed of various letters, and "Easy Lessons" are very much expanded and fill about fifty pages of the total text pages, 3–95. The Easy Lessons are composed of extracts from the Bible, and of didactic proverbs and platitudes. Most of the cuts representing birds, animals, and sacred scenes are found as in the Newbery Primer, though evidently reëngraved in many cases. But pages 76–80 have a series of cuts of sailing vessels which have been found in no other primer, a ship, brigantine, snow, schooner, and sloop. Running on at the bottom of these five pages is a poem by Addison entitled: "An Ode to Almighty God, on a Deliverance at Sea." The book ends at page 95 with Dr. Watts's "Divine Song of Praise to God, for a Child," page 96 being used to advertise another publication by Chattin.

The *Pennsylvania Gazette* does not contain any advertisement of the Chattin Royal Primer in 1753, and no advertisement of it as a separate publication has been found. But the *Gazette* of February 26, 1754, has a list of "Books printed and sold by James Chattin, at his Printing-Office, next Door to Hugh Roberts's in Church-Alley, Philadelphia, viz.; . . . The royal primer improv'd, neatly bound, 6d. Ditto, bound different, 8d." [28] This was repeated in the issues of March 12 [29] and April 11, 1754. [30]

In Boston the earliest known reprint of the Royal Primer is that of William McAlpine in 1768, a copy of which is in the Rosenbach collection, with the imprint: "Boston: Printed and sold by W. McAlpine, between the Governor's and Dr. Gardiner's Marlborough-Street, 1768." Evans (IV, 10761), records a McAlpine edition as Boston, 1767, but no copy has been located. The record was apparently made from a sale catalogue, or similar source, and there may have been some confusion with the New England Primer, of which McAlpine did publish two editions in 1767.

The Rosenbach McAlpine copy of 1768 is incomplete, ending with page 44. Judging from a later McAlpine edition it should have fifty-six pages. So far as it goes, it follows the Newbery Royal Primer closely, the variations in general being due to compressing the material into a smaller number of pages, and to the reëngraving of cuts.

The files of the *Boston News-Letter* contain various advertisements of primers, beginning as early as 1752, commonly referred to as imported either from London or Scotland, but no definite conclusions can be drawn as to whether they were Royal Primers or New England Primers. In the case of the Scotch importations however it seems more than probable that they would be the latter. In the *News-Letter* of July 3, 1752,

28. Page 2/3. 29. Page 4/1.
30. Page 4/1. The Royal Primer was also advertised by Chattin in the issues of October 17, October 31, and December 5, 1754.

John and Thomas Leverett "opposite to the Stationer's Arms, in Cornhill," gave notice that they had just imported, and offered for sale, a long list of books including "Psalters, Primers, Spelling-Books, &c. . . ." [31] July 16, 1752, William McAlpine advertised books "Lately Imported from Scotland" among which were Psalters, Psalm Books and Primers.[32] Thomas Rand in Cornhill, on May 22, 1755, advertised as "Just imported from London . . . Psalters and Primers . . ." [33] June 10, 1756, Joshua Blanchard gave notice that he had just imported Primers.[34] Thomas Leverett, June 8, 1758, offered Primers which he had imported,[35] and January 17, 1760, and January 29, 1761, John Leverett had imported Primers for sale.[36] July 1, 1762, Philip Freeman offered Primers,[37] and on the same day William Lang announced an offering of "Primmers" imported from Glasgow.[38]

While no specific advertisement of the McAlpine 1768 edition has been found, the *Boston Gazette* of November 21, 1768, contained a general advertisement reading: "William M'Alpine Informs his Customers and others, That, being obliged to raise a Sum of Money in a few Months — he intends to dispose of his Stock under the common Wholesale Prices if applied for soon. Most of the Books are of his Printing & Binding, and will be warranted good. Among which are . . . New England Primers, Royal Primers. . . ." [39] The *Boston News-Letter* of August 24, 1769, carried an advertisement by Zechariah Fowle, with whom Isaiah Thomas served his apprenticeship, which is of interest both on account of its offering of children's books and for the opportunity which it afforded to any aspirant to the trade of printer and book-seller.[40] It reads: "The

---

31. Page 2/2.   32. Page 2/2. Repeated July 23, p. 2/2.
33. Page 2/2. Repeated May 29, p. 4/2, and June 5, p. 4/2.
34. Page 2/2.   35. Page 3/1. Also November 2, 1758, p. 3/3.
36. Pages 4/1 and 3/2.   37. Page 1/1.   38. Page 4/2.   39. Page 2/3.
40. Page 2/3. This advertisement appeared also in the *Massachusetts Gazette*, August 31, 1769 (p. 2/1), and September 21, 1769 (p. 2/3).

following Books to be sold By the Groce or Dozen, By Zechariah Fowle, In Back-Street near the Mill Bridge, Boston. . . .
The following Books for Children. The School of Good Manners, The Royal Primer, with Cuts, History of the Holy Jesus,
Dr. Watts's Divine Songs. . . .

"Said Fowle has to dispose of his Printing-Press, which is
compleat, and his Printing-Types, consisting of a Fount of
Double-Pica, English, and Small-Pica, with an Assortment of
large Letters, Flowers etc., and a very great Variety of Cuts
suitable for Ballads and such Books as are designed for the
Amusement of Children and others: Together with all Uten-
sils necessary for carrying on the Printing-Business. Any
Person inclining to purchase the above, may apply to said
Fowle." He eventually appears to have found a purchaser in
the person of his former apprentice, Isaiah Thomas, who became his partner in 1770. In Thomas's History of Printing he
wrote that: "This connection was dissolved in less than three
months, and Thomas purchased his press and types." [41]

In 1770 there appeared another American edition of the
Royal Primer, with the imprint: "Boston Printed for, and
Sold by John Boyles, in *Marlborough Street*, 1770," of which
only one copy has been located. The publisher was John
Boyle, also the publisher of several editions of the New Eng-
land Primer, a native of Marblehead who appears to have
begun life as Boyles. The records of St. Michaels Church,
Marblehead, contain the entry: "Boyles, Jo[hn] , s. Jo[hn] and
Lydia, bp. Mar –, 1745–6." [42] Among the marriage records is
the entry: "Boyles, John, and Lydia Gale, July 31, 1744." [43]
In the year 1773 he dropped the final letter of his family name.
The *Boston News-Letter* of August 26, 1773, had an advertisement of a new publication to be sold by John Boyles in Marlborough Street. [44] The issue of the *Boston Post Boy* for Mon-

41. Second Edition, 1874, i, p. 135.
42. Marblehead Vital Records, i, 62.
43. Id., ii, 48.
44. Page 4/2.

day, August 30 to Monday, September 6, 1773, contained a notice of a book: "This day Published, and to be sold by John Boyle, in Marlboro-street . . . ." [45] After this time the final *s* is very rarely, but still occasionally, to be seen.[46]

Isaiah Thomas, in his History of Printing, wrote that "John Boyle served an apprenticeship with Green & Russell. He purchased the types of Fletcher of Halifax,[47] and began business as a printer and bookseller in Marlborough St. in 1771, and printed a few books on his own account. In May, 1774, Boyle formed a partnership with Richard Draper, publisher of the *Massachusetts Gazette*, or *Boston News-Letter*. Draper died the following month, but the widow continued the newspaper, etc. Boyle was in partnership with the widow until August following; they then dissolved their connection and Boyle returned to his former stand. In 1775, Boyle sold his printing materials, but retained his book store, which he continued to keep in the same place." [48] As a matter of fact Boyle began the business of bookselling some two years earlier than the time stated by Thomas. The *Boston Post Boy*, June 26, 1769, contains the first mention of him as a bookseller. Four sermons by Samuel Stillman were advertised as "published, and Sold by Ezekiel Russell, at the New Printing Office, a few Doors Northward of Concert Hall, by Philip Freeman . . . by Philip Freeman, Jun'r . . . and by John Boyles, in Marlboro'-Street." [49] In the *Post Boy* of November 20, 1769, and again on November 12, 1770, Boyle advertised "Primers" in conjunction with other books which he offered for sale.

45. Page 3/2. Repeated in the next two issues of the Post Boy.

46. Heartman lists two issues of the New England Primer in 1774, one "Printed and sold by John Boyle's in Marlborough-street"; the other "Printed and sold by John Boyle, in Marlborough-street" (p. 43).

47. Thomas stated that Fletcher "remained at Halifax until 1770, then sent his printing materials to Boston for sale, and returned himself to England." (History of Printing, 1874, i, 361.)   48. Id., i, 170, 171.

49. Page 4/3. This advertisement had already appeared in the *Massachusetts Gazette* on June 5 and June 15, 1769, but without Boyle's name. In the issue of June 29 his name appeared together with the names of the three other sellers.

Boyle's reprint of the Royal Primer also follows the Newbery Primer closely. The slight typographical variations in the
text are such as would naturally come about in type-setting
and in reducing the number of pages,[50] but the general contents and arrangement in sequence are the same. The cuts are
cruder, but in general the variations in the details and positions
of the animals and birds represented might naturally be expected in reëngraving from the originals. Only once is a
totally different cut employed, in illustrating "The Rewards
of Virtue," where a large single figure is represented instead of
a small group of figures. There is, however, one curious variation among the cuts of animals. The Lion in the Newbery
Primer has the massive head and heavy mane of a lion. In the
Boyle Primer the head of the animal has a striking resemblance
to a human face and it does not have the shaggy mane which
would be expected as a marked characteristic of a lion, and
which would be very easy to reproduce. This fact taken in
conjunction with the last couplet of the descriptive verse:

> "The *Lion* ranges round the wood,
> And makes the lesser beasts his food:
> Thus Tyrants on their subjects prey,
> And rule with arbitrary sway."

arouses the probably fanciful but not unnatural conjecture,
whether any political satire was intended in view of the events
of the preceding year of 1769.

In 1773 McAlpine published another edition of the Royal
Primer. Valentine Hollingsworth of Boston has a perfect copy,
formerly the A. L. Hollingsworth copy. The imprint reads:
"Boston, Printed and Sold by William McAlpine, in *Marlborough-Street* where may be had a Variety of entertaining and
instructive Books for Children, MDCCLXXIII."[51] In its

50. The Newbery Primer used for purpose of comparison has seventy-two pages.
The Boyle edition has fifty-six only, but the pages are both taller and wider than in
the Newbery copy.

51. Title-page and frontispiece (cut of King George III), reproduced by George
E. Littlefield in his Early New England Schools, Boston, 1904, pp. 150, 151.

contents this edition corresponds to the Newbery Primer very exactly, though the subject matter is contained in fewer pages, which are both taller and wider than in the English edition.

A comparison of the McAlpine, 1773, and Boyle primers shows probably beyond a reasonable doubt that both were printed by the same printer. It will be remembered that the imprint of the Boyle primer reads: "Boston: Printed for, and Sold by John Boyles, ..." Except for a difference in making up the first five pages [52] they are almost identical, though an occasional variation in a line of text shows that the type had been reset for the 1773 edition. Both end with page 56. The single figure cut for "The Rewards of Virtue" is employed in each, as well as the cut of the Lion with what resembles a human face. In both, the cuts of animals, birds, sacred scenes, etc., are enclosed in borders composed of typographic flowers. At first glance the borders seem to be identical in the two primers, but a closer examination shows that while the same flowers are employed there are variations both in their combination and use.

Isaiah Thomas of Worcester in 1787 published an edition of the Royal Primer as one of his reproductions of the Newbery children's books. Dr. Charles L. Nichols, who has a perfect copy, has stated that "In 1784 Isaiah Thomas wrote to Thomas Evans of London for a large assortment of the Newbery books, evidently having in mind the plan of reproduction which was carried out in the following year." [53] This edition closely resembles the Newbery Primer, as would naturally be expected. The most noticeable differences are that the cut of the Royal Arms on the Newbery title-page is replaced by a cut containing the American eagle, shield, and motto; the description of "The Wicked Man" and Dr. Watts's "Divine Song of Praise to God," which appear about in the middle of the New-

52. Boyle edition: the first two leaves lacking; p. 5, title-page; p. 6, alphabet. McAlpine edition: p. 1, blank; p. 2, cut of George III; p. 3, title-page; p. 4, blank; p. 5, cut of a Boy and Girl at Prayers, with the verses; p. 6, alphabet.

53. Isaiah Thomas Printer, Writer & Collector. Boston 1912. Page 24.

bery Primer, are carried over toward the end of the Thomas Primer, and a poem of four verses entitled "An Evening Song," which is not found in the earlier primers, is added on the last page of text. The first and last pages of the book contain advertisements of Thomas publications. A "List of Juveniles" in the manuscript catalogue of the Library of Isaiah Thomas, in the possession of the American Antiquarian Society,[54] records two editions of the Royal Primer as having been printed, but no copy of the other reprint is known. The 1787 edition is an excellent specimen of the Thomas typography. The cuts, which in general closely follow those of the Newbery Primer, are very good, and rather better executed.

In 1796 the latest known issue of the eighteenth-century American editions made its appearance: "Printed and sold by Samuel Hall, No. 53, Cornhill, Boston. — 1796." The American Antiquarian Society possesses a perfect copy. It seems to have been reprinted from the Thomas 1787 edition, and is very much like it in appearance. The cut of the Arms on the title-page is the same, the Wicked Man and Divine Song appear in the same relative positions, and the Evening Song is on the last page of text. It does not contain any advertisements.

It will be observed, as has been stated earlier, that the New England Primer had not affected, nor reacted upon, the Royal Primer. Aside from the Chattin 1753 edition which stands in a class by itself, the inclusion of "An Evening Song" in the Thomas and the Hall editions is the only textual addition to be found in the course of nearly fifty years, with the trifling exception that Thomas had included among the alphabets on page 4 a set of what he termed "Old English Black" capitals. Since the Plimpton copy of the Newbery Primer has at the bottom of page 4 "Old English Black" lower case letters, it may be conjectured that the English edition from which Thomas reprinted also had Old English letters.

54. Isaiah Thomas, etc., pp. 132, 133.

Returning to the Newbery Royal Primer, it should be said that no copy with a dated imprint has been seen. Only two fairly safe conclusions can be drawn with regard to the probable time of issue of the various editions. First: Any primer which has in the imprint the name J. Newbery either alone or in conjunction with other booksellers, was, in all probability at least, printed before Newbery's death in 1767.[55] Second: Any copy which has an owner's name and date written in it was presumably published as early as the written date.[56] It is entirely unsafe to draw the deduction from the statement on the title-page: "Authoriz'd by His Majesty King George II. To be used throughout His Majesty's Dominions," that the edition was published prior to the death of the King in 1760. The Boyle edition of 1770, and McAlpine editions of 1768 and 1773, all have this statement. As a matter of fact it meant exactly what it said, that the book had been authorized by the King, and it was merely a simple form of copyright. This was clearly pointed out by Charles Welsh who wrote: "These little books were many of them published by the King's authority, which was the manner in which copyright was secured at that period, as witness the following announcement from the *Mercurius Latinus*, August 9, 1746: — 'George R., George the Second, by the Grace of God, King of Great Britain, &c., to all whom these presents shall come, Greeting. Whereas our trusty and well-beloved *John Newbery of London*, Bookseller, hath with great expence and much labour, compiled a work intitled '*The Circle of the Sciences; or, The Compendious Library*,' digested in a method entirely new, whereby each branch of *Polite Literature* is rendered extremely easy and instructive. We being will-

55. John Newbery died December 22, 1767, at the age of fifty-four (Bookseller of the Last Century, p. 70).

56. This statement is qualified on account of the possible chance of the owner having made a clerical error in setting down the date. It does not seem probable however that in the case of a book with no particular value at the time of its acquisition any one would be likely to date his book back with prophetic foresight of its enhanced value to posterity.

ing to encourage all works of public benefit, are graciously
pleased to grant him our royal privilege and license for the
sole printing, publishing, and vending the same.

> *Given at St. James', the 8th of December* 1744.
> *by His Majesty's Command,*
> Holles Newcastle.'

But owing to the laxness of the copyright laws at that period,
or possibly to the fact that Newbery did not renew his licenses
when they expired, many of the books were pirated by printers
in York, Newcastle, Dublin, and other provincial towns, and
often in terribly mutilated and travestied forms."[57]

Six Newbery Royal Primers have been located in this country and examined. Four are very much alike textually, but the
other two, which are both in the private collection of Dr.
A. S. W. Rosenbach, have noticeable variations. The first,
formerly the D. Huntington copy, has a presentation inscription on the fly-leaf dated 1755. This is probably the earliest
edition among the six primers. It has only sixty-four pages
instead of the customary seventy-two, and does not contain
the pictorial alphabet, the short Scripture Catechism, the
Scripture-names in the New Testament, or the Rewards of
Virtue. It does include a short moral sketch of two pages
entitled the "Force of Good-Nature," which is headed by the
cut employed in the other copies for the Rewards of Virtue.
The second, formerly the James W. Ellsworth copy, has
seventy-eight pages, doubtless accounted for by the fact that
both types and page are slightly larger. The principal variation, however, is found in the pictorial alphabet where only five
out of the twenty-four illustrative cuts which are found in the
other primers have been used. For instance, Ape is substituted

57. Bookseller of the Last Century, p. 111. Sales of the Newbery Primer alone
must have run into hundreds of thousands. Welsh cites a statement from B. Collins's
Account Book that "20000 of these were sold from October, 1771 to October 1772,"
and this was over twenty years after its first appearance. (Id., p. 302.)

for Apple, Bee-hive for Bull, Camel for Cat, and so on. The imprints of the several editions differ somewhat,[58] while the general cuts show minor variations, largely from reëngraving, which are unimportant and do not call for particular comment.

As to other English editions, the Boston Public Library has a copy of 'The New Royal Primer' authorized, according to the title-page, by King George III, and "Printed by R. Bassam, No. 53, St. John's Street, West Smithfield." It is undated but has on the outside of the front cover a cut of the Princess of Wales, and on the back cover the Prince of Wales's crest.

Below the cut of the Princess of Wales is the fervent, though somewhat ungrammatical, aspiration: "Long live her Offsprings," a wish which was quite fully realized. At page six the same cut is used again under the heading "The Princess Royal of England." The Princess Royal was presumably the oldest daughter of George III, born September 29, 1766, and the Princess of Wales, who died February 8, 1772, was his mother. This would seem to establish the time of its first appearance somewhere between these two years. It follows in a general way the Newbery Primer but with many variations. It has a running headline, "Royal Primer." The first set of verses which are found on the frontispiece, as in the Newbery edition, appear again in a variant on the pages of the pictorial alphabet:

> "He who learns this Book throughout,
> Shall have a Horse to ride about:
> And She who learns these Letters fair
> Shall have a Coach to take the Air."

58. 1. London: Printed for J. Newbery, at the Bible and Sun, in St. Paul's Church-yard, and B. Collins at Salisbury. (Rosenbach.) 2. London: Printed for John Newberry. (N Y P L). 3. London: Printed for J. Newbery, at the Bible and Sun, in St. Paul's Church-yard, and B. Collins at Salisbury. (Nichols.) 4. London: Printed for J. New[bery at the Bible] and Sun, in St. Paul's [Church-yard and] B. Collins at Salisbury. (Plimpton, title-page defective). 5. London: Printed for J. Newberry, at the Bible and Sun, in St. Paul's Church-yard. (Rosenbach.) 6. London: Printed for John Newbery. (Merritt.)

It conforms to the Newbery Primer fairly closely for the first thirty-one pages, after which the changes are very marked. The birds and animals represented in the various cuts are nearly all different from those in the Newbery book, while the cuts of sacred scenes and events vary considerably. It also has an addition in the form of "An Hymn, by Mr. Addison."

In the Victoria and Albert Museum, South Kensington, there is an undated copy of the Royal Primer, with the imprint: "Brentford, Printed by P. Norbury, nearly opposite the Market Place. (Price Three Pence.)"

The Huntington Library has a copy of the Royal Primer published by D. Wogan, Dublin, 1813, which probably contains nineteenth-century additions as it has ninety-five pages, 32mo. There are several copies known of 'The Royal Primer: or, the First Book for Children. Adapted to their tender Capacities. Authorized by His Majesty King George III. To be used throughout His Majesty's Dominions. . . . Dublin: Printed by William Jones, 75, Thomas-Street. 1818.' This edition has ninety-six pages, and while it contains some of the features of the Newbery Primer it is much changed for the worse. It has a number of alphabets, some styled "Enticing," didactic "Easy Lessons" for children, several collections of Proverbs and Precepts, as well as additions to the cuts of animals and birds. The distinction and interest which pertained to the eighteenth-century primers is gone.

A simple check-list is appended with full realization of its incompleteness.

Check-list of Royal Primers

John Newbery Editions, 1750–17—?

1750   Advertised in *Pennsylvania Gazette*, November 15, 1750.

[*1755*?]   Rosenbach, formerly D. Huntington.
           Has presentation date of 1755.

[*1757*?]   N Y P L.

[*1760*?]   B M.

           Nichols: Imperfect, lacks frontispiece and pp. 65–72.

           Plimpton: Title-page defective, lacks pp. 49–50, 71–72.

           Rosenbach.

           Merritt: Pages 11–12 supplied by leaf from a New England
           Primer.

American Editions, 1753–1796

1753   *The Royal Primer Improved*, James Chattin, Philadelphia.
           Rosenbach.

1768   *The Royal Primer.* William McAlpine, Boston.
           Rosenbach: Lacks pp. 45–56.

1770   *The Royal Primer.* John Boyles, Boston.
           Merritt: Lacks first two leaves.

1773   *The Royal Primer.* William McAlpine, Boston.
           Huntington: Lacks pages 7–8.
           Valentine Hollingsworth: Perfect.

1787   *The Royal Primer.* Isaiah Thomas, Worcester.
           A A S: Imperfect.
           Nichols: Perfect.

178–?   Another Thomas' edition, date and copy unknown.

1796   *The Royal Primer.* Samuel Hall, Boston.
           A A S: Perfect.
           M H S: Imperfect.

Other English Editions, 1766?–1818

1766–1772? *The New Royal Primer.*   R. Bassam, West Smithfield.
           B P L.

1770–1800? *The Royal Primer.* P. Norbury, Brentford, England.
           B M.
           Victoria and Albert Museum, South Kensington.

1813   *The Royal Primer.* D. Wogan, Dublin.
           Huntington.

1818   *The Royal Primer.* William Jones, Dublin.
         B M.
         Pequot Library.
         Merritt.

The British Museum Catalogue also lists three editions of Royal Primers as:

London [1854?].   4°.
"   [1858].   24°.
"   [1870?].   8°.

A *good* Boy *and* Girl *at their Study.*

HE who ne'er learns his *A, B, C,*
     For ever will a Blockhead be;
But he who to his Book's inclin'd,
Will foon a golden Treafure find.

CHILDREN, like tender
     Oziers take the Bow,
And as they firft are fashion'd always
     grow:
For what we learn in Youth, to that
     alone,
In Age we are by fecond Nature
prone.

THE
Royal Primer;
Or, an eafy and pleafant
GUIDE
TO THE
ART of READING.
Being an Introductory Part of
the *Circle of the Sciences.*
Publifh'd by AUTHORITY.
LONDON:
Printed for J. NEWBERY, at
the *Bible* and *Sun,* in St. *Paul's*
Church-yard, and B. COLLINS
at *Salifbury.* (Price bound 3*d.*)

From the copy with inscription dated 1755

THE NEW ENGLAND PRIMER

By WORTHINGTON CHAUNCEY FORD

Of the Massachusetts Historical Society

AMONG the words in common use and understanding, the origin of which has never been determined, is the word "Primer." The ordinary sense of "first or primary book" does not agree with its historical growth. One of the Day Hours of the Western Church was known as "Prime" and, specifically, it was one of the Little Hours, said to have been introduced at a later time than the Greater Hours. A primer in its first forms was a prayer-book or devotional manual intended not for the priests but for the laity, and in the fourteenth and fifteenth centuries, in its simplest form, it contained the Hours of the Blessed Virgin, Psalms, the Litany, the Office for the Dead, and the Commendations. After the English Reformation the contents were altered to conform to the Book of Common Prayer, first issued in 1553 and continued with changes till 1783. Long before the Reformation, however, the word was applied to a little book by which children were taught to read and pray. The A B C, Pater Noster, Creed, Decalogue, and certain prayers would constitute such a primer, but the form and contents were not uniform, and a volume could be written on the subject even if confined to the products before the beginning of the seventeenth century.

The primer was thus originally a religious book, a manual of devotion, and, by a natural progress, and with alphabet and syllabary added, became a school-book, but with the religious feature still dominant.[1] We are told that after 1600 the main purpose of the primer appears to have been educational, and it

---

1. In 1564–65 Alde printed a ballet, "an a b c with a prayer," and printers were fined for binding primers "contrary to the orders" of the Stationers' Company; *Registers*, I, 269, 274.

was used as a first reader, as in Scotland down to about 1800. Sanctioned by royal authority, the little book took on a political function, for Church and State were in close union. In the disturbed conditions in both Church and State of the seventeenth century, and in the hands of printers compiling their own A B C's or primers, the possible extension of purpose was limited only by the purpose in the mind of the compiler. It was a long way between the privilege or monopoly given to Seres of printing the primer for little children, and just a century after the freedom taken by Benjamin Harris in his 'New England Primer.' The alphabet might be attached to the catechism and so serve religion and education, and catechisms were imported into Boston from London in the second half of the seventeenth century. The first idea of a New England primer, however, arose in the mind of an obscure London printer, apparently without any connection with Massachusetts or New England.

In the Stationers' *Register* (Eyre and Rivington, III, 199), under date October 5, 1683, was entered by John Gaine, "for his Booke or Coppy entituled the New England Primer or Milk for babes." What little is known of John Gaine and his publications throws no light upon the entry or its origin. The book was presumably printed, for the fee of six-pence would hardly be warranted by the registration of merely a title. Some information that such a publication had been made drifted to Boston, for Usher wrote in 1684 or 1685 about it to Chiswell, the noted London publisher and bookseller, who replied in April, 1685: "There is not one New England Primmer in London, if they will Take of Ten Grose and send over a book to print it by, they may be furnished, less than that Number will not Answer the Charge." Catechisms had been prepared in New England, so there is no impossibility in supposing that a primer might also be. Yet here is an entry of a title exactly suited to such a publication, emanating from a printer who could not have got the suggestion from Boston. Usher would have known of the preparation in Massachusetts of such a work; had there been any profit in it he or another Boston bookseller would have handled it. He wrote to London, however, and one of the largest and best-known publishers of that city could not supply a single copy. If Gaine did issue his 'Primer' not a copy has survived, a fact by no means strange, even where many editions of a book were made.

This discovery of Gaine's entry somewhat shook the claim generally made that Benjamin Harris originated the New England primer. Harris came to Boston in 1686 after a somewhat stormy career in London, where his publishing activities had deeply involved him with the courts. On one subject he was almost a fanatic — on the cruelty and wickedness of the Pope and Roman Catholics. By tracts, newspapers, and playing cards he had sought to express the dangers threatened to the State by the Popish following, and he had prepared a volume intended to inspire the young with a wholesome fear of Rome and her works. In 'The Protestant Tutor,' first issued in 1679–80, Harris compiled a volume intended to serve as a first reader for children and an unfailing encouragement to persecute Roman Catholics. The title of this production reads:

The | Protestant | Tutor. | Instructing Children | to spel and read En- | glish, and Ground- | ing them in the True | Protestant Religion | and Discovering the | Errors and Deceits | of the Papists. || London: Printed for Ben Harris under the Piazza | of the Royal Exchange at Cornhill, 1679.

From this publication the 'New England Primer' issued by Harris in Boston between 1687 and 1690 was believed to have been derived.

In an advertisement in Harris' *Protestant (Domestick) Intelligence*, February 27, 1680, the contents of the first issue of the 'Protestant Tutor' are given, and from them it is seen that the volume was a bitterly partisan tract, in which the educational features were reduced to a minimum. In a country still quaking from the terrors of Oates and Popish plots, torn by disputes on the State church, such a publication would find a place; and Harris sought favor by dedicating a second edition, put forth in January, 1681, to the son of the Duke of Monmouth. It was highly recommended for use in all Protestant schools as an antidote to Popery. Outside of England, however, it would find no market, for its reading matter and crude wood-cuts were intended for English youth and no others. The illustrations did not appear in the syllabary nor in any of the pages for instruction in reading, — as in the 'New England Primer,' — but were associated with the articles most concerned with the misdoings of the Papists.

One year before Harris came to Boston a little tract was printed in that town by Samuel Green, for John Griffin, a bookseller of no great account. It bore the title 'The Protestant Tutor, for Children.' From a fragmentary copy in the American Antiquarian Society it is seen to have been composed of two divisions, a catechism and Mr. Rogers' Verses, both of which were in Harris's 'Protestant Tutor' and may have been borrowed from that work. It was a catechism against Popery, and reads strangely on New England soil — quite out of place. Griffin's venture could hardly have proved a success. No mention of it is known in records of the time, and there is no hint of later issues. The catechism could serve no useful purpose, and the martyrdom of the fictitious Rogers awakened little or no interest. One year later Harris appeared in Boston and in time thought he saw an opening for a primer — a true New England primer. He entirely discarded his 'Protestant Tutor,' rejecting even the two selections which Griffin had taken into his 'Tutor.' In the first 'New England Primer' neither the catechism nor the Rogers verses appeared: the war against Rome had disappeared. In the second edition, advertised in 1690, the Verses of Rogers and a Prayer of King Edward VI were inserted, but the prayer soon dropped out, as unsuited to the political or churchly atmosphere of New England.

Thus the Rogers lines, and possibly the syllabary, were the only parts of the 'New England Primer' that were drawn from Harris's 'Protestant Tutor.' The 'Tutor' was a political tract and the 'Primer' was a school-book. It is difficult to see how a definite connection between the two can be made. Though Harris was responsible for both, it is rather a tribute to his business acumen that he could throw off so completely his English compilation, recognizing its unfitness for the New England people. In retaining the Rogers verses he kept one of the chief claims of the 'Primer' to remembrance. As Mr. Eames has done so much to clear our knowledge of New England primers and catechisms, I have thought it a proper opportunity to make this record of late developments.[2]

2. See my Boston Book Market, 1679–1700, 29, and Massachusetts Historical Society *Proceedings*, LVII, 45.

DES
PRISONS
DE
PHILADELPHIE.

PAR UN EUROPÉEN.

PHILADELPHIE.

Imprimé & ſe trouve chez MOREAU DE Sᴛ-MÉRY, Imprimeur-
Libraire , au coin de Front & de Walnut ſtreets , Nº. 84.

Jᴀɴᴠɪᴇʀ 1796.

CHEZ MOREAU DE SAINT–MÉRY, PHILADELPHIE

By HENRY W. KENT

Of the Grolier Club, New York

With a List of Imprints enlarged by George Parker Winship

SEVERAL years ago, a friend who knew my interest in Bodoni and his press at Parma, sent me a beautiful uncut square quarto by the Papal printer, which I regarded as a gift having a double value, since it dealt with a subject, also, in which I had an interest. The title of the book ran like this: 'Discours sur l'utilité du musée établi à Paris; prononcé dans sa séance publique du 1er décembre 1784, par M. L. E. Moreau de Saint-Méry, ex-Secrétaire perpétuel de ce musée . . . A Parme. Imprimée par Bodoni, MDCCCV.' I read the essay as well as I was able, without cutting the leaves, but I used the book chiefly to gratify my eye. Having had time hanging on my hands lately, I have read the essay again, carefully, and then I began to wonder who the author might be, with so long a sheaf of titles and honours gathered on the title-page after his name: Conséiller d'Etat, l'un des commandants de la Légion d'Honneur, Administrateur Général des Etats de Parme, Plaisance, Guastalla, etc., etc., and member of seven societies, including La Société Philosophique de Philadelphie. The "museum" concerning which Saint-Méry wrote was established in 1782, in the rue Ste. Avoye, at Paris, by Pilâtre de Rozier, an interesting young man who met his death at the age of thirty-one in a tragic and most unfortunate manner, by a fall from a balloon.[1] The museum, which was really a kind of

---

1. Upon his tomb-stone one may read:

    Ci-git un jeune téméraire
    Qui — dans son généreux transport
    De l'Olympe étonné franchissant la barrière
    Y trouva le premier et la gloire et la mort.

incubator for revolutionary ideas, and not a museum in the usual sense of the word at all, was known by his name until it was changed to Lycée Républicain, and again to Athénée de Paris, under which it had an interesting history. The preface to the book tells this. But why was the essay not published until 1805! What had happened to the author between these dates? This curiosity was easily satisfied by a reference to the 'Biographie Universelle'; in an article signed by B. L. the facts appear, and, abridged and translated freely, they are as follows:

Moreau de Saint-Méry was born January 13, 1750, at Fort Royal, Martinique. Sprung from a good family, originally of Poitou, he was still young when he lost his father, and he received but an imperfect education. When he was nineteen he went to Paris, and was admitted into the King's guard, and succeeded, without neglecting the service, in being enrolled an *avocat au parlement*. Returning to Martinique, he found his fortune considerably diminished, and, in order to reëstablish it, he set off to Cap Français to practise as an advocate. About 1780, he was admitted to the Superior Council of San Domingo.

Taking advantage of such leisure as his duties permitted him, he occupied himself in classifying the abundant materials he had collected on the laws, the description, and the history of the French colonies. He explored the registers and archives of the Antilles, and, on one of his excursions, discovered the tomb of Christopher Columbus which he restored at his own expense. Returning to Paris, he was warmly welcomed by the learned world, and it was then that he became associated with Pilâtre de Rozier in founding the Museum of Paris, of which the greater part of the men of letters of the period were members. When the Revolution broke out, he was chosen President of the Electors of Paris, and twice made an address to Louis XVI. He also, it is said, persuaded his colleagues to choose Lafayette as chief of the National Guard. In 1790, as Deputy for Martinique, he was a member of the Constituent Assembly, where he occupied himself more particularly with the affairs of the Colonies. In 1791, he was a member of the Judicial Council, established in connection with the Ministry of Justice. A few days before the tenth of August, he was attacked by a band of fanatics, and forced to retire to the little Norman town of Forges. Having been arrested with the Duc de la Rochefoucauld, he escaped the scaffold, thanks to the devotion of one of his guards, to whom he had once rendered a favor. He then fled to the United States with his family. Returning to France in 1799, he obtained from his friend, Admiral Bruix, the post of Historiographer of Marine, and a commission to prepare a Maritime Penal Code. Nominated Councillor of State in 1800, Moreau de Saint-Méry was dispatched in 1801, in the capacity of Resident, to the Duke of Parma; and, on the death of that Prince, he became Administrator-General of the Duchies of Parma, Piacenza, and Guastalla. He used the very considerable power delegated to him with wisdom and moderation, protected all industrial establishments, and encouraged letters; enjoying, doubtless, an acquaintance with Bodoni, whom he now employed to print the 'Discours' of twenty years before! But unfortunately, the Administrator habitually lacked firmness, and was too prone to forget he was not the Sovereign of the States confided to his care. In 1806 he was recalled by Napoleon, and fell into complete disgrace. The cause assigned for this was the weakness with which he had repressed a mutiny of the Militia companies of Parma, who had refused to march to the camp at Bologna. The Emperor showed a lively irritation, and dispatched Junot with unlimited powers. The instigators of the revolt were shot, and two villages which had sided with them, burnt. As to Moreau de Saint-Méry, he lost not only his place of Administrator, but his position as Councillor of State, and even the sum of 40,000 francs due him, which they refused to pay. Napoleon having addressed him on the subject in a loud voice, with a certain asperity, he allowed himself to reply: "Sire, I do not ask you to reward my uprightness; I only beg that it be tolerated. Do not be afraid — this disease is not catching!"

Up to the year 1812, Moreau lived entirely upon the kindness of the Empress Josephine, his distant relative; after that period he was allowed a pension which hardly sufficed for his necessities. In 1817, Louis XVIII, having been told of his distress, sent him a present of 15,000 francs. He died January 28, 1819, at Paris, at the age of sixty-eight. He belonged to most of the learned societies of Paris.

Here is a life that reads like a romance! Few novelists, however, would have thought of the touch about Columbus's grave, which gives an American a feeling of proprietary interest in the gentleman from the Antilles. But we have still to supply in its chronological place a paragraph apparently unrecognized by the biographer which is calculated to awaken this kind of interest in earnest.

When Saint-Méry came to America, it appears that at first he earned his bread, painfully, as a clerk in the employment of a New York commission merchant, the future Administrateur Général des Etats de Parme, Plaisance, etc., etc., rolling barrels of pork and all sorts of things, and loading vessels. Later he went to Philadelphia, where he opened a book-shop at 84 S. Front Street, to which he presently added a printing press! Saint-Méry became a printer and bookseller, and it is this episode in his career which concerns us chiefly, and not that of the really famous refugee, the friend of the most distinguished of his countrymen who came to live in the United States, or to visit here. The list of his callers, visitors, friends, and correspondents includes such men as John Adams, Beaumerg, William Cobbett, Gouvain, Goynard, General Kosciusko, La Rochefoucauld Liancourt, Talleyrand, Van Braam, and many others. Our printer's own interesting account of his travels in this country and his stay in Philadelphia is found in a volume of his Journal entitled: 'Voyage aux Etats-Unis de l'Amerique, 1793–1798,' edited by Professor Stewart L. Mims of Yale University, and published in 1913. What an interesting *rendezvous* his shop in Philadelphia was, with Talleyrand and the other frequent visitors coming and going; as headquarters for the publication of the *Courrier de la France et des colonies*, edited by another San Domingan, Gatereau, and as a common ground for the meeting of the *émigrés*, the diary duly relates. But, full as it is on other subjects, this important record is provokingly reticent regarding the work of the book-shop and the press. Gleaned from the text of Professor Mims' book, its meager references to the "complete printing office" are given here to save some one else the trouble of weeding them out.

In October, 1794, Saint-Méry employed as clerk a man named Descombatz, who had had a shop in San Domingo, and in November he hung out a sign in English and French, "ma belle enseigne," reading:

MOREAU DE ST. MÉRY AND CO. BOOKSELLER
PRINTER AND STATIONER
NO. 84 FRONT STREET

MOREAU DE ST. MÉRY ET COMP. LIBRAIRIE
IMPRIMEUR ET PAPETIER
NO. 84 1ere RUE

The shop, which was on the south side of Front Street, on the corner of Chestnut, where nearly all of the best goldsmiths, watchmakers, booksellers, and printers were located, was opened on December 10, and on March 1, 1795, a catalogue of the stock was published. The list of books and other wares offered for sale shows Saint-Méry to have been a discriminating buyer in a field calculated to appeal to the French people, as well as others in Philadelphia; and a note shows that he was prepared to offer engravings, stationery, mathematical instruments, maps, charts, and music, as well as English, Italian,

Spanish, German, Dutch, and French books. In April of the same year, the printing equipment, "L'imprimerie," ordered from London, arrived. Trouble with his partner, the Baron Frank de la Roche, whose acquaintance he made in New York and who advanced the capital for the business, began early. In May, he promised de la Roche to efface the words "et compagnie" from his sign, and he adds in the Diary, "Je ne sais quel prix il mettait à ce sacrifice." The legal dissolution of the company occurred in August of the same year.

In June, the types ordered from London were about to be shipped, and in August they were received. Descombatz was taken into service in September of the same year. La Grange, a printer, first in Paris and then in San Domingo, became *maître ouvrier* in the printing office, and one Despioux, a Bordelais, also from the island, was employed as compositor. There seems also to have been another clerk, named Jules, who was born in Paris. Early in September, 1797, the shop was moved to a less desirable location, the unfashionable Northern Liberties, Callow Hill Street, corner of Front and Walnut Streets, and there Saint-Méry remained during the rest of his stay in Philadelphia.

The first volume issued from the press, an 'Essay on Improving the Breed of Horses,' appeared in October, a month after La Grange and Despioux began work. The real purpose of the printing press, however, was to enable the author-printer to issue his own work on San Domingo, one of the most important contributions to the history of this island; but the works of certain of his friends and visitors came in remarkably pat as fillers-in until his own performances were ready for the press: of William Cobbett, the English political writer who translated the 'Description of the Spanish Part of San Domingo'; of Van Braam, the Dutch ambassador of the East India Company; and of La Rochefoucauld Liancourt, the distinguished philanthropist.

A list is added of such of the books issued from the press as have been located in New York, Philadelphia, Boston, or Providence libraries. The notes from the file of the *Courrier Français et des Colonies*, at the Boston Athenaeum, have been added by Mr. Winship. The books were printed in a Caslon of a clear, clean appearance, their title-pages showing the nice French touch, particularly in the use of an eighteenth-century cypher in 'Des Prisons,' and a *cul-de-lampe* in the 'Despatch.' The map in the 'San Domingo,' engraved by Vallance, and the plates in the Van Braam 'Voyage' are much more pretentious and far better done than those issued in most American publications of the period.

Saint-Méry was not exactly above his business, but he appears to have had a clear idea of his own importance, and the affairs of the big world interested him more than anything else. The comings and goings of his many visitors, the suppers and dinners which he gave and was given, the visits he paid — all very properly a part of the life of a person accustomed to the ways of French society — could not have left him much time for work behind the counter. Add to all these distractions the disorders occasioned by the epidemic of yellow fever which raged in Philadelphia in 1797, and it is not surprising that when Saint-Méry was about to return to France, going home for good in August, 1798, he was obliged to sell all his belongings because he was hard up, the business not having paid, "car mon commerce n'allait plus."

As a printer, brief as the period of his activities was, Saint-Méry conferred distinction upon the history of the art in America, and he is entitled to a high place in our list of early publishers, wherever historians assign him as patriot, historian, and governor.

Publications of Moreau de Saint-Méry

1795

(Moreau de St.-Méry.) Catalogue of Books, Stationary, Engravings, Mathematical Instruments, Maps, Charts, and other Goods of Moreau de St.-Méry & Co.'s Store, No. 84, South Front-Street, Corner of Walnut, Philadelphia, 1795.　　　　　　　　　　　　12 mo, pp. ix, 76.　(1)
Issued in March.

Prospectus . . . un journal sous le titre de *Courrier de la France et des Colonies* . . . paraîtra le 15 de ce mois. [signed] Gaterau. Philadelphie ce 1er. Octobre 1795. Printed by Moreau de St.-Méry, Printer and Book-seller, corner of Front and Walnut Streets, Philadelphia.
　　　　　　　　　　　　　　　Small 4to. Broadside.　(2)
Reprinted from the copy at the John Carter Brown Library in The Papers of the Bibliographical Society of America, 1920, xiv, 125–126.

Courrier de la France et des Colonies. No. 1 [to 66] Publié, à Philadelphie, par Gaterau. Du Jeudi 15 Octobre 1795 [to 31 Decembre].
　　　　4to, pp. 1–264 & 1 p. Supplement to No. 64. Each issue 4 pp.　(3)
The Boston Athenaeum Library has the complete file; see Winship, 'French Newspapers in the United States before 1800' in Papers of Am. Bib. Soc., xiv, part II, which states that "no copy has been seen." The advertisements which throw additional light on the subject of this paper are reprinted below, with the date when each first appeared. Nearly all were repeated in subsequent issues, apparently whenever there was space to be filled.

(Moreau de St.-Méry.) Essay on the Manner of Improving the Breed of Horses in America. October.　　　　　　　　　　　　　　　　(4)
The month of publication is usually given on the title page of Moreau's editions

Essai sur le manière de améliorer l'éducation des chevaux. Novembre.
　　　　　　　　　　　　　　　8vo, pp. iv, 39.　(5)
Announced in *Courrier*, No. 4, 19 Octobre. "Le prix est d'un quart de gourde (25 cents), en français ou en anglais."

Nouvelle Constitution Française.　　　　　　　　　　　　　　(6)
The following announcement appeared in the *Courrier*, No. 29, 17 Novembre: "On met actuellement sous presse, à l'imprimerie de cette feuille, la *Nouvelle Constitution francaise*, arrivée par le dernier bâtiment venu du Havre. Elle paraîtra en même tems en anglais, imprimée par Benjamin Franklin Bache." No copy has been seen, and the fact that, unlike all of the other advertisements of the printer, this does not appear again, may mean that the project of printing it was given up.

1796

Courrier de la France et des Colonies . . . par Gaterau. No. 1 [to 63]. Du Vendredi 1 Janvier 1796 [to Lundi 14 Mars].   4to, pp. 1–252. (7) No. 63 begins with a brief statement that the ill-health of the editor will make it impossible for him to continue the publication.

La Rochefoucauld-Liancourt, F. A. F. de. Des Prisons de Philadelphie. Par un Européen. Janvier.   8vo, pp. 44. (8)

—— On the Prisons of Philadelphia.   8vo, pp. 46. (9) This was deposited for copyright on January 2, 1796, and the certificate is printed in the *Courrier*, No. 8, January 9, and later issues. In No. 19, January 22, "Moreau de St.-Méry, a l'honneur de prévenir le public qu'il metre en vente aujourd'hui un pamphlet (etc.). Le prix de l'exemplaire est d'un quart de gourde, en française ou en anglois." A brief statement of its contents was printed in the paper of the 25th, and subsequently. Reprinted, Amsterdam, 1799.

Moreau de St.-Méry. Description topographique et politique de la partie espagnole de l'isle Saint-Domingue. 8vo, 2 vols.: pp. xlix, 307; 311. (10) This was announced in No. 1 of the *Courrier*. The price was three dollars for the two volumes, and would be four dollars to those who did not subscribe in advance of publication; 200 had already subscribed, and the work was to go to press as soon as 500 subscriptions were received; the first volume was to appear in November. The printed List of Subscribers contains 136 names, one of which is "Un François, Cent Exemplaires" and another "Un Américain, Deux Cents Exemplaires," these two friends making the publication possible, apparently. It was deposited for copyright on January 2, and the certificate, with a résumé in French, was printed in the *Courrier*, No. 8, January 9, and subsequent issues. The completion of vol. I is announced in No. 49, February 26: "Le travail de la gravûre de la Carte n'étant pas encore terminé, cette Carte (quê doit itre mise à la fin du 1er. volume), ne sera delivrée qu'avec le second." About 300 copies remained in June, 1798.

Moreau de St.-Méry. A topographical and political description of the Spanish part of Saint-Domingo. Translated by William Cobbett.   2 vols., 80, pp. 8, 8, liv, 314; 318, (1). (11) The *Courrier* on February 26 stated that "la traduction anglaise . . . dont plus des deux-tiers sont déjà imprimée, paraîtra incessament." The final issue announced on March 14 that "La traduction Anglaise du Ier. volume de la Description . . . sera mis en vente le 25 de ce mois; le 2ème volume est actuellement sous presse, ainsi que sa traduction en Anglais." In June, 1798, about 500 copies of the English edition were left. Reprinted, London, 1798.

Bordes, J. Marie de. Défense des colons de Saint-Domingue; ou, Examen rapide de la nouvelle Déclaration des droits de l'homme, en ce qu'elle a particulièrement de relatif aux colonies.   12mo, pp. x, 179.   (12)

The *Courrier* on March 4 announced "Souscription Proposée pour un ouvrage intitulé [as above] Par . . . habitant, propriétaire à Jérémie. Le prix . . . est d'une gourde [one dollar], et dès qu'il y en aura cent-vingt, l'ouvrage sera mis sous presse . . . sera de 100 à 120 pages"; it has 179.

Moreau de St.-Méry. Danse. Article extrait d'un ouvrage de M. L. E. Moreau de St.-Méry. Ayant pour titre: Répertoire des Notions Coloniales. Par Ordre Alphabétique.   8vo, pp. 8, 62.   (13)

Reprinted by Bodoni at Parma, 1801 and 1805.

James Quicksilver; pseudonym of James Philip Puglia. The Blue Shop or Impartial and Humorous Observations on the Life and Adventures of Peter Porcupine. August.   8vo, pp. 55.   (14)

Cobbett published his *Porcupine's Gazette* at Philadelphia in 1797-1799.

—— The Political Massacre, or Unexpected Observations on the Writings of our Present Scribblers. September.

8vo, p. 29, cartoon frontispiece.   (15)

—— The Disappointment, or Peter Porcupine in London: A Comedy in Three Acts, Written by James Quicksilver, Author of the Blue Shop, Political Massacre, &c.   (16)

The last paragraph of ' The Blue Shop ' promises "in three weeks from this date, I will publish a Comedy on the transactions of Peter Porcupine in London . . . and I pledge my honour that it will be as interesting, instructive and humourous Production as you could expect on the subject. Its title will be" as above. At the end of ' The Political Massacre ' is a full-page advertisement of this title as "Shortly will be published From the press of Moreau de St.-Mary," followed by a page announcing ' The Blue Shop ' as "Just Published From the press of Moreau de St.-Mery, and to be had at his and other principal Bookstores in this City." This is not mentioned, although another "Complete Disappointment" of 1808 in manuscript is given, in the list of his publications at the end of ' Forgery Defeated by James Ph. Puglia,' Philadelphia, 1822, in which the two preceding titles are described. Moreau does not allude to this episode in his Journal.

Moreau de St.-Méry. Idée Général, ou Abrégé des Sciences et des Arts à l'usage de la Jeunesse. October.   16mo, pp. xi, 408.   (17)

From the work by M. Forney, 1783.

Of the edition of 1000 copies, about 300 were left in June, 1798.

[The same] translated into English by Michael Fortune.

16mo (?) pp. 380.   (18)

About 300 copies were left in June, 1798.

Moreau de St.-Méry. De nouvelles Etrennes spirituelles à l'usage de Rome. October.   12mo, pp. 290.   (19)

In June, 1798, about 150 copies were left.

1797

Tanguy de la Boissiere (C. C.). Observations sur la dépêche écrite le 16 janvier 1797, par M. Pickering . . . à M. Pinkney.   8vo, pp. 50.   (20)

—— Observations on the Dispatch written the 16th. January 1797, by Mr. Pickering . . . to Mr. Pinkney. Translated from the French by Samuel Chandler.   8vo, pp. 50.   (21)

Moreau de St.-Méry. Description topographique, physique, civile, politique et historique de la partie française de L'Isle Saint-Domingue.
Large 4to, 2 vols., pp. 788 & 856, map, table.   (22)
The final issue of the *Courrier*, on March 14, 1796, announced that "Moreau de St.-Méry ouvrira incessament une souscription pour la Description de la partie Française de Sait-Domingue dont il est l'auteur." 1000 copies were printed, of which 300 remained in June, 1798.
The advertisement of June, 1798, states that "le 1er. volume est déjà traduit & publié par un libraire d'Harlem."

Braam Houckgeest (A. E. van). Voyage de l'Ambassade de la Compagnie des Indes Orientales Hollandaises, vers l'Empereur de la Chine, en 1794–1795.   4to, 2 vols. Maps & plates.   (23)
In June, 1798, Moreau advertised that he was "au moment de terminer l'impression du second volume du voyage de la Chine." An English translation, by Moreau, appeared in London in 1798.

Moreau de St.-Méry. Description of the Spanish Part of San Domingo.
4to, 2 vols., pp. 312; 319; maps & plates.   (24)
Translated by William Cobbett. Also, London, 1798.
The following extracts from Moreau's Journal refer to this publication: Mai 17, 1796. A la racommandation de Talleyrand, je fis une visite â M. Van Braam. Mai 23. Je convins avec M. Van Braam d'être l'Editeur de son voyage . . . et de la publier imprimé.
The first volume was announced for sale in the Leyden newspapers on October 6.

ADVERTISEMENTS

The following advertisements appeared in the *Courrier* on the dates given, and in various subsequent issues:
October 23, 1795. MOREAU DE ST.-MÉRY a l'honneur de prévenir qu'il vient de recevoir d'Europe un nouvel assortiment de plus de deux mille volumes français, au nombre desquels se trouvent:
La Vie du Général Doumourier, *qu'il ne faut pas confondre avec ses Mémoires.*
Les Mémoires posthumes de général Custine.
Le tableau des Prisons du tems de Robespierres. Et un grand nombre d'autres ouvrages sur les événemens présens.
On peut y choisir aussi, une fonde de Romans agréables & intéressans, &c. &c.

November 4. Moreau de St.-Mery a l'honneur de prévenir qu'il a de la musique Française dès meilleurs maitres pour le Forte Piano & la Harpe. Il a aussi pour la saisan présent, des pièces de l'espèce de lainage Anglais, appellé *fleecy hosiery*, & notamment des chaussons, des pièces d'estomac, des bas, des caleçons, des chemises d'hommes & des femmes.

November 25. Moreau de St.-Mery vient de recevoir de Londres par l'Ann et Mary, differens ouvrages, notamment:

Discours sur la Révolution, par Durand.

L'Expedition de Quiberon, par un officier Français à bord de la Pomone.

Aperçu des événemens, &c.

Histoire secrete de Coblentz.

Paris pendant l'année 1795.

Nouvelle lettre aux français, sur les évenemens depuis juillet, 1794.

Dangers which threaten Europe.

Letter to the Prince of Wales.

Chronological events of the French Revolution.

A Sketch of the politics of France; &c. &c.

February 1. Moreau de St.-Mery vient de recevoir le *Calendrier Parisien* pour l'an IV de la République Française, auquel on a joint un tableau chronologique des operations de la Convention — L'hymn du 9 Thermidor, le Réveil du Peuple &c. Prix: un quart de gourde:

Et des numèros de l'ouvrage périodique, Paris pendant l'année 1795.

March 14, the last issue. Moreau de St.-Méry a l'honneur de prévenir le public en général & ses amis en particulier, qu'il continue & continuera à imprimer tout ce qu'on voudra bien lui confier, soit en Anglais, soit en Français, sans différence pour le prix relativement à l'un ou l'autre language.

During June, 1798, an advertisement appeared in several issues of the *Courier Francáis* of Philadelphia,[1] announcing that "Moreau de St.-Mery étant au moment de terminer l'impression du second volume du voyage de la Chine par Van Braạm, dont il est l'Editeur; et de son second volume de la Partie Française de Saint-Domingue; veut vendre,

1°. Une imprimerie complette avec laquelle on peut entreprendre également la publication de plusieurs ouvrages, soit en français, soit en anglais.

2°-6°, 8°. [The remainders of his several publications, as noted above.]

7°. Des exemplaires de son Atlas de St.-Domingue. [Paris, 1795.]

9°. Quelques livres qui lui restent du fond de sa librairie.

10°. Un Forté-Piano.

11°. Un Violon de Renaudin.

12°. Plusieurs meubles & objets dont le détail serait trop long. Enfin Moreau de St.-Mery cedera aussi plusieurs ouvrages de sa bibliothèque personelle & quelques-unes de ses cartes.

1. Reprinted in The Papers of the Bibliographical Society of America, xiv, 118.

QUIENES FUERON LOS AUTORES, HASTA AHORA IGNORADOS, DE DOS LIBROS INGLESES QUE INTERESAN A AMERICA

By JOSÉ TORIBIO MEDINA

Of Santiago de Chile

PARA nadie medianamente versado en Bibliografía es un secreto que el ramo más difícil de esta ciencia es la averiguación de los autores de los libros anónimos o pseudónimos, y que, especialmente, sin duda, por eso, es también la parte de ella que se halla menos adelantada. Aportar una noticia siquiera que contribuya a aumentar el acervo de los que hasta hoy han sido resueltos no puede carecer de cierto interés, sobre todo si se trata de obras que tengan relación con la historia o literatura americanas. Quiera el lector pasar los ojos por las líneas siguientes y juzgar si he acertado con los nombres de los autores de los dos libros ingleses de que voy a tratar.

Sea el primero de ellos el que se intitula 'The Vale of Guasco: or the Maid with seven lovers. A romance in verse. In seven cantos.' London: Printed for J. J. Stockdale, 41, Pall-Mall. 1813. 8vo., 320 pp.

Bien se deja comprender que este libro toca a Chile por el título que lleva, 'El Valle del Guasco,' como si dijéramos aquel que primero encontraron Almagro y sus compañeros en su jornada de descubrimiento, que es, cabalmente, lo que el autor expresa al darnos en compendio el argumento de su poema en los términos siguientes: "Al leer la historia de Chile y compararla con la de Felipe II, tuve la idea de poner de relieve esta especie de conexión entre el Mundo Nuevo y el Viejo en su principio, bajo cierta especie de pintura imaginaria, del todo diferente, sin embargo, de aquel alegórico ropaje bajo el cual Barclay mostró en su 'Argenis' asuntos de ese período. La figura capital en el pequeño romance que sigue es un emigrante inglés, a quien se supone, después de una serie de aventuras (no frecuentes, aunque no del todo improbables) haber logrado una concesión de tierras y alcanzado relaciones de familia en esta parte de Chile, que fué más tarde el primer escenario de la crueldad española."

El espíritu en gran manera religioso que transpira toda la obra y las frecuentes referencias que contiene a 'La Araucana' de Ercilla me hicieron sospechar desde el primer momento que el autor debió de ser algún eclesiástico protestante y, a la vez, fervoroso admirador de aquel poema; y, en efecto, por lo que a este último toca, a la vuelta de la página final de la obra se halla la siguiente noticia: "Lista para la prensa, por el autor del 'Vale of Guasco,' una traducción de 'La Araucana,' poema español, por Ercilla y Zúñiga, que viene a ser continuación del tema del 'Vale of Guasco.'"

Pues bien: traductores ingleses de esa epopeya española no ha habido sino dos: William Hayley y el reverendo Henry Boyd, y pues no podía ser aquél el autor de la obra que se decía hallarse lista para la prensa por cuanto los fragmentos que tradujo de 'La Araucana' se habían publicado treinta años antes, no quedaba, así, más candidato que Boyd para la paternidad del manuscrito ofrecido. Añadiré que esa traducción completa del vate español nunca vió la luz pública, salvándose sólo de ella los fragmentos que se insertaron como apéndice a la versión inglesa de la 'Historia de Chile' del Abate Molina, impresa en Middletown (Estados Unidos), en 1808.

Respecto a su autor, diré que era irlandés; en 1785 había publicado la traducción del 'Infierno' del Dante, que completó, en 1802, con la de toda 'La Divina Comedia.' "En 1805," refiere Nichols ('Dictionary of National Biography,' t. VI, p. 91) Boyd "andaba en busca de un editor para su traducción de 'La Araucana,' extenso poema, que era empresa demasiado grande para un editor de Edimburgo, y para la cual hizo sin resultado gestiones |para hallar un comprador en Londres. Falleció el 18 de Septiembre de 1832."

Cualquiera que sea el mérito literario que corresponda a esa obra de Boyd, por la importancia que reviste para el conocimiento de uno de los períodos más interesantes de la historia de la América Española, queda muy por debajo de la que en los últimos meses de 1831 se publicaba, también en Londres, en tres volúmenes en 12mo, con el título de 'Campaigns and cruises in Venezuela and New Grenada, and in the Pacific Ocean: from 1817 to 1830; with the narrative of a march from the River Orinoco to San Buenaventura on the coast of Chocó; and Sketches of the West Coast of South America from the Gulf of California, to the Archipelago of Chiloé. Also Tales of Venezuela: illustrative of revolutionary men, manners and incidents,' que sospecho debe haberse impreso en tirada muy reducida, porque ni Lowndes, en 1834, ni Bohn, en 1837, mencionaron el libro en el nutridísimo 'Bibliographer's Manual.'

A referir esos últimos particulares están consagrados los tomos II y III, que, aunque tan bien escritos e hilvanados, que se leen como la más entretenida de las novelas, no alcanzan, ni con mucho, la valía que corresponde al I, dedicado que estaba a referir los sucesos históricos de aquella época interesantísima de las guerras de la Independencia en la América española.

En una Advertencia plena de modestia, el autor afirma que todo lo que relata le consta de propia información, y cuando de ajena, de fuentes insospechables, como en efecto sucede, salvo en contadísimos casos de escasa entidad, que no es del momento apuntar aquí. A gala tuvo el autor ocultar toda referencia a su nombre. Resulta de todo punto inútil repasar las páginas de su libro para ver modo de descubrirle en alguna de las muchas incidencias en que le tocó figurar; digo mal, en una en que se nombra, — lo que comprobamos a posteriori, — la alusión que hace a su persona está de tal manera disimulada, que sería materia de adivinanza saber que de él se trata. ¿A qué se debió semejante ocultación? Ni siquiera lograron averiguarlo sus contemporáneos. El traductor francés de la obra, al paso que observa que "cuando se publicó en Londres, los órganos más acreditados de la prensa le tributaron, unánimemente, los más brillantes elogios," pero no pudieron adelantar una palabra respecto a quien fuera el autor. Ese mismo traductor, también anonimo, pero cuyo nombre han logrado descubrir los bibliógrafos, — Alphonse Viollet, — a pesar de que escribía en 1837, digamos, por consiguiente, apenas seis años después de haber aparecido el original inglés, tuvo que guardar silencio respecto a quien perteneciera la obra que divulgaba en Francia. Halkett y Laing ni siquiera pudieron hacer caudal del libro en su 'Dictionary of the anonymous and pseudonymous literature of Great Britain.' Sabin, en Estados Unidos, en su 'Dictionary of books,' etc., (n. 10193) citó el libro inglés, pero sin decir palabra acerca de quien fuera el autor, y Cushing ha incurrido en la misma omisión; ¡y apenas necesito decir que Blanco Fombona en el prólogo que puso al frente de la traducción castellana del libro inglés, tomándola de la francesa, no adelantó en un punto la averiguación del anónimo, limitándose a expresar, para salir del paso, que si no firmó el autor inglés, ello debe atribuirse al escepticismo de que estaba dominado!

Diré, por último, que Barros Arana no recuerda tampoco en su 'Catálogo de obras anónimas' las 'Campaigns and cruises,' etc.

Ensayaré por mi parte el ver modo de resolver este problema envuelto hasta ahora en el misterio, tomando por punto de partida algunos de los hechos en que el autor nos dice haber figurado, haciendo caso omiso de todos aquellos que atañen a su permanencia en el servicio de Venezuela, para concretarme al tiempo que militó bajo las banderas de Chile.

Cuenta, pues, que hallándose en Guayaquil con licencia de Sucre, a cuyas órdenes había servido, para dirigirse a Europa, llegó allí Lord Cochrane al mando de la escuadra chilena y que habiendo recibido de él el ofrecimiento de incorporarse a una de sus naves con el mismo grado que tenía en el ejército de Colombia, se embarcó a bordo de *La Independencia* el 1° de Noviembre de 1821: dato del mayor interés para descubrir su nombre, pero que viene a complicarse con la circunstancia de que en el mismo caso se halló el teniente G. Noyes; por fortuna, la duda de si podría atribuirse a éste la paternidad de la obra se mantiene por un instante, pues en nota cuida de advertirse que ese oficial falleció en Valparaíso en 1825. Queda, pues, así, como candidato al intento que buscamos uno solo de los dos oficiales que ingresaron a la escuadra allí en Guayaquil.

En términos más generales, se cuenta en el libro que su autor tomó parte en las excursiones a las costas de México y California, cuya relación ocupa todo el capítulo primero de la obra; en las dos expediciones a Chiloé, que refiere también por extenso, y, sin otros muchos particulares que sobran al intento que perseguimos, cómo había militado a las órdenes inmediatas de Freire cuando en.1823 se trasladó de Talcaguano a Valparaíso, a bordo de *La Independencia*.

Después que todo esto sabemos, léase ahora el siguiente documento y júzguese si calza, diré así, en todo y por todo con esos antecedentes.

Excmo. Señor Director Supremo. — Don Ricardo Longeville Vowell, capitán de tropa de la Marina de Chile, ante V. E. con el mayor respeto parezco y hago presente que por los certificados que tengo el honor de acompañar, firmados por los Jefes y Contadores con quienes he navegado (*sic*), consta que ha estado siempre de servicio actual en la dicha clase, desde Noviembre de 1821 hasta la fecha, durante que tiempo he presenciado las campañas de México y California y con los bloqueos de Chiloé, teniendo el honor de servir a bordo de *La Independencia* cuando vino V. E. de Talcahuano acá en 1823; en fin, en toda expedición . . .

Resultaría tedioso y, además, redundante para un artículo como el presente que fuéramos comprobando tales datos con citas de las páginas del libro de Vowell; y en cuanto a los antecedentes biográficos suyos, en él están para quien desee conocerlos. Limitaréme, pues, a decir que partió de Inglaterra en los comienzos de 1817, con el grado de oficial del Primer Regimiento de Lanceros venezolanos, y que después de haber militado en Venezuela y Nueva Granada, en ocasiones viéndose en inminente riesgo de perder la vida, y de soportar en todo momento las penurias consiguientes a tan duras campañas, durante cuatro años, arribó a Guayaquil, según se dijo ya, con licencia de su jefe para regresar a su patria, enfermo de un agudo reumatismo. Allí entró al servicio de Chile, en el cual permaneció hasta Noviembre de 1829, fecha en que se embarcó en Valparaíso, para llegar por fin a su patria, después de una travesía por el Cabo de Hornos y el Brasil, en la primavera de 1830, al cabo de trece años de ausencia.

THE LITERARY FAIR IN THE UNITED STATES

By CHARLES L. NICHOLS

Of Worcester, Massachusetts

WITH the foundation of the United States of America, a new chapter in the history of the book trade of this country was begun. The printing restrictions and trade regulations of Great Britain were at an end, but new difficulties opened before it; new dissensions arose. The first printers' strike in America was that in the office of James Rivington of New York in 1776. From that time such disagreements between printers and their employers were common and gradually typographical societies were formed in the large cities by the journeymen printers with the twofold object of arranging wage scales for their benefit caring for their sick and poor.

An interesting summary of the development of the book trade during these early years was published in *The Evening Star*, for October 30, 1810:

> For many years after the peace of 1783, books could be imported into the United States and sold cheaper than they could be printed here and in deed until 1793 nothing like a competition with English Printers and Booksellers could be maintained. The war then raging in Europe and added duty on paper made some difference but it was not until the union of Ireland and England (in 1801) that a decided advantage was ascertained to exist.

This statement was made by the striking printers of Philadelphia and was followed by an outline of their grievances. The state of the book trade as thus described, the unrest and the union of the printers, and the isolation of the publishers caused much concern among the larger minds in the trade. In December, 1801, Mathew Carey of Philadelphia, after several years of study of his plan, sent a circular to the principal booksellers of the country calling attention to the need of greater uniformity in the book trade. He suggested the foundation of an annual book fair, after the custom in Leipsic and Frankfort which had been in operation for many years and had materially benefited the booksellers of Germany. Carey proposed that a fair be held in New York the first of June, 1802, and asked all dealers to express their opinion and accept the invitation.

While this plan was being considered, an important matter came up requiring immediate concerted action and the steps taken showed that the tendency toward unity of effort was becoming a reality. On April 2, 1802, E. T. Andrews, of the Boston firm of Thomas & Andrews, wrote to Isaiah Thomas: [1]

I have received a circular letter from a committee of Booksellers &c. of Baltimore requesting a union of the trade here in presenting a memorial to Congress requesting them to lay an additional duty on books imported. I should like something of the kind restricted to certain classes of books. What do you think of a measure of that kind? Bibles ought to be included though I do not think it would do to lay an additional duty on them only, as serious people might think they intended to prohibit religion or embarrass it.

Three days later he wrote:

I have my doubts about the utility of laying an additional duty on books until we are prepared in a more effectual manner to answer the demand of the public. But few of the books used in the colleges have yet been printed here and to tax them would be burdening literature. It would help booksellers and prices at the expense of the public. I have not viewed the subject thoroughly but I think there are weighty objections to the measure on a general scale. The booksellers meet this evening to consider the circular letter on the subject. I do not feel much inclined to go to the Book Fair, I do not altogether like the plan. Fear that it will do more harm than good.

On April 5, 1802, Thomas & Andrews sent a letter to Carey (Bradisher's 'Life of Carey,' p. 23) urging the formation of associations of the booksellers in every considerable city to regulate prices and the printing of books in place of increasing the duties on foreign books.

In spite of his uncertainty regarding the fair, Andrews went, for in a letter to Thomas from New York, June 4, he says:

1. Mss. letters in collections of the American Antiquarian Society.

The fair in this city has assumed more consequence than I anticipated though I still have my doubts of its utility unless care is taken to regulate it. We have, this day, dined together, at Barden's Hotel, to the number of about fifty and among them several very respectable booksellers such as Messrs. Gaine, Beers, Collins, Kollock, Pritchard and others. The entertainment went off very well and I believe it is the first time that so many booksellers ever dined together in America.

The *New York Gazette and General Advertiser* of June 2 says:

Yesterday agreeable to public notice was held the first American Literary Fair at which were present a considerable number of printers and booksellers from different parts of the country. The proceedings of the meeting were opened by the appointment of Hugh Gaine, the oldest printer and bookseller in the United States, as President and Mathew Carey as Secretary after which committees were appointed to frame rules for the management of the business of the fair.

The *Independent Chronicle* (Boston) of July 19, in an account of this first Literary Fair, printed the following resolutions passed by the booksellers who attended the fair on June 7th:

1. Resolved that it is earnestly recommended to the printers and booksellers throughout the United States, to use their utmost endeavors to improve the quality of the books they publish, in order to establish and support the reputation of the American manufacture of books and render it deserving the patronage of the friends of their country.

2. Resolved that it be likewise recommended to our brethren to avoid, as much as it may be, any interference with the interests of each other by the republication of books already printed in the United States and of which there is a sufficient supply to be had on reasonable terms.

3. Resolved that it be recommended to the importers of books to discontinue the importation of all books of which good and correct editions are printed in this country and on which a liberal discount is made by the publishers.

4. Resolved that the continuance of the Literary Fair be strongly recommended to all persons interested in the publication of books in this country and that it be held twice a year — on the first Tuesday of April in New York and on the first Tuesday of October in Philadelphia.

5. Resolved that it be recommended to the booksellers in the principal cities of the United States to form themselves into associations for the purpose of corresponding with each other in order to promote the general interest and that every person publishing a book be requested to forward specimens of the printing and paper with terms of sale to the secretaries of such associations for the information of the members.

Then a committee was appointed, consisting of two members from Philadelphia, M. Carey and J. Conrad, two from Boston, E. T. Andrews and John West, and two from New York, J. Collins and J. Swords, to prepare rules and regulations for the future government of the fair.

The Presidential address of Mr. Gaine has been preserved and in it he expresses the hope that this will be the beginning of a new era of good will among the members of the trade, and expresses great confidence in such an outcome.

The second meeting was held at the Franklin Hotel in Philadelphia in December of this year, as was noticed in the *Aurora* of December 7, the regular meeting being postponed until this time because of yellow fever in that city during October. This fair closed with a dinner at which seventeen toasts were offered.

On June 21, 1803, Andrews again wrote Thomas from New York:

There are a large number of booksellers here and probably will be more tomorrow. The fair is assuming more order and system and may become an important institution. I have hardly seen the whole company yet and done no business, yesterday being pretty much taken up with preparation and arrangement.

In the 'Chronological Record of Printing' kept by Joel Munsell of Albany, we find an entry of June 18, 1804:

The fourth meeting of the American Company of Booksellers was held in the city of New York when the following officers were chosen, for the coming year: Mathew Carey, President; Isaac Collins, Vice President; and Thomas S. Arden, Secretary. There was a very general attendance of the members of the company and the business transacted greatly exceeded that of any former year. During the meeting new articles of association and bylaws were adopted for the government of the company.

Among the directors chosen this year was E. T. Andrews and it was voted to have all meetings in the future held in the village of Newark, New Jersey.

In *The Library, or Philadelphia Literary Reporter* of July 28, 1804, we read:

At the fourth meeting of the American Company of Booksellers, held at New York, June 18th, 1804, the following resolution was adopted:

"Resolved, that the premiums to be offered for the present year shall be a gold medal of the value of $50 for the best specimen of printing, no less than 300 pages, executed on American paper and with American ink and the edition of which such specimen is part, to consist of no less than 500 copies, all executed in the same style. A gold medal of $20 for the second best specimen of like printing, of no less than 150 pages and the edition to consist of not less than 300 copies, all executed in the same style. A gold medal of like value for the best sample of American printing paper, the quantity to be not less than 50 reams, of which the sample is a part. A gold medal of the value of $25 for the best piece of American binding executed in American leather to be exhibited on a book of American printing of no less than 300 pages. And a gold medal of like value for the best sample of American printing ink, to be exhibited in a printed volume of no less than 300 pages and the quantity of which such sample is a part, to consist of not less than 500 weight."

This was signed by Mathew Carey, President.

Joel Munsell's Diary, with date of 1805, states:

The annual fair of the Booksellers was held at Newark which closed on the 20th of June. Exchanges to a large amount were transacted. The premiums offered at the previous meeting were awarded as follows: for the best specimen of printing ink, a sample of 500 weight, a gold medal of the value of $25 was awarded to Jacob Johnson, of Philadelphia. For the best specimen of binding executed in America, a like medal was awarded to William Swain of New York. The medals for printing and paper were held over to the next meeting.

There is in existence an octavo sheet folded, dated June Fair, 1806, entitled, 'Warner & Hanna's Exchange List' which was used at the fair of that year and which is the last evidence of these meetings.

The primary object of the book fair was to facilitate the exchange of books published in the different sections of the country by exhibiting them at these gatherings and taking orders for them and, as we have seen, the plan worked well for several years. Later, in spite of the precautions taken by the officers of the organization to raise the standards, the market was flooded with large editions of poorly printed books which came into competition with the finer and more costly issues of the better publishers and these, largely in the cities, withdrew from the organization. It is not known when the meetings ended, but the above date, 1806, is the last reference that the writer has been able to find.

A striking illustration of the difficulties that followed this ineffectual attempt at organizing this important branch of business, and the length of time required to overcome the resulting evil, prolonged without question by the War of 1812, is seen in a letter written to Isaiah Thomas, by Littell & Henry of Philadelphia and dated June 24, 1819:

> Booksellers have suffered so much in this city and in New York and to the south of us, by auctions and by irregular persons who sold at large discounts at retail, that for several years past fewer books have been printed, editions have been smaller and a call for new ones has not been readily answered. This has led to a scarcity of books and now, therefore, this fact is producing a more regular and orderly course of business. Books are becoming a better stock than they were and we hope that industry and honesty will be able to compete advantageously with speculation and knavery.

One important result, in addition to the meetings already described, did follow and this alone would have been sufficient justification for the effort. In the circular letter sent to Carey, dated April 5, 1802, and later endorsed at the first meeting of the fair, was the suggestion of Thomas & Andrews that local associations be formed in the principal cities for the benefit of their local trade. A number of these were established, the most active being that of Philadelphia, and called the Company of Printers of Philadelphia. Founded in 1794, it is the oldest known organization of employers in this country; its constitution has been used as a model many times; and, although its active existence lasted but two years, it is considered to be the connecting link between the merchant guilds of the Middle Ages and the employers' associations of to-day. Early in the nineteenth century it was revived as the Philadelphia Company of Booksellers and at once took an active part in affairs. In 1804, a newspaper of four pages was published by this company entitled, *The Library, or Philadelphia Literary Reporter*. It contained advertisements and lists of books, imported and domestic, which were for sale by the members of that association. It was published every two weeks at the beginning, No. 1 being dated Saturday, February 25, 1804, and later only once in six weeks. One extract from this paper has been quoted above, but with that exception and a few notices of the book fair it contained only notices and lists of books.

In January, 1809, the Philadelphia *Library Reporter* appeared, published by David Hogan, under the auspices of a number of Philadelphia booksellers. It was published monthly to September of that year at least, the last number seen by the writer bearing this date.

The New York Society of Printers was another similar organization, formed in 1805. The Lexington, Kentucky, papers of this year announced that on the first Wednesday of October the printers and booksellers of the Western country were called upon to hold a meeting for the purpose of taking such measures as might be thought advisable to form an organization among themselves similar to those in the Atlantic States to facilitate the interchange of works of merit.

In Boston a similar organization was formed as early as 1805, for we find, in the archives of the American Antiquarian Society, a printed circular, dated June 13, 1805, from the Society of Printers of Boston and Vicinity, signed by Benjamin Russell, President, soliciting membership, as well as a manuscript copy of a 'Constitution and By-Laws of the Association of Printers and Booksellers.' In 1808 the name of this society was changed to the Faustus Association and the objects of the organization were stated to be

the elevation of the printing art, the regulation of trade and prices, the preservation of good fellowship in the profession and the formation of a Fire Society for the protection of printing offices.

This fire society, suggested by Mr. Andrews, continued its useful existence until the reorganization of the Boston Fire Department in the year 1826, while the Faustus Association ceased to exist as such in 1815, the older name, the Society of Printers, being taken when later the organization was revived.

The original plan of a literary fair was, as Carey stated, derived from those held in Frankfort and Leipsic, in which cities several weeks were devoted to them. The records of that at Frankfort contain much of interest to-day. In the year 1579, for example, Plantin and his stepson, Moretus, traveled to the Lent Fair with six boxes of books for sale and returned with but 1600 of the more than 5000 they had brought. John Bill of London bought books there when purchasing for Sir Thomas Bodley; while Estienne of Paris, Froben of Basle and Elzevir of Leyden have left records of their experiences at these fairs.

Before A.D. 1156 the fairs at Leipsic were in existence. They still are in active operation, although they have been omitted or curtailed in their activities at times such as the period of the Thirty Years' War.

In the spring of 1922, according to 'The Leipzig Book Fair,' by T. W. Koch, the 522d fair was held, at which there were 155,000 buyers, 32,000 of whom were foreigners, and more than 12,000 were exhibitors, these figures applying to all departments but showing the number of possible purchasers. In August, 1922, 100,000 were present and in the Book Department 165 publishers, in addition to booksellers, were represented.

The contrast here suggested will show where lay the cause of failure of the American Book Fair. The small number of members of the organization in consequence of the limited trade of that period, and the lack of an international basis to stimulate the interchange of ideas and products are sufficient reasons for its brief existence, but this early attempt to raise the standards of our country's book trade should have a fitting record in history. It is hardly necessary to call attention to the fact that neither of these reasons exist to-day and that organized effort might result, through a revival of this institution, in a more uniform elevation of the standards of book production in this country.

THE BALLAD OF LOVEWELL'S FIGHT

By GEORGE LYMAN KITTREDGE

Of Harvard University

THE oldest extant text of the ballad of "Lovewell's Fight"
— "Of worthy Captain Lovewell, I purpose now to sing"
— is that published at Concord, New Hampshire, in Farmer
and Moore's *Collections, Historical and Miscellaneous; and
Monthly Literary Journal* for February, 1824,[1] and there entitled "Lovewell's Fight. A Song." The piece has been often
reprinted,[2] but the reprints are in every instance derived, medi-
ately or immediately, from the *Collections*. Farmer and Moore
acknowledge indebtedness to "a friend" for "a copy of the
song" — apparently a manuscript copy, and they remark that
the ballad "was written about one hundred years since." "For
many years," they add, "it was sung throughout a considerable portion of New-Hampshire and Massachusetts, and probably served more than anything else to keep in remembrance
the circumstances of this desperate engagement." The Fight
took place on May 8, 1725.

The friend from whom the editors of the *Collections* received
the song was Joshua Coffin (1792–1864), the genealogist and
antiquary, celebrated in Whittier's poem "To my Old Schoolmaster" and honorably known as the author of 'A Sketch of
the History of Newbury' (Boston, 1845). He was at the time
the head of a school at Tyngsborough, Massachusetts, formerly
a part of Dunstable.[3] A letter from Farmer to Coffin, dated
December 20, 1823, contains the following passage:

I have, for several years, been endeavoring to find a copy of a song in
memory of the heroic exploits of Capt. Lovewell and his brave companions
at Pequawkett, which I remember to have heard sung in my early years.
It ought to be preserved as a curiosity. It was written about an hundred
years since, and for more than half a century was sung in memory of the
events it commemorated. I have a fragment of it. The first stanza is —

"The worthy Captain Lovewell my purpose is to sing
"How willingly he served his country & his King;
"He and his jolly soldiers did range the wood full wide;
"Much hardship they endured, to quell the Indians' pride."

Perhaps Col. Bancroft may have a copy of it. This we should like to publish.

This letter I found among the Coffin MSS in the library of the Essex Institute (III, 4). Coffin's reply containing or enclosing a copy of the ballad is unfortunately not preserved, but it must have been despatched before January 22, 1824.[4]

The historical accuracy of the ballad, combined with the express statement of Farmer and Moore as to its age and oral currency, has resulted in its general acceptance as the work of some contemporary of Lovewell's. As to its oral currency in two New England states, their testimony may be accepted without scruple: we must believe that either the editors or their informant, or both, really knew that the ballad was much older than 1824 — that it was at least fifty years old. And if so, the probability that it was contemporary with the event is very strong.[5] One other point too, is hardly open to doubt: the copy furnished by Coffin was either a printed text (a broadside) or a text derived from good manuscript authority. It is too faithful to the facts and too little corrupted in form, to have been a recent transcript from a long line of oral tradition.

When all is said and done, however, we still need one specific piece of evidence — namely, direct proof that some ballad describing Lovewell's Fight was actually written soon after the event. If this can be established, we have a basis for comparison between the extant text and the presumable form and contents of the contemporary product — and, if the extant text stands the comparison, we shall be justified in inferring that the Farmer ballad is really as ancient as its editors supposed.

Such direct evidence exists in the form of an unassailable record. In his invaluable catalogue of Massachusetts broadsides, issued in 1922 by the Massachusetts Historical Society,

Mr. Worthington C. Ford prints the following advertisement (p. 73) from the *New-England Courant* of May 31, 1725 (No. 200): "Just Publish'd, and sold by J. Franklin in Union-Street, The Voluntier's March; being a full and true Account [of] the bloody Fight which happen'd between Capt. Lovewell's Company, and the Indians at Pigwoket. An excellent new Song."

Mr. Ford does not suggest any connection between this advertisement and the extant ballad, which, indeed, he does not mention. In a recent note,[6] however, I have dared to conjecture that the lost broadside issued by James Franklin contained the ballad preserved by Farmer and Moore. A closer scrutiny tends only to substantiate this inference. In discussing the question I shall for convenience designate the "new Song" advertised in the *Courant* as "the Franklin ballad" and the text in the *Collections* as "the Farmer ballad."

We know positively that the Franklin ballad was written shortly before Monday, May 31, 1725, the day on which it was announced in the *Courant* as "Just Publish'd." The first contingent of survivors (twelve in number[7]) did not get to Dunstable until May 13 "at Night." [8] Their report of the engagement reached Lieutenant Governor William Dummer at Boston on the 14th and 15th.[9] On the 17th there appeared, in the *Boston Gazette*, the first printed account of Lovewell's Fight.[10] Obviously, then, the earliest conceivable date for the composition of the Franklin ballad is May 14 or 15. But we can come nearer than that. Like Benjamin Franklin's "Blackbeard" and "The Lighthouse Tragedy," both of which were prompted by the business sagacity of brother James,[11] the ballad on Lovewell was made to sell: it was meant for immediate hawking about the streets. Hence it was undoubtedly set up as soon as copy was available. It was certainly not in type, and probably not in existence, on May 24, or it would have been advertised in James Franklin's *Courant* of that date. Manifestly the extreme limits for its composition are May 25 and May 31, 1725.

It was based, therefore, on such tidings as had come to Boston by Monday, May 24, or, in other words, on the long item published on May 24 in the *New-England Courant.*[12] This was as follows:

Boston May 24.

Last Week came to Town Lieutenant Wyman and several others who were in the late Fight between the Indians and Capt. Lovewell's Company at Pigwocket, by whom we have a more particular and certain Account of the Fight than has yet been publish'd, and is as follows.

Early on Saturday Morning, the 8th Instant, the English discover'd an Indian on a Neck of Land which run into a Pond, and by his Actions judg'd there were a considerable Number of Indians near the Pond, and that he was set on purpose to draw the English upon the Neck: They therefore laid down their Packs (that they might be ready to receive the Enemy's Attack) when they had about two miles to travel round the Pond, to come at the Indian upon the Neck. When they came within Gun Shot of him, he fir'd two Guns, and slightly wounded Capt. Lovewell *and one of his Men with Beaver Shot. Several of the English immediately fir'd upon him, kill'd and scalp'd him; and returning to the Place where they left their Packs, before they could reach it, one of the English discovered an Indian, and calling out to the rest, the Indians rose up from their Ambush, shouted and fir'd, as did the English at the same Instant. The Indians were reckon'd at least 80 in Number, and Capt.* Lovewell's *Company consisted of but 34, Nine Men and the Doctor being left about 50 miles distant with a sick man. After the first Fire, the Indians advanc'd with great Fury towards the English, with their Hatchets in their Hands, the English likewise running up to them, till they came within four or five Yards of the Enemy, and were even mix'd among them, when the Dispute growing too warm for the Indians, they gave back, and endeavour'd to encompass the English, who then retreated to the Pond, in order to have their Rear cover'd, where they continu'd the Fight till Night. During the Fight the Indians call'd to them to take Quarter, but were answer'd that they would have it with the muzzles of their Guns. About two Hours before Night the Indians drew off, and presently came on again; and their Shout then being compar'd with the first, it was thought half their Number at least were kill'd and wounded. Of the chief among the English, Capt.* Lovewell, *Lieut.* Fairwell, *and Ensign* Robins, *were mortally wounded at the beginning of the Fight, and Mr.* Fry, *their Chaplain, in about five Hours after, having fought with undaunted Courage, and scalp'd one of the Indians in the Heat of the Engagement. Eight of the English dy'd on the Spot, and 9 were wounded, 4 of which Number were just expiring when they came away at Night, and the rest they brought off several miles, but were oblig'd to leave them with what Provision they had, when they were unable to travel with them. Sixteen of our men are return'd tho' they had no Provision but what they caught in the Woods, the Indians having got all their Packs before the Fight. 'Tis thought that not above 20 of the Indians went off well at Night: But tho' we cannot have a certain Account of their Loss, yet it is evident that 'twas very great, and they were afraid of another Engagement; for tho' our men staid several Hours after the Fight, and the Indians knew they had no Provision, yet they neither endeavour'd to keep them there, nor waylaid them in their Return Home. His Honour the Lieut. Governour has been pleas'd to grant a Captain's Commission to Lieut. Wyman, who distinguish'd himself with great Courage and Conduct during the whole Engagement.*

N. B. The Article of the late Fight publish'd in the last Week's Gazette, was design'd likewise for this Paper, but omitted by Mistake.

This morning it is confidently reported that Capt. Lovewell and Mr. Fry are got to some of our Frontier Towns, tho' very much wounded.

The next *Courant*, that of May 31, contains the following item:

The Report of Capt. Lovewell's being alive, proves groundless; but we have certain Advice, that Eleazer Davis, one of the 4 wounded Men who were brought off several Miles by the English, is arriv'd at Berwick. The other three, who were not able to travel as fast as himself, he left in the Woods, of whose Return we are not yet out of Hopes. The Indians not venturing to follow the Track of these wounded Men, is a further Confirmation of their entire Defeat.

Now let us turn to the ballad published by Farmer and Moore in 1824 and asserted by them to have been "written about a hundred years since."

If we compare the Farmer ballad with the *Courant* of May 24 and 31, we shall find that the ballad follows the item of the 24th closely, not only in statements of fact, but even in phraseology. Indeed, it is to all intents and purposes a versification of that item, though it adds two or three details. And we shall also find that the balladist, — whoever he was and whenever he poetized, — though he had the *Courant* of May 24 on his table, had not seen the *Courant* of the 31st. Thus it becomes evident that the Farmer ballad, like the Franklin ballad, was composed after May 24 and before May 31. The inference is unescapable: the two ballads are identical: the ballad published by James Franklin on or just before May 31, 1725, still exists, though no man living has ever seen one of the original broadsides. A copy of the text, probably a manuscript, came into the hands of Farmer and Moore and was published by them in their *Collections* in February, 1824.[13]

Some of the details that establish this identity will now be specified. In making our comparison, we shall consider also the 'Lovewell Lamented' of the Reverend Thomas Symmes, published at Boston on July 1, 1725; [14] for the agreement of the Farmer ballad and the *Courant* item of May 24 in points in which both of them differ from Symmes's fuller and more accurate narrative, will serve to emphasize the dependence of the Farmer ballad on that item.

(1) In the ballad (stanza 2), as in the *Courant* item of May 24, the Indian whom Lovewell's men spied "upon a neck of land" early on Saturday morning, May 8, is the same who is killed and scalped (stanzas 5, 6). In Symmes the two are quite distinct.

(2) The ballad and the item both report that the savage fired first, discharging two guns:

> "They came unto this Indian, who did them thus defy,
> As soon as they came nigh him, two guns he did let fly,
> Which wounded Captain Lovewell, and likewise one man more,
> But when this rogue was running, they laid him in his gore.

> "Then having scalp'd the Indian," etc.   — Stanzas 5, 6.

"When they came within Gun Shot of him, he fir'd two Guns, and slightly wounded Capt. Lovewell and one of his Men with Beaver Shot. Several of the English immediately fir'd upon him, kill'd and scalp'd him." — *Courant*, May 24.

In Symmes the Indian (the second Indian in this case) is not said to have had two guns, and it is the English who open fire:

> "They all squat, and let him come on: presently several Guns were Fir'd at him; upon which the *Indian* Fir'd upon Captain *Lovewell* with *Bever*-Shot and Wounded him Mortally (as is supposed) tho' he made little Complaint, and was still able to Travel, and at the same time Wounded Mr. *Samuel Whiting*: Immediately *Wyman* Fir'd at the *Indian* and Kill'd him; and Mr. *Frie* and another Scalp'd him." — Symmes, p. vi; (Kidder, p. 32).

The curious detail of the two guns (in the ballad and the item; not in Symmes) challenges attention. Manifestly it is a mistake: Lovewell and Whiting were wounded at a single discharge, the beaver shot scattering. It is worth noting that, when the *News-Letter* of May 27 repeated the *Courant* item of May 24, "one Gun" was substituted for "two Guns." We might infer that the Farmer ballad was written before May 27, and thus we should reduce the limits of its date from May 25–30 to May 25–26; but this point need not be pressed. It is enough for our present purpose to observe that the balladist follows the *Courant* of May 24 in a mistaken statement.[15]

(3) For coincidence in phraseology we may take, as one specimen out of many, the following instance:

"Therefore we'll march in order, and each man leave his pack,
   That we may briskly fight them when they make their attack."
                                                          — Stanza 4.

"They therefore laid down their Packs (that they might be ready to receive the Enemy's Attack)." — *Courant*, May 24.

Contrast Symmes:

"The *Captain* . . . Ordered the Men to lay down their Packs, & March with greatest Caution, and in utmost readiness." — P. v (Kidder, p. 32).

(4) A striking agreement between the ballad and the item, both in incident and in phraseology, concerns the temporary lull in the fighting:

"'Twas ten o'clock in the morning, when first the fight begun,
   And fiercely did continue until the setting sun;
   Excepting that the Indians some hours before 'twas night,
   Drew off into the bushes and ceas'd a while to fight.

"But soon again returned, in fierce and furious mood,
   Shouting as in the morning, but yet not half so loud;
   For as we are informed, so thick and fast they fell,
   Scarce twenty of their number, at night did get home well.

"And that our valiant English, till midnight there did stay,
   To see whether the rebels would have another fray;
   But they no more returning, they made off towards their home,
   And brought away their wounded as far as they could come."
                                                     — Stanzas 12–14.

"About two Hours before Night the Indians drew off, and presently came on again; and their Shout then being compar'd with the first, it was thought half their Number at least were kill'd and wounded . . . . 'Tis thought that not above 20 of the Indians went off well at Night . . . tho' our men staid several Hours after the Fight, . . . yet they neither endeavour'd to keep them there, nor waylaid them in their Return Home."

Symmes says nothing of a temporary cessation of fighting and a renewed attack, and therefore, of course, he does not contrast the shouting on the two onsets.

(5) A plain indication that the Farmer ballad was written soon after the event is the language used in recording Seth Wyman's promotion to a captaincy: "Wyman's Captain made" (stanza 17). This is as much as to say, "Wyman has been made Captain." The *Courant* of May 24 remarks: "His Honour the Lieut. Governour has been pleas'd to grant a Captain's Commission to Lieut. Wyman, who distinguish'd himself with great Courage and Conduct during the whole Engagement." So Symmes: "HIS *Honour*, Our Excellent Lieutenant *Governour* has been Pleas'd to give Ensign *Seth Wyman*, a Captain's Commission, since his Return, as a Reward of His Valour."[16] Nobody who was writing after Wyman's death (which took place on September 5, 1725) would have said "Wyman's Captain made" or "Wyman *has been made* Captain." Such a form of speech implies that Wyman is still alive and in the enjoyment of the commission which has recently been granted him.[17]

(6) The sixteenth stanza of the ballad runs thus:

"Our worthy Captain Lovewell among them there did die,
They killed Lieut. Robbins and wounded good young Frye,
Who was our English Chaplain, he many Indians slew,
And some of them he scalp'd when bullets round him flew." [18]

The minstrel, then, was certain that Lovewell and Robbins were dead, but, so far as he could tell, the Chaplain (Jonathan Frye), though wounded, was still in the land of the living. Now it was known in Boston as early as May 17 that Lovewell and Robbins must be dead, for the first contingent of the survivors, who reached Dunstable on the 13th, had reported that these two were "mortally wounded by the Indians first shot from their Ambushments," and that, if not actually dead when the survivors started on the homeward march, they were at the point of death and had been unable to move from the field; and this report was confirmed by Wyman's account when he arrived at Dunstable on the 15th. But the fate of four of the men — Lieutenant Josiah Farwell, Chaplain Jonathan Frye, Josiah Jones, and Eleazer Davis, — who, though wounded, had started with the others on the return march but had been left behind after the party had travelled some distance, was still in doubt when the *Courant* printed its report on May 24.[19] On the 27th Davis got to Berwick [20] and Jones to Saco,[21] but both Frye and Farwell died on the way home. Davis reported, on his arrival at Berwick, that Frye was certainly dead [22] — he had been forced to leave him *in articulo mortis;* but hope of Frye's return had not been abandoned in Boston on the 31st.[23] When the details of Davis's story became known,[24] however, there could be no question that the chaplain had perished. Unless the balladist had written soon after the Fight, he would hardly have left the matter doubtful.

(7) In stanza 15 the balladist states that "Sixteen of our English did safely home return," which accords with the *Courant* of the 24th: "Sixteen of our men are return'd." This figure — *sixteen* — is almost if not quite enough by itself to fix the date of the Farmer ballad as somewhere between May 20 and May 31, and it certainly indicates a date before the 31st. On the 20th the *News-Letter* was still putting the number of survivors at *twelve* [25] (in an item which was a mere reprint of that in the *Gazette* of the 17th); on the 24th, as we have seen, the *Courant* raised the figure to *sixteen;* on the 31st the *Courant* reported the return of Eleazer Davis on the 27th, making *seventeen,* but knew nothing of the return of the *eighteenth* man, Josiah Jones, who arrived at Saco on the 27th, and whose safety was chronicled by the *News-Letter* of June 3. In Symmes's book, published on July 1, the safety of the whole eighteen is duly registered.[26]

There are, it is true, a few details in the ballad that are lacking in the *Courant* item of May 24. None of these, however,
is of any consequence, except the statement (in the concluding stanza) that Wyman "shot the old chief Paugus." For this
the ballad is our sole authority. Both Symmes and Penhallow
inform us that Paugus was killed, but they do not tell who shot
him.

   "*Since* the Action," writes Symmes, "Col. *Tyng* with a Company, have
been on the spot, and found and Buried Twelve of our Men. They also
found where the *Indians* had Buried Three of their Men, and when they
were dug up, One of them was known to be the *Bold* Paugus, who has been
such a Scourge to *Dunstable*; but if he be gone to his own place, He 'll cease
from Troubling." [27]

Penhallow's account is to the same effect. The inference seems
to be that Wyman, on whose narrative the *Courant* report of
May 24 is based, did not claim the credit of killing the old
chief, and, indeed, that nobody except the Indians was certain
that Paugus had been shot until Tyng dug up his body about a
fortnight after the battle.[28] One significant thing, however,
which must have been a feature of the story that Wyman told
in Boston on his arrival there just before May 24, was ignored
in the *Courant* item of that date. It is thus recorded by
Symmes on Wyman's own authority:

   "At one time, Captain *Wyman* is Confident, they [the Indians] were got
to Powawing, by their striking on the Ground, and other odd Motions, but
at length *Wyman* crept up toward 'em and Firing among 'em, shot the
Chief Powaw and brake up their Meeting." [29]

Perhaps the town talk, or the balladist himself, confused "the
Chief Powaw" with Chief Paugus; perhaps the minstrel was
indulging in a little poetic licence. It is even possible that
"Paugus" for "Powaw" is an editorial improvement on the
authentic text.[30] Anyhow, the statement, be it true or false, in
no wise affects the validity of the evidence already given that
the *Courant* item of May 24 was the minstrel's chief source of
information, and that he had finished his song before the
Courant of May 31 was published.[31] The proof that the

Farmer ballad is the Franklin ballad ("The Voluntier's March") remains unshaken.

Let us recapitulate: One limit for the Farmer ballad is fixed by the fact that the author follows so closely, both in facts and in phrases, the report in the *Courant* of May 24, 1725: he cannot have written before that date. The other limit is fixed more and more narrowly by a series of considerations. If he had written after September 11, 1725 (when the *Courant* reported Wyman's death on the 5th), he would not have spoken as if Wyman were still alive and had just been promoted. If he had written after seeing Symmes's book, which was published on July 1, he would have told a different story of the Fight. If he had written after June 3, he would have known from the *News-Letter* that there were eighteen survivors, not sixteen. If he had written after May 31, he would have known from the *Courant* that at least seventeen men had returned. If he had written after the *News-Letter* of May 27 came out, he would have known that the Indian who shot Lovewell had one gun, not two. It follows, then, that the earliest possible date of composition is May 24, and the latest May 27 or (if the detail about the guns be waived) May 31, 1725. These limits accord with those of the Franklin ballad, which was clearly not in existence on May 24 and was advertised on May 31 as just published. The Farmer ballad and the Franklin ballad are one and the same.

Finally, I hazard the conjecture that the author of "The Voluntier's March" was James Franklin himself. That he was a fluent versifier is shown by the poems which he contributed to the early numbers of the *Courant* and the authorship of which has been proved by Mr. Ford in an extraordinarily interesting paper in the Massachusetts Historical Proceedings for April, 1924 (LVII, 336–353). But there is another Richmond in the field — Joseph Jewett of Groton. The main facts in this regard, for a knowledge of which I am indebted to the kindness and antiquarian learning of Mr. S. Harrison Lovewell, may be briefly summarized.[32]

In 1736 John Lovell (Lovewell) of Dunstable gave a note to Joseph Jewett of Groton:

> Dunstable Septemb^r 8th 1736:
> Whereas Joseph Jewett of groton hath Deliuer'd to me the Subscriber the Verses he made of Capt John Louells killing the ten Indians & them he made when Capt Louell was kil'd:
> I the Subscriber promise to pay to the S^d Joseph Jewett Five pounds passible mony or deliver to s^d Joseph Jewett or Leaue at his house in groton twenty ballads of each Sort of s^d Verses in print at or before December next as witness my hand
>
>
> his
> John L Louell
> mark
>

Jewett sued Lovewell in the Inferiour Court of Common Pleas held at Concord, Massachusetts, August 29, 1738, for £10 damages, alleging that Lovewell had neither paid the money nor delivered the verses. The jury found for the plaintiff — £5 damages and cost of court (£4, 19 shillings). Lovewell appealed to the next session of the Superiour Court of Judicature, held at Charlestown on the last Tuesday of January, 1739, but he lost his case and had to pay costs taxed at £17, 14 shillings.

At this time there were living in Groton two Joseph Jewetts, father and son. The father was born on September 14, 1685, the son on October 9, 1708.[33] The Jewett ballads were probably written in 1725, immediately after the events, when the younger Joseph was less than seventeen years old. Perhaps, therefore, the elder Joseph is the better candidate for such poetical honors as attach to their composition. In support of his claim we might also urge the fact that the author is styled "Joseph Jewett" in all the documents and not "Joseph Junior," though this is by no means conclusive. Mr. S. Harrison Lovewell decides in favor of the son.

Anyhow, it is certain that one of the two Joseph Jewetts of Groton composed a pair of ballads on Captain Lovewell. One

related to the exploit of February 21, 1725, when Lovewell's
Company surprised and killed ten Indians, receiving £1000 as
scalp money. This has perished. The other, described in the
promissory note as the verses "made when Capt Louell was
kil'd," may or may not have been "The Voluntier's March."

II

The literary history of the old song of "Lovewell's Fight,"
to which we have now confidently restored its original title of
"The Voluntier's March," has been intimately associated for
a hundred years with another ballad, also called "Lovewell's
Fight," which begins —

> "What time the noble Lovewell came,
>   With fifty men from Dunstable,
> The cruel Pequa'tt tribe to tame,
>   With arms and bloodshed terrible."

This was published for the first time in Farmer and Moore's
Collections for March, 1824,[34] the next monthly number to
that which contains the old song; and it is there expressly
designated as a contribution to that periodical: "For the
Monthly Literary Journal. Lovewell's Fight. A Ballad."
"The Monthly Literary Journal" was a special department of
the *Collections*. The receipt of the poem is mentioned by
Farmer in the same letter to Joshua Coffin (February 4, 1824)
in which he announces that the old song "is inserted in the
February Number of the Collections." Farmer writes: "I
have just received an Excellent Ballad on Lovewell's Fight
written in the style and manner of *Chevy Chase*, which will
probably appear in our next" (Coffin MSS, III, 4). He does not
name the contributor.

The author had certainly read Symmes's 'Historical Mem-
oirs,' for he based his poem on the text of Symmes reprinted in
the first volume of these same *Collections* (1822). Here he had
found a narrative at variance with the old ballad in several
particulars, and he retold the story accordingly. Now that

text of Symmes was reprinted, not from either of the two original issues (1725), but from the Fryeburg edition of 1799. This was prepared and printed by Elijah Russell, who modified the language to suit his fancy and made a number of interpolations without notice.[35] One of these is important. Symmes, in announcing the safe return of Josiah Jones, states the bare fact that "*Josiah Jones* another of the Four, came in at *Saco*." [36] Russell continues with an account of Jones's sufferings in the woods and his subsequent recovery [37] and adds a long passage, quite unknown to Symmes — the story (often repeated since) of the conversation between Chamberlain and Paugus at the pond, of their firing at almost the same moment, and of the fall of the Indian.[38] To this he appends the apocryphal tale of the attempt made by a son of Paugus to kill Chamberlain "after it had become a time of peace," [39] and another anecdote about a night encounter between Chamberlain and a prowling savage at a sawmill. This last item includes the remark that Chamberlain "used to say that he was not to be killed by an Indian."[40] We now perceive that it was from Russell's interpolation that the poet derived the material for his eighteenth stanza:

> "But Chamberlain, of Dunstable,
>   (One whom a savage ne'er shall slay,)
> Met Paugus by the water side,
>   And shot him dead upon that day."

Stanza 8 refers to the Indian who was first spied by the English and was supposed by them to be a decoy:

> "The Savage had been seeking game,
>   Two guns and eke a knife he bore,
> And two black ducks were in his hand,
>   He shrieked, and fell, to rise no more."

The direct source of this stanza is an extract from Belknap's 'History of New Hampshire' (1791) [41] given by Farmer and Moore in a footnote to their reprint of Russell's edition of Symmes.[42]

The only statements, indeed, which our modern balladist did not get from Russell's edition of Symmes concern John Harwood and his wife. Symmes says that Harwood was killed on the spot.[43] The tender parting between him and his wife when he left home, and the death of Mary Harwood soon after she heard of the disaster, are additions made by the poet.

The date of the modern ballad we have fixed as early in 1824. Its author is commonly supposed to be the Rev. Thomas Coggswell Upham. Though he never publicly acknowledged the poem, the circumstantial evidence is strong, and, as we shall see presently, he did acknowledge it in a private letter.

Upham was born at Deerfield, Massachusetts, on January 30, 1799, but his parents removed to Rochester, New Hampshire, in his infancy. He grew up, therefore, in a region where, as he himself tells us, traditions about Lovewell's expedition were rife. In noticing the first volume of the *Collections* in the *North American Review* for January, 1824, he refers especially to the reprint of Symmes: "Among the accounts, which have appeared in the Historical Collections, the narration of the contest with the savages, commonly called 'Lovewell's Fight,' is particularly interesting. The story of Lovewell's Fight is one of the nursery tales of New Hampshire; there is hardly a person that lives in the eastern and northern part of the state, but has heard incidents of that fearful encounter repeated from infancy." [44] An extract from this notice was probably included along with the poem in the author's manuscript as sent to the editors of the *Collections;* at any rate, it is printed as a footnote to the ballad.

At the moment of publication (March, 1824) Upham (who graduated at Dartmouth College in 1818 and at the Andover Seminary in 1821) was minister of the church at Rochester, and the same volume which contains the poem twice records the date of his ordination there, July 16, 1823.[45] On May 29,

1825,[46] his Rochester pastorate terminated, for he had accepted a call to a Professorship of Mental and Moral Philosophy at Bowdoin College — a position which he occupied until his resignation in 1867. He died in 1872.

From December 27, 1817, to December 4, 1819, the *Columbian Centinel* prints many poems contributed by Upham, all but one ("Dark-Rolling Connecticut") labelled "For the Columbian Fount" (the Poet's Corner on the fourth page of that journal),[47] and all but two ("Susan and Jack" and "The Green Mountain Lad") signed "A. K." The two last mentioned are signed "Oscar."[48] In 1819 Upham publicly acknowledged these A. K. poems as his own by including several of them in a little volume of verses entitled 'American Sketches,' issued in February at New York with his name on the title-page.[49]

Afterwards he used the same title, 'American Sketches,' in the *Centinel* as a general heading for other poems that he contributed during 1819. Most of the latter he did not include in any of his subsequent volumes of verse, and they have never been collected, so far as I know. I find nothing by Upham in the *Centinel* after that year. Two of the poems in Upham's volume of 'American Sketches' (1819) deal with Lovewell's Fight — "Lovellspond" (a lyric) and "The Birchen Canoe."[50]

The former was first printed in the *Centinel* of January 31, 1818,[51] with the usual signature "A.K.", and was introduced by an editorial compliment: "We recognize in the following another of the emanations of a rural muse, which have been copied from *The Fount* into most of the respectable papers in the Union. We think our correspondent sounds the shell of Clio as fitly as he breathes the strains of the Shepherd's reed." The poem was reprinted by Farmer and Moore in the first volume of their *Collections*, immediately after Symmes's narrative.[52] "The following stanzas," the editors remark, "are from the pen of *Thomas C. Upham*, a New-Hampshire poet. They were written on visiting the scene of Lovewell's fate, and are worthy the fine taste and genius of the author." Longfellow's earliest known poem, "The Battle of Lovell's Pond," which appeared in the Portland *Gazette* of November 17, 1820, was certainly inspired by Upham's lyric, to which it bears a striking resemblance both in ideas and in phraseology. The Harvard College Library has Longfellow's own copy of Upham's 'American Sketches' of 1819.[53]

"The Birchen Canoe" is accompanied in Upham's volume by a significant note: "It is related as a tradition, that one of the soldiers who fought at Lovellspond in 1725, on being desperately wounded, crept into a birchen canoe, and in that condition was wafted to the other side beyond the reach of the conflict; and the probability is, considering how few escaped to tell the issue of that day's sanguinary encounter, that his life and sufferings were ended beneath the wave." [54] This note not only brings Upham into connection with local traditions about Lovewell's Fight, but also proves that when he printed it (1819) he had not yet seen either Symmes's or Penhallow's narrative, for Symmes expressly records the safe arrival of Solomon Kies (Keyes) at Dunstable on the thirteenth of May,[55] 1725. The interpolated text of Symmes, which our balladist uses in "Lovewell's Fight," was made accessible to Upham, as we have seen, in 1822, in Farmer and Moore's *Collections.*

The oftener Upham and the *Collections* can be brought together in some way, the stronger the probability that the ballad is his. The *Collections* was a periodical. Volume I was made up of five numbers that came out at intervals in 1822 (April,[56] June, August, October, December). Volumes II and III were issued in monthly parts throughout 1823 and 1824. Now Mr. Upham is present, in one way or another, in every volume. He may fairly be styled a regular contributor. The first number of all, as we have just noted, reprints his lyric on Lovewell's Pond "Ah! where are the soldiers that fought here

of yore?" with a well-deserved editorial compliment. To No. 3
of volume I he contributed, under the general heading of
"American Sketches," a long poem called "The Farmer's
Fireside," modelled on "The Cotter's Saturday Night," with
a rather skilful application to New England country life as he
knew it in his boyhood at Rochester. This was printed anonymously in the *Collections*, and (also anonymously) in a little
pamphlet: 'American Sketches. Farmer's Fireside. A Poem.
Concord, N. H. Printed by Hill and Moore. 1822.' Hill and
Moore were the publishers of the *Collections* — the Moore of
the firm being Jacob B. Moore, co-editor with John Farmer of
that periodical. In the pamphlet "The Farmer's Fireside" is
printed, page for page and line for line, from the type already
set for the *Collections*.[57]

"The Farmer's Fireside" furnishes direct evidence of Upham's interest in the Indian wars in general, and mentions
Paugus particularly. Upham represents himself and other
young people as "teazing" a "grandam" of eighty for stories:

> "She told of Mog,[58] Madockawando,[59] all
> From Hopehood[60] down to Paugus' frantick yell,
> And, as her lips the bloody deeds recall,
> And, as with upturned gaze we heard her tell,
> Unconsciously the chrystal tear-drops fell,
> For, from our infancy, we'd heard and read
> Of chiefs from Canada, and knew full well
> Of Sachem's wrath, that feasted on the dead,
> And shook the haughty plume and arm with life-blood red." [61]

With "Paugus' frantick yell" it is proper to compare stanza 17
of the ballad which we are trying to prove is Upham's:

> "'T was Paugus led the Pequ'att tribe; —
> As runs the Fox would Paugus run;
> *As howls the wild wolf, would he howl,*
> A large bear skin had Paugus on." [62]

In volume II (1823) of the *Collections* Upham cuts a considerable figure. In the February number the editors prefix to
"An account of the voyage of the Plymouth Pilgrims" a poetical motto from "Upham" (page 33),[63] and they reprint (page

58) his poem of "Susan and Jack," ascribing it to "'OSCAR,' a New-Hampshire bard." Oscar was the signature under which it had appeared in the *Columbian Centinel* of February 25, 1818.[64] Again, in the same February number of the *Collections*, the editors acknowledge the receipt of "a poem, entitled 'THE WINTER EVENING,' from the author of the 'Farmer's Fireside,' which originally appeared in these Collections," and they promise to print it in the next number.[65] The March number, accordingly, contains "American Sketches. The Winter Evening," labelled (like "Lovewell's Fight" in volume III) "For the Literary Journal." [66] No author's name is given, but the poem is known to be Upham's.[67] It has much about the telling of Indian stories,[68] relates the famous incident of Waldron's murder,[69] and embodies the following significant stanza:

> "Nor, Lovewell, was thy memory forgot!
> Who through the trackless wild thy heroes led,
> Death, and the dreadful torture heeding not,
> Mightst thou thy heart-blood for thy country shed,
> And serve her living, honor her, when dead.
> Oh, Lovewell, Lovewell, nature's self shall die,
> And o'er her ashes be her requiem said,
> Before New-Hampshire pass thy story by,
> Without a note of praise, without a pitying eye."[70]

This stanza, one notes with interest, Upham omitted in the revised form of "The Farmer's Fireside " which he published in 1843[71] and again in 1850-51.[72] Was this omission due, perhaps, to the fact (for it *is* a fact) that he was determined not to acknowledge the authorship of "Lovewell's Fight"? To reprint the stanza under his own name would certainly have tended to foster the belief that the ballad, too, was from his pen.

Returning to the *Collections* for 1823, we find, in the May number,[73] a commendatory review of Upham's translation of Jahn's 'Biblical Archaeology,' which had just come out.[74] He is named and is described as "Assistant Teacher of Hebrew and Greek in the Theol. Sem. Andover."

Thus we arrive at the *Collections* for 1824 — the last volume. Here Upham's ordination as minister at Rochester on July 16, 1823, is twice recorded: in the March number, and again in the April number.[75] Between the records appears, in the March number, the modern ballad of "Lovewell's Fight,"[76] marked as a special contribution to the periodical, and accompanied by a quotation from Upham's commendatory notice of volume I — which appeared in the *North American Review* for January.[77]

A minute but significant detail is the mention of Agio[co]chook in stanza 2 of the ballad:

> "Then did the crimson streams, that flowed,
>   Seem like the waters of the brook,
> That brightly shine, that loudly dash
>   Far down the cliffs of Agiochook."

Mr. Upham was fond of this Indian name for the White Mountains. In "Passaconaway" he writes:

> "And oft the sprites who deck Agiocochook,
>   With nightly lamps and carbuncles, repair,
> When churchyard gleams illume thy grassy nook,
>   To trim their fires and pay their worship there."[78]

To the *Centinel* of August 11, 1819, he contributed a poem called "Sprite of Ajocochook."[79] The name recurs in "The Winter Evening."[80]

Upham's habit of composing verses about the Indians makes a sound argument *a priori* for his authorship of the modern "Lovewell's Fight." His addiction to such subjects comes out strikingly, not only in "The Farmer's Fireside" and "The Winter Evening," but in a score of other poems, some of which have already been mentioned. The list is rather impressive: — "Lovewell's Pond" ("Lovellspond");[81] "Tychou Mingo: or, The Voluntary Sacrifice";[82] "Lucinda" (on the murder of Miss McCrea);[83] "The Indian Scholar";[84] "Philip's Dream";[85] "Passaconaway";[86] "The Indian on Pegasus";[87] "Sprite of Ajocochook";[88] "Obookiah";[89] "Her Cherub's arms are round her breast";[90] "Wohawa";[91] "Madockawando";[92]

"The Iroquois"; [93] "Onontague"; [94] "The Birchen Canoe"; [95] "Isle of Wococon"; [96] "The Three Mounds"; [97] "The Soldier of Hadley"; [98] "The Algonquins"; [99] "The Daughters of the Sun." [100]

In this regard it is notable that a warm admirer of A.K. looked upon him as especially the poet of the Indian. This admirer is "Orolio," who addressed some verses "To A.K." in the *Centinel* for July 7, 1821. These begin:

> "I know that lyre whose thrilling sound
> In magic spell my heart has bound."

Then, after celebrating several of A.K.'s poems by name or in some easily recognizable allusion, Orolio continues:

> "But strongest, wildest sound its strings,
> And deepest are the notes it flings,
> When in its native forests wild,
> It echoes to the Forest Child.
> Oh! then it rolls such minstrelsy
> As none can wake — save only Thee."

Finally I may quote Upham's own words in his notice of volume I of the *Collections* — a notice which appeared (unsigned, of course) in the *North American Review* for January, 1824. Here, under the veil of anonymity, he feels free to allude to several of his own poems on Indian subjects.

"We do not know that poetry has found many votaries among the sons of New Hampshire, but we have at times seen specimens of their efforts, which show that her mountains and lakes are beheld by some, who can inhale the breath of their inspiration, and rejoice in the surrounding sublimities of nature. There are few portions of the Union, which can furnish more to gratify and to excite the powers of an imagination truly poetic, one that is fond of the marvellous in incident, and of the wild and enrapturing in scenery. The wonderful stories, which were told in the primitive times, of Passaconaway the Penacook, of Paugus the chief of the Pequacketts, of Wohawa, who, though a Frenchman by birth, invaded the frontier settlements with more than the cruelty of a savage, are yet remembered and repeated with interest. Even Jocelyn and Darby Fields are not forgotten, and many an untutored lad has been more than half persuaded to leave the unpoetic roof of his forefathers, and emulate the marvellous wanderings of those early adventurers, by going to search for carbuncles on the *Chrystal Hills*." [101]

All the circumstances make it easy to believe that Upham is indeed the author of the modern ballad of "Lovewell's Fight." We should note, too, that in style and manner that piece resembles four ballads which he acknowledged: "Destruction of the Willey Family,"[102] "Death of Colonel Hayne,"[103] "Yanko, the Noble Negro,"[104] and "The Frozen Family of Illinois."[105]

Frederic Kidder, in quoting the first stanza of the ballad in 1865, remarks that it was "written by a gentleman that has obtained some celebrity as a poet, who is still living, but has never allowed his name to accompany it."[106] Mr. George W. Chamberlain, in editing his reprint of Kidder's monograph in 1909, inserts (in brackets) "Prof. Thomas C. Upham of Bowdoin College, Brunswick, Maine," after "poet,"[107] and Williamson ascribes the ballad to Upham without qualification.[108] The authorship must have been known to Farmer and Moore in 1824, and it seems to have been suspected by Willey in 1855.[109] Probably it was an open secret among Upham's friends. He was a very modest man, and somewhat addicted, withal, to innocent mystification. One of his warmest admirers describes him, in a memorial address, as "reticent about himself even to colleagues of forty years close companionship."[110]

Ten years after Upham's death the following memorandum was drawn up. It is now in the possession of Mr. C. W. Lewis, whose investigations in the matter of Lovewell's Fight are gratefully acknowledged by Parkman in his chapter on the subject in 'A Half-Century of Conflict.' I am indebted to Mr. Lewis for my knowledge of this memorandum and for his kindness in furnishing me with a copy.[111]

18 Somerset Street, Boston, Mass.

August 8, 1882.

This is to certify that in a letter (now destroyed) which I received from Thomas C. Upham he stated that the poem commencing with the line What time the noble Lovewell came and referred to by me on page 119 of my History of The Expeditions of Capt. John Lovewell, was written by him. He also stated in the same letter that he was the author of the poem which commences with the words, Ah! where are the soldiers, etc., and which I give on pages 122–123 of my history referred to above.

Frederic Kidder.

This certifies that the above-named letter was shown me by Mr. Kidder and that his statement of the contents is correct.

John Ward Dean.

Upham's reluctance to acknowledge the ballad may have had something to do with the sentiments expressed in one of its liveliest stanzas—sentiments which perhaps seemed to him a little indecorous in his maturer years, when he had become well known as a Christian philosopher and as the author of many religious sonnets and devotional poems: —

> "Good heavens! Is this a time for pray'r?
> Is this a time to worship God?
> When Lovewell's men are dying fast,
> And Paugus' tribe hath felt the rod?"

Some years after the publication of the ballad, Upham became a convert to the extreme doctrine of non-resistance. He wrote 'The Manual of Peace' (New York, 1836), widely circulated by the American Peace Society in an edition issued at Boston in 1842. In this treatise he maintained that every kind of war is wrong, even war in defence of one's country, and he devoted a whole chapter to proving "that ministers of the Gospel cannot innocently and lawfully exercise the office of military chaplain." [112] Such views accorded ill with the meed of praise bestowed by the ballad upon Chaplain Jonathan Frye, who certainly belonged to the church militant. "Chaplain though he was," writes Parkman, "he carried a gun, knife, and hatchet like the others, and not one of the party was more prompt to use them." [113]

NOTES

1. Vol. III, 64–66. A strange error, which has more than once emerged in print, may be corrected here—not because it is likely to pervert anybody who is at all versed in the works of our early historians, but because it affords an amusing (if somewhat disconcerting) instance of the pitfalls that beset the path of the literary investigator. Tyler, in A History of American Literature, 1879, II, 52, note 1, remarks that the ballad of Lovewell's Fight is printed "in Samuel Penhallow, Indian Wars, 129–136." In G. C. Eggleston's American War Ballads and Lyrics, I, 14, the editor avers that it "has been preserved in Penhallow's History of the Wars of New England with the Eastern Indians, 1726" (no page reference). In Burton E. Stevenson's Poems of American History, p. 684, we read: "This ballad . . . has been preserved in The | History | of the | Wars of New England with the Eastern Indians, | or a | Narrative | of their continued perfidy and cruelty, | from the 10th of August, 1703, | to the Peace renewed 13th of July, 1713, | and from the 25th of July, 1722, | to their Submission 15th December, 1725, | which was Ratified August 5th, 1726. | By Samuel Penhallow, Esqr. | Boston, 1726. | This was reprinted at Cincinnati, Ohio, in 1859, and the ballad occurs on page 129." The fact is that Penhallow neither preserves nor mentions the ballad, which is, however, appended to the text of his History, with a careful reference to Farmer and Moore's Collections, III, 64–66, on pages 129–131 of the Cincinnati reprint of 1859. See a note by Mr. C. W. Lewis (signed "Observer") in the Boston Evening Transcript, July 25, 1914, Part 3, p. 10.

2. S. G. Drake, Church's Indian Wars, 2d edition (Boston, 1827), Appendix, pp. 330–334 (and later editions; not in 1st edition, 1825); Samuel L. Knapp, Lectures on American Literature (New York, 1829), pp. 157–159 (four stanzas omitted); S. G. Drake, The Book of the Indians, 5th edition (Boston, 1837), book III, pp. 132–133 (and later editions); R. W. Griswold, Curiosities of American Literature (preface dated 1843), appended to D'Israeli's Curiosities of Literature (New York, 1846), pp. 27–28; C. J. Fox, History of the Old Town of Dunstable (Nashua, 1846), pp. 124–127; E. A. and G. L. Duyckinck, Cyclopædia of American Literature (New York, 1855), I, 427–428 (Simons's edition, Philadelphia, 1875, I, 444–446); Cincinnati reprint, 1859, of Penhallow, The Wars of New England with the Eastern Indians, pp. 129–131; N. Bouton, The Original Account of Capt. John Lovewell's "Great Fight" (Concord, New Hampshire, 1861), pp. 38–41; F. Kidder, The Expeditions of Capt. John Lovewell (Boston, 1865), pp. 116–119, cf. p. 105 (reprint, 1909, in Extra Number 5 of The Magazine of History, II, 95–97, revised by G. W. Chamberlain); Elias Nason, History of Dunstable (Boston, 1877), pp. 51–54; E. C. Stedman and Ellen M. Hutchinson, A Library of American Literature (New York), II (1888, 1892), 294–296; G. C. Eggleston, American War Ballads and Lyrics (New York [1889]), I, 14–18; Henry M. Perkins, Dunstable, in Hurd's History of Middlesex County (Philadelphia, 1890), I, 745; E. E. Hale, New England History in Ballads (Boston, 1903), pp. 69–75; Burton E. Stevenson, Poems of American History (Boston, copyright 1908, 1922), pp. 106–108; the Same, The Home Book of Verse (New York), VI (1915), 2345–2348 (1918, II, 2412–2415); Boston Evening Transcript, July 18, 1914, Part 3, p. 10; R. P. Gray, Songs and Ballads of the Maine Lumberjacks, with Other Songs from Maine (Cambridge,

1924), pp. 127–133. Professor Gray alone reproduces the text exactly as printed in the Collections, letter for letter and point for point.

3. "I have found a letter addressed by Mr. Farmer to my brother, Rev. Joseph B. Hill, dated Concord, Sept. 2, 1823. 'Have you ever met with the song written soon after Lovewell's defeat in 1725? We ... should much like to obtain and publish it.' Mr. Farmer subsequently obtained a copy of the song, as he informed me, from Mr. Coffin, the Principal of the Tyngsborough Grammar School, after an inquiry for it of more than eight years. He published it in the N. H. Historical Collections and I published it, with introductory remarks, in the Constellation and Nashua Gazette." So testifies John B. Hill in a letter to E. H. Spalding, September 24, 1877; see Bi-Centennial of Old Dunstable (Nashua, 1878), p. 51. For this reference I am indebted to Mr. C. W. Lewis. For a notice of Coffin see New England Historical and Genealogical Register, xx, 267–270. A Brief Memoir of Rev. Joseph Bancroft Hill by the Rev. Edwin R. Hodgman was published at Boston in 1868.

4. On February 4, 1824, Farmer wrote to Coffin acknowledging the receipt of a letter of January 22, and adding "The Song of Lovewell is inserted in the February number of the Collections, with a few preliminary observations" (Coffin MSS, III, 4). This letter of January 22 is preserved among the Coffin MSS (ibid.), but it does not contain the ballad.

5. The only writer who has impugned the ballad's claims to antiquity, so far as I know, is Mr. George W. Chamberlain, in his essay on "John Chamberlain, the Indian Fighter at Pigwacket" (Maine Historical Society, Collections and Proceedings, 1898, 2d Series, IX, 1–14). He is concerned to vindicate the tradition which ascribes the killing of Paugus to Chamberlain, and it is a part of his case to discredit the testimony of the song that it was Wyman who "shot the old chief Paugus." Mr. Chamberlain styles the piece "an anonymous ballad of uncertain age and veracity" (p. 5) and "an anonymous ballad first published ninety-nine years after the battle it describes occurred" (p. 11). In reprinting his essay in Extra Number 5 of the Magazine of History (1909), he is careful to remark that John Chamberlain is not an ancestor of his. The antiquity of the ballad is accepted (with or without qualifying phrases) by most of those who have reprinted it and also (among others) by Palfrey, History of New England, IV (1872), 442, note; T. W. Higginson, Winsor's Memorial History of Boston, II (1881), 110; Parkman, A Half-Century of Conflict, 1892, I, 258, note 1, 260, note 1; J. L. Onderdonk, History of American Verse (Chicago, 1901), p. 61.

6. In Gray's Songs and Ballads of the Maine Lumberjacks with Other Songs from Maine (Cambridge, 1924), p. 128.

7. Before the twelve arrived, the first news of the Fight had been brought to Dunstable by Corporal Benjamin Hassell, who had decamped as soon as the Indians made their attack and was therefore unable to tell who were dead and who were alive. He seems to have reached Dunstable on May 11, on which day he wrote a brief report to Lieutenant Governor Dummer, preserved in the Massachusetts Archives, LII, 168 (Kidder, p. 75; Baxter, p. 268), which was sent by Col. Eleazar Tyng in a letter in which he gave a fuller report derived orally from Hassell (Tyng to Dummer, May 12, Archives, LII, 169; Kidder, pp. 75–76; Baxter, pp. 268–269). Dummer received Tyng's communication on May 13 in the morning (Dummer to Tyng, May 13, first draught, Archives, LII, 173; second draught, Archives, LII, 171–

172; only the second printed by Kidder, p. 77, and Baxter, pp. 270–271: see also Dummer to Col. John Wentworth, May 13: Archives, LII, 170; Kidder, p. 76; Baxter, p. 270). This was the first news to reach Boston. For convenience I attach to the citations from the Archives references to Kidder (The Expeditions of Capt. John Lovewell, 1865) and Baxter (Documentary History of the State of Maine, Vol. x, 1907), but I must add that neither affords accurate transcripts of the documents.

8. Symmes, Lovewell Lamented (Boston, 1725), p. ix (Kidder, p. 35).

9. Dummer to Tyng, May 14, 1725: "I have this moment receved your Express of this Day with Blanchards acc! of the action between Lovells men & the Indians, taken from Melvin" (draught, Archives, LII, 175; Kidder, p. 78; Baxter, p. 272). There were two Melvins of Concord, Massachusetts (David and Eleazar) among Lovewell's men and neither received any "considerable Wound" (Symmes, pp. iv, viii; Kidder, pp. 30, 34). On the 14th Tyng sent another of the twelve to Dummer as the bearer of a letter in which Tyng acknowledges the receipt of orders contained in Dummer's letter of the 13th cited in note 7, above: "I have also sent one of Capt Lovewells men the Bearer hereof who was in the whole Engagement a man who by the account the rest gave of him behaved himself couragiously to the last" (Tyng to Dummer, May 14, 1725, Archives, LII, 174a; Kidder, p. 78; Baxter, p. 272). I assume that this messenger got to Boston on the 15th.

10. Reprinted by Kidder, p. 85. This same account, James Franklin tells us, was to have been printed in the Courant of May 17, but was "omitted by Mistake"! (Courant, May 24.)

11. Autobiography, Writings, ed. Smyth, 1, 239–240.

12. The same item was very likely published in The Boston Gazette of May 24, but no copy of that issue has been found. The next number of the Gazette after No. 286 (May 17) that is known is No. 294 (July 19). See Colonial Society of Massachusetts, Publications, IX, 115, 172.

13. That Farmer and Moore printed from a manuscript copy, not from one of the original Franklin broadsides, is clear. Otherwise they would in all probability have noted the imprint, — unless, to be sure, the original broadside had no imprint, — and, in any case, they would have kept the original title, "The Voluntier's March." Farmer and Moore say nothing of the advertisement in the Courant of May 31, 1725.

14. It is advertised in the News-Letter of July 1, 1725, as published "this Day." On July 15 the News-Letter announced that "a Second Impression is now just out of the Press." See Green, 2 Massachusetts Historical Proceedings, XI, 181–182. My quotations are from the first edition. For convenience, references are appended to Kidder's reprint of the second edition (Historical Memorial) in his monograph, The Expeditions of Capt. John Lovewell (Boston, 1865).

15. Cf. Paul Coffin, Ride to Piggwacket, 1786 (Collections of the Maine Historical Society, IV [1856], 290).

16. Page x. Contrast the tense form used in the Courant of Saturday, September 11, 1725 (No. 215) in recording Wyman's death: "On Sunday Night last dy'd at Woburn Capt. Seth Wyman, very much lamented. He was a Man of Religion, Probity, Courage and Conduct, and hearty in the Service of his Country against the Indian Enemy. He was an Ensign under Capt. Lovewell in his several Marches to

the Eastward; and for his uncommon Bravery at the late memorable Fight at Pig-wacket, his Hon. the Lieut Governour granted him a Captain's Commission." Cf. Penhallow, 1726, p. 117: "Mr. *Wyman*, who distinguish'd himself in such a signal manner, was at his return presented with a Silver hilted Sword and a *Captains* Commission."

17. For "Wyman's captain made" most of the reprints since Farmer and Moore read erroneously "Wyman captain made." Parkman has this wrong reading and therefore remarks that "the popular ballad, written at the time and very faithful to the facts, says that, the other officers being killed, the English made Wyman their captain." (A Half-Century of Conflict, 1892, 1, 259, note.) Our forefathers knew well enough that Wyman, who was an ensign, was ranking officer on the retreat and needed no further commission to lead the survivors. They knew also that captaincies were not conferred by popular election.

18. With the last two lines of this stanza compare the following passage from The Mournful Elegy of Mr. Jonathan Frye:

> "He listed out with courage bold,
> And fought the Indians uncontroled;
> *And many of the rebels slew*
> *While bullets thick around him flew.*
> At last a fatal bullet came,
> And wounded this young son of fame."

The Elegy was certainly composed soon after Frye's death, and it is believed (with good reason) to be from the pen of Susannah Rogers of Andover, the *very* young lady to whom he was engaged to be married. The printed Franklin ballad may well have circulated in Andover, where Frye's parents were living. Anyhow, the coincidence in phraseology is worth noting, though "slew" and "bullets flew" make a sufficiently obvious rhyme. The contents of the Elegy show that it was written at least some days later than the ballad — after the details of Frye's death had become known from Eleazer Davis (see p. 101). The Elegy was first printed by T. C. Frye in The New England Historical and Genealogical Register, 1861, xv, 91. It is reprinted (not quite exactly) by Bouton in his edition of Symmes, pp. 35–37; by Kidder, pp. 120–122 (ed. 1909, pp. 99–101), and (very imperfectly) by Bailey, Historical Sketches of Andover, pp. 191–193. See also S. L. Knapp, Lectures on American Literature (New York, 1829), p. 157; Williamson, Bibliography of Maine, 11, 375; Parkman, A Half-Century of Conflict, 1892, 1, 261.

19. There was a rumor in Boston on the morning of May 24 that Lovewell and Frye were "got to some of our Frontier Towns, tho' very much wounded" (Courant, May 24, see above). This was in part corrected in the Courant of May 31: "The Report of Capt. Lovewell's being alive, proves groundless; but we have certain Advice, that Eleazer Davis, one of the 4 wounded Men who were brought off several Miles by the English, is arriv'd at Berwick. The other three, who were not able to travel as fast as himself, he left in the Woods, of whose Return we are not yet out of Hopes." Meanwhile the Captain's father (John Lovewell, Senior) in his petition of May 20 speaks of "the Death of his Son in the Service of his Country" (Archives, LXXII, 236), and on May 27 Dummer, in a speech to the General Court, referred to Lovewell as certainly dead: — *I Recommend to your Compassion the Widow of Capt. Lovewell and those of his Men who dyed bravely in the late Action at Piggwackett, in*

the Service of their Country" (Journal of the House of Representatives, Boston, 1725, p. 7).

20. The arrival of Eleazer Davis at Berwick on May 27 was reported to Dummer by Wentworth (who calls him Ezekiel) in a letter written from Portsmouth on the next day (Archives, LII, 194–195; Kidder, p. 99; Baxter, pp. 283–284): "I have him at Portsmouth . . . I have sent you what was taken from his mouth Yesterday." The following document (not heretofore printed) is in the Archives, LXXII, 239; it was apparently enclosed: —

Portsmouth May $\tilde{y}$ 27th/1725 An Account of the Mens Names that were kill'd in Capt Lovewell's Late fight with the Indians, at Pigwocket, as taken from the mouth of Eliaz^r Davis, who came in to Berwick this Day —

> Imprim^s: Capt: Lovewell
> Leiut: Farewell
> Mr Fry $\tilde{y}$ Chaplain
> Daniel Woods of Groten
> Thomas Woods of D^o
> John Jeffs of D^o.
> Josiah Davis of Concord
> Jacob Farrer of D^o.
> Solomon Kies of Bilrica
> & one Kitteridge of D^o.
> Jacob Fullum of Westown
> Jonathan Robbins of Dunstable
> Robt Usher of D^o.
> Ichabod Johnson of Woburn
> Josiah Jones of Concord; Lost in $\tilde{y}$ Woods, much wounded, $\tilde{y}$ Next day after the fight, being the Sabbath; & $\tilde{y}$ 9th Instant.

Eleaz^r Davis Gott in at Lovewells fort on friday $\tilde{y}$ 25th Instant & at Keys Garrison $\tilde{y}$ 27th D^o. att Berwick

[Docketed:] List of Men Kill'd w[ith] Capt Lovewell May 27. 1725.

21. News-Letter, June 3; Courant, June 7; cf. Symmes, p. x (Kidder, p. 37). Kidder, p. 104, erroneously credits the News-Letter item to Wentworth's letter to Dummer, May 28 (see note 20, above).

22. See note 20.

23. See note 19.

24. Symmes, p. ix (Kidder, p. 36); cf. Kidder, p. 99.

25. That is, the twelve who reached Dunstable on May 13 (note 8) plus the four (including Ensign Seth Wyman) who got there on Saturday, May 15 (Symmes, p. ix; Kidder, pp. 35–36). Wyman came to Boston during the week of May 16–22 (Courant, May 24) — perhaps not before the 19th, since the News-Letter of the 20th merely repeats the Gazette item of the 17th and makes no mention of the safety of Wyman and his three companions.

26. Pages ix, x (Kidder, pp. 35–37).

27. Page x (Kidder, p. 37). Cf. Penhallow, The History of the Wars of New-England with the Eastern Indians (Boston, 1726), p. 116.

28. Tyng left Amoskeag on his march to Pigwacket on May 19 (Tyng to Dummer, May 19, Archives, LII, 182a; Kidder, p. 80; Baxter, p. 277). On June 4 the

House Journal (p. 21) records that "*Penn Townsend* Esq; brought down a Letter from Col. *Eleazer Tyng*, Dated at *Dunstable*, *June* 3d. 1725. Giving an Account of his late March to *Piggwackets*, which His Honour thought proper to Communicate." The Courant of June 7 contains the following item: "We have Advice from Dunstable, that a Company of Men under the Command of Coll. Tyng have been upon the Spot at Pigwacket, where the late Fight happen'd, and found three of the Indians buried; and by the Blood they saw on the Ground, and other Circumstances, judge the Loss of the Indians to be very great, and that the rest of their Dead were carry'd off in Canoes." This does not mention Paugus. On June 10, however, the News-Letter records the discovery of his body: "We have Advice here, That a Company of Men under the Command of Col. Tyng have been upon the Spot at Pigwocket, where the late Fight happen'd, and found Three of the Indians buried; One of which was known by several particular Marks to be *Paugus*; and by the Blood they saw on the Ground, and other Circumstances, judge the Loss of the Enemy very great, and that the rest of their Dead were carry'd off in Canoes." The Courant of July 10 prints a Vote of the House of Representatives, June 17, 1725: "That there be allowed and paid out of the publick Treasury the Sum of Three Hundred Pounds for the Three Indians found kill'd by Capt. Lovewell and Company, to them or their lawful Representatives, although their Scalps were not produced." See the printed Journal of the House (Boston, 1725), p. 48. Cf. Westbrook's letter to Dummer, June 22, 1725 (Archives, LII, 205; Baxter, p. 289; W. B. Trask, Letters of Colonel Thomas Westbrook, Boston, 1901, p. 118). It must be permitted me to doubt whether the body in question was that of Paugus after all. If the Indians carried off any of their dead, would they have left their chief's corpse to be disinterred and perhaps scalped by the next band of white men that might come to Pigwacket? That Paugus was killed seems certain, for he was never again heard of in the land of the living. But is it not likely that the body was that of some less important warrior tricked out with the dead chief's insignia to deceive the enemy?

29. Page vii (Kidder, p. 33); not in Penhallow. We remember that Wyman was one of the three who signed the "Attestation" printed at the end of Symmes's narrative (p. xii).

30. In writing to Farmer on January 22, 1824, Coffin remarks: "In my last letter you probably noticed an error, 'Pawwaw' for 'Paugus'" (Coffin MSS, III, 123, Essex Institute). By "my last letter" Coffin means the letter (now lost) in which he had communicated the ballad. It is an easy conjecture that the text as received by Farmer read "shot the old Chief Pawwaw," that Coffin afterwards decided that "Paugus" ought to be substituted, and that this erroneous emendation was adopted by Farmer.

31. The other statements that the ballad adds to the Courant item of the 24th are (1) that the fight began about ten o'clock; (2) that the sixteen survivors "safe arriv'd at Dunstable the thirteenth day of May"; (3) that there were "two logs" which "close together lay" behind the Indians; and (4) that "young Fullam" fought well, and "fell a sacrifice" while "endeavouring to save a man." None of these need disturb us. (1) Ten o'clock is mentioned in the Gazette report of May 17, 1725. (2) Twelve of the sixteen did arrive at Dunstable on the 13th; four more came in on the 15th. (3) (4) The matter of the logs and the attempt of Fullam to save a

comrade were probably a part of Wyman's story and therefore well known in Boston when the balladist wrote, though the Courant ignored them, just as it did the incident of the powowing, which certainly was reported by Wyman. That Fullam was killed on the field was of course known to all of the sixteen survivors who had returned when the ballad was written. Symmes mentions the death of Fullam early in the fight but says nothing of his endeavoring to save a man (p. vi; Kidder, p. 33). Penhallow remarks: "Mr. *Jacob Fullam*, who was was an Officer and an only Son, distinguish'd himself with much bravery. One of the first that was kill'd was by his hand; and when ready to encounter a second, it's said, that he and his Adversary fell at the very instant by each others shot" (pp. 114–115). The "logs," by the way, are a trifle puzzling. Dr. E. E. Hale (New England History in Ballads, p. 75) silently emends to "bogs," which may, however, be a misprint (like his "flew" for "slew" in stanza 16); but there *was* a bog (see Belknap, 5 Massachusetts Historical Collections, 11, 398).

32. Mr. S. Harrison Lovewell called attention to this singular case in a note (signed "S. H. L.") in the Boston Evening Transcript, September 15, 1917, Part 3, p. 4, identifying the defendant with Captain Lovewell's father and the plaintiff with Joseph Jewett, son of Joseph. The defendant's mark in his signature to the note resembles the initial L in the signature "John Lovewell" affixed to a petition of the Selectmen and inhabitants of Dunstable, May 20, 1725 (Archives, LXXII, 235), which, by the way, in no wise resembles the signature "John Lovewell" attached to another petition of the same date which is certainly from the Captain's father (Archives, LXXII, 236). This latter signature bears a strong family likeness to the Captain's own signature (Archives, LII, 141). The case is entered as No. 109 in the records of the Inferiour Court (Middlesex), Book of August, 1738–December, 1739, in the Clerk's Office at East Cambridge. The documents are partly in this office, partly in the Suffolk Files at the Court House in Boston. In the Suffolk Files are (1) the original writ, August 9, 1738, containing the plaintiff's declaration and the defendant's answer (Vol. CCCLI, No. 54821); (2) an attested copy of the judgment with a statement of the appeal (Vol. CCCX, No. 47208); (3) the final bill of costs (Vol. CCCXV, No. 48163). In the Clerk's Office at East Cambridge are (1) the original note; (2) the original verdict in the Inferiour Court; (3) the first bill of costs; (4) an attested copy of the appeal. The records of the Superiour Court of January, 1739, seem to be missing, but the result of the appeal is shown by the fact that the final bill of costs (including 16 shillings for the "appeles trauel 80 miles out & Back" and one pound for "his attendance 10 days") is docketed "Jewett Bill Coast against louell Pd.". As to "Capt John Louells killing the ten Indians" (February 21, 1725), see the Captain's journal (Kidder, p. 17); Archives, LXXII, 284 (cf. Kidder, p. 84), 325–328, 368–369 (cf. Kidder, p. 18); New-England Courant, March 1, 8, and 15, 1725; Penhallow, p. 110.

33. Frederic C. Jewett, History and Genealogy of the Jewetts of America, Boston, 1908, 1, 53–54, 99.

34. Vol. III, 94–97. Reprinted: S. G. Drake, Indian Biography (Boston, 1832), pp. 237–243 (only in part; also only in part in 2d–4th editions, 1833–35); same, 5th edition, 1837 (Book of the Indians), book III, pp. 129–132 (complete; also in later editions); C. J. Fox, History of the Old Town of Dunstable (Nashua, 1846), pp. 128–131; Benjamin G. Willey, Incidents in White Mountain History (Boston, 1856,

1858), p . 218–221; Francis Chase, Gathered Sketches from the Early History of New Hampshire and Vermont (Claremont, New Hampshire, 1856), pp. 33–38; the Cincinnati edition of Penhallow, 1859, pp. 132–136; N. Bouton, The Original Narrative of Capt. John Lovewell's "Great Fight" (Concord, New Hampshire, 1861), pp. 42–46; B. E. Stevenson, Poems of American History (Boston, copyright 1908, 1922), pp. 108–109; Boston Evening Transcript, September 12, 1914, Part 3, p. 11; R. P. Gray, Songs and Ballads of the Maine Lumberjacks (Cambridge, 1924), pp. 134–139. Professor Gray alone reprints the poem exactly as it stands in the Collections. Cf. S. G. Drake, New England Historical and Genealogical Register, January, 1853, VII, 61, 64; Kidder, The Expeditions of Capt. John Lovewell (Boston, 1865), p. 119 (reprint, 1909, p. 97); Nason, A History of the Town of Dunstable (Boston, 1877), p. 54; R. B. Caverly, History of the Indian Wars of New England (Boston, 1882), pp. 294–295; the Same, Battle of the Bush (Boston, 1884–85), pp. 274–275; Williamson, Bibliography of the State of Maine, II, 545.

35. See Williamson, A Bibliography of the State of Maine, II, 495; G. W. Chamberlain, Collections and Proceedings of the Maine Historical Society, 2d Series, IX, 5, 9. Others besides the balladist have been misled by Russell's interpolated text of Symmes: for example, Wilkes Allen, The History of Chelmsford (Haverhill, 1820), p. 37; Folsom, History of Saco and Biddeford (Saco, 1830), p. 220; S. G. Drake, in his reprint of Church's Indian Wars, 2d edition (Boston, 1827), p. 334, note; the Same, Indian Biography (Boston, 1832), pp. 240–242; C. J. Fox, History of the Old Township of Dunstable (Nashua, 1846), p. 127; N. Bouton, whose edition of Symmes (Concord, New Hampshire, 1861) adopts Russell's text as genuine; Stedman and Hutchinson, A Library of American Literature (New York), II (1888, 1892), 293–295, whose extract from Symmes takes in the interpolation.

36. That is, of the four badly wounded men who were left behind by the main party on the way back (see above). Symmes, p. x (Kidder, p. 39).

37. Page 23 (Collections, I, 33).

38. Pages 23–24 (Collections, I, 33). Cf. William Lincoln, The Worcester Magazine, October, 1825, I, 23. See Green, Groton during the Indian Wars, pp. 140–141; notes by C. W. Lewis (signed "Observer") in the Boston Evening Transcript, August 15, 1914, Part 2, p. 4; August 29, 1914, Part 2, p. 4; April 7, 1917, Part 3, p. 15.

39. Page 24 (Collections, I, 34). See S. G. Drake, Indian Biography (Boston, 1832), pp. 240–241; Caleb Butler, History of the Town of Groton (Boston, 1848), pp. 107–110; G. W. Chamberlain, as above, IX, 12.

40. Page 24 (Collections, I, 34).

41. Vol. II, 65, note (not in Russell). Belknap seems to have got his information on this point from Captain John Evans, and he, in turn, "from one of the Indians that was in the fight" (Belknap's Tour to the White Mountains, 1784; 5 Massachusetts Historical Collections, II, 397, 398).

42. Collections, I, 29, note.

43. Page vi (Kidder, p. 33).

44. North American Review, XVIII, 35.

45. Collections, III, 82, 119.

46. See McDuffee, History of the Town of Rochester (Manchester, 1892), I, 240, 243; II, 606.

47. The first A. K. poem printed in the Centinel ("A New-Year's Present") appeared on December 27, 1817, with an editorial preface indicating that it was the author's earliest contribution: "The following has been sent to the FOUNT from *New-Hampshire*, as an original composition: — If it be such, it is one of the finest effusions of the pastoral muse we have met with in our country. — It would not detract from the merits of SHENSTONE, CUNNINGHAM, GOLDSMITH or COWPER. We bid a cordial welcome."

48. Oscar = A. K. = Upham is an equation proved by the letter communicating "The New-Hampshire Hunters" along with "Susan and Jack." This letter was printed in the Centinel of February 21, 1818, along with A. K.'s "New-Hampshire Hunters" (a poem which Upham later included in his American Sketches, New York, 1819, pp. 31–32). "Susan and Jack" was printed, as by the same author as "The New-Hampshire Hunters," in the next number of the Centinel (February 25, 1818), though it is signed "Oscar." The following poems that had been published in the Centinel under the signature of A. K. are included in Upham's 1819 volume: "Dark-Rolling Connecticut" (pp. 21–22; Centinel, April 1, 1818; also in Fireside Poetical Readings, Boston, 1843, pp. 143–144, and American Cottage Life, Brunswick, Maine, 1850–51, pp. 65–66); "The New-Hampshire Hunters" (pp. 31–32; February 21, 1818); "So Recall not the Soul" (p. 50; revised, "When the Wings of the Soul," March 14, 1818; further revised, "The Departing Christian," The Religious Offering, for MDCCCXXXV, pp. 111–112, and Fireside Poetical Readings, p. 296); "Montgomery's Return" (p. 53, completely rewritten; July 29, 1818); "Lucinda" (pp. 60–61; October 17, 1818); "A New-Year's Present" (pp. 70–72; December 27, 1817); "The Voluntary Sacrifice" (pp. 80–82; August 12, 1818); "Lovellspond" (pp. 110–111; January 31, 1818). All but one of these ("Dark-Rolling Connecticut") are labelled "For the Centinel Fount." This appeared in the Centinel on April 1, 1818, without this label, but with the following editorial comment: "The following beautiful little ballad has been copied into several papers from the *Port Folio* without the signature which it ought to bear of a New-Hampshire Correspondent, to whom the Fount of the CENTINEL has been indebted for numerous rich effusions." The poem was, in fact, first published in the Port Folio (Philadelphia) for February, 1818 (4th Series, v, 161). It is marked "For the Port Folio" and is signed "A. K."

49. The Centinel of March 17, 1819, remarks: "We have received a copy of a beautiful little work entitled 'American Sketches,' published in New-York, by THOMAS C. UPHAM. Several of them originally appeared in the *Centinel Fount*, and were copied with high commendation in various papers." In a footnote to "several of them" the notice specifies "Camilla" (*i. e.*, "A New-Year's Present"), "Lovell's Pond," and "Montgomery's Return." The Centinel extracts three poems from this volume, with due credit: "The Indian Scholar" (March 20, 1819); "Oh, it is sweet to run with thee" (March 24); "How sweet the scene" (April 10).

50. Pages 110–111, 57–58.

51. "Lovell's Pond. *The scene of* [sic] *1725 of a desperate encounter with the savages.*" It begins, "Ah! where are the soldiers that fought here of yore?" As published in Upham's volume of American Sketches (1819), pp. 110–111, the poem has been to some extent rewritten: it begins "In earth's verdant bosom, still, crumbling, and cold."

52. Collections, I, 35–36.

53. Another poem on the same subject — styled by the correspondent who sent it to the newspaper a "poetic effusion from a young gentleman of *Maine*, occasioned by a visit to the ever memorable battle ground near Lovell's Pond, . . . a fine specimen of mature genius" — was printed in the Centinel of November 10, 1819. It is modelled on Gray's Elegy and begins —

> Saw ye that spirit move along the wave
> And tread in silence through the hallow'd air?
> 'T was the dim spectre of the warrior brave
> Who comes to brood him o'er his ashes there.

On Longfellow and Upham see C. W. L[ewis]., Boston Evening Transcript, May 5, 1886, p. 6.

54. Upham, American Sketches, 1819, p. 116.

55. Page ix (Kidder, p. 35). Cf. Penhallow, 1726, pp. 115–116.

56. See J. B. Moore, Collections of the New Hampshire Historical Society, VI, 40.

57. Pages 169–177 of Collections, vol. I; pp. 3–11 of the pamphlet. The poem, revised, is included in two of Upham's later publications: Fireside Poetical Readings (Boston, 1843), pp. 53–62 (issued anonymously), and American Cottage Life (Brunswick, Maine, 1850–51), pp. 13–30. The latter volume was afterwards republished (with an excellent portrait of the author) at Boston (no date) by the American Tract Society, to which Upham assigned the copyright. In this edition the title runs: A Book for the Home. American Cottage Life.

58. Whittier's "Mogg Megone," begun in 1830, was published in The New England Magazine for March and April, 1835, VIII, 161–170, 266–273, and appeared as a volume in 1836.

59. Upham had already contributed a poem called "Madockawando" to the Columbian Centinel of November 13, 1819.

60. Upham's poem beginning "Her Cherub's arms are round her breast" (Centinel, September 11, 1819) concerns a tragic incident of the expedition of "two French partizans, Artell and Hopehood, alias Wohawa" against Salmon Falls in 1690. Another poem of his, "Wohawa," is in the Centinel of October 30, 1819.

61. Stanza 12.

62. Collections, III, 96.

63. It consists of two thirds of his poem called "The Pilgrims" (American Sketches, pp. 22–23).

64. See p. 108, above.

65. Collections, II, 64.

66. Ibid., II, 83–90.

67. See notes 71, 72.

68. Stanza 9.

69. Stanzas 11–14. A part of this passage is quoted as from "Upham's Sketches" in the Collections of the New Hampshire Historical Society for 1827, II, 46, note.

70. Stanza 15. Collections, II, 86.

71. Fireside Readings, pp. 71–80.

72. American Cottage Life, pp. 31–40.

73. Collections, II, 159–160.

74. It ran through several editions.

75. Collections, III, 82, 119.

76. Ibid., 94–97.

77. The review was of course unsigned, but it is known to be Upham's (Cushing, Index to the North American Review, p. 149).

78. Columbian Centinel, May 29, 1819. He appends an explanatory footnote with a reference to Belknap's History of New-Hampshire, I, 121.

79. The poem is accompanied by an interesting note about the famous carbuncle and "Darby Fields" and the many attempts made to find the treasure (see p. 113).

80. See stanza 33, p. 111.

81. Columbian Centinel, January 31, 1818; American Sketches, 1819, pp. 110–111; Farmer and Moore's Collections, I (1822), 35–36; Drake's reprint of Church's Indian Wars, 2d edition, Boston, 1827, Appendix, pp. 335–336 (and later editions); Cincinnati reprint of Penhallow, 1859, p. 136; N. Bouton, The Original Account of Capt. John Lovewell's "Great Fight," Concord, New Hampshire, 1861, Appendix, pp. 47–48; Kidder, The Expeditions of Capt. John Lovewell, Boston, 1865, pp. 122–123 (reprint, in Extra Number 5 of The Magazine of History, 1909, II, 101–102); Edwin D. Sanborn, History of New Hampshire, Manchester, 1875, pp. 106–107; Nason, A History of the Town of Dunstable, Boston, 1877, pp. 54–55; The Illustrated Webster Fryeburg Memorial, Fryeburg, 1882, pp. 30–31.

82. Centinel, August 12, 1818; American Sketches, pp. 80–82.

83. Centinel, October 17, 1818; American Sketches, pp. 60–61. Upham's poem is not included among the poems on Miss McCrea collected by W. L. Stone in his Ballads and Poems relating to the Burgoyne Campaign (Albany, 1893), pp. 134–207. Similarly Stone ignores Upham's poem "The Burial of Fraser" (Centinel, July 17, 1819) in his collection of "Ballads on the Death of General Fraser" in the same volume, pp. 114–127.

84. American Sketches, pp. 89–90 (91–90 by error); reprinted, Centinel, March 20, 1819 ("From Upham's American Sketches"). Suggested, apparently, by Freneau's poem, "The Indian Student; or, Force of Nature."

85. Centinel, April 21, 1819.

86. Ibid., May 29, 1819.

87. Ibid., June 5, 1819.

88. Ibid., August 11, 1819.

89. Ibid., September 4, 1819.

90. Ibid., September 11, 1819. See note 60.

91. Ibid., October 30, 1819.

92. Ibid., November 13, 1819.

93. American Sketches, pp. 54–55.

94. Ibid., p. 67. This poem may have been inspired by Mrs. John (Anne Home) Hunter's famous lyric, "The Death Song of an Indian Chief," which Upham could have found in Ritson's English Songs, 1783, I, ii, note 5 (also in Park's edition, 1813, I, iii, note); The American Museum for January, 1787, I, 90; the Salem Mercury, March 3, 1787; The American Musical Miscellany (Northampton, Massachusetts, [ca. 1798]), pp. 114–115; Mrs. Hunter's Poems (London, 1802),

pp. 79–80; The Warbler (Augusta, Maine, 1805), p. 19; The Nightingale or Ladies' Vocal Companion (Albany, 1807), p. 38; The Songster's Companion (Brattleborough, Vermont, 1815), pp. 90–91 — and elsewhere. The ascription of the poem to "P. Freneau" in the third edition of vol. I of The American Museum (1790, I, 77) has misled several scholars (it is anonymous in the first and second editions of that periodical, both 1787); but the blunder was corrected long ago: see Duyckinck's Cyclopædia of American Literature, 1855, I, 341, note; T. P. Cross, Modern Philology, XVII, 235.

95. American Sketches, pp. 57–58.

96. Ibid., pp. 91–92.

97. Ibid., pp. 95–98.

98. Ibid., pp. 101–103.

99. Ibid., pp. 104–105.

100. Fireside Poetical Readings, Boston, 1843, p. 153.

101. XVIII, 39. Cf. Upham's note to his "Sprite of Ajocochook" in the Centinel, August 11, 1819 (note 79, above).

102. The Religious Offering, for MDCCCXXXV (New York, 1835), pp. 167–176; Fireside Poetical Readings (Boston, 1843), pp. 122–130. Upham contributed to the Collections of the New Hampshire Historical Society for 1832, III, 266–280, a long account of "the destruction of the Willey Family, in the Notch of the White Mountains" in the form of a letter to John Farmer dated September, 1828. Cf. J. B. Moore's account in the same volume, pp. 224–232.

103. Fireside Poetical Readings, pp. 114–121; American Cottage Life (Brunswick, Maine, 1850–51), pp. 51–58.

104. Fireside Poetical Readings, pp. 131–136; American Cottage Life, pp. 59–64.

105. Fireside Poetical Readings, pp. 137–142.

106. The Expeditions of Capt. John Lovewell, p. 119.

107. Extra Number 5 of The Magazine of History, II, 97.

108. Bibliography of the State of Maine, II, 545.

109. "The following ballad stanzas were published originally in the work entitled 'Collections' [etc.]. The author's name is not given; but it is conjectured that they were written by a personal friend of the learned and excellent editors, who was then young and not much practised in writing, and who is said to be still living somewhere in the State of Maine." Benjamin G. Willey, Incidents in White Mountain History (Boston, 1856, copyright 1855), p. 218.

110. Alpheus S. Packard, Address on the Life and Character of Thomas C. Upham (Brunswick, Maine, 1873), p. 9.

111. Cf. Mr. Lewis's notes (signed "Observer") in the Boston Evening Transcript, July 25, 1914, Part 3, p. 10; November 7, 1914, Part 3, p. 14.

112. Edition of 1842, chapter 15, pp. 167–171.

113. A Half-Century of Conflict, 1892, I, 251.

THE PRINTERS beg leave to acquaint their Subscribers and the Public, that the TYPES with which THIS Paper is printed are of AMERICAN manufacture, and should it by this means fail of giving such entire satisfaction to the judicious and accurate eye, they hope every patriotic allowance will be made in its favour, and that an attempt to introduce so valuable an art into these colonies, will meet with an indulgent countenance from every lover of his country.--------We are sensible, that in point of elegance, they are somewhat inferior to those imported from England, but we flatter ourselves that the rustic manufactures of America will prove more grateful to the patriot eye, than the more finished productions of Europe, especially when we consider that whilst you tolerate the unpolished figure of the first attempt, the work will be growing to perfection by the experience of the ingenious artist, who has furnished us with this specimen of his skill, and we hope the paper will not prove less acceptable to our readers, for giving him this encouragement.

We beg leave further to observe, that as one of the eastern mails is now dispatched from Boston, in such time as to arrive here on Thursday (instead of Saturday as formerly) we have judged it expedient to change our day of publication to Friday, by which alteration we expect to have an opportunity of furnishing the most early intelligence from that interesting quarter. We trust this will be a sufficient apology for making that only deviation from the assurances given the public in our proposals, nor will any other alteration be admitted unless manifestly tending to the advantage and entertainment of our Subscribers.----We return thanks to those gentlemen in this and the neighbouring provinces, who have kindly countenanced our intentions, and obligingly assisted us by taking in subscriptions, &c. for the PENNSYLVANIA MERCURY and UNIVERSAL ADVERTISER, and would beg them still to continue such, their friendly offices, and those who have not yet sent us their lists of subscribers names will please to transmit them and the Papers shall be immediately forwarded.

Philadelphia, April 3, 1775.

Messrs. STORY and HUMPHREYS,
IF you think the inclosed juvenile Production has merit enough to fill a corner of your entertaining Paper, by inserting it you will oblige your constant Reader and Well-wisher.   B------.

THOUGHTS on FRIENDSHIP.

THE FIRST WORK WITH AMERICAN TYPES

By LAWRENCE C. WROTH

Librarian of the John Carter Brown Library

O N April 7, 1775, there appeared in Philadelphia the initial issue of Story & Humphreys's *Pennsylvania Mercury*. This newspaper was referred to by a contemporary diarist as "The first Work with Amer. Types" and with certain qualifications, later to be made, it seems to be entitled to the distinction of priority implied in this descriptive phrase. Type founding in the colonies went through those phases of tentative effort, complete failure, and partial achievement which are normal to the beginnings of great industries, and before going on with the story of the font of type from which the *Pennsylvania Mercury* was printed, it is proposed to give briefly an account of earlier attempts at the establishment of letter founding in English America.[1] By doing this it will be possible to secure correctness of sequence and of relationship among the several elements of this study in origins.

The first font of types cast in English America was that which resulted from the painful efforts of Abel Buell, a silversmith and lapidary of Killingworth, Connecticut. As early as April 1, 1769, Buell cast a small font of letters, crude in design and in execution, from which proofs were taken for the examination and the criticism of his friends. In October of the

---

1. Type founding in Spanish America began earlier than in the English colonies. The Indian converts of the Jesuits in Paraguay cast type, probably of tin, as early as 1705. In 1770 occurred the first known use in a commercial publication of a letter cast in the Western Hemisphere. The book was the Descripcion del Barreno Inglès, by Joseph Antonio de Alzates y Ramirez. Mexico, Joseph de Jauregui, 1770. Its title-page asserts that the letters employed in the book had been manufactured in Mexico City at the expense of the publisher by Francisco Xavier de Ocampo. A copy of this rare volume, Medina 5322, is in the John Carter Brown Library.

same year, using a different and much better type of his own making, he presented to the Connecticut Assembly a printed petition in which he asked that body for financial assistance in his proposed establishment of a letter foundry. In reply to this memorial he received a loan from the colony for the purposes of his venture, and soon afterwards he removed to New Haven and prepared to manufacture type for the printers of a continent.[2] The story of his failure at this time, and of his success on a much smaller scale twelve years later, is a part of the present study only in the sense which has been indicated in the introductory sentences.

Buell was not without a rival in his ambitious plans. David Mitchelson of Boston, possibly acting under the direction of John Mein, a printer of that city, is reported by a contemporary newspaper writer to have attained as great a degree of success as the Connecticut silversmith in the difficult art of letter casting. In the *Massachusetts Gazette and Boston Weekly News-Letter* for September 7, 1769, there appeared among the local news items a report on recent developments in American manufacturing activities in which are certain sentences of interest in the story of colonial type founding. "We are assured by a Gentleman from the Westward," said the writer, "that Mr. Able Buell, of Killingworth in Connecticut, Jeweller and Lapidary, has lately, his own Genius, made himself Master of the Art of Founding Types for Printing. Printing Types are also made by Mr. Mitchelson of this Town [Boston] equal to any imported from Great-Britain; and might, by proper Encouragement soon be able to furnish all the Printers in America at the same price they are sold in England." The absence of a known specimen of Mitchelson's letters or of any specific infor-

2. The story of Abel Buell's type-founding venture exists in manuscript in the Connecticut State Archives, from which source certain documents have been published in the Colonial Records of Connecticut. Further information is found in Extracts from the Itineraries and other Miscellanies of Ezra Stiles, 1755–1794. Ed. by F. B. Dexter, New Haven. 1916.

mation as to his operations is enough, however, to require a verdict of "not proved" on any claim to priority in American type casting that has yet been made on his behalf.

Because of the unfruitful nature of the enterprises which have been spoken of, the year 1770 found the American printer still dependent upon European importation for his printing type, and at the moment there existed little prospect of relief from a situation which in the years of the Revolution was to become a hardship rather than the simple inconvenience of the earlier period. The policy of non-importation, however, was stirring the colonies to the establishment of local manufactures, and under the whip of necessity, type founding, among other essential industries, was to take its rise in the United States. The carrying to success of this manufacture in Pennsylvania in the year 1775 was undoubtedly assured by the political and economic situation of the country, but its beginning, which must first be described, had its cause in a set of circumstances of a more general character.

"The secular history of the Holy Scriptures," wrote Henry Stevens, "is the sacred history of printing." In these words the Vermonter gave sententious expression to the truth that the printing of the Bible has been in all ages an appreciable factor in the development of typography. The successful beginnings of type founding in English America, it is believed, may be traced to the desire of Christopher Sower, Jr., of Germantown, Pennsylvania, to issue a third edition of that German Bible which first had made its appearance at the pains and expense of his father in the year 1743. It is said that the younger Sower's dissatisfaction with the conditions of type importation from Germany led him to conceive the idea of importing thence matrices and moulds instead of finished type, and with these placed in the cunning hands of Justus Fox, his journeyman, of casting his own letters for use in the proposed edition of 'Die Heilige Schrift.' An enterprising man, a religious zealot and the proprietor of one of the most extensive printing offices in America, he was able, partly at least, to carry out his intention.[3]

The exact date of the first use by Sower of locally cast German letters evades determination. Sometime in the year 1770, he began the publication of the "second part" of a periodical known as *Ein Geistliches Magazien*. The title-page of No. 1, Part II, of this early religious magazine tells us that it was printed by Christopher Sower at Germantown in the year 1770, and the undated colophon of No. xii of the series contains a piece of information of singular interest in the words, "Gedruckt mit der ersten Schrift die jemals in America gegossen worden." With this statement of the publisher before us, the problem of the date of No. xii becomes one for which a solution should be sought, even though the foreign type-face employed in its printing and the fact that its letters were cast from imported matrices and moulds render it a document of secondary importance in an inquiry devoted to the origins of native type founding. The evidence supplied by certain dated numbers of the periodical enables us to fix with moderate assurance the time of publication of the important number in question. Hildeburn says that Part I of *Ein Geistliches Magazien*, begun in 1764, came to an end with its fiftieth number sometime in the year 1770, a rate of issue which means that the separate parts must have appeared at intervals of six weeks throughout the period. That this frequency of issue prevailed also in the publication of Part II is attested by the circumstance that the colophon of No. x of the second series bears as its date the year 1771. In the normal course of things, there-

3. The account of Sower by Isaiah Thomas in his first edition of the History of Printing in America includes a reference to his type-founding operations, while in the second edition a very full story of his activities in this field is given on the basis of the material communicated to the author from 1812 to 1814 by William McCulloch, a Philadelphia printer who was acquainted with Sower's sons. One of Sower's descendants, W. K. Sowers, made up the type of this volume of essays into pages.

fore, No. xii, with its American-cast letters, would have been published late in 1771 or early in the following year.[4]

It is sometimes said that, from this beginning, Sower went on with letter founding until he had cast type in such quantity as to enable him to maintain standing an entire edition of the Bible, as well as to supply with German type other printers who made use of that character in their publications. Dr. Julius Friedrich Sachse, the historian of the Pennsylvania Germans, thought that this tradition had no basis in fact. In his refusal to accept it he went to the other extreme and asserted positively that at no time in his career had Sower engaged either directly or indirectly in letter founding.[5] The evidence has never been studied by any one skilled in the discrimination of typographical printing surfaces, but for the sake of the record such an investigation should be undertaken. It is enough for our present purpose to know that in a publication owned and printed by Sower in the year 1771 or 1772 eight pages of German text were printed in a locally cast letter; that a persistent tradition credits him with having continued for several years his activities in letter casting; and that when his estate was sold in 1778 there were found among his effects letter moulds, crucibles, and a large quantity of antimony.[6] The actual amount of fraktur which he cast is a matter of secondary importance in this investigation; for when in the year 1776 there appeared the Bible for which the new type is said to have been made, Roman letter of local design and man-

4. Hildeburn 1998, Seidensticker, p. 66, Evans 9676. Of the second part there are known to exist only a few scattered numbers in the Typographic Library and Museum of the American Type Founders Co., Jersey City, including the only known copy of No. xii, a collection formerly in the library of Dr. Julius Friedrich Sachse. A small number of issues of Part ii has recently been secured by the American Antiquarian Society, including No. x, with its dated colophon.

5. The German Sectarians of Pennsylvania, 2 vols., Philadelphia. 1899-1900. 2:45. It should be said that Dr. Sachse leaves his statement without the support of evidence or of argument.

6. Pennsylvania Archives, 6th Series, 12:887-919.

ufacture already had become an article of commerce in Philadelphia.

The initiatory efforts of Sower, however, have a particular significance in the story of American type founding; for the tradition is that while engaged in the casting process of type making in the Germantown foundry, Justus Fox and Jacob Bay learned the more difficult mysteries of an art in which later they attained proficiency. Because of the link of continuous effort thus formed between Sower's initiation of the business in 1770 and the later cutting and casting of Roman letter by these artisans, there must be conceded to him the distinction of having begun in English America the industry of type manufacturing, regardless of whether or not his casting of German letter from imported matrices was as extensive as has been supposed.

Our knowledge of Fox and of Bay is derived largely from the 'Additions to Thomas's History of Printing,' a body of tradition of uneven reliability transmitted to Isaiah Thomas by William McCulloch, a Philadelphia printer active in the early years of the century.[7] It is not a difficult matter occasionally to find McCulloch tripping over the line which divides hearsay from fact, but it is much to the purposes of this study to find that he possessed and made use of unusual opportunities to obtain correct information as to the craftsmen who are the subject of our interest. The facts which he records of Justus Fox [8] he obtained from Emmanuel, the son and partner in type founding of that artisan. He was indebted to various relatives

7. Parts of the six communications that McCulloch wrote in the years 1812 to 1814 were incorporated by Thomas in the manuscript from which the second edition of the History of Printing in America was printed in 1874. The whole series of letters was published in the Proceedings of the American Antiquarian Society for April, 1921, pp. 89–247, under the title, William McCulloch's Additions to Thomas's History of Printing.

8. Dr. Charles L. Nichols has brought together from McCulloch and from other sources the available information concerning Fox in Justus Fox, a German Printer of the Eighteenth Century, reprinted from the Proceedings of the American Antiquarian Society for April, 1915.

of Bay, among them a sister, "a plump lady of 68," for the account of him which is found in the pages of the 'Additions.' It is possible to compare various items in McCulloch's sketches of these men with records unknown to him, but available to us, with results so little at variance that one is inclined to accord a high degree of credence to all that he wrote concerning their activities.

According to McCulloch, at the time of Sower's importation of German equipment, he had among his journeymen an ingenious general mechanic, Justus Fox, whom he charged with the responsibility for casting the letters to be used in the great Bible. In April, 1772, he employed a newly arrived Swiss silk weaver, Jacob Bay,[9] to assist Fox. Two years later Bay left Sower's service and set up a foundry on his own account in a near-by house in Germantown. Fox remained in Sower's establishment, presumably engaged in casting the large font of type required to keep standing an edition of the Bible. In addition to this routine work he is said to have cut and cast an unspecified amount of Roman letter before 1774, the year of Bay's separation from the Sower establishment. Working in his separate foundry, it is recorded that Bay "cast a number of fonts, cutting all the punches, and making all the apparatus pertaining thereto, himself, for Roman Bourgeois, Long Primer, etc."

That this reported activity in type casting in Germantown about the year 1774 was not a play of the imagination on the part of its historian is made certain by the definite statement that occurs in one of the non-importation resolutions of the Pennsylvania Convention. On January 23, 1775, the Conven-

9. McCulloch, p. 181, gives the middle of December, 1771, as the date of Bay's arrival in Philadelphia. In Rupp's Collection of Thirty Thousand Names of German, Swiss, Dutch, French, and other Immigrants in Pennsylvania from 1727 to 1776, p. 398, Jacob Bäy is among the arrivals on the Brig *Betsey* on December 1, 1771. The name is spelled Bey by McCulloch, Bäy by Rupp, and Bay in various lists and documents in the Pennsylvania Archives. The last-named spelling is used in the present study on this authority.

tion "Resolved unanimously, That as printing types are now made to a considerable degree of perfection by an ingenious artist in Germantown; it is recommended to the printers to use such types in preference to any which may be hereafter imported." [10] Referring somewhat vaguely to this resolution, both as to content and as to origin, McCulloch tells us that even at the time of its passage Fox and Bay each claimed the honor implied in its terms, and to this day the identity of the "ingenious artist" remains uncertain.

It is not clear by what evidence it was known to the Convention that "a considerable degree of perfection" had been attained in the making of type in Germantown. The only known specimen of letters cast there before the meeting of the Convention in January, 1775, is the fraktur employed in Sower's periodical, *Ein Geistliches Magazien,* and it is not likely that this or any other specimen of German type would have led the Convention to a recommendation as sweeping as that which has been quoted from its journal. It could only have been a Roman letter that the delegates had in mind for a usage so general as was indicated in their resolution, and we must remain in doubt as to what specimen or specimens they had seen of locally cast type in this character. It is certain, however, that at the time of their action a font of Roman letter had been completed, or at any rate, that it was then in the process of casting. It is quite possible that a trial specimen of this font had been submitted to the Convention for its examination and approval.

It is a satisfaction to be able to introduce the new font through the medium of a contemporary reference to its use. We are indebted to the correspondence and to the diary of the Rev. Ezra Stiles of Newport, later President of Yale College, for some important information on early American type founding.

10. Journal of the House of Representatives of the Commonwealth of Pennsylvania . . . (1776–1781). Volume the First. Philadelphia, 1782, p. 33.

Excited by Buell's efforts to make type in the year 1769, his interest in the manufacture seems to have remained in being, for on May 9, 1775, he appended the following comment to an entry in his Diary: "Extracted from the Pennsylvᵃ Mercury, whose first Nᵒ was pub. the 7th of April last: printed with types of American Manufacture. The first Work with Amer. Types: tho' Types were made at N. Haven years ago." [11] The fact that Ezra Stiles was one of the earliest patrons of Abel Buell's venture in letter casting, supported as this fact is by his interest in American manufactures generally, lends a certain amount of weight to any observation that he might make on the subject of American type founding, although it is probable that he was ignorant of Sower's partial achievement of the art, just as Sower some years earlier in his claim to priority had seemed to be unaware of Buell's technically successful effort. If we may interpret Dr. Stiles's words as meaning that Storey & Humphreys's *Pennsylvania Mercury* [12] of April 7, 1775, Vol. 1, No. 1, was the first published work printed in Roman letter which had been cut and cast in English America, we may unhesitatingly repeat his description of it as "The first Work with Amer. Types."

The Philadelphia newspaper which has been referred to is one of the rarest of American journals of the period. The only complete file, covering its brief existence from April 7 to December 27, 1775, is that which is found in the Library of Congress. From the first page of its first issue the publisher's announcement is reproduced on page 128.

A glance at the pages of the newspaper in which the new Roman letter was first used makes us feel that in his commendable willingness to admit imperfection the publisher paid small tribute to the skill of his "ingenious artist." The letters of

11. Stiles, Ezra: Literary Diary. Ed. by F. B. Dexter. 3 vols. New York, 1901, 1:549.

12. Story & Humphreys's Pennsylvania Mercury, and Universal Advertiser. Evans 14477. No copy seen by Hildeburn.

"rustic manufacture" were far from perfect, it is true, and in later issues of the newspaper it is observable that they had not worn especially well, but none the less they composed agreeably and they were sufficiently well executed to entitle them to something more than the half apology with which they were offered to the public. Their interest, however, as the first American-made Roman type to be used in a publication intended for circulation transcends considerations of worth and of appearance. One would like to know whether it was from this font or from another that the book was printed which was advertised in the *Mercury* for June 23, 1775, as "Just Published and Printed with Types, Paper and Ink, Manufactured in this Province." Its title was 'The Impenetrable Secret,' and no copy of it has been recorded. The possibility of finding some day the "hitherto unknown" and "probably unique" copy of the first book printed in the United States with type of native manufacture is one of the dreams which brighten the coming years.

Isaiah Thomas says that the *Pennsylvania Mercury* was established with the backing of Joseph Galloway as a substitute for the *Pennsylvania Chronicle*, that disastrous earlier venture in journalism in which the Quaker politician had engaged with William Goddard. If this was the case, certain features of the new publication must have been displeasing to the silent partner, for Galloway the Tory could hardly have rejoiced with the publishers in their virtuous encouragement of native type founding, with all its patriotic implications. Furthermore, from an advertisement of John Willis and Henry Vogt in the first issue of the paper one learns that the publishers were making use of other articles of printing equipment made by these general craftsmen, who here announced their ability to make presses and any and all of the mechanical appurtenances required in a printing shop. This well-advertised Americanism of the publishers, however, seems not to have availed them in the attainment of success, and after their establishment had been destroyed by fire in the closing days of the year the business was never resumed.

It is not certainly known who was the maker of the significant Mercury types. Benjamin Franklin Bache brought his type-founding equipment from France to Philadelphia sometime in the year 1775, but of course the letters used in the *Mercury* were in process of manufacture many months before their appearance in the issue of April 7th of that year. Assuming that Sower's foundry was in full operation at this time, we must assume also, in the absence of knowledge to the contrary, that its principal activity was in the manufacture of German letters for the great Bible, and that Sower would not have been likely to engage in the making of Roman type on a large scale until this work had been completed. Because of our ignorance of other possibilities there remain to be considered only the two craftsmen, Fox and Bay, as the probable makers of this first successful American letter. According to McCulloch, Fox had cut and cast Roman letter at some period before the year 1774 while still working for Sower. This statement contains all that is known of his efforts at making Roman type during the years that he remained with Sower, but there is the chance to be taken into account that the Mercury font was the result of his experimentation during this period in an art which later he pursued with no small degree of local success. On the same authority it is said, it will be remembered, that Jacob Bay had left Sower in 1774, and in a near-by house in Germantown had set up a type foundry on his own account. In this separate establishment, it is likely that he was able to devote to the business such time and energy as would be required in making a font of sufficient size to accommodate the needs of such a newspaper as the *Pennsylvania Mercury*. The fact of his separate foundry having been established sometime in 1774, the reference in the Convention resolution of January, 1775, to the "ingenious artist" at Germantown and the appearance in April, 1775, of the new font of type acclaimed by the publishers as "an attempt to introduce so valuable an art into these colonies" are considerations which, taken in their order, seem to give ground for an assumption that it was Jacob Bay who cut and cast the letters for "The first Work with Amer. Types." Until proof is forthcoming, however, this must remain an assumption and nothing more.

It is certain that both Fox and Bay maintained their interest in letter casting for many years. At the sale of Sower's confiscated property in the year 1778 both of these artisans were present as purchasers of type-making tools and material.[13] Bay especially seems to have taken advantage of the opportunity to secure equipment at this dispersal of his old master's goods. Among other purchases which he made at the sale of what was probably at the time the largest typographical establishment in the country were "a lot of letter moles" at £3, "a Box with 9 Crusibles" at £5 15s., a quantity of worn type at 8d. a pound and antimony worth £8 18s. 3d. He was living at the time in a house rented from Sower,[14] and at the sale of the printer's real property in September, 1779, he purchased another house belonging to the estate for £4200, a sum which he paid in two installments before October 28, 1779.[15] In recording from tradition the fact that Bay secured at this time one of the Sower houses, McCulloch asserts that he purchased it from John Dunlap, the printer, whom he paid in type of his own making. It is possible that he borrowed the purchase price from Dunlap on this or a similar basis of repayment, a transaction that would explain McCulloch's version of the story. It is said that he conducted his foundry until the year 1789, and

13. Pennsylvania Archives, 6th Series, 12:887–919.

14. McCulloch's statement is borne out by the inventory of Sower's real estate in Pennsylvania Archives, 6th Series, 12:872–873.

15. Pennsylvania Archives, 6th Series, 12:918–919.

that between this year and 1792 he sold the business to Francis Bailey. Fox continued the making of type until his death in the year 1805, when his son and partner Emmanuel Fox sold the equipment to Samuel Sower of Baltimore, the son of Christopher Sower, the Second, of Germantown, whose enterprise was the determining cause of its existence.

The type-founding operations of Fox and of Bay have greater importance in the history of the art in America than is usually conceded them. When they are referred to at all by general writers, their activities are mentioned briefly or in such a manner as to give one the impression that their efforts were sporadic or tentative. It is with the work of the Scotch founder Baine, using imported equipment, that the story of American type founding is usually begun, but with the Mercury font before us, cut and cast thirteen years before Baine's first operations, and with assurances by McCulloch that Fox cut and cast the letters used in the McKean edition of the 'Acts of the Pennsylvania Assembly,' printed by Francis Bailey in 1782,[16] and with references by McCulloch to other fonts produced by Bay, it seems certain that there exists material which will require a revision of the story of American type-founding origins. Beginning with the incontestable fact of the successful Mercury font of 1775 and accepting McCulloch's relation of later events as a working hypothesis, there is seen to exist a field for research which should prove productive of discoveries, inasmuch as the fact and the tradition indicate a continuous activity on the part of one or the other of these early Pennsylvania founders, Fox and Bay, from 1775 to 1805. In the course of these years other founders, better known to us, began their work, and between the years 1796 and 1801, more than one hundred American printers, from Massachusetts to Georgia,

16. McCulloch gives the date indefinitely as about the year 1784. His father, John McCulloch, from whom he received much information embodied in the Additions, was at one time foreman in Bailey's shop.

purchased type from the foundry of Binney & Ronaldson of Philadelphia.[17]

The identification of the various fonts of locally made type used in Pennsylvania in the quarter century following "The first Work with Amer. Types" would form an interesting chapter in the story of early American type founding.

17. One Hundred Years. MacKellar, Smiths and Jordan Foundry, Philadelphia, Pennsylvania (1896), p. 12, where is given a list of printers found in Binney & Ronaldson's ledgers from 1796 to 1801. The original books are now in the Typographic Library and Museum, Jersey City, N. J.

A MARYLAND TRACT OF 1646

By LATHROP COLGATE HARPER

Of New York

ONE of the earliest books relating to Maryland, and one that seems to have escaped the notice of bibliographers, is a small quarto tract of sixteen pages, with the following title, unpromising enough as far as American interest is concerned:

A | Moderate | and | Safe Expedient | To remove *Jealousies* and *Feares*, of any | danger, or prejudice to this State, by the | Roman Catholicks | *of this Kingdome*, | And to mitigate the censure of too | much severity towards them. | With a great advantage of Honour | and Profit to this State and Nation. | [6 small ornaments.] Printed in the Year of our Lord, | 1646. Collation: A–B⁴. Title, 1 leaf, verso blank; pp. 3–16.

Even a casual glance through the pages of this publication, however, shows that it contains matter of exceptional importance on the early history of Maryland. It seems to be the only work relating to Maryland, printed in English, between the two 'Relations' of 1634 and 1635, and the 'Lord Baltemore's Case' issued in 1653.

In brief, it is a tract setting forth a plea for enacting suitable laws that will allow the Roman Catholics to sell their estates in England, remove to Maryland and settle there. It is divided into two parts. The first, with the heading "A Moderate and Safe Expedient," occupies the six pages following the title. The second, with the heading "Objections Answered touching Mariland," fills its remaining eight pages.

The author opens with a plea for granting the Catholics liberty of conscience, or as much toleration as is given them in Holland, but in case Parliament shall not see fit to do this, to give them free leave to transplant themselves to Maryland. He strengthens this suggestion with the argument that the Catholics are considered dangerous persons to the State, according to the policy and religion of the present Government;

that they should either be given the rights and liberties of free-born subjects, or allowed to emigrate to another country; that the planting of the Roman Catholics in Maryland will add much honor and profit to the Nation; that as they cannot subsist without yearly supplies, it will mean much to the trade of England.

The second part consists of a discussion of the plan in the form of five "Objections," with an "Answer" to each, as follows:

First. That the Laws against the Roman Catholics were made to free England from Popery, and that to allow them to depart to Maryland would take away all hope of their conforming to the Church of England. *Answer.* That these Laws were passed more for reasons of state than for conformity of religion. That there are numerous other dissenting sects against which there are no such laws, which differ as much as the Roman Catholics from the doctrines of the established church.

Second. That it would seem to be a kind of toleration of Popery. *Answer.* Banishment to Maryland, even if voluntary, would be in a way a persecution. That divers malefactors have chosen rather to be hanged than to go to Virginia.

Third and Fourth. That the King's revenue would be impaired and that the wealth of the Kingdom would be reduced. *Answer.* That the number of Catholics is not so great that it would take much wealth out of England, and that the future increase of trade would be a great advantage.

Fifth. That a large Catholic settlement in Maryland might be dangerous to New England and Virginia. That they might unite with Spain to suppress the Protestants in those colonies. *Answer.* This is refuted at length. The writer gives interesting particulars of the other American colonies, closing with the argument, that all ships going to Maryland must enter by way of the mouth of Chesapeake Bay, which is a part of Virginia.

The reasons for writing this tract open up an interesting field for conjecture. The author shows an intimate acquaintance with American affairs, not only in Maryland, but also in Virginia and New England. The tract bears evidence of that duality of motive which animated the early Lords Baltimore in their colonization venture; that is, the desire to provide a refuge for their co-religionists and to establish for themselves a durable and prosperous domain. The year 1646 was a critical time in the affairs of Maryland. The so-called "pirate" Richard Ingle, claiming to act for the Parliament, had overturned the Proprietary government and had driven Governor Leonard Calvert into exile. In England, on the other hand, there seemed a chance that the Roman Catholics and the Independents would come together in an agreement which would secure toleration for the recusant body. If in addition to toleration of the Papists, or in lieu of it, the Parliament should pass an ordinance permitting them to sell their property and emigrate to Maryland, thus giving official recognition to the colony as a place of refuge, the Ingle rebellion would lose its strength and its significance. Furthermore the colony by this action would gain immediately in numbers and in wealth. The time seemed well chosen for the publication of such a pamphlet as has been described.

We find the second part of the tract in question, the "Objections Answered" quoted in full both by Bradley T. Johnson in his 'Foundations of Maryland' and by the Reverend Thomas J. Hughes, S. J., in his 'History of the Society of Jesus in North America,' cited in each case from the Stonyhurst College MSS. Johnson supposes it to have been in manuscript, but Father Hughes states that it is a printed pamphlet, pages 9 to 16. Father Hughes, however, never having seen the complete work, was unaware that it had been published as late as the year 1646. From the sense of it he assumed, as Johnson had done, that it was written about the year 1633 as a defense of the Maryland charter, not yet passed by the Privy Council.

A close reading of the "Objections Answered" convinces one of two things with regard to its matter: first, that it was of Jesuit authorship, and second, that its composition was earlier in date than that of the "Moderate and Safe Expedient" with which it was published in 1646. The latter tract was a plea to the victorious Parliament for toleration of the Roman Catholics in England, or, lacking this, for the enactment of an ordinance which would permit them to emigrate to Maryland, and more particularly to sell rather than to forfeit their property in England before removing thence. The "Objections Answered," it is true, constitute an extension and an enforcement of its argument, but while the "Moderate and Safe Expedient" assumes that the colony of Maryland is a place and government in being, the "Objections Answered" speak of it, particularly in the last paragraph, as a colony not yet established. The first is a plea addressed to the Parliament; the second is an argument addressed, as its phraseology shows, to the old Royal government. The form of the second, with its anticipated questions given in full with answers conditional upon them, seems to mean that it had been intended originally for the private instruction of Lord Baltimore in defending his charter in its passage of the Great Seal. In that form it would hardly have been presented to the Privy Council as a document in the case.

Both Bradley Johnson and Father Hughes attribute the "Objections Answered" to a Jesuit source, and both, in ignorance of its date of publication, assume that it was written in 1633 in defense of Lord Baltimore's plan to establish a Roman Catholic colony. Even with the date of publication before us, the sense of the document persuades us that they were not far out in their guess, certainly in so far as it is a question of its original intention. One concludes that in this troubled year of

1646, when the Catholics stood in need as always of alleviation of their disabilities, and Maryland stood in need of colonists of that belief, the pamphlet was published by Lord Baltimore or in his interest, with this double purpose to be served. Remembering the shrewd presentation of the case for emigration presented in the "Objections Answered," it was probably decided to make it the basis of the plea to Parliament. Accordingly the old manuscript, for it is as such that we must think of it, was brought out and put into type as part of the pamphlet issued in this crisis. It is understood that these are assumptions made in an effort to account for the appearance in print at this time of a document, clearly of a private nature, which must have been composed to meet an emergency twelve years before.

The authorship of the "Objections Answered" is not known. It has every mark of the Jesuit method and of the Jesuit logic. Father Hughes accepted it as a Jesuit document, and its printed pages, 9–16, detached from the first part of the pamphlet, were found among the Stonyhurst papers. It has been attributed to the pen of Father White, but it is not the sort of writing that we associate with what is known of this man of action, this devout and zealous missionary. Its cool clear logic speaks rather of some member of the order accustomed to political thought and writing, and it is likely that it was the work of Father Richard Blount, the Provincial of the English Society, a priest who is known to have acted as adviser to Lord Baltimore in the furthering of his venture in its early stages.

The tract seems to be very rare. It is not in the Thomason collection of Civil War tracts in the British Museum, or in the Gay collection at Harvard College. There is no copy in the Lenox or Huntington Libraries, and it is not mentioned by Rich, Sabin, Winsor or Mathews. Aside from the copy here described, and the imperfect one at Stonyhurst College, the only other that I have been able to locate is in the John Carter

Brown Library at Providence, a copy purchased in London in 1889.

The subject of the tract, its publisher's anonymity and the absence of a copy from the Thomason collection are facts which indicate a surreptitious printing. It may have been issued from some obscure country press, but it is more than likely that it was the product of an unprivileged London establishment. There were plenty of these in existence, so many in fact that in 1643 the Parliament had found it necessary to re-impose the Restriction Act of the Star Chamber in all save its most severe features, and within a few years the most rigorous of the old regulations were embodied in a new act. Such eminent publishers as George Thomason occasionally had dealings with the brotherhood of the secret press. On the other hand, the tract may have come from the shop of a licensed printer. Even the boldest of these would not have been anxious to put his name to a publication so pregnant with unpleasant potentialities. In typographical appearance it is as good as the average of the metropolitan product of the day.

I hope that the printing of this paper will bring out some information as to the purposes, authorship, and publication of this pamphlet of a more definite nature than these brief speculative deductions from the book itself.

THE SURREPTITIOUS PRINTING OF ONE OF COTTON MATHER'S MANUSCRIPTS

By THOMAS J. HOLMES

Librarian of William G. Mather's Library, Cleveland, Ohio

A N annotated bibliography of surreptitious editions might
be more than a curiosity, if it could trace the uncertain
steps of the errant manuscript from the parental domicile by
devious path of transcription to the portal of unauthorized
publicity; especially if it recorded the author's emotion when
the wanderer, unwashed of his errors, unkempt, his native imperfections not hidden but magnified in a suit of orderly print
naïvely walks up the front steps and in sight of an astonished
world extends, unabashed, his filial greetings.

John Cotton's 'Way of the Churches of Christ in New England,' because some brethren disagreed with it, had long been
suppressed, while still in manuscript, and a later work along
similar lines had been more satisfactorily set forth in his since
famous 'Keyes of the Kingdom of Heaven,' which he published in London in 1644.

A copy of his earlier manuscript of 'The Way' had been
taken by a "brother going for England" and had been read
and discussed there; but some years had elapsed since John
Cotton had heard anything of it; and since the work was now
superseded he hoped that it was suppressed. The copy that
had thus gone for England, however, was by no means suppressed. "Abrupt in the entrance and imperfect otherwise"
though it turned out to be; when least needed, this doubly defective offspring brazenly appeared in print in London the year
after the publication of the 'Keyes.'

"Which when I saw" says its embarrassed author, "it
troubled me not a little as knowing that the discrepant Expressions in the one, and in the other, might trouble Friends, and

give Advantage to Adversaries. I suffered both to stand . . . seeing I could not help it, the *Book of the way* being published without my Consent, and both the *Way* and the *Keys* past my revoking."

Many a good story might such a bibliography bring to light; and it might show how some surreptitious editions were such only in seeming; that many manuscripts considered to have been lost or stolen, then published as foundlings, really received parental secret aid and guidance to carry them to their journey's end in the print shop.

There have been enough of such, especially in the sixteenth and seventeenth centuries, to justify Dr. Samuel Johnson's pungent averment that

there is surely some reason to doubt the truth of the complaints so frequently made of surreptitious editions . . . . It is easy to convey an imperfect book, by a distant hand to the press, and plead the circumstance of a false copy as an excuse for publishing the true, or to correct what is found faulty or offensive, and charge the errors on the transcriber's depravations. This is a stratagem, by which an author panting for fame and yet afraid of seeming to challenge it, may at once gratify his vanity, and preserve the appearance of modesty.

However frequently this may have been true it is well known that it did not happen to apply to the work that called it forth, the 'Religio Medici' — the most celebrated instance of an aberrant manuscript intended only for private circulation, having stolen into print.

But even Dr. Johnson, had he been interested, would have found no difficulty in absolving another author, Cotton Mather, from responsibility in the design to publish the confidently and hopefully written and willingly though privately circulated manuscript of his observations on the "witchcraft" case of Margaret Rule; at least in the form and frame in which it finally appeared. And our bibliography of surreptitious editions might record a note, inadequate though it would be, of the agonies with which this author came later to contemplate the public forthcoming of his work.

The manuscript was copied by Robert Calef or by some one under his name and then pilloried in Calef's bitter scathing criticism of Mather and others. This miscellaneous compilation of excerpts, letters, and criticisms, as if in ironical derision of Mather's 'Wonders of the Invisible World,' he entitled 'More Wonders of the Invisible World,' taking the title from the second clause of the heading of Mather's manuscript.

The incident that brought about the writing of this manuscript was in itself of trifling moment, but it has given more advantage to Mather's adversaries and for that reason more trouble to his friends than any other event of his career. On September 10, 1693, Margaret Rule fell into convulsions and began to see spectres, which in those days of primitive diagnosis were easily defined as the work of witchcraft, though the evil spirits of rum seem to have played some part in the witchery. Samuel P. Fowler in 1861 thought it a case of delirium tremens.

The young woman appears to have been an attendant at Mather's church. He pleaded "that as she belonged to his flock and charge, he had so far a right unto her as that he was to do the part of a minister of our Lord for the bringing of her home unto God." (Mather's MS 'Another Brand . . .,' Sect. x.) At any rate on the evening of September 13, after sundown, he and his father Increase with their party first visited Margaret Rule. Others drawn by curiosity also came. "In the whole there were about thirty or forty persons" present. Among them was Robert Calef, a cloth merchant of Boston, who afterward wrote down his impressions of the meeting. These notes reflected discredit on Increase and especially on Cotton Mather. Again on the 19th, Calef visited the afflicted girl. Cotton Mather, who had been there earlier on the same day, had already left. Calef reports some of the gossip he heard there, again working in insinuations discreditable to Mather.

This paper of reports Calef showed around. News of it came to Cotton Mather, who threatened Calef with arrest for slander. Calef thereupon wrote Mather a note dated September 29, in which he proposed a meeting "at Mr. Wilkins's or at Ben Harris's"; where for the professed purpose of verifying or correcting his reports, he offered to read his paper to Mather in the presence of one witness on either side.

In reply to this, Mather seems to have written a letter to which Calef briefly refers as, "that long letter only once read to me." This letter so far as I know has not yet been found. However, Mather sent word agreeing to meet Calef at Mr. Wilkins's, but later changed his mind and with his father began the threatened suit in court charging Calef with "scandalous libels." Calef was bound over for trial at the sessions. Before the trial Mather again changed his mind, dropped the suit, and invited Calef to consult books in his library, a privilege that Calef scornfully spurned.

Meantime Margaret Rule was, from September 10, "in those torments," "too hellish to be sufficiently described," "confining her to her bed for just six weeks together," that is, until about October 22, says the MS, Sect. IV. It was after this date, then, that Mather wrote his manuscript of observations of the case and entitled it, 'Another Brand Pluckt out of the Burning, Or more Wonders of the Invisible World.' It probably was not written until after the receipt of Calef's second letter, that of November 24; for that writer does not mention it therein, though he does make reply to it in his next letter, of January 11.

The manuscript, it is clear, was Mather's method of replying to his adversary's letters and report of the meetings at Margaret Rule's house. The text of the work itself corroborates this view. Sections XI and XII, and some other parts of the document are certainly aimed indirectly at Calef, though without name; and Calef in his letter of January 11 accepted the references, even repeating Mather's epithets with which he characterized Calef's group as "Saducees," and as "our learned witlings of the coffee-house." The work has the appearance and tone of an attempt by its author to defend himself against insistent goads and stings of criticism. He says:

> ... must I be driven to the necessity of an apology? Truly the hard representations wherewith some ill men have reviled my conduct, and the countenance which other men have given to these representations, oblige me to give mankind some account of my behaviour. (Sect. XII.)

This description of the sufferings and hallucinations of Margaret Rule, observed by or told to Cotton Mather and written down by him in his hyperbolical style, supported, as it was later in Mather's letter of January 15 to Calef, with whatever proofs that Mather's six witnesses could adduce to Margaret Rule's spiritualistic levitation, could well satisfy Mather and his friends whose beliefs about witchcraft were similar to his own. But it cannot be denied that it was a poor defense for him to make against such an antagonist as the obtuse, unimaginative, sceptical, cynical Calef.

That it was a defense, its form indicates, and the chronology of Calef's documents, I think, proves. The manuscript therefore we may conclude was as much a result of Calef's critical activities as of Mather's wish to vindicate his views. It was merely one, probably the fifth, written in the series of Calef-Mather papers. Mather handed it out to his friends, as Calef had exhibited his own insinuating notes.

A desire for some form of exposure of the witchcraft fallacies as he saw them probably burned in Calef's brain anterior to the Margaret Rule case. The cases of 1692 still fresh in every one's memory kindled a resolution in Calef's consciousness. It is likely his mind flamed with purpose when he attended the meeting at Margaret Rule's house; and he doubtless planned to use his observations there to further the project already in hand, though it was as yet probably without definite form. Cotton Mather's impulsive nature, unguarded actions, confident manner and too ample speech, readily tripped him into Calef's trap. The Margaret Rule incident was Robert Calef's good opportunity; and he thoroughly utilized it.

Calef's report does not read, at least to my view, like an unbiased, spontaneous impression of the meeting. The repeated suggestion of indecency seems forced, proceeding as much from the recorder's own made-up mind as from Mather's actions before the eyes of thirty to forty witnesses. Mather calls the report "an indecent Traversty." It has a malicious twist that makes truth a lie, and betrays an intense hatred not specifically for Mather's witchcraft ideas but for Mather himself and for all that he represented. Increase Mather prays too long to suit the critic. Nothing the Mathers could have done would have pleased Calef.

Down to the writing of his second letter to Mather, November 24, Calef had nothing tangible to show for his labor except his own two letters and his notes of the Margaret Rule meeting. But sometime between November 24 and January 11 there came into his hands, possibly by Thomas Brattle, a copy of Mather's manuscript. This probably determined the shape Calef's efforts would take.

Calef's book originated in a great emotion, but no one will hold it to be great literature; and few will regard it, except Parts III and v, scarcely as history. It is as a whole a literary gallows. The author apparently aimed to show that the folly, passion, superstition, malice, injustice, futility and blindness of the witch trials and executions of 1692 were the indirect result of the erroneous doctrines taught by the ministers. These doctrinal errors it was his purpose to expose, and to show

whether the witches . . . have been the cause of our miseries. Or whether a Zeal governed by blindness and passion, and led by president [precedent], has not herein precipitated us into far greater wickedness (if not Witchcrafts) than any have been yet proved against those that suffered. To be able to distinguish aright in this matter, to which of these two to refer our Miseries is the [purpose of the] present Work. (Calef's 'Epistle to the Reader.')

In the execution of this fair-seeming design, impervious to the thought of any error in his own position, he burned with an unquenchable zeal intense as that which a little earlier had fired the devil hunters and witch baiters themselves. If the advantage of his position enabled him in turn on his own part to do a little harmless baiting he was not averse to doing it. Gathering strength and boldness as he went along doubtless he enjoyed the prospect of crucifying in his book those he held responsible for the more material damages of 1692.

So contagious is human feeling and so inflaming are words that the animus which pointed Calef's "quill under a special energy" to write his letters and compile this work, has ever since then animated some of the readers who have shared his views as to the origins of the witchcraft of 1692, to feel as he felt, to burn inwardly and to hate, as he sometimes did, and vicariously to enjoy the grillings he gave the ministers, while his manner has moved to impatience those readers who see his deficiencies even though they might sympathize with his larger aims, and admire him in some of his attitudes. If his purpose were as he said, "to prevent, as far as in my power, any more such bloody victims or sacrifices," no witches have been hung in New England since. But any one can close the stable door.

His labor in the direction of prevention, as is common with noble intentions, completely failed by being too late — eight years too late. He did not extinguish the smallest flame, not to say any conflagration of the witchcraft frenzy, that is traceable now. Circumstances so fell that the fire was all out, the error of the proceedings realized, before the date of Calef's earliest recorded public effort. His book published in London by Nathaniel Hillar arrived in Boston about November 15, 1700. His activities, before that time, were merely those of a then obscure private letter-writer and compiler, which could scarcely have exercised any far-reaching public influence.

What effect the letters might have had if written during the trials and before the witches were hung, in the summer and early autumn of 1692, it is idle to speculate. Calef was silent then. It will be only charity to suppose that he was not lacking in valor to protest. Possibly, like most of his neighbors, he may have learned some of his wisdom after the occurrences, and through them. It is fairly certain, however, that he did not begin to write until almost a year after the last witch was hung, and four months after the last of the trials. He has much feeling and many opinions, but apparently no first-hand knowledge of any of the witchcraft incidents on which he writes except his first visit to Margaret Rule.

Cotton Mather's praying with Margaret Rule, or in the earlier case with Mercy Short, might be regarded as reasonable, charitable acts designed to aid mentally and physically distressed individuals, and his writings of their babblings as an attempt to record the curious phenomena connected with the devil's operations in the material world, as Mather himself viewed his work; or his efforts might be regarded as pitiably credulous, fatuous performances, as his opponents have held. But in either case he was not engaged in commencing any new furor of witch persecution; for he permitted no accusations to be made upon which any possible public punitive action could be begun. It required little effort, indeed, on Calef's part to stop a new persecution that was never started.

This is not a suitable occasion nor have I any desire to disinter the remains of the Upham-Poole controversy, yet it may be said that Mather's own defense on this point still stands:

that the Name of *No one* good Person in the World ever came under any blemish by means of any *Afflicted* Person that fell under *my* particular cognisance, yea no one Man, Woman or Child ever came into any trouble for the sake of any that were *Afflicted* after I *had once begun* to look after 'em. ('Another Brand . . .,' Sect. XII.)

Even Calef never contradicted this statement. Calef was orthodox enough to say, "That there are witches is not the doubt," but he was heterodox in that he denied, "that a witch can commissionate devils to afflict mortals," because, says he (pp. 17, 26), "The devil's bounds are set, which he cannot pass." So wicked and "full of malice" was the devil that no witch could make him any worse, believed Calef; and hanging witches could not lessen his power. On the other hand the magistrates and ministers and most of the general public seem to have held the ancient belief that witches actually made compacts with the devil to injure human beings.

If Cotton Mather was an enthusiast in his purpose to rout the devil and his agents, conversely, Calef was no less so in his design to further the acceptance of his views. In his letter to Mather of November 24, in opposition to the ministers he set up his own "doctrinals." Of these he goes so far as to say, "These last Sir, are such Foundations of Truth, in my esteem, that I cannot but own it to be my duty to ascert them, when call'd, tho' with the hazard of my All." ('More Wonders,' 1700, pp. 17–18.)

The martyr spirit here shown and his antipathy to the ministers, his bitter tongue, his attitude toward capital punishment, his estimation of education in classical literature as being a source of poison (see Preface and elsewhere), his incessant demand for Scripture authority for doctrines of witchcraft, seem strongly suggestive of Quaker influence in the background, a Quaker too, probably living in Salem, who doubtless provided Calef with that portion of his Salem and Salem Village material that he did not owe to Cotton Mather. Was the Quaker Thomas Maule? It is known that Calef had aid and it seems certain that there were others than Thomas Brattle with him.

Though Thomas Brattle was not a Quaker but an Episcopalian, nevertheless when all the facts behind the authorship of this work become known, considering the main work and not the postscript, it is possible that the book may yet be seen to owe some of its inspiration to the long-drawn-out conflict between the Quakers and the Puritans, even if parts of it do not eventually take their place in one of the side skirmishes of that struggle. Mr. John H. Edmonds, State Archivist of Massachusetts, states that he is inclined to think that some identity of authorship may lie behind 'Truth held forth' and 'More Wonders.' Might not Calef himself have held Quaker leanings?

"If I err, let me see it by Scripture," Calef repeatedly flung at the ministers. None answered him, he said. Cotton Mather was the only minister who attempted to argue with him; with what result the book bears witness.

Calef addressed seven letters to Cotton Mather, one to Benjamin Wadsworth, one to Samuel Willard, one 'To the Ministers in and near Boston,' and one even 'To the Ministers whether English French or Dutch,' and asked them to inform him what Scripture authority they had for their doctrine that witches could "commissionate devils." In these letters he made extracts from or references to works that dealt with witchcraft such as Cotton Mather's 'Wonders' and his 'Memorable Providences'; Increase Mather's 'Cases of Conscience' and his 'Essay for the Recording of Illustrious Providences'; and Richard Baxter's 'Certainty of the World of Spirits'; which quotations seemed to have allowed the devil greater power than he ought to have according to Calef's views. In derision he asks interpretations of these passages.

Calef scraped together this correspondence, somewhat one-sided though it was, containing his "doctrinals," his gibes, his quotations from Scripture and from the works of the Mathers and Richard Baxter. With these letters he included his report of the Margaret Rule meeting. To these he added a selection from, but not the whole of the documents concerning the differences between some members of the church of Salem Village and their pastor, the Reverend Samuel Parris, in whose house the witchcraft accusations of 1692 began. These differences arose over the charges made by four members bereaved by the trials; they concerned the responsibilities of the minister in aiding to bring out the accusations in the early stages of the troubles. After five years of agitation, these differences terminated in the dismissal of Mr. Parris.

To this accumulating material, Calef brought his most important addition, 'An impartial account of the most memorable matters of fact touching the supposed witchcraft in New-England'; which contained an outline history of the beginnings and development of the frenzy in the household of the Reverend Samuel Parris; with notes on some of the Salem trials, and with illustrative letters, confessions and indictments of some of the accused, with signed letters and attestations of some of their friends. To these he added extracts from Mather's 'Wonders of the Invisible World' containing in full his summary of five of the trials.

To this collection is appended a Postscript — almost certainly from a different writer than he of the letters, though written in collaboration with him or with his material in hand. The postscript contains a piquant review of Mather's 'Life of Sir William Phips' (Pietas in Patriam) published at London in 1697. The review is written in an unreserved, acrimonious, querulous, almost scurrilous vein, with an apparent purpose less of reviewing the book than of driving at Increase and Cotton Mather — condemning the new charter, the work of the one; and "the kindling those flames" of witch persecution, as much the indirect work of the other. ('More Wonders,' pp. 150–152.)

Though there is truth in the reviewer's charge that Mather used the occasion of the book to extol himself over the witch trials and his father over the agency, still it should be stated that the defense fits in the story and it is likely would offend few at the time other than the hypersensitive reviewer and the charter opponents. If Dr. Elisha Cooke, the disgruntled agent and the opposer of Phips for the governorship, did not write this review, he had indeed a great deal to do with it. ('More Wonders,' pp. 146–150.)

This whole bag of collected heterogeneous materials Calef hung high in his published work, to invite the mingled admiration, pity, sorrow, hate, and scorn of the ages. Not because of its preëminent importance among the other documents, but because it was regarded as an example of the erroneous witchcraft doctrines of an eminent Puritan minister, calculated to bring obloquy and ridicule upon its author, Cotton Mather's manuscript on Margaret Rule is exhibit A in this gibbetry.

Perhaps the reputation of no character in history has suffered so much and so unjustly through a surreptitious printing as has the author of the manuscript of 'Another Brand Pluckt out of the Burning, Or more Wonders of the Invisible World.'

ELIZABETHAN AMERICANA

By GEORGE WATSON COLE, L.H.D.

Librarian of the Henry E. Huntington Library, San Gabriel, California

OSCAR WILDE, in a letter written in June, 1897, says: "I am going to write a Political Economy in my heavier moments. The first law I lay down is: 'Wherever there exists a demand there is no supply.'" The book-collector chooses his field and starts out bravely to cover it. He soon learns that of certain works, the possession of which seems necessary to his happiness, "there is no supply."

Rarity in books is due to several causes. Some are merely *ghosts* that have crept into bibliographies. Many such, we are inclined to believe, have found their way there through printers' errors arising from illegible copy. Of these there is, of course, absolutely "no supply."

Then, there are *lost books* known only by allusions to them or from quotations in the writings of contemporaneous authors. These lost books sometimes come to light as did the First Edition of Shakespeare's 'Titus Andronicus' a few years since; or the copy of the earliest edition of 'The First and Second Partes of King Edward the Fourth,' by Thomas Heywood, now in the library of Charles W. Clark, of San Mateo, California. This latter volume doubtless owes its preservation, as have many others, to its having been included in a bound volume of tracts.

There are also *unrecorded books or editions*. These occasionally turn up in the most unexpected places, as did a considerable number in the Isham find of 1867, when a collection of Elizabethan books was found by Charles Edmonds at Lamport Hall, Northamptonshire, in an old lumber-room. Among the books there found were several the very existence of which had never even been suspected and editions of others previously unknown or supposed to be hopelessly lost.

Books, heretofore unknown, occasionally appear in sales as did the 1595 edition of Robert Greene's 'Pandosto' at the sale of the Newdigate Library in 1920. This unique volume now graces the shelves of the Henry E. Huntington Library. Examples similar to this show that though there may always be a demand there is "no supply."

Many books, especially those of small bulk usually termed pamphlets, have completely disappeared beyond all possibility of recovery. Of the perishable nature of these waifs of the printing-press every book-collector is but too painfully cognizant. Many such copies owe their preservation to the fact that they were bound in volumes with works of a similar nature. Examples of some of these are to be found in the works named below.

A book may be termed excessively rare if but a single copy of it is known, or at most two or three copies. The rarity of such a book is, of course, liable to be affected by the discovery of other copies. The late Dr. William Frederick Poole was accustomed to say he did not care to purchase a book until the fact of its rarity had been made public and such publicity had caused the owners of other copies to search their shelves and on finding copies to place them in the market.

In explanation of our title it should be said that we have extended the term Elizabethan to include works printed from about 1520 to 1641.

Of these early books relating to America a score or so have been selected of which no other, or at most only an extremely limited number of other, copies are known; or, of those which from their importance demand more than ordinary attention. Of these nearly one half deal with the discoveries and explorations of the Western Hemisphere. The remaining moiety were written to encourage emigration thither or to give accounts of the experiences and privations of the early colonists. Of those herein named all are to be found in the Henry E. Huntington Library. For convenience of reference a chronological arrangement has been followed.

I. *ca.* 1520. The earliest work in our language relating to America appeared at Antwerp about 1520. It is entitled: 'Of the newe la[n]des and of yᵉ people founde by the messengers of the kynge of Porty[n]gale named Emanuel.'

A single leaf only [A ii] describes a voyage to America (therein called "Armenica") made "in the yere of our Lord God. M.CCC.C.XCVI." This leaf in the Huntington Library copy is, fortunately, original and genuine. The rest of the volume, of which several leaves are in facsimile, describes various parts of Africa, Asia, and the East Indies. The entire work is decorated throughout with quaint woodcuts. This copy formerly belonged to the late E. Dwight Church, but was acquired by him too late to be inserted in his Catalogue of Americana.

The only complete copy is in the British Museum. The Bodleian Library possesses only a fragment, consisting of but two leaves, the 17th and 22d. It was reprinted by Edward Arber in 1885 in his 'First Three English Books on America' (pp. xxvii–xxxvi). Ten photostatic copies, from the British Museum copy, have been made and distributed in this country to that number of subscribing libraries and collectors.

II. 1569. The earliest book written and printed in the English language that relates the adventures and explorations of any Englishman in any part of America was written by Sir John Hawkins. It gives an account of his third voyage and was published under the title, 'A true declaration of the troublesome voyadge of M. John Haukins to the parties of Guynea and the west Indies, in the yeares of our Lord 1567. and 1568.' It was published in London in 1569.

All earlier books in English relating to America are translations from other languages. Hawkins was the first Englishman to engage in the slave trade. His book is a vigorous and direct narrative of his experiences and is full of shrewd observations.

The only other copy we are able to trace is in the British Museum. Arber reprinted it in his 'English Garner,' 5 (1882), 213–225. It also appears in the 1903 edition of that work (*Voyages and Travels*, 1: 91–103). Sabin (8: no. 30954) says he never saw a copy and was sceptical of its existence, believing that "it is only to be found in Hakluyt's Collection."

Knowledge of the extent of the North American continent from east to west was, during the sixteenth century, very vague. The Verrazano map (1529) represents the shore of the Pacific Ocean as extending inland in a vast indentation or bay almost to the eastern shore of the continent. The deep bays and large tidal rivers of the Atlantic coast, accentuated by this idea of Verrazano's, naturally stimulated exploration with a view of finding a navigable passage through the continent by which the English could extend their trade to the East Indies; the routes by Cape Good Hope, and Magellan's Straits and Cape Horn having already been monopolized by the Portuguese and Spaniards. Various expeditions were therefore undertaken by the English for the purpose of discovering such a passage.

The idea that the continent of North America was comparatively narrow from east to west prevailed among a few geographers even as late as 1612, when Sir Dudley Digges in his little work 'Of the Circumference of The Earth' (p. 23) computes the breadth of the American continent to be "about 6. Degrees, or 300. English Miles betweene *Virginia* and *Noua Albion*," "where Sir *Francis Drake* his *Noua Albion* should bee."

One of the most notable series of voyages to discover a navigable passage through the North American continent was undertaken by Sir Martin Frobisher. His first voyage, made in 1577, was promoted by the Earl of Warwick and other adventurers. Needless to say the expedition failed of its object. One of the sailors carried home a piece of black pyrite, which, in defiance of the London goldsmiths, an Italian alchemist declared to contain gold. A gold craze ensued; another expedition, and still a third, was sent out to follow up this supposed discovery. Hence followed Frobisher's second and third voyages, made in 1577 and 1578. Accounts of both these voyages are among the rarest of works relating to America.

III. 1577. An account of Frobisher's Second Voyage, entitled, 'A true reporte of the laste voyage into the West and Northwest regions, &c. 1577. . . . by Capteine Frobisher' (London, 1577), was written by Dionysius Settle.

Of this work two editions appeared the same year. The first has survived in only two other copies besides that in the Huntington Library. They are in the British Museum and John Carter Brown Library.

During his second voyage Frobisher was specially directed to search for more of the gold ore. As a result persistent efforts for the discovery of the Northwest Passage became a subordinate consideration. Settle's narrative was reprinted in 1868 for private distribution by John Carter Brown in an edition limited to fifty copies.

IV. 1578. Works describing Frobisher's Third Voyage (1578) are of even greater rarity than the volume just described. Thomas Ellis wrote an account of it which he entitled, 'A true report of the third and last voyage into Meta incognita: atchieued by the worthie Capteine, M. Martine Frobisher, Esquire. Anno. 1578.'

This, though undated, appeared the same year that Frobisher returned. Of this work only the Church-Huntington copy can be traced.. Hazlitt in 1876 (p. 482) described a copy which he may have seen, perhaps the identical one later acquired by Mr. Church. The Third Voyage was primarily fitted out to secure more gold ore as that procured during the second voyage had proved to be poor. The mineral gathered during this last voyage also turned out to be worthless. As a result public opinion turned against Frobisher, and his voyages in search of gold and of the Northwest Passage came to an ignominious end.

V. 1578. The first book in Spanish relating to America, Enciso's 'Suma de geographia,' became known to English readers through John Frampton's translation, entitled 'A Briefe Description of the Portes, Creekes, Bayes, and Hauens, of the Weast India.' This appeared at London in 1578.

Frampton in his dedication says the original was "vvritten by *Martin Fernandes Denciso*, aboute *Anno*. 1518 . . ., and after called in aboute tvventie yeares past, for that it reuealed secretes that the Spanish natiõ vvas loth to haue knovven to the vvorld." This goes far to prove what had long been surmised, that it was the policy of Spain to maintain the strictest secrecy regarding her possessions in the New World.

Copies of Frampton's translation are of even greater rarity than those of the original; for, of the First Spanish Edition (1519; Church, *Americana*, no. 42) seven copies are known and of the two editions of 1530 at least four can be traced, one of them, the Second Edition, being in the Huntington Library (Church, *Americana*, no. 61). The copy of Frampton's translation now in the Huntington Library was offered for sale in 1916 by Christie-Miller, in the catalogue of the Americana portion of his magnificent library. There is also another copy (the Lenox) in the New York Public Library.

VI. *ca.* 1579. Mention has already been made of the rarity of works relating to Frobisher's voyages. Thomas Churchyard, in 1579, published 'A Discovrse of The Queenes Maiesties entertainement in Suffolk and Norffolk' (autumn of 1578).

The American interest of this little work consists of the "adioyned" twenty-page poem written, as stated on the title-page, in "commendation of *Sir Humfrey Gilberts ventrous iourney*" of discovery and colonization. At the last moment Churchyard appended four leaves more, in verse, containing "A welcome home to Master Martin Frobusher." Frobisher, who had set out on his third voyage in May, 1578, returned in October of that year while this work was passing through the press. Churchyard, to celebrate the event, added this long poem, "written," as he says in its caption, "since this Booke was put to the Printing, and ioyned to the same Booke, for a true testimony of Churchyardes good will, for the furtherance of Mayster Frobushers fame." The poem occupies a single sheet of four leaves and follows a blank leaf at the end of the Gilbert poem. It is said to be lacking in more than one of the existing copies. There are other copies in the British Museum and the Bodleian Library. The Church and Devonshire copies are in the Huntington Library. The Epistle Dedicatorie varies but little in different copies. In the Church and Devonshire copies it is addressed to "Maister Gilbert Gerard, the Queenes Maiesties Attourney General." In others it is addressed to William Jarret. The British Museum possesses copies of each. Richard Heber also possessed copies containing these variations.

VII. 1582. Allusion has just been made to Churchyard's poem on the "ventrous iourney" of Sir Humphrey Gilbert. In 1582 there appeared, from the pen of Stephanus Parmenius, a Latin poem entitled, 'De Navigatione Illvstris Et Magnanimi Equitis Aurati Humfredi Gilberti.'

Parmenius was a learned Hungarian and a writer of elegant Latin verses. He accompanied Gilbert on his last voyage and was drowned near Newfoundland, August 29, 1583, when the *Delight*, one of Gilbert's fleet, ran aground and was lost with nearly one hundred men.

The only other copy of his work we can trace is that in the British Museum. It was reprinted by Hakluyt in his 'Principal Navigations,' 3 (1600): 137–143, with other works relating to Gilbert's 'Traffiques and Discoueries.'

VIII. 1587. Exploration of the territory now known as New Mexico was made by Antonio Espejo in 1582 and 1583. The original narrative of his expedition, in Spanish, appeared in Madrid in 1586. During the same year editions in both Spanish and French appeared in Paris, the former at the expense of the famous geographer, Richard Hakluyt. A translation into English entitled, 'New Mexico. Otherwise, The Voiage of Anthony of Espeio, who in the yeare 1583. with his company, discouered a Lande of 15. Prouinces,' was published by Thomas Cadman in the following year (1587).

The Epistle Dedicatory of this little work is dated and signed: "London this 13. Aprill 1587. . . . A. F."

The only known copy of this translation appeared for the first time at the sixth Heber sale (no. 2250) in the spring of 1835, and was even then described as "very rare." It was acquired by William Henry Miller, the founder of the Christie-Miller or Britwell Court Library, a library that is now being dispersed. In 1916 Mr. Sydney Richardson Christie-Miller, its present owner, decided to dispose of the American portion and this volume was included as no. 89 in the sale which was to have taken place in August of that year. The owner, however, reserved the right to dispose of the collection by private treaty before the date of sale and sold it to the late George D. Smith, the Napoleon of book-auction rooms, who in turn passed it over to Mr. Huntington. This copy is believed to be unique.

Sir James Lancaster, one of the leading seamen of the reign of Queen Elizabeth, returned in May 1594 from a voyage to the East Indies. During this voyage he had broken the monopoly of the East India trade of the Portuguese by passing around the Cape of Good Hope, plundered their vessels, and returned with much booty. His success led to the formation of the East India Company. Realizing that the Portuguese could be profitably plundered nearer home, the aldermen and merchants of London fitted out three ships for that purpose and placed Lancaster in command. He sailed the following October for Pernambuco. During the voyage thither he seized many Spanish and Portuguese vessels, and on his arrival captured the town. Loaded with plunder he sailed for England and arrived in the Downs in July, 1595.

IX. *ca.* 1595. An account of this voyage by H. Roberts, entitled 'Lancaster his Allarums, honorable Assaultes, and supprising of the Block-houses and Store-houses belonging to Fernand Bucke in Brasil,' appeared the same year.

This work is known by only two copies. These vary. A copy of the first issue is in the John Carter Brown Library. That in the Huntington Library is of the second issue and may be distinguished by the added leaf between folios C2 and C3. This extra leaf contains a long commendatory notice of Captain Randolph Cotton who was slain at Pernambuco. It would seem that after the pamphlet had been printed it was considered that not enough credit had been given him, so an extra leaf was added to supply the omission. Unfortunately the binder of the Huntington copy mistook this leaf for a cancel and destroyed leaf C3. The text of the missing leaf has been supplied by a photostat from the copy in the John Carter Brown Library. An account of Lancaster's expedition appeared in Hakluyt's 'Voyages,' 3 (1600): 708–715, and was reprinted by the Hakluyt Society, 46 (1877): 35–56. This later account is based on Roberts's text, many passages, notably at the beginning, being repeated word for word.

We now arrive at a period when the character of Americana changes. Thomas Harriot's 'A briefe and true report of the new found land of Virginia' (1588) was the second original English production relating to America given to the English reading public. Though of the utmost importance, it is by no means as rare as many other books mentioned in this paper, no fewer than a dozen copies being known.

In 1597 there appeared a volume that sprang into instant popularity. This book, not usually thought of as belonging with works relating to America, is Gerard's 'Herball Or Generall Historie of Plantes.'

On page 752, in a description "Of Indian Swallow woort," appears a contemporaneous notice of Sir Walter Raleigh's Virginia colony of 1585. In speaking of the place where this plant is to be found he says: "There groweth in that part of Virginia, or Norembega, where our Englishmen dwelled (intending there to erect a Colony) a kind of *Asclepias* or Swallow woort, which the Sauages call *Wisanck*," etc. Lower down on the page, he further says: "It groweth, as before is rehearsed, in the countries of Norembega, and now called Virginia by the H. Sir *Walter Raleigh*, who hath bestowed great summes of monie in the discouerie thereof, where are dwelling *at this present* [the italics are our own] English men, if neither vntimely death by murdering, or pestilence, corrupt aire, bloody flixes [*sic*], or some other mortall sicknes hath not destroied them." This volume is perhaps the first to record American plants. In it are described 28 varieties, some of them indigenous.

No account of Elizabethan Americana should fail to mention three important works, though not one of them is of such rarity as those herein enumerated. We refer to Harriot's 'Virginia' (1588), mentioned above; Brereton's 'A Briefe and true Relation of the Discouerie of the North part of Virginia; . . . Made this present yeere 1602, by Captaine Bartholomew Gosnold' (1602), of which there are two impressions. Copies of both are at San Marino; and Rosier's 'A Trve Relation of the most prosperous voyage made this present yeere 1605, by Captaine George Waymouth, in the Discouery of the land of Virginia' (1605). The last two Henry Stevens characterized in 1874 as the "Verie two eyes of New England history."

X. 1610. (Gainsford.) The earliest mention of Columbus noticed in any work of English poetry occurs in Thomas Gainsford's 'Vision And Discovrse Of Henry the seuenth' (1610).

This, his earliest work, possesses little merit as a poem. The best passage of the whole production is perhaps that in which he relates the discouragement of Columbus in England and elsewhere in finding aid to his projected voyage of discovery. This work has long been considered one of the choice nuggets of English Literature, but not until copies of it came into the Huntington Library was it discovered to have an American interest. Corser, in his 'Collectanea Anglo-Poetica' (pt. 6:403), failed to note this feature of the work. The passage in which reference is made to Columbus occurs on page 21 and reads as follows:

> "Once to *Columbus* we gaue little heede,
>   When he made proffer to the English nation
>   That if we did but furnish him with ships,
>   All *Europes* glorie we might soone ecclipse.
>   He said he knew there was another world,
>   And to the same he would the Pilot be:
>
> . . . .
>
>   But we esteem'd his speech an idle dreame,
>   And after long delay his suite denied."

Of this work we are only able to trace three copies; the Huth, now in the Huntington Library, that in the British Museum, and the Bridgewater House copy, formerly in the Huntington Library, but the present location of which is unknown to us.

We had no idea when selecting the present topic for this paper that such a considerable number of the works to be recorded would relate to the Bermudas, a locality about which the present writer has had much to say elsewhere. This, however, is a mere coincidence. Early works relating to Bermuda are of extreme rarity. Major-General J. H. Lefroy, sometime governor of the Bermudas and an authority on its history, says: "So far as the writer has been able to learn, there is no British colony of the seventeenth century whose social history can be so fully traced, or dates from so early a stage of settlement; and it presents a more faithful picture of the habits, manners, and morals of the mother country than might at first be expected." Discovered under most disastrous circumstances, and supposed from early discoveries of ambergris, abundance of turtle, fish, fowl, etc., to possess unusual natural resources, "the Somers Islands" enjoyed for a few years a reputation incommensurate with that which they really deserved. These facts naturally led the participants in the perils incident to their discovery, and others of imaginative minds, to place on record these impressive events. Several contemporary writers penned their experiences and naturally found ready publishers. Few copies of these works, however, have survived the vicissitudes of time.

XI. 1610. The earliest separate publication of this character is Silvester Jourdain's 'Discovery Of The Barmvdas, Otherwise called the Ile of Divels' (1610).

Jourdain, or Jourdan as his name is sometimes spelled, was a townsman of Sir George Somers. In 1609 he embarked with him, and Sir Thomas Gates and Captain Newport, deputy governors of Virginia, on their voyage thither. The *Sea Venture* in which they sailed was wrecked on the Bermuda Islands, July 28, 1609. After remaining there ten months, until they had constructed two small vessels, they embarked for Virginia, May 10, 1610, and reached there on May 23. Jourdain in his narrative gives a most vivid description of the shipwreck, an event which has been thought by some to have suggested to Shakespeare his idea of 'The Tempest.'

The Britwell copy, now in the Huntington Library, and that in the British Museum are the only ones we have been able to locate. This tract was reprinted three years later, with additions but without due credit given to the author, under the title, 'A Plaine Description Of The Bermudas, Now Called Sommer Ilands.' The dedication to this later issue is signed "W. C.," initials thought by Alexander Brown ('Genesis of the United States,' 2 : 621) to be those "of the Rev. Wm. Crashaw"; though Sabin (3 : no. 9759), with less probability, questions whether they may not be those of William Castell. This latter tract is not as rare as the first edition, as some eight or more other copies of it can be traced.

Incidentally, attention may here be called to the fact that the Bermudas were the first part of the Western Hemisphere to be mapped from an actual survey; that made by Richard Norwood in 1618 and published about 1622. Norwood made a later survey of the Islands in 1662–63. His map corresponds most surprisingly with the latest Admiralty charts, showing the skill and accuracy of that distinguished surveyor, who was among the first to undertake the measurement of the earth's circumference by surveying, with a chain, the distance from London to York in 1639.

XII. 1610. In 1610 also appeared another little work relating to the Bermudas. This was written by R. Rich, who describes himself as "one of the Voyage." It is written in doggerel verse and is entitled, 'Nevves from Virginia. The lost Flocke Triumphant.'

This pamphlet describes the shipwreck of Sir Thomas Gates, Captain Newport, and Sir George Somers on the Bermudas and their final escape to Virginia. So rare is this little poem that for a long time the copy in the Huth Library was supposed to be unique. Later, however, another copy turned up and passed into the Church Library. These two copies are the only ones known.

When, by the will of Alfred Henry Huth, the British Museum was permitted to select fifty volumes from his library before it was dispersed at public auction, this little poem was among those selected. So important was the addition made by this provision that it was declared to be "the most important gift that has been made to the library of the British Museum since the bequest of the Grenville Library in 1846."

XIII. 1615. The Reverend Lewis Hughes was the first clergyman appointed by the Virginia Company to go to Bermuda. He probably reached there in July 1612. He seems to have been of a disputatious disposition, for in 1615 he was imprisoned for opposing the six governors. He was one of those whose opposition to some parts of the English liturgy finally led, in 1620, to the adoption of the liturgy of Guernsey and Jersey. He returned to England in 1620 to secure more clergymen for the colony and to give the Bermuda Company an account of the grievances of the people. He returned to Bermuda in 1621 and again, for the last time, in 1625. In 1615 he published 'A Letter, Sent into England from the Svmmer Ilands.'

This was signed, and dated, "From the Summer Ilands this 21. of December. 1614." Of this we are able to trace only three other copies, those in the British Museum, the Bodleian, and the New York Public Library, the latter being the Lenox copy. Lefroy in his 'Memorials of Bermuda' reprints much of this tract.

XIV. 1618. Copies of works issued by William Brewster from the Pilgrim Press at Leyden during the years 1617–1619 are exceedingly rare. Of the twenty titles recorded by Harris and Jones ('Pilgrim Press,' pp. 72–87) only 47 copies in all have thus far been located, seven of these being known by single copies only. The authors of 'The Pilgrim Press' locate but 37 of the 47 copies known, the other ten being located by George Ernest Bowman as in the possession of the Massachusetts Society of Mayflower Descendants. These represent six different titles and four duplicates. Among these is Laurence Chaderton's 'A Frvitfvll Sermon Vpon the 3. 4. 5. 6. 7. and 8. verses of the 12. chapter of the Epistle of Paul to the Romanes' (1618).

The Huntington Library has a perfect copy though some leaves are cropped at the top. The only other copy known is that in the Yale University Library, which lacks the title-page and the ten following leaves. This impression, as seen by resemblances in spelling and spacing, was reprinted by Brewster from the Waldegrave edition of 1589. Chaderton came of a Roman Catholic family. While in Trinity College, Cambridge, he became a Puritan and was disowned by his father. He attained distinction as a preacher and died in 1640 at the extreme age of 103 or 104 years.

XV. *ca.* 1618. A lost work, long known only by contemporary mention on the title-page of a work by William Euring, in answer to it, is T. Draxe's 'Ten Covnter-Demavnds Propounded to those of the Separation (or English Donatists), to be directly, and distinctly answered' (*ca.* 1618). Dexter, in the Appendix to his 'Congregationalism,' records the work on the strength of the title-page to Euring's work, entitled 'An Ansvver To The Ten Covnter Demands, Propovnded By T. Drakes.'

The only copy of the 'Ten Covnter-Demavnds' is now in the Huntington Library; while of Euring's 'Ansvver' thereto (one of the last of the books printed at Leyden by the Pilgrim Press) we know of only two copies, those in Dr. Williams's Library, London, and the Dexter copy in the Yale University Library.

The 'Ten Covnter-Demavnds' was a bibliographical ghost, the very existence of which was questioned until 1911, when a copy came into the possession of Mr. Henry N. Stevens, who first identified and described it. It was acquired by Mr. Huntington at the sale of Colonel Charles L. F. Robinson's library in April, 1917, at a price commensurate with its excessive rarity, $1050. Before leaving England it was examined and transscribed by Mr. Champlin Burrage who reprinted it in full in his 'Early English Dissenters' (2: 140-145). The work itself, as shown by Mr. Burrage, is an answer to Francis Johnson's "Seven Questions," appended to his 'Treatise of the Ministery of the Church of England.' Of the 20 publications of the Pilgrim Press the Huntington Library possesses nos. 5, 6, 9, 15, 16, 19, as well as a photostat of the Yale University copy of no. 18, Euring's book mentioned above.

XVI. 1621. The Reverend Lewis Hughes's 'Letter, Sent into England' (1615) has already been mentioned. Six years later (1621) another pamphlet emanated from his pen, entitled 'A Plaine And Trve Relation Of The Goodnes Of God towards the Sommer Ilands.'

In this latter work he gives an interesting account of the first night he spent at Coopers Island in the Bermudas. He speaks of the abundance and incredible tameness of the birds. So confiding were "the silly wilde birds" that they came into his cabin, and went so familiarly between his feet, and round about his cabin, and into the fire, as if they bade him take, kill, roast, and eat them. This tameness he interpreted (in accordance with the pious custom of the time) as "a manifest token of the goodnesse of God, euen of his loue, his care, his mercy and power working together, to saue this people from staruing." Incredible as this account seems, it has been confirmed by the experiences of other naturalists in their visits to other uninhabited islands. The only other copies of this tract recorded are in the British Museum and in the Library of the Duke of Devonshire.

XVII. 1621. Another little pamphlet of the utmost rarity is an English translation of the Charter of the West India Company. It is entitled 'Orders And Articles Granted By The High And Mightie Lords The States General Of The Vnited Provinces, Concerning the erecting of a VVest India Companie.' This appears to be a translation of the 'Ordonnantien Ende Articvlen,' described in no. 51 of Asher's 'Bibliographical and Historical Essay on the Dutch Books and Pamphlets relating to New-Netherland' (p. 98). The Church-Huntington copy is the only one of which we have any knowledge, except that in the British Museum.

XVIII. 1622. The Reverend Patrick Copland was chaplain of Captain Martin Pring's ship, the *Royal James*. Sir Thomas Dale had interested Copland in Virginia while they were serving together in the East Indies. When the *Royal James* was at the Cape of Good Hope a subscription was raised "towards the building of a free Schoole in Virginia." Of the £70 8s. 6d. there subscribed Captain Pring contributed £6 13s. 4d. and his chaplain £5. The amount thus raised was increased to £100 by the generosity of an unknown contributor. By additional subscriptions the amount was later increased to a total of £192 1s. 10d. This was paid over to Henry, Earl of Southampton, for the Virginia Company at a General Court held November 21, 1621; the Court adding 1000 acres at Charles City to be called "The East India School" (Brown, 2: 973). Of this little pamphlet by Copland, 'A Declaration how the Monies . . . were disposed' (1622), we know of no other copy than that formerly in the Church Library.

Copland is better known by his sermon 'Virginia's God Be Thanked,' preached at Bow-Church in Cheapside before the Honorable Virginia Company, April 18, 1622. This was published the same year; but only some nine copies can be traced.

XIX. 1625. The next work to engage our attention contains an urgent plea for the peopling of the British colonies. It relates chiefly to the colonization of New England. It was written by Captain John Hagthorpe and is entitled 'Englands-Exchequer. Or A Discovrse Of The Sea and Navigation with some things . . . concerning Plantations.'

This is an eloquently written tract interspersed with poetry. A sample of Hagthorpe's poetry appears in the laudatory verses prefixed to Captain John Smith's 'Sea Grammar,' published two years later. In his own work, to which attention is here called, he devotes much space to the attractions of Virginia, New England, and Newfoundland as suitable places for plantations. His preference is for the latter and he sets forth his reasons in detail (p. 31). These he states to be, " 1. For conueniency and temprance of the Clime, agreeing with this of ours. 2. For the safety of the Planters, both from inward and outward Enemie. 3. For the goodnes of the place, abounding with all things necessary to mans sustenance. 4. For the facilitie of transportation, and supplies of all necessaries." Other copies are in the British Museum, Bodleian, University Library, Cambridge, and the John Carter Brown Library.

XX. 1630. Thomas Morton occasioned the Puritan settlers so much trouble by his dissolute ways and illegal sale of arms and ammunition to the Indians that Governor Endicott called a meeting on July 28, 1629, at which it was agreed to petition the King and Council to renew the Proclamation of King James I, of November 6, 1622, preventing the sale of arms and powder and shot to the savages. This petition was favorably received by Charles I who, on the 24th of November, 1630, renewed the Proclamation of his "deare Father King James of blessed memorie," with the insertion of additional beneficial clauses. This is entitled 'A Proclamation forbidding the disorderly Trading with the Saluages in New England in America, especially the furnishing of the Natives . . . with Weapons, and Habiliments of Warre.'

Nine copies of the earlier of these proclamations can be traced, the only ones in this country being those in the Henry E. Huntington and

John Carter Brown Libraries. Of the latter, beside the two copies in the Huntington Library, there are others in the Privy Council Office, the Public Record Office, the Society of Antiquaries in London, and the library of the Earl of Crawford, at Haigh Hall.

XXI. 1630. Another early mention of Columbus in a book of English poetry occurs in Baptist Goodall's 'Tryall Of Travell.'

This was a rare book over a hundred years ago. In the 'Bibliotheca Anglo-Poetica' (1815) it was priced at 12 guineas. The collection there recorded formerly belonged to Thomas Park, the English antiquary and bibliographer. But three or four other copies are known to us, those in the British Museum, University Library of Cambridge, and the Harvard College Library. Another, the Jolley copy, was sold in the Huth sale.

XXII. 1638. In August, 1638, the West India Islands were visited by a violent storm or hurricane, as so often happens during the summer months. This event was recorded, the same year, in a little pamphlet of extreme rarity, entitled 'Newes and strange Newes from St. Christophers of a tempestuous Spirit, which is called by the Indians a Hurry-Cano or whirlewind.'

Following this account in prose, in which two of its ten pages give an account of Sir George Summers' shipwreck on the Bermudas, is a four-page poem entitled "A true Relation in Verse, of the strange accident which hapned at Withycombe in Devon-shire." This latter event was described in two other contemporary pamphlets, both in prose, entitled 'A trve Relation,' etc., and 'A Second And Most Exact Relation,' both printed by G. M. for R. Harford, 1638. Another account of the Widecombe storm, also in verse, by the Vicar, the Reverend George Lyde, is given in Robert Dymond's 'Widecombe in the Moor,' pp. 104–108. A comparison of Lyde's verses with those in our St. Christopher pamphlet show them to be different works. We pause to mention these, as, owing to the rarity of the poem in the St. Christopher pamphlet, they were thought to be identical. The entry in the Stationers' Register for December 4, 1638 (Arber, 'Transcripts,' 4:446) ascribes the authorship of the latter to John Taylor, the Water Poet. Thus is added a new title and one of American interest, to the long list of the works written by Taylor. The copy in the Huntington Library (Britwell: 1916, no. 271) is believed to be unique.

To summarize, it will be seen that of the 22 books above enumerated only 59 copies are at present known or can be located. Besides the 24 copies in the Huntington Library, five of which are unique, there are only 8 other copies in American libraries. All of the 59, save three or four, are in public libraries. Such being the case, what possible chance has a collector of Elizabethan Americana of adding a single one of these books to his collection?

We thus see that the law laid down by Oscar Wilde applies most rigidly in the case of all of these books, and so can realize more than ever that while there is a demand for such books, there is "no supply." Little wonder that when a stray book of known rarity happens to come into the market the competition for its possession is of a most aggressive character and prices soar to unprecedented heights. Regarding "record prices" it should be borne in mind that in the auction room there are always underbidders, eager, often opulent, and it is really their demand that determines the high prices that at present prevail. The successful bidder, if he is bound to secure the prize, has only to go the underbidder one better.

The question naturally arises, Where is all this to end? More and more book rarities are finding their way into public libraries and are thus being permanently withdrawn from the market, so that however strong may be the desire of a collector to place them on his shelves, the law as laid down by Oscar Wilde steps in and says, Nay. It may, therefore, in his paradoxical phrase be said that in innumerable instances "Wherever there exists a demand there is no supply."

SUMMARY

Serial Number	Date	Author	Title	Photostats of T. p., &c.	No. of copies known	Location of other copies	Other copies in America
1	ca. 1520		¶Of the newe lādes	3	3	BM, Bodl. (frag.)	
2	1569	Hawkins	True declaration	1	2	BM	
3	1577	Settle	True reporte	1	3	BM, JCB	1
4	1578	Ellis	True Report ... third ... voyage	1	1	HEH (unique)	
5	1578	Frampton, tr.	Briefe Description ...	1	2	NYP (Lenox)	1
6	ca. 1579	Churchyard	Discourse, ... (HEH, 2)	2	5	BM(2), Bodl.	
7	1582	Parmenius	De Navigatione	1	2	BM	
8	1587	Espejo	New Mexico	1	1	HEH (unique)	
9	ca. 1595	Roberts	Lancaster his Allarums	1	2	JCB	1
10	1610	Gainsford	Vision and Discourse	2	3	BM, Bridgewater copy	1?
11	1610	Jourdain	Discovery of the Barmudas	1	2	BM	
12	1610	Rich	Newes from Virginia	1	2	BM	
13	1615	Hughes	Letter sent into England	1	4	BM, Bodl., NYP	1
14	1618	Chaderton	Fruitful Sermon	1	2	Yale (imperfect)	1
15	ca. 1618	Draxe	Ten Counter-Demaunds	1	1	HEH (unique)	
16	1621	Hughes	Plaine and True Relation	1	3	BM, Devonshire	
17	1621		Charter W. India Co.	1	2	BM	
18	1622	Copland	Declaration how the Monies were disposed	1	1	HEH (unique)	
19	1625	Hagthorpe	Englands-Exchequer	1	5	BM, Bodl., ULC, JCB	1
20	1630	Charles I.	Proclamation (HEH, 2)		6	Privy Council, Soc. Antiq., Pub. Record Office, Crawford	
21	1630	Goodall	Tryall of Travell	1	5	BM, ULC, Harvard, Jolley copy	1
22	1638	Taylor	Newes ... from St. Christophers	2	2	Worcester College, Oxf. (Hazlitt, 6:378)	
				26	59		8

THE ELIOT INDIAN TRACTS

By GEORGE PARKER WINSHIP

Librarian of the Harry Elkins Widener Collection, Harvard College Library

THE eleven seventeenth-century pamphlets which are commonly grouped as the 'Eliot Indian Tracts' still await adequate bibliographical treatment as a series. Mr. Eames showed how the work should be done, in the description of two of them under the author entry, Thomas Shepard, in Sabin's 'Dictionary,' nos. 80205 and 80207; and his solution of the confusing issues of 'Strength out of Weakness' of 1652 may be anticipated when the 'Dictionary' reaches the name of Henry Whitfield. Dr. Cole also provided descriptions of the first eight tracts in the Catalogue of the E. Dwight Church Library, 1907, in accordance with the most elaborate bibliographical canons. The present contribution does not propose to supply the missing details, but merely to bring together a few items of information, relating to the printing of certain of the tracts, which have come to light more recently.

The first record book of the Corporation supplies most of the following notes. This book, containing entries for the years 1656 to 1686, was sold by auction at Boston in 1871, by Henry Stevens. He had previously tried to induce Mr. Lenox, Mr. John Carter Brown, and others of his correspondents to buy it at what he regarded as a fair price. The result of these negotiations was that he spoiled the market for this item when it appeared in his public sale, and it was knocked down to a collector not widely known as interested in this field, Mr. James Frothingham Hunnewell. In his library, which in course of time passed to his son, it remained hidden until 1915, despite the persistent, practically uninterrupted efforts of Mr. Eames and of every one whom he could enlist in the search, to discover what had become of it. It lay wrapped in a torn and sun-dried brown paper on the topmost shelf in a vault which Mr. James Melville Hunnewell had built for his rarer books in his house on Beacon Hill, Boston, when, very late one evening in the autumn of that year, he asked me if there was anything else I would like to look at before I said good-night. My eye caught the dust-colored paper and mechanically I reached for it, conversing of other things. As mechanically I opened it, and noticed the words "Meeting of the Corpo: for Ppagating ye Gospel." I closed the book and looked more carefully at the label on the binding, which had already reminded me of old "G. M. B." Stevens. Then I said, thinking hard and wondering whether hand or voice was betraying my excitement, — for I did not want to raise false hopes in the owner, — that it was too late to look at it carefully, but that some day I wanted to see it again.

"Take it with you if you want," said he. I did. Mr. Eames was far away and sound asleep, I hope, but I knew that Mr. Frederick Lewis Gay would still be reading in his Brookline study, with a telephone beside his chair. So I sought the nearest public telephone booth. When he and I had finished talking, and I had answered all the test questions he put to me to make sure that I had the volume we had so often discussed longingly, it was a night-owl cabby who conveyed me home, who can hardly have guessed how unusual and how precious a fare he had that night.

Mr. Gay soon arranged to have the volume photostated and then transcribed. It was printed by the Prince Society, of which he had been president, after his death, in 1920. This present paper might be considered as an appendix to the Introduction which I prepared for that volume.

In addition to the Record Book, the Prince Society printed the Ledger of the New England Company for the years 1650–1660, from the manuscript preserved in the archives of the State of New Jersey. This supplies some figures giving the

cost of the Eliot tracts issued during that decade, and incidentally enables us to prove that the clerk of the Corporation made
a mistake in one entry — the most important entry in the
whole volume for students of the history of printing.

Although the Ledger balances from the year 1650, and apparently includes the accounts from the beginning of the Society's active operations, those for the years 1650–1653 are
summarized on a single page, from the "Book of Disbursements," or Day Book kept by the Treasurer's clerk. The detailed accounting begins with the reorganization of the Corporation after it secured a large amount of money in the spring
of 1653. The entries which may be pertinent to the subject of
this paper, on the first or summary page, raise more questions
than they answer.

The very first entry under "Contra Creditor" reads "1650
Aug: 22 By Bookes paid for to Mr. Thomas Jenner in pte
as by the perticulers of them in ye Booke of Disbursements
Fo 5 li 0030 00 00." Thomas Jenner was an active book- and
printseller in London from 1623 to 1666, but his name does
not appear on any book with which the Corporation was concerned, and there is no reference elsewhere to the purchase of
books to be sent to the missionaries at this time. There were
three publications which the Corporation presumably paid for,
or helped to pay for, at this time. The Act of Parliament in-
corporating the Society was printed in two forms in 1649, both
of them "for Edward Husband, Printer to the Parliament of
England." One of these was the regular official black-letter
form, paged consecutively with other acts; but the other was
clearly intended for distribution by the Corporation to those
whom it engaged in the task of collecting money, and who
would certainly not be asked to pay for this evidence of their
public authorization. The other publication of the same year
in which the Corporation may be supposed to have had at least
a subsidizing interest is the 'Glorious Progress' tract, which

was "printed for Hannah Allen in Popes-head-Alley." Mrs. Allen was the widow and the mother of London booksellers who issued books of interest to the Puritan public, and it is not easy to think of a reason why the Corporation might have dealt with or through Jenner rather than directly with her, if the payment quoted above was on account of this tract. There is of course a possibility that Jenner might have taken over the account and carried it as a favor or for a consideration, until funds came into the Company's treasury; but this is purely a conjecture offered for lack of anything better.

An entry dated August 23, 1651, reads "Paid Mr. Nicholas Hayward in full for Bookes" £34. The word "books" in the records, ten years later, ordinarily means the blank books which were furnished to the collectors throughout the counties, in which they were expected to keep account of all moneys received or promised. The sum seems large for books of this sort, unless they were got up much more elaborately than would be expected. On the other hand, it is not easy to connect the entry with this year's tract, 'The Light appearing more and more towards the perfect Day,' which was "Printed by T. R. & E. M. for John Bartlet, and are to be sold at the Gilt Cup, neer St. Austins gate in Pauls Church-yard." This tract was entered at Stationers Hall on the preceding January 22, and Thomason dated his copy on February 18. These two dates probably tell when the letters from New England reached London, and about the time it took to get a 54-page pamphlet through the press. The amount paid Hayward may be compared with the cost of the 48-page tract of 1659, £24. Hayward's name does not appear in Plomer's 'Dictionary of the Booksellers and Printers who were at work in England, Scotland and Ireland from 1641 to 1667,' London, Bibliographical Society, 1907.

There is only one other entry for 1650–1653 which might cover whatever payment was made on account of the tracts of these years, all the remaining entries specifying that they were for "Goods bought and sent to New England." This is under date of Decemb. 27, 1653, "By Disbursments paid foreth att tymes As by ye Book of Disbursmts it appeares in, £0359:07:05." A similar entry of £260 03s 01d balances the account for 1653–1654, on September 2 of the latter year, preceding the annual meeting for elections. Doubtless this included a payment on account of 'Tears of Repentance . . . Published by the Corporation for propagating the Gospel there, for the Satisfaction and Comfort of such as wish well thereunto. London: Printed by Peter Cole in Leaden-Hall, and are to [be] Sold at his Shop, at the Sign of the Printing-Press in Cornhil, near the Royal Exchange. 1653.' An observation may be added here, concerning the spelling of the Treasurer's clerk; his inconsistencies are explained by the fact that he added or omitted letters as he found helpful in making each line of an entry come out even — a practice that does not imply a lack either of education or of intelligence.

There is more definite information concerning the next tract in the series: 'A Late and Further Manifestation of the Progress of the Gospel amongst the Indians in New-England . . . Published by the Corporation, established by Act of Parliament, for Propagating the Gospel there. London: Printed by M. S. 1655.' The entries of the payment for this appear in the treasurer's statement for 1655–1656 as the first items after the regular outlay for goods shipped to the colony:

By Moneys paid Mrs. Symonds for paper and printing of Three Thousand Books Intituled. A late & further manifestation of the progresse of the Gospell & As appeares ye 8th of Sept 1655 in ye Book of Disbursments
58   0012 14 00
By Moneys paid Mr. Lee for blew & Marble paper & for covering & stitching the 3000.Books above menconed As appeares the 15 of Sept: 1655 in ye Booke of Disbursments 58   0007 12 00

'A Late and Further Manifestation' is a thin tract of only 32 pages, four quarto sheets, calling for eight 4-page forms or runs on the press, for each copy. The figures show that the tract cost just over a penny a copy — 3048 pence — for type-setting, press-work, and paper, or a farthing a sheet, with four shillings for extras; and rather more than half as much — 3648 half-pence — for binding in the original blue or marbled paper. Adding these two, the tract as distributed cost 4872 pence, or about one and three-fifths pence each.

Mrs. Mary Simmons was presumably the widow of Matthew and mother of Samuel Simmons; for her activity as a printer from 1656 to 1667 bridges the interval between the death of the elder in 1654 and the earliest record found by Mr. Plomer for the younger in 1666. The two men are best known as the printers of the writings of the Puritan politician, John Milton. All three were frequently employed by Independent writers. Mr. Plomer notes that Mrs. Simmons, on the evidence of the hearth-tax roll for 1666, had larger premises than any other London printer.

It is a significant fact that the disintegration of the Common-wealth did not appear to disturb those who were directing the affairs of this missionary society. Their next printed appeal was 'A further Accompt of the Progresse of the Gospel amongst the Indians in New-England and of the means used effectually to advance the same. Set forth in certaine Letters sent from thence declaring a purpose of Printing the Scripture in the In-dian Tongue, into which they are already Translated. London, Printed by M. Simmons for the Corporation of New-England, 1659.' The entry of payment for this reads:

May 27, 1659 By Moneys paid Mrs. Symonds for paper and printing 3000. Bookes, Intituled A further Accompt of the progresse of the Gospell amongst the Indians in New England, and for fine blue Paper & stitching the said bookes   0024 00 00

'A further Accompt' is a 48-page pamphlet, six quarto sheets. The cost per copy was 1.92 pence (3000 for 5760 pence). That of the 32-page tract of 1655 was 1.624 pence (3000 for 4872 pence) — proportionately considerably more.

The 1655 tract cost 8 shillings per page for composition, press-work, and paper.

At the 1655 rate of a farthing a sheet for printing and paper, the 18,000 sheets of 1659 would have cost £18 15s, leaving £5 05s for the binding, as against the £7 12s paid for binding the smaller 1655 tract. If Mrs. Simmons bought her paper at the price paid by the Corporation in 1660, 3s 10d a ream, the 24 reams needed for the 1655 tract, with no allowance for waste or run-over, would have cost £4 12s; and the 36 reams for that of 1659, £6 16s. In 1655 this left her £8 2s for composition and presswork, or about five-eighths of a farthing per sheet.

In general, and with a full realization that none of these seventeenth-century craftsmen figured their costs as accurately as we now would like to have them, these figures seem to show that paper cost rather more than half the amount charged for composition and press-work; that is, more than one-third of the usual printer's bill, not including binding. The covers and sewing of a pamphlet cost about half as much again as the paper, these two being something over half the total cost of the publication. It also seems clear, more specifically, that Mrs. Simmons printed the 1659 tract for substantially less than she received for that of 1655. This is the more noticeable because the later one was, for reasons to be explained, which will also show why these costs have been analysed so minutely, an unusually difficult piece of composition for the typesetters.

The Record Book adds some details concerning the history of the 1659 tract. At a meeting on February 5, which was presumably as soon as the members could be notified to assemble after the arrival of a ship from Boston bringing letters dated as late as December 28, the record states:

That ye Generall letter Mr. Endecott & Mr. Eliot of ye 11 of x[decem]ber 1658 together with ye Printed Shett Intituled helps for the Indians &c And the Epitomy of Exhortacon Delyvered by ye Indians att a fast & the abreviacon of Mr Mahews Manuscript bee presented unto Mr Reynold that hee would please to Drawe up a short Epistle to the same & Methodize the whole for the presse And this is especially recommended to the care of Mr Floyd Mr Ashurst & Mr Clerke.

Mem Mr Smyth propounded to speake with a Printer & to report.

On February 26 Mr. Floyd reported that he had

attended Doc. Reynolds with the letter & Papers & that the sd Dr. is willinge to peruse & methodize & prepare an Epistle & that his heart is in the work. [It was also voted] that 3000 of the bookes in Dr. Reynolds hands bee printed. To acquaint ye Dr yt ye Bible is printinge in the Indian Languige yt hee would mencon in ye Epistle &c.

That ye New Testament bee printed in the Indian Language first before the Old.

That John Hooper speake with Mrs. Symondes about ye printinge of the 1500 bookes.

At the meeting on March 19 the Committee previously appointed were requested

to attend Dr. Reynolds & let him understand that the Corporation doe not thinke fitt to print Mr Mahews Manuscript & to give him thankes in the Corporations name for his panes.

That ye title [the word "Page" is cancelled] of the booke bee referred to Dr. Reynolds & that one of the last bookes bee presented unto him.

That ye Dedecacon of the new booke bee accordinge to ye effect of the last booke.

That there bee a Postscript att the End of the booke now to bee printed to intimate that the bible is now alsoe about to bee printed in the Indian Language.

That when ye Corporacon wayte upon his Highnes with the bookes, That they desire him to graunt the duty of Custom & Excise for paper to bee free in reguard of their Charge of printinge ye Bible.

The only vote of interest on May 7 was "That 50 bookes bee sent to ye Commissioners for the United Coloneys in New England to bee disposed as they thinke fitt." On the 13th, 25 copies were ordered sent to the President of the Corporation, this probably giving the date when the tract was delivered by the printer, whose bill was paid on May 27. A month later, on June 18, the decision to ask Mr. Cludd to carry on the collection of funds in Nottinghamshire was accompanied by the provision "that a booke bee sent unto him which was last printed."

There are a few later votes ordering that "books be sent" to various ministers and others who were asked to look after the moneys collected for the missionary work; but it is not clear whether this means the printed tracts or the blank memorandum books provided for the recording of subscriptions and the payment of contributions. The other entries quoted above show clearly how the tracts were distributed, although there is no entry which would give the information most to be desired, specifying exactly how the rest of the edition was disposed of. It may be taken for granted that each member of the Corporation not only received a copy for himself, but that he also took away from the meeting other copies for such of his acquaintances as were likely to be interested, and that copies also were promptly dispatched by the clerk to all who had made, or were thought likely to make, substantial contributions to the cause.

There is no entry on the debit side of the Ledger which might contain receipts from the sale of any copies. If, as seems both possible and likely, copies could have been found in the shops of St. Paul's Churchyard, whatever money was received from the booksellers may have been treated as petty cash, not amounting to enough to figure in the yearly balance-sheet. It may be noted, as strengthening the impression that these pamphlets did not appear in the shops as ordinary publications, that none of those issued after 1652 are found in the Thomason Catalogue or on the Stationers' Register. It is a fair inference also that those sent to Massachusetts were not distributed widely, for not one of them is found in the Library of the Rev. Thomas Prince "begun to be collected upon his entering Harvard College in 1703" and, what remains of it, now deposited in the Boston Public Library.

The next tract of the series is presaged by the record of the meeting on October 17, 1659, when the Corporation acknowledged the arrival of a letter from Eliot enclosing two manuscripts. On the 22d a committee of three was requested "to peruse the 2 Manuscriptes sent from New Eng & see whether the same bee fitt to bee printed, and report." Two months later, on December 20,

The Corporacon havinge perused the Manuscripts lately sent from New England concer: the Indians confessions before their admittance into the Church, Doe think fitt that the sd Manuscripts bee printed & in order heerunto Mr Treasurer is desired with such other of the Members of this Corpor: as hee shall thinke fitt to repare unto Mr Caryll ye Minister that hee would please to drawe & prepare an Epistle to ye same.

Treasurer Ashurst, who was at this period the dominating member of the Corporation, reported on January 21 "that hee hath wayted upon Mr. Caryll concerninge the drawinge of an Epistle to the Manuscripts &c & that hee is ready and willinge to doe the same." "Ye Dedicatory Epistle Drawen & prepared by Mr. Caryll" was read at the meeting on March 17 and "approved & that the same bee printed with the Indians confessions, & that 1500 bee printed by Mrs. Symones, or such others as shall print the said bookes cheaper, & that the same bee referrd to Col. Puckle to take care heerof."

Colonel Puckle reported promptly a week later that "hee hath agreed with Mr. —— Maycoke a Printer to print ye Indianes Confessions at a farthinge per sheete, and that hee hath bought 20 reames of Paper at 3s 10d per reame." The sum of £3 16s 8d was forthwith ordered paid to Mr. John Cade for the paper. As the Treasurer entered the payment on the same day, March 24, a guess is justified that Colonel Puckle secured the paper at what he believed to be a low price, partly by promising a prompt cash payment. As will appear, there is an important error in the clerk's record which is quoted above. Another error in what may be assumed to have been Colonel Puckle's expectations when he purchased the paper for the Corporation, instead of leaving it to the printer to provide this, will be explained below.

This tract is entitled 'A further Account of the progress of the Gospel . . . being A Relation of the Confessions made by several Indians. Sent over to the Corporation . . . by Mr. John Elliot. London, Printed by John Macock. 1660.' It is the longest of the series, 76 pages of text preceded by 8 preliminaries and followed by one added page. A blank leaf presumably completed the last sheet, making 88 pages or 11 quarto sheets.

Macock's charge, £8 12s 6d, was ordered paid at the meeting on July 27. It is entered by the Treasurer under the date September 5, when he was closing the year's accounts, so that the actual payment may have been made more promptly. This amount makes 8280 farthings, and 1500 copies of an 11-sheet pamphlet call for 16,500 sheets. Macock therefore charged just half what he should have, at the rate specified by the clerk's record of what Colonel Puckle reported. As has been shown above, the rate of a farthing a sheet is approximately what was paid Mrs. Simmons for the printing and paper in 1655. The agreement with Macock called for composition and press-work only, the paper being furnished by the customer, who also attended to and paid for the binding. As these latter items easily figure over half the total cost, there can be little doubt that the agreement with Maycock was at the rate of half a farthing a sheet, and that the clerk made a mistake in noting the exact rate. It is possible that Colonel Puckle explained the transaction at length, describing with much detail how he was expecting to save the money of the Society by depriving the printer of his commissions on the paper and binding, and that the clerk lost interest before the explanation ended.

The twenty reams of paper bought in March proved insufficient, and on April 27 the Treasurer entered "By more moneys paid Mr. John Cade for paper, 0002 17 06." This would pay for fifteen reams at 3s 10d each. The thirty-five reams bought from Cade would be 17,500 sheets; the 1500 copies required 16,500 sheets, without allowing for the normal wastage and for an ordinary over-run on each of the twenty-two times the forms were put on the presses. On this job it may be noted that Macock had no incentive to see that the workmen were careful about the amount of paper they used, except the expectation of acquiring whatever may have been left over of the two extra reams for which the Corporation paid.

The payment for the binding is entered under the joint dates May 5 and June 27: "By moneys paid Mr. Richard Westbrook for fouldinge, pastinge & cuttinge of 1500 Bookes, £4 05s." This is approximately two-thirds of a penny each; but in comparing this price with that paid for binding the 1655 tract, it should be remembered that the latter was made up of only four sheets, and this of eleven, requiring nearly three times as much sewing. There is no mention of blue paper for the wrappers, so this was probably issued without covers. Paper and binding together cost £10 19s 2d, as against £8 12s 6d for composition and press-work.

John Macock, who got this job away from Mrs. Simmons, had one of the larger London establishments. Some years later it consisted of three presses, three apprentices, and ten workmen. In this same spring of 1660 he had secured the appointment as printer to the Parliament, in company with the Col. John Streator who had dared to oppose Cromwell in 1653.

A comparison between the tract printed by Macock in 1660 and that produced by Mrs. Simmons a year earlier justifies some interesting reflections. Mrs. Simmons made up a full page with 34 lines; Macock with 32; each page measuring six and a half and six inches respectively. Macock's type may be very slightly larger, but this is not certain, both being what was known as "English," approximating 13-point according to the scale now in use. He used a wider "set," supplying his compositors with spaces for use between the words of nearly twice the thickness of those used by Mrs. Simmons. The result of this was that each of his full pages contained between 320 and 330 words, whereas hers held from 350 to 365. Macock accomplished this in spite of the fact that his "copy" called for a much larger proportion of italic than appears in the 1659 tract, and italic sets much more compactly than roman letters. But he more than made up for this by the fact that his "copy" consisted of short sections with one-line headings, and with his shorter pages this frequently made it necessary to leave a few lines at the foot of the page blank because there was not room enough to begin a new section without having it look badly. Macock also spread his main headings in larger type, so that he occupied one and three-quarters inches with 32 words, while Mrs. Simmons used only one and three-eighths for 45 words.

In these various ways, Macock filled at least one full sheet for each tract more than his less sophisticated competitor would have done. Without noticeable compression, set to correspond with the two preceding tracts of the same series, this one could have been put into nine and a half sheets, 76 pages. This would have netted a saving of four and a half reams of paper; of three forms, or runs, on the press; and a corresponding reduction in the cost of sewing for the bindings.

In two other ways Macock was helped to make more profit than Mrs. Simmons had in 1659. He, or his author, omitted all side-notes, always a troublesome detail. She also had to struggle with ten and a half pages of Abraham Peirson's 'Some Helps for the Indians,' which was in the American language with interlinear English text in a very small type. It would not be surprising if she had asked for some additional compensation, or named a higher figure when she was asked to estimate on another similar publication.

The good people of England had many other things to think about, more absorbing than the conventionalized professions of faith of native American converts to Christianity, during the summer of 1660. Charles II had returned to London in May, and was crowned King in the following April. The "late pre-

tended Corporation," as it carefully and somewhat ostenta-
tiously described itself, secured a new charter, but otherwise
carried on its affairs without noticeable interruption. It had
acquired during the Commonwealth a valuable property from
a Royalist absentee, and successfully maintained its title in a
prolonged legal proceeding. Before the withheld rents could be
collected, the Plague and Fire of London brought a new succession of complications. Not until September, 1669, is there
any reference to another publication. Then the official letter
from New England mentions "the accomptes of Mr. Eliott,
Mr. Bourne & Mr. Mahew senior of the present State of the
Indians." A year later Eliot alluded to this "brief Tract of the
present state of the Indian work" as having "fallen short of its
end."

His next letter, dated September 20, 1670, formed the last of
the "Eliot Indian Tracts." This is the shortest of the series,
having only 11 pages, and is by far the scarcest. It was
"Printed for John Allen, 1671," and contains nothing except
the text of Eliot's letter. There is no reference to it in the Corporation records, and Allen may well have undertaken to print
it on his own account or for some individual patron. It was not
entered on the Stationers' Register.

THE NEW YORK PRINTERS AND THE CELEBRATION OF THE FRENCH REVOLUTION OF 1830

By RUTH SHEPARD GRANNISS

Librarian of The Grolier Club

THE so-called "Revolution" in France, of the "three glorious days of July," 1830, was brought about largely through the influence of public opinion as expressed by the press, under the fearless leadership of M. Thiers, editor of the *National*. It marks the beginning of the power of the Fourth Estate over modern politics. The absolute freedom of the press established in France by the great Revolution had been checked by various restrictions, until the charter of Louis XVIII restored its liberty, only to meet further restrictions. Finally, in 1830, came the Ordinances of St.-Cloud, the first of which dealt with the suspension of the liberty of the press, and was violently opposed by Thiers and his followers. The defeat of this and other tyrannical measures, the consequent abdication of Charles X, and the new constitutional monarchy with Louis Philippe as King of the French (not King of France), were hailed with delight in many countries of Europe. Interest was perhaps even more keenly manifested in the United States, where constitutional liberty was still so new and gratitude toward the French still so warm that enthusiasm for the one and admiration for the other were hearty and spontaneous.

Preparations were soon set in motion by the "working men of the city of New York" to "express their admiration and esteem for the brave and magnanimous daring of their brother mechanics and working men of Paris," by a great celebration. The affair, however, was postponed on account of approaching elections, which being well over, and people of all ranks having been invited to participate, in order to "render the celebration more effective and to divest it of all party feeling," a meeting of a committee of two hundred citizens was held at Tammany Hall on November 12. James Monroe, "late President of the United States," consented to preside at the meeting, with Albert Gallatin, Thomas Hertell, and Walter Bourne, vice-presidents, and November 25, the anniversary of the evacuation of New York in 1783, was fixed upon as the date of a stupendous procession. Philip Hone was made chairman of the Committee of Arrangements. During the remainder of November, the New York newspapers were filled with the great event.

From the first, the printers manifested especial interest in the proposed celebration. On November 17 the members of the New York Typographical Society held a meeting at the Shakespeare Hotel to consider plans, one of their resolutions being:

That as this brilliant revolution originated with and was principally effected by the talents, patriotism, enterprise, and undaunted public spirit of our *typographical* brethren in Paris, it particularly becomes *us* to unite in the proposed celebration of the 25th instant.

Soon followed meetings of the Benevolent Association of Journeymen Bookbinders, the Typefounders and Casters, the News Carriers, the Daily Journal Printers, and numerous other societies.

The *Morning Courier and New York Enquirer* of the 17th announced that the celebration bade fair to be the "greatest display got up in this city for many years." "It springs," continued the column, "from a generous and manly feeling, a feeling of sympathy for the revival of Liberty in France, brought about, in a great measure, by the firmness, moderation, and *amor patriæ* of our own, our devoted Lafayette. . . . The petty jealousies and groans of the grunters have been drowned in the cry of exultation." That there were, indeed, grunters is proved by the following which appeared on the same day: "A grumbler in the *American* last evening, finds fault with the French celebration because the 'Workies' originated it. The 'Workies' of Paris effected the revolution itself; of course it cannot please all."

Then follows the notice of a ball, a "splendid pageant," set for the 26th, "which is beginning to excite considerable interest among the ladies," and where the French ladies "intend to make a great display of the taste for which they are famous." A far different note is struck by a letter, almost side by side with the gay predictions of the ball, from "A Subscriber and Bankrupt," begging the Committee to devise a way by which "poor but honest debtors, confined in prison for not performing the impossible, can be permitted to look at the procession through the iron gates of their prison, or be bound hand and foot and set down under guard where it would pass."

The morning of the 25th, alas! dawned with a strong east wind and rain, and the postponement of the celebration as prearranged was inevitable. Friday, too, threatened to be lowering, but the newspapers announced that the parade would take place if the weather should possibly permit, the presence in the city of the many strangers who had come for the occasion, and the hazard to public safety through the incapacity of fire engines, which had been placed on platforms ready for the march, making further delay most undesirable. "Let no one stay at home," admonishes the morning paper, "in consequence of the streets being wet, as Mr. Bloodgood, the Street inspector, has a large corps of labourers engaged, who will scrape every street through which the procession will pass."

The *Morning Courier and Enquirer* announced that, should the procession take place, no paper would be issued from its office on Saturday. Consequently, it is not until the issue of Monday, the 29th, that we have its account of what actually took place; but then neither space nor eloquence was spared. We read that Friday morning was ushered in by a roar of artillery, announcing to "at least 250,000 persons that the inhabitants of this great commercial emporium . . . would suspend their usual avocations and unite in testifying to their admiration for the conduct and moderation of the people of France, who in three days drove their oppressors from power."

At nine o'clock the procession began to form, in Canal Street, and at ten the marshal started, preceded by a squadron of cavalry, "elegantly uniformed and mounted upon beautiful chargers," and followed by a barouche, wherein sat the vice-presidents of the Committee. President Monroe, who was to have accompanied them, was too feeble to join the company until it reached Washington Square.

Then followed various officials, a group of elderly French patriots, who were enthusiastically and tearfully applauded, five hundred French citizens of New York, trustees of the various colleges, and a company of infantry, immediately behind which marched the printers and members of the Typographical Society, and the Typefounders. The printers were led by their "venerable Marshal, John Lane, one of the Proprietors of the *Gazette*, . . . connected with the press of this city for more than forty years." Directly behind him marched those connected with the morning and evening papers, "bearing a large and beautiful banner, having for device a Clymer printing press, over which soared an American eagle holding in its talons a bust of Franklin, and in its beak the motto, *Vérité sans peur*; at the right, the Goddess of Liberty, at the left, the figure of a slave in chains, who had burst the shackles from one arm and laid hold on the press for emancipation; behind him a crown reversed, and a sceptre broken into three pieces, in allusion to the late Revolution."

The body of printers followed with various banners, and, in their midst, two platforms, each drawn by four horses, one of them carrying two printing presses, busily printing an ode written for the occasion by Samuel Woodworth, copies of which were thrown among the spectators by printers' devils dressed in green frocks and three-cornered cocked hats. The other platform bore "one of the new invented printing presses, also in operation at intervals, throwing off various publications." The *Advertiser* adds that the platforms were carpeted and tastefully decorated with the tri-color, festooned and beautifully ornamented, and that the presses were made by Messrs. Rust and Hoe, and were gilded for the occasion.

But what about the ode which was printed, distributed, and sung along the route? A badly printed broadside, lately presented to the Grolier Club, gives the answer, and is responsible for this retelling of the well-nigh forgotten events of November 25 and 26, 1830. The text, within a border of printers' ornaments, is headed:

Ode | for the | Celebration of the French Revolution | in the City of New York, November 25, 1830. | Written at the Request of the Printers of New-York, | By Samuel Woodworth, Printer. | Tune — Marsellois Hymn.

At the foot of the seven stanzas and chorus, we read:

The foregoing ode was printed on a moveable stage, on the 25th of November, 1830, and distributed to the citizens, during the procession in honour of the triumph of liberal principles in France. It was afterwards sung, on a platform erected for that purpose, in the centre of Washington Square, by all the vocalists of the Park Theatre, accompanied by the whole orchestra of that establishment.

It is particularly requested by the Music Committee, that all who join in the *Procession*, will unite in the Chorus.

Stereotyped by James Conner, Franklin Buildings.

A stanza will suffice to show the character of the poem, which is occasionally included in collections of poems of the press:

Thy chartered rights, with lawless daring,
Beneath oppressors' feet were trod,
Till startled despots heard, despairing,
The people's voice, the voice of God!
Their sovereign will was loudly spoken,
The *PRESS* proclaim'd it to the world —
Till Freedom's ensign waved unfurled,
And Gallia's galling chain was broken.

CHORUS

Then swell the choral strain,
To hail the blest decree;
Rejoice! Rejoice! The *PRESS* shall reign,
And all the world be free.

That all New York of the period was not exigeant as to the quality of its poetry is proved by the following which appeared in the *Courier and Enquirer* a few days before the celebration:

Mr. Woodworth has published a very beautiful small edition of his Poems, Songs, &c. embellished with plates and engravings. Mr. W. deserves the patronage of the public. He is a genuine native poet. He is altogether free from the satanic fustian which too frequently characterizes the poetry of the day. His poetry is plaintive, sweet, simple and pathetic. . . . He is not only the father of a numerous family of pretty poems, but he is also the author of a dozen of the finest children which ever was presented to a blooming and flourishing republic. . . . Let us patronize the tribe of married poets, and put down if possible these bachelor drabs — these satanic-moping, pineing-touchy-testy-blue-deviled bachelor *literati*, who monopolize the world of taste and fashion.

That the author of the immortal "Old Oaken Bucket" was a printer may be news to many. He chose the profession at an early age and bound himself as apprentice to Benjamin Russell, of Boston, editor of the *Columbian Centinel*. His first independent business venture was in New Haven, where he issued a weekly journal, the *Belles Lettres Repository*, of which he was "editor, publisher, printer, and more than once carrier." It failed after a few weeks, and his later editorial efforts in New York were little more successful. He was, however, highly esteemed as an honourable citizen, his "many gracious qualities of head and heart" making his home in Duane Street the resort of many of the literary men of the day, among them Cooper and Fitz Greene Halleck. It is also interesting to note that the various notices of meetings of the Typographical Society, appearing in the newspapers in connection with the great celebration, are signed by Woodworth as secretary.

The first collection of his poems appeared in 1826, and a second was published by the author in 1830. This is the little volume advertised so flatteringly, the title running, "Melodies, Duets, Trios, Songs and Ballads, Pastoral, Amatory, Senti- mental, Patriotic, Religious and Miscellaneous." That he was a popular poet for "occasions" is proved by such efforts as the "Ode on the Opening of the Lafayette Circus," for which he was awarded "a silver cup of fifty dollars value," and the "Ode for the Grand Canal Celebration." The latter was printed for the first time during the great land procession of November 4, 1825, and was distributed among the spectators in much the same way as the ode on the French Revolution. It, too, is en- thusiastic in its praise of printing, "the art which unshackles the soul." Indeed, a surprising number of poems included in the little 1830 edition deal with the art of printing and the free- dom of the press — so many that in the collection edited by Woodworth's son in 1861 they are grouped together as "Typo- graphical Odes," and number nearly a dozen. The poem of our broadside appears, also, in the 1861 edition, where it is entitled "The French Revolution."

Returning from this digression to the order of the procession, we find that the typefounders, who followed the printers, wore badges containing likenesses of Washington and Lafayette, and carried a banner on which appeared a workman casting types. At the top of the banner were "likenesses of the three reputed fathers of the profession, Guttenberg, Faust, and Schaeffer."

Among the delegations of all conceivable trades that fol- lowed, one of the most impressive must have been that of the manufacturers of steam engines and boilers, whose "beautiful steamboat ploughed our streets instead of our waters without intermission." The procession marched from Canal Street "down Broadway to the Park, around the Park," through Chatham Street, the Bowery, and Broome Street, up Broad- way to Fourth Street, and thence to Washington Square (or Parade Ground) where the ceremonies of the day took place.

"Among other scenes which attracted much curiosity," wrote the *Daily Advertiser*, "were the several presses at work upon their cars in the open field, while the ceremonies were performing, and thousands crowding around them eager to obtain an ode." Owing to an accident, according to another paper, the cars with the printing presses had not been able to get into line until the procession reached Broadway; but to make up for it, we are told, the printers, with the two platforms, paraded the length of Broadway, after the ceremonies, printing and distributing their ode.

Space fails for an adequate description of the ceremonies at Washington Square. Countless details may be found in the journals of the day, as well as in a little book by Myer Moses, entitled "Full Annals of the Revolution in France, 1830. To which is added a full account of the celebration of said Revolution in the City of New York" (New York, 1830). Of the ode, which he quotes in full, Moses writes: "Immediately after the oration, the following Ode, written by Samuel Woodworth, Esq., — a production of no ordinary merit — was sung by the entire band of choristers attached to the Park Theatre." The ceremonies were concluded at about three o'clock by the singing of the Marseillaise hymn and a *feu de joi* by the troops, after which, Mr. Moses tells us, "Dinner parties, balls, routes, and theatres — all these had their votaries and all were liberally patronized."

The only one of these festivities which concerns us is the Printers' repast at the Shakespeare Hotel, "prepared at a moment's notice in the host's usual style of profusion and elegance." The guests of honor were the members of the delegation of Albany printers, who had early voted to take part in the celebration, embodying in their resolutions, "That as printers we regard the influence of the Press in the event we celebrate as a signal instance of the benign effects flowing from our art."

Charles P. Webster, Chairman of the Albany delegation, gave the first toast: "The press — its liberty the pride of our citizens and the palladium of our rights — may it speedily be equally the pride and boast of every civilized country!"

John Lang, the leader of the printers in the procession, proposed "Worn-out types that have never been used for licentious purposes"; Samuel Woodworth gave them "The Civic Procession of November 26, 1830"; and another of the many toasts was to "Our Typographical Brethren of Paris — the men who quit their *shooting-sticks* for muskets, their *bodkins* for bayonets, their *mallets* for battering rams, their *balls* for bullets, whose *first proof* was a *correct impression*."

It is further reported that the printers separated at a seasonable hour, pleased with themselves and their guests, and "duly impressed with the taste, skill and accommodating spirit of their provider, — Mr. Stoneall."

The newspapers of the Monday following the procession predicted that all the participants and spectators would report it to their children's children as the most splendid pageant ever witnessed in the New World; and all this while the recollection of the unprecedented glories of the Erie Canal celebration of 1825 were still fresh in the minds of the citizens! Alas for the memories of departed splendor! The celebration of the French Revolution of 1830 is mentioned barely, if at all, in works on New York, and, besides the newspaper accounts, we have but Myer Moses's little-known volume, and a worn broadside or two, to recall in any fullness that "splendid pageant."

The Typographical Library and Museum, at Jersey City, has Woodworth's Ode in an entirely different setting from that of the broadside in the Library of the Grolier Club. It is elaborately printed in blue and red, on white satin, with a cut of a printing-press at the top, the paragraph asking all to unite in the chorus is omitted, and the last line reads: "J. Booth & Sons, Printers, New York." After some speculation on these variations, it was interesting to discover, among the advertisements of the *Morning Courier* for November 24, the following paragraph: "*Celebration Ode.* — The patriotic ode which has been written for this occasion, by S. Woodworth, will be printed on a moveable stage, and several thousand copies distributed to the citizens, during the grand procession, on the 25th inst. It will afterwards be sung, on the platform, in Washington Square, by all the vocalists of the Park Theatre, accompanied by the whole orchestra of that establishment, which have been obtained through the politeness of Mr. Simpson. Those who wish a copy with the music adapted can be supplied by Messrs. Firth and Hall, 358 Pearl Street, on Thursday morning. It is also understood that beautiful, *tri-coloured* copies, both on satin and paper, will be for sale at the office of the New York Mirror, Franklin Building, corner of Nassau Street and Ann Street, printed by Messrs. *Booth & Sons, solely* for the *benefit of the Author.*" Search has, so far, failed to reveal any of the tri-coloured copies on paper, as well as those with the "music adapted."

A copy of the broadside, from the Henry Cady Sturges collection, is now owned by the Library of Congress, and is like the one belonging to the Grolier Club. The Ode, in Woodworth's handwriting, is in a manuscript volume in the New York Public Library, as well as a copy of his Erie Canal broadside, already mentioned. The New York Historical Society possesses a broadside poem similarly printed during the celebration held in New York on July 23, 1788, in honor of the adoption of the Federal Constitution.

Thanks are gratefully expressed for information received from I. N. Phelps Stokes, from Thomas W. Hotchkiss, from Beatrice L. Becker, Acting Librarian of the Typographical Library and Museum, Jersey City, from H. H. B. Meyer of the Library of Congress, from Victor Hugo Paltsits of the New York Public Library, and from Alexander J. Wall, Librarian of the New York Historical Society. The kind interest of many librarians who have aided in the search for further copies of the broadsides is also acknowledged with much appreciation.

WALL–PAPER NEWSPAPERS OF THE CIVIL WAR

By CLARENCE S. BRIGHAM

Librarian of the American Antiquarian Society

ONE of the most interesting curiosities of the American Civil War, so far as printed matter is concerned, is the newspaper printed on wall-paper. Forced by scarcity of paper to print his journal on ledger paper, wrapping-paper and tissue paper, the enterprising Southern editor finally seized upon wall-paper as the final and despairing solution of his problem. Compelled to print on one side of the paper only, and frequently shorn of his advertisements, he gave to his readers only the military information, the local news, and occasional quotations from other journals. But in these newspapers published under such adverse conditions, there was a freshness of expression and a nearness to events quite a bit more interesting than the labored and prepared thought of earlier issues. And when the Union soldiers entered some of these Louisiana and Mississippi printing-offices, then the papers suddenly became Union organs for the time being, giving in their pages most graphic reminders of the fortunes of war.

When the subject of Civil War newspapers printed on wall-paper is mentioned, one primarily thinks of the famous *Vicksburg Daily Citizen* of July 4, 1863, which, because of its numerous facsimiles, is known rather generally. In fact most libraries, even those with the pretense of good newspaper collections, have only this one wall-paper journal, either occasionally in an original or, more likely, in a reproduction. Yet there were at least twelve other newspapers which in 1863 or 1864 were printed on wall-paper, and of these thirty-one different issues have been found. Doubtless this is but a small proportion of the total number of issues so printed. These papers are exceedingly scarce. They were published in small towns, the size of the edition was even smaller than usual, and the unsettled condition of affairs, with the male members of the family absent on the fighting line, was not conducive to the preservation of historical literature. The fact that nearly all of the numbers located are the only known issues indicates the rarity of those which have survived.

Of course it was the scarcity of print paper that forced the editors to use wall-paper. The South was almost entirely dependent on the North for paper. Of the 555 paper-making establishments in the United States in the year 1860, only 24 were in the South, and even these were mostly incapacitated by the war. What print paper could be secured was held at high prices. Paper which at the beginning of the war was eight cents per pound rose in November, 1862, to seventeen cents, and in 1863 to twenty-five cents and over. Other substitutes besides wall-paper were used. The *Opelousas Courier* of August 30, 1862, was printed on brown wrapping-paper, as was the *Port Hudson Freeman* of July 14, 1863. The *Natchitoches Union* extra of April 1, 1864, was printed on tissue paper, and the same journal of April 4, 1864, used a blue ledger paper. All these papers were of Louisiana, and of the copies seen the first three are in the Library of the American Antiquarian Society, and the last in the Library of Congress.

Why this wall-paper printing of newspapers was confined to Louisiana and Mississippi is not clear. Perhaps it was because there were no paper-makers in any of the Gulf States, what few factories there were in the South being located in the Atlantic seaboard states and in Tennessee. The newspapers of the North also had their difficulties with paper supply. They reduced the size of their sheets, imported paper from Europe, and even tried substitutes. The *Boston Journal*, for example, printed its entire edition of January 15, 1863, on a paper made from wood pulp, — basswood, — one of the earliest instances of what is now the universal practice.

Newspapers have occasionally been compelled to use substitutes for print paper even in more recent times; two examples of this are to be found in the Antiquarian Society collection. The *Whiting News*, of Whiting, Indiana, because of a railroad strike, printed its issue of July 6, 1894, on a bright-colored wall-paper; and the *Cowlitz County Advocate*, of Castle Rock, Washington, because of the high price of print paper, brought out an edition in November, 1916, on shingles, one of the greatest curiosities in American newspaper history.

There has been no attempt to consult all of the libraries in the country in the preparation of the list which follows. Most of the larger libraries have been visited or written to, as well as a few of the Southern libraries and private collections of Civil War Literature. It is to be hoped that the publication of this tentative list may bring to light additional copies, and even new titles. The abbreviations for the names of libraries used in the list follow:

AAS. American Antiquarian Society.
BA. Boston Athenæum.
BPL. Boston Public Library.
LC. Library of Congress.
LLL. Loyal Legion Library, Boston.
MHS. Massachusetts Historical Society.
Y. Yale Library.

Checklist of Issues

Alexandria, La. *The Pictorial Democrat*, April 15, 1863. No publisher's imprint or volume numbering. AAS, Y.
Editorial apologizes for paper upon which the issue is printed and promises "regular edition" soon. Alexandria was occupied by the Union troops May 7, 1863.

Alexandria, La. *The Southern Sentinel*, March 21, 1863, vol. 1, no. 1, T. G. Compton, Proprietor.
The editorial announcement in no. 1 apologizes for the quality of the paper, and states that all job work will have to be executed on the same paper. It says:
"Even the apology for printing paper which we are forced to use to print one page on, and which we will change for the better as soon as possi-

ble, costs us four and five times as much as a full sheet of four pages would have done two years since, and we are assured by our neighbor of the Democrat that each half sheet on which he now prints his paper costs him here 14½ cents, which is at the rate of $2.88 for paper alone, and as its subscription price is only $5. it is clear his expenses must be paid and his profits come from other sources — such as Government printing, advertising and job work — the first of which we do not expect, and of the last can do but little for want of proper paper."

—— Mar. 28, 1863, vol. 1, no. 2.   AAS.
—— Apr. 4, 1863, vol. 1, no. 3.   MHS.
—— May 16, 1863, vol. 1, no. 8.   LC.
A note in no. 8 says that, the editor having seceded, the paper is in charge of Wilson Millor, Lieut. & Sup. Govt. Printing. The Union forces entered Alexandria on May 7, but departed May 15, 1863.

—— Oct. 24, 1863, vol. 1, no. 34, T. G. Compton.   MHS.

Franklin, La. *Attakapas Register*, Mar. 5, 1863, Extra edition, vol. (?), no. 10. Upper right quarter only.   BA.
Franklin, La. *The Planters' Banner*, Feb. 5, 1863, Extra.   AAS.
No imprint or volume numbering. Entirely given over to President Jefferson Davis's Message of Jan. 12, 1863. The copy in the AAS has written upon it in pencil, "Found when Northern Troops entered Franklin."
    The Boston Athenæum has copies of this paper for Mar. 14 and Apr. 11, 1863, published by Daniel Dennett, but neither on wall-paper.

Franklin (Attakapas), La. *The Weekly Junior Register*, Feb. 12, 1863, vol. 2, no. 7, Jona. C. White & Son, Proprietors.   AAS.
—— Feb. 26, 1863, last half only.   BA.
—— Apr. 25, 1863, vol. 2, no. 16, published by White & Wing (Jona. C. White and Chas. G. Wing).   LLL.
This was a Union publication, as the Union troops had entered Franklin on April 14.
—— May 2, 1863.   BA.
—— May 9, 1863.   BA.

Montgomery, Ala. *Montgomery Daily Mail*, 1863–1864.
A file complete from Feb. 2, 1863 to Dec. 31, 1864, offered for sale by the A. H. Clark Co. in 1916, contained five issues printed on wall-paper. This file cannot now be traced.

Natchitoches, La. *Natchitoches Union*, Apr. 2, 1864 [no volume numbering]; Lt. Thos. Hughes, editor; Sgt. H. R. Crenshaw & Co., proprietors.   LC.
The Union troops entered Natchitoches March 31, 1864, and on April 1 brought out an Extra of the *Natchitoches Union*, on a poor grade of paper. Although the names of the Confederate publishers — Col. J. S. Brisbin as editor and L. Duplex as proprietor — were given in the imprint, the Extra was issued by Union soldiers. A copy is in AAS. Then came the wall-paper issue of April 2, 1864. The issue of April 4, 1864, a copy of which is in LC, was printed on blue ledger paper.

New Iberia, La. *Unconditional S. Grant*, Oct. 31, 1863, vol. 1, no. 2, publ. by Serg'ts Thorpe & Whitlock, of the 130th Ills. Regt. MHS.
The Union troops occupied New Iberia in October 1863, and brought out their own paper.

Opelousas, La. *The Opelousas Courier*, Dec. 13, 1862, vol. 11, no. 2, published by Joel H. Sandoz. LC.
In English and French.
—— Apr. 22, 1863, vol. 11, no. 22, publ. by Joel H. Sandoz. BPL.
In English and French. The French title "Le Courier des Opelousas" is dated Apr. 18, 1863.
The first issue after the arrival of the Union troops. Editorial reads: "We print this paper just as the form was left for us when the Confederate troops abandoned the town, merely adding for the benefit of the community such later items of news as have reached us through Southern sources. The picture they represent, though not cheerful, is of course the most favorable for their side."
—— April 25, 1863, vol. 11, no. 24, published by Joel H. Sandoz.
AAS, MHS.
This was the second issue brought out by the Union troops, after their occupation of Opelousas, April 20, 1863. Sandoz was one of the previous editors of the paper, and many of the advertisements of Southern residents were continued. The paper was conducted by officers of the 41st Massachusetts regiment.

St. Martinsville, La. *The Courier of the Teche*, Jan. 3, 1863, vol. 14, no. 1, published by R. T. Eastin & A. Dore. AAS.
Half English and half French, with the French title "Le Courier du Teche."
A Confederate issue.

Thibodaux, La. *La Sentinelle de Thibodaux*, Oct. 17, 1862, vol. 2, no. 29, published by François Sancan. AAS.
In French and English. A Confederate issue.
—— Oct. 25, 1862, vol. 2, no. 31. MHS.

Thibodaux, La. *The Stars and Stripes*, Feb. 24, 1863, publ. by McCloud and Lewis. AAS.
Edited by two Union soldiers during the occupation of Thibodaux. In their salutatory, they say "This is our first issue and it may be our last."

Vicksburg, Miss. *The Daily Citizen*, June 18, 1863; J. M. Swords, Proprietor. LC.
—— June 20, 1863. LC.
—— July 2, 1863. AAS.
The original issue of July 2, 1863, before the Union troops captured Vicksburg, does not have the "Note" of July 4, 1863 at the bottom of the last column.
—— July 2, 1863 ("Note" at bottom of last column, dated July 4, 1863);

J. M. Swords, Proprietor.   AAS, LC, MHS, etc.
The issue of July 4 is the same as the issue of July 2, except for the sub-
stitution of several new articles in the last column. When the Federal
troops entered the city, they found the paper set up for publication, and
they issued it, with an additional "Note" dated July 4, 1863, at the
bottom of the last column, stating the facts of the Federal occupation,
and concluding, "This is the last wall-paper edition, and is, excepting
this note, from the types as we found them. It will be valuable hereafter as a curiosity."

There are many facsimiles of the original, some of them difficult to
distinguish, as they were printed a half-century ago on early wall-paper,
and faithfully attempt to copy the type. Numerous defects in type or
spelling, however, identify the original, among them the following: in
the original the first word of the seventh line of the third paragraph of
the last column is spelled "Secossion"; the fourth word in the second line
of the second article of the last column is spelled "whisttle"; the last
word in the last article in the last column, preceding the "Note," is
printed with the quotation mark misplaced: 'dead' instead of dead."

Among the facsimiles noted are the following. The location of only
one copy is given.

1. An issue which is the nearest in facsimile of all the reproductions.
It does not possess the distinctions noted above, however, and prints the
last word in the second line of the poem in the second article of the last
column, thus: "a 'frightened." The copy seen has written upon it,
"This Paper is an exact copy of the papers printed in Vicksburg, during
the siege by Gen. Grant. I. B. Greenman, Jr."   AAS.

2. An issue with larger type for the article headings, thirteen dots in
the imprint between "J. M. Swords" and "Proprietor"; and "The
Recent Federal Losses at Vicksburg" as the second article of the last
column. This is probably the earliest reproduction. The copy in MHS
has written on the back, "J. Mason Warren, from Mrs. Joshua Davis,
1863"; the copy in AAS was given to the Society Jan. 28, 1867.
                                                              AAS, MHS.

3. An issue with "Vicksburgh" in the imprint of the first column, a
different line set-up, an absence of hand-pointers before the paragraphs,
and with the article heading "Yankee News From All Points" at the
bottom of the second column.   AAS.

4. An issue headed in large type "Fac-simile of the Daily Citizen."
Follows no. 2 in set-up.   AAS.

5. Supplement to the San Francisco Daily Report.   AAS.

6. "The Grant Edition of the Vicksburg Daily Citizen"; copyrighted
April 16, 1885. An additional fifth column contains the news of Grant's
death, and states that this paper can be obtained from Rider & Reynolds,
agents, Dunkirk, N. Y.   AAS.

7. "The Grant Edition of the Vicksburg Daily Citizen." No mention
of copyright and no fifth column. Abbreviated in the subject matter.
Different type and set-up from no. 6.   MHS.

8. Supplement to the Chicago Herald. AAS copy has pencilled "Aug. 1, 1885." AAS.

9. Supplement to the San Francisco Evening Bulletin, Aug. 8, 1885. AAS.

10. A facsimile which has in the last column only "Yankee News from all Points," "Gone Out," and the "Note" of July 4, 1863.

11. "The Vicksburg Daily Citizen. Set up for print July 2, 1863, before the surrender to Grant, and issued by his order July 4th. Copyright, 1886. Price, Five Cents." MHS.

12. Inserted article in the last column, entitled "Little Coquette." On the back a printed notice: "Keep this as a Memento of the War. It is a copy of the last newspaper printed on wall-paper in Vicksburg, Miss., during the siege. This valuable curiosity is presented to you by Hettie Bernard Chase, whose charming play, 'Little Coquette,' is founded upon incidents narrated in these columns." MHS.

13. "The Wall Paper Citizen. A facsimile reproduction of this famous paper issued in Vicksburg, Miss., July 4, 1863." One of the "Little Coquette" issues, with that article in the last column. LLL.

14. Similar to the two previously listed, but without the notice on the back or the descriptive heading. There may be other variants of this "Little Coquette" issue. AAS.

15. A facsimile with two printed lines at the top: "A facsimile copy of the last Vicksburg Rebel newspaper"; and on the upper left margin two lines: "Sold for the benefit of a one-armed soldier. Price 10 cts." LLL.

16. A facsimile with the following note at the bottom of the page: "This paper is copied from the original, printed by the Confederate Printer, Mr. Swords, at Vicksburg, Miss., on wall-paper, in 1863, and sold at that time for 20 cents a copy. Was taken possession of by the 8th Illinois (known as Oglesby) Regiment, to do the Government printing in," etc. AAS.

17. Facsimile reprinted and given away by Edmund N. Hatcher, author of "The Last Four Weeks of the War," which was published at Columbus in 1892. AAS.

18. Facsimile reprinted by A. F. Curchia, Melvern, Kansas. AAS.

19. Photographic facsimile issued as a Supplement to "Pep," October 1919. AAS.

20. The Grant edition of the Vicksburg Daily Citizen set up for print July 2, 1863, before the surrender to Grant, and issued by his order July 4th. On lower margin: "Souvenir G.A.R. Encampment, Indianapolis, Ind., September 20th to 25th, 1920." LLL.

Mr. President,—what is it, that has made England a sort of general banker for the civilized world? Why is it, that capital, from all quarters of the globe, accumulates at the centre of her empire, and is thence again distributed? Doubtless, sir, it is because she invites it, and solicits it. She sees the advantage of this. She manifests no weak or pretended jealousy of foreign influence, from the freest intercourse with the commercial world; and no British minister ever yet did a thing so rash, so inconsiderate, so startling, as to exhibit a groundless feeling of jealousy towards the introduction or employment of foreign capital.

Sir, of all the classes of society, the larger stockholders of

Mr. President,—what is it, that has made England a sort of general banker for the civilized world? Why is it, that capital, from all quarters of the globe, accumulates at the centre of her empire, and is thence again distributed? Doubtless, sir, it is because she invites it, and solicits it. She sees the advantage of this. She manifests no weak or pretended jealousy of foreign influence, from the freest intercourse with the commercial world; and no British minister ever yet did a thing so rash, so inconsiderate, so startling, as to exhibit a groundless feeling of jealousy towards the introduction or employment of foreign capital.

Sir, of all the classes of society, the larger stockholders of

Mr. President,—what is it, that has made England a sort of general banker for the civilized world? Why is it, that capital, from all quarters of the globe, accumulates at the centre of her empire, and is thence again distributed? Doubtless, sir, it is because she invites it, and solicits it. She sees the advantage of this; and no British minister ever yet did a thing so rash, so inconsiderate, so startling, as to exhibit a groundless feeling of dissatisfaction at the introduction or employment of foreign capital.

Sir, of all the classes of society, the larger stockholders of

Mr. President,—what is it, that has made England a sort of general banker for the civilized world? Why is it, that capital, from all quarters of the globe, accumulates at the centre of her empire, and is thence again distributed? Doubtless, sir, it is because she invites it, and solicits it. She sees the advantage of this; and no British minister ever yet did a thing so rash, so inconsiderate, so startling, as to exhibit a groundless feeling of dissatisfaction at the introduction or employment of foreign capital.

Sir, of all the classes of society, the larger stockholders of

Test passages from Webster's Speech at Worcester in 1832.

ANALYTICAL METHODS IN BIBLIOGRAPHY

Applied to Daniel Webster's Speech at Worcester in 1832

By CLIFFORD BLAKE CLAPP

Of the Henry E. Huntington Library, San Gabriel, California

THE early collectors of Americana set 1800 as the later limit of their practical interest. At the present time, fifty or seventy-five years later, it is logical to extend that interest at least to the end of the American Civil War. There is abundant material of bibliographical interest in pamphlets of 1800 to 1865. The present paper is written to illustrate the fact that the intelligent and curious bibliographer may find in the study of a plebeian pamphlet of the nineteenth century the same sorts of difficult and fascinating work that he finds in studying books connected with the achievements of printing and of a national literature, and with the early expansion of geographical knowledge, books which rank as the royalty and nobility of the bibliographical field.

We are dealing with an American political pamphlet of 1832, of which there were two title editions and two type editions, the four of which were crossed and recrossed by textual variations. The title editions in their normal form are as follows:

(1) Speech of the Hon. Daniel Webster at the National Republican Convention, in Worcester, Oct. 12, 1832. Boston: Stimpson & Clapp, 72 Washington Street, [J. E. Hinckley & Co., Printers, No. 14, Water Street] 1832. Octavo in fours; 6 sheets. 43 pp.

(2) Journal of the Proceedings of the National Republican Convention, held at Worcester, October 11, 1832. Boston: Stimpson & Clapp, 72 Washington Street. J E. Hinckley & Co., Printers, 14 Water Street, 1832. Octavo in fours; 10 sheets. 75 pp. Webster's speech occupies sheets 5–10, *i.e.*, pp. 33–75.

These two titles will be called for convenience the 'Speech' edition and the 'Journal' edition.

When these pamphlets were first under consideration, an inspection of several copies seemed to show that existence of these title editions in their normal forms with perfect pagination was the exception rather than the rule. The following collations were found:

1–43.   1–72, 41–43.   1–40, 9–43.   1–40, 73–75.   1–41, 74–75.

This confusion was caused chiefly by the combination of sheets from the 'Journal' edition with sheets from the 'Speech' edition; or at least by the combination of sheets having the 'Journal' pagination with sheets having the 'Speech' pagination.

A superficial examination showed remarkable variation in page-endings, and about a dozen copies were found to differ each in some respect from all the others. The deeper the penetration of the subject the greater grew the mystery, for textual variations were found on pages beginning and ending the same. Some of these variations were merely verbal changes such as Webster was in the habit of making, but in one case a passage was either added or deleted.

The study of these abnormalities has been absorbing and perplexing, so bewildering in fact that, time and again, the writer has despaired of coming to any presentable conclusions regarding the cause of the trouble and the order of the issues.

It was necessary to resolve the pamphlets into their several component sheets and treat each sheet as if it were a separate book. The speech itself, in whichever edition, is printed on six sheets — five with four leaves each and the last a half-sheet, or really a quarter-sheet, with two leaves. Sheets 1 to 6 of the 'Speech' edition correspond with sheets 5 to 10 of the 'Journal' edition, and, as was found after some study, are printed from the same settings of type. In this paper the sheet numbers are those of the speech portion unless designated as 'Journal' sheets 1 to 4; sheets 5 and 6 are either 5 and 6 of the 'Speech' or 9 and 10 of the 'Journal.'

There are variations in page-endings in each of the six sheets, running from two each in sheets 4 and 5 to eight in sheet 2. An early step in the examination of the sheets consisted in placing the copies in order by sameness or likeness of page-endings or other characteristics of one or another page. By numerous experiments it was found that in any attempt to arrange all the copies of sheet 2 in order by one or two characteristics the copies were thrown out of order by some other characteristic, the characteristics that seemingly ought to agree alternating or more often going back to the starting-point. There seemed to be no way to break into these circles but by concluding that there were two distinct editions not corresponding to the 'Journal' and 'Speech' editions, or else that there had been some monstrous practices in printing the sheets. The former was in fact the case. But the latter alternative led the writer into a most interesting study of the "half-sheet" or "work and turn" method, which was that by which these pamphlets were printed, and a tentative hypothesis regarding these issues, which ultimately ran into absurdity.

Too much reliance on page-endings had blinded the writer to the fact that there were two type editions, and led to neglect of opportunities for procuring and comparing copies, and the consequences of this mistake have not yet been fully remedied by adequate photostat evidence.

The pamphlets are printed in a small pica type of two slightly different varieties, so similar as not to be readily distinguished, so far as most of the characters are concerned. In the type that we shall call A the roman g is remarkable for its small head, and the question mark has a straight shaft; but in type B the question mark is curved throughout, and the upper and lower parts of the g are relatively of one size.

It was found, after a time, that differences in page-endings were due in part to the fact that two presses, using these different types A and B, were in operation at the same time: one apparently copying the composition of the other, giving parallel but not identical results. The differences in endings were due also to textual variations. The discovery of both or all textual variants in both type editions was the longest step toward a satisfactory analytical study of the pamphlet.

Each textual variant, or rather for convenience each combination of such variants on a single page, in each type (in whichever of the two page-numberings) became a unit character to be branded and always recognized; and each copy of the pamphlet had to be analyzed for its unit characters and its pedigree determined by the successive variations these units went through. In this study thirteen copies (here designated by letters of the alphabet), all different, most of them seen "in the flesh" or in part by photostat, and a few of them merely reported to the writer, have come under the knife on the bibliographical dissecting table.

A few of the textual variations may be noted by way of example without taking the space to explain an entire combination making up a page or unit character, or to indicate the page-endings or other brands used to trace them in the writer's tabulation. In the first full paragraph on page 13 (page 45 of the 'Journal') in sheet 2, there occurs in some copies a passage reading: "She [England] manifests no weak or pretended jealousy of foreign influence, from the freest intercourse with the commercial world." Other copies lack this passage and have another difference in the same paragraph. Both textual versions of this paragraph occur in type *A* and in type *B*; both versions occur in copies of the pamphlet having the paging and title-page of the 'Speech' edition. Both versions occur in copies having the title-page of the 'Journal' edition; but this sheet, when with the 'Journal' pagination, has been found only in type *A* and without the "freest intercourse" passage. In one copy having this passage the words are "by reason of the freest" instead of "from the freest."

Elsewhere on the same page there are verbal corrections occurring in both type editions. One version reads "and this, in time, will" where the other reads "and this, will"; one has "scarcity for money," the other "scarcity of money"; and one reads "And all this, on the pretended" where the other reads "And all this is to be suffered, on the pretended." Such verbal alterations to meet Webster's exacting taste occur throughout the speech. A few only can be mentioned: on page 10 we find either "shows that" or "makes good that assertion"; on page 11, "maintain it" or "maintain that system"; on page 14, "by the people of the United States" or "by the people"; and on page 16, "derived from" or "derived, as is supposed, from." Every sheet in the speech has examples of these slight changes, but it is in sheets 1, 4, and 5 that, because of identical beginning and ending of pages in identical type, small textual changes are the least easily discovered. In one case, when a change was made on page 40, the syllable "com" slipped out of the word "command" and joined with another word forming "com-| moderation"; it is curious that in the other type- and title-editions there are copies with the spelling "moder-| tion."

When the language of the speech is improved, either by smoothing or strengthening, in characteristic Websterian fashion, and when the better language is identical with the version in the collected editions of Webster's speeches, the improved form is in all probability the later. There are enough such alterations to give us a basis for an almost certain judgment between most of the issues of the unit characters occurring in the same type, and therefore between the issues of the pamphlets in which the sheets are entirely or mostly in a single type. As between the two types, however, and as between the 'Journal' and the 'Speech,' it is most difficult to assign an order of printing and issue. As to the types, nothing has yet been discovered that *proves* one type edition to have been copied from the other in any particular sheet; but the observed uniformity of the two editions, as well as the convenience to the compositors and binders, makes it probable that one was copied from the other.

That one title-edition was converted into the other is absolutely certain from the fact that the type of the 'Journal' and the 'Speech' have the same setting and have the same broken letters and typographical slips. Two cases of page-numbering, one where an 11 is inverted, the other where a leaf is numbered on the recto 41 and on the verso 74, have some bearing on this conversion.

Judgment on the order of type- and title-editions may in some degree be based on interpretation of the curiosities in the method of binding the sheets together. The singularities of pagination are mentioned at the beginning of this paper. In several copies of the speech, sheets with types A and B have been found mixed as follows:

$$A\ A\ A\ A\ A$$
$$A\ B\ B\ B\ B\ B$$
$$B\ B\ B\ B\ B\ B$$
$$B\ B\ B\ B\ B\ A$$
$$A\ B\ B\ B\ B\ A$$

In the four sheets, 'Journal' 1–4, preceding the 'Speech,' the types have so far been found only in the order $A\ A\ B\ B$.

No final judgment on the order of issue of copies of the entire pamphlet can yet be made. Certain versions of portions of the text reported to the writer are still a mystery. Certain sheets, notably the last, seem to recur absurdly in older versions after being supplanted by the newer. There would almost seem to have been a studied avoidance, on the part of the binder, of providing a complete inviolate copy of the 'Journal.'

On the basis of all the factors mentioned in this study, the present writer has come to an approximate decision as to the order of events in the offices of the printers. It seems to him that in the beginning two presses were put to work on the 'Journal,' press A printing the first and second sheets and press

B the third and fourth. Either *A* or *B* went on with the six 'Speech' sheets. One press seems to have copied from the other. The demand for the 'Speech' had already begun, and no sheets of the speech portion were printed at this time with the 'Journal' pagination; but 'Speech' sheets 1 to 6 of type *A* with the earliest version of the text were set aside to be bound with the first four 'Journal' sheets. They were not actually issued until after five varieties of the 'Speech' had been put out. The first four varieties, known to the writer as A, B, C, and D, are mostly, but not purely, *B* types, and are chiefly distinguished by their including two versions of sheet 6 in type *A* and two in type *B*. The fifth variety of the pamphlet, called E, is a pure *A* type. It has a second version of page 13 and the second version of page 42 in type *A*. Following the issue of this variety of the pamphlet, the convention 'Journal' must have been bound and issued, using the first sheets set aside, consequently with wrong paging and an already incorrect textual version. Next appeared a new variety of the speech in the *B* type, which we have named H, this copy noticeably with changed versions of pages 13 and 19 for this type.

Up to this time the "freest intercourse" passage on page 13 had remained. It was now taken out by both presses, and K and L were issued in the *A* and *B* types respectively, except that the last sheet of L is in type *A*. Three further type *B* varieties followed, probably in the order called by the writer M, R, and Z. One or another of these had changes in every sheet from the forms of 'Speech' H; sheet 2 being altered in L, sheet 3 in L and again in M, sheets 4 and 5 probably in L, and sheet 6 in Z.

The remaining remarkable point is that sometime during the publication of these *B* type 'Speech' pamphlets another 'Journal' issue appeared entirely in the *A* type, but with the last sheet in the 'Speech' edition, while the 'Speech' varieties R and Z in the *B* type have the last sheet in the 'Journal' paging, the one in the *A* and the other in the *B* type. The second 'Journal' issue involved, of course, the changing of page numbers.

The final textual version of the pamphlets was probably reached between K and N in type *A*, and (except for sheet 6) between L and M in type *B*.

The causes of all this varying printing and promiscuous binding are more readily to be discerned than the detailed facts given above might seem to indicate. In 1832, it was only two years since Webster had made himself the master of American statesmen in the contention between Union and Secession, between Constitutionalism and Nullification. By his great 'Reply to Hayne,' delivered in the Senate on January 26, 1830, he had so captivated popular admiration that about forty thousand copies of that speech were issued from the *National Intelligencer* office and perhaps twenty different editions were printed elsewhere. Webster's fame as orator and statesman, with the existing political situation, was sufficient to produce a demand for the speech at Worcester in October, 1832, that was difficult for the printers to meet.

Even with the insistent demand, however, there was nothing in the speech or in the method of printing it that need have caused so much confusion in the publication office or the printer's shop, had it not been for the orator himself. Webster must have stepped in several times, as was his habit, to stop the presses and make alterations in the text of his speech. He used to prepare his manuscripts himself for the printer, and there is adequate evidence not only that he was careful of their original form but that their details were the ground of much solicitude. If he saw a chance to improve them, either by clarifying the thought or by strengthening the rhetoric, he would make changes, whether before or during printing or on the occasion of republication in after years.

Most of the changes found in the Worcester speech are

merely matters of style; that concerning freedom of intercourse must be considered in the light of the politics of the time and the remainder of the speech. It would be too long to explain here, but when so considered it is evident that the passage on "freest intercourse" was deleted for fear it should be misinterpreted as a commendation of free trade, whereas it was not so intended. That it was deleted is shown also in the fact that it does not occur in the collected editions in which this speech is found, which had the approval of Webster himself.

It is apparent that the demand for copies of the speech interfered with the plan of issuing the 'Journal' at the start, so that it was issued later using unrevised 'Speech' sheets having the pagination of the 'Speech' edition. It was later reissued with revised sheets, the 'Speech' settings having their page numbers altered; but this issue has so far not been found with the 'Journal' numbering of the last sheet. It is apparent that both presses were put to work on the entire speech, and that the demand was so insistent that whatever sheets were immediately available, whether old or revised, were put together and sent out. Sometimes press *A* was ready with sheets and sometimes *B* was ready, but it was not thought to matter so long as the sheets were there. Webster interfered two or three times, going through the entire speech at least once to make small changes, and the discarded sheets could not always be kept from publication when the revised sheets were not ready. This was particularly the case with the last sheet, number 6, which is wrongly bound with other sheets at least a third of the time and has not yet been noticed in the 'Journal' edition bound with other 'Journal' sheets.

The two title editions, the two type editions, the urgent demand for copies, and the revision by the author while the work was being printed, present a remarkable, perhaps unique, case, and we may never see anything else in modern printing quite so intricate.

Proposals

By MILLS DAY, *New-Haven*,

FOR PUBLISHING BY SUBSCRIPTION,

AN EDITION OF THE

HEBREW BIBLE,

FROM THE TEXT OF

VAN-DER-HOOGHT.

PROSPECTUS.
....

BIBLICAL criticism, which, during the infancy of our country, has been left, almost exclusively, to the men of learning in Europe, is beginning to assume a new aspect in the United States. Theological controversy, though often conducted with a spirit unfavourable

CAPUT II.

ו/ ויכלו השמים והארץ וכל צבאם : ויכל אלהים ביום

2/ השביעי מלאכתו אשר עשה וישבת ביום השביעי מכל

3/ מלאכתו אשר עשה : ויברך אלהים את יום השביעי

ויקדש אתו כי בו שבת מכל מלאכתו אשר ברא

4/ אלהים לעשות : אלה תולדות השמים והארץ בהבראם

5/ ביום עשות יהוה אלהים ארץ ושמים : וכל שיח השדה

טרם יהיה בארץ וכל עשב השדה טרם יצמח כי לא

המטיר יהוה אלהים על הארץ ואדם אין לעבד את

6/ האדמה : ואד יעלה מן הארץ והשקה את כל פני האדמה :

7/ וייצר יהוה אלהים את האדם עפר מן האדמה ויפח באפיו

8/ נשמת חיים ויהי האדם לנפש חיה : ויטע יהוה אלהים

MILLS DAY'S PROPOSED HEBREW BIBLE

By OSCAR WEGELIN

Of New York City

THE first edition of John Eliot's translation of the New Testament in the Mohegan dialect was the earliest version of the Scriptures printed in the English colonies in any language. This epoch-making volume was issued from the press of Samuel Green and Marmaduke Johnson, at Cambridge, Massachusetts, in September, 1661. The Old Testament was added to it two years later. In the latter part of the seventeenth century (about 1695) the justly celebrated Cotton Mather projected what he called a 'Biblia Americana,' and issued a prospectus asking support for printing it. No printer could be found in the colonies, however, who would, or could, undertake so hazardous an enterprise,[1] and it was not until 1743 that a Bible or part of the Scriptures was printed in a European language in the colonies. This was the well-known 'Sauer Bible,' the printer of which was one of the most enterprising of colonial typographers. His establishment was at Germantown, near Philadelphia. There the first version of Holy Writ in an Old-World language was printed in German.

In or about 1752, a Bible is supposed to have been printed in the establishment of Kneeland and Green, in Boston. This book bore, according to Isaiah Thomas,[2] the imprint of a London printer. No copy that can be authenticated has been unearthed, although a Bible purporting to be a copy of this edition, and bearing date of 1752, was sold in Part VI of the McKee sale on May 12, 1902. It sold there for $2025.[3]

1. O'Callaghan, American Bibles. Albany, 1861.

2. History of Printing in America. Worcester, 1810. Second edition, Albany, 1874.

3. Dr. Charles L. Nichols discussed this Bible in "Is there a Mark Baskett Bible of 1752?" Transactions of the Colonial Society of Massachusetts, 21:285–291.

A Bible was projected by John Fleming of Boston, who issued a prospectus which states that it is (or was to be) the first Bible ever printed in America. This was about 1760. Fleming was a Scotchman, and ran a printing office in Boston.

In 1777 Robert Aitken printed in Philadelphia the New Testament, and this was the first version of the Scriptures in English that bears an American imprint. In 1782 Aitken printed his celebrated Bible, containing both the Old and the New Testaments.

William Woodhouse of Philadelphia issued in 1788 'The Christian's New and Complete Family Bible.' This book was, however, printed at Berwick, England, and the sheets sent to America. It is very rare, and O'Callaghan, who had not located a copy, gives the date as 1790. A copy is in the collection of the American Bible Society.

The first Roman Catholic Bible was issued by Mathew Carey in Philadelphia. The first number was published December 12, 1789. It appeared complete on December 1, 1790. It is believed to be the first quarto Bible published in English in the United States.

Hugh Gaine printed a New Testament in New York in 1790, and Hodge, Allen & Campbell issued the Holy Bible in the same year in that city. Isaac Collins of Trenton, New Jersey, printed the first Bible issued in that state in 1791.

The first Greek Testament printed in the United States was issued from the establishment of Isaiah Thomas, Jr., of Worcester, Massachusetts, and is dated April, 1800. The first French (New) Testament was issued from the press of J. T. Buckingham, in Boston, in 1810.

It was not until 1814 that an edition of the Bible in Hebrew was printed in the United States, and it remained for Thomas Dobson, an enterprising publisher of Philadelphia, to have the honor of having been the pioneer in issuing the Scriptures in the original tongue. The title of this book is:

[Line in Hebrew] Hebraica, Secundum ultimam Editionem Jos. Athiæ, a Johanne Leusden Denuo recognitam, Recensita Variisque Notis Latinis illustrata ab Everardo Van Der Hooght, V. D. M. Editio Prima Americana, sine punctis Masorethicis. Tom. I. Philadelphiæ: Cura et Impensis Thomæ Dobson edita ex Ædibus Lapideis Typis Gulielmi Fry. MDCCCXIV. 2 volumes, 8vo.

Mr. O'Callaghan, in a note to this title, writes:

In 1812 Mr. Horwitz had proposed the publication of this edition of the Hebrew Bible, the first proposal of the kind in the United States; early in 1813 he transferred his right and list of subscribers to Mr. Thomas Dobson, who published, soon afterwards, the 1st volume; the title page and preface were furnished with the 2d volume; with which they are bound in some instances.

Several years prior to the printing of the above, an attempt had been made to issue a Hebrew Bible in America, and had the project succeeded, it would not only have had the distinction of being the first issue of the Scriptures in that ancient tongue in America, but it is more than probable that had it appeared, it would have deterred Dobson from issuing his edition. All that is known of this early attempt is a "Proposal," with Chapter I and part of Chapter II of Genesis, which were printed as a specimen of the type to be used.

The title may be seen on the accompanying facsimile of the first page. The prospectus, including the sample specimen of type, consists of eight pages. The 'Conditions' are dated New-Haven, March 20, 1810. Beneath these 'Conditions,' which state that the work will be in "two volumes of about 500 pages each, and costing the Subscribers $3.25 per volume," is a blank for the names of prospective subscribers, the number of copies which they would subscribe for, and their place of residence.

In the prospectus before the writer are two names of subscribers, written in ink. They are Joab Bruce, Wethersfield and John Hyde, Hamden. Each was put down for one copy. Several other copies of this prospectus have been examined, and none of them contained more than five or six names of those who were interested in subscribing for a copy of the Bible. This seems proof conclusive that the publisher met with little success in his attempt to obtain subscriptions.

Subscription papers were "to be returned to Walter, Austin & Co., Booksellers, New-Haven, by the 1st of July." "If papers with but a single name affixed, are transmitted, it will enable the publisher to ascertain, with greater precision, the demand there will be for the books." The books were to be "transmitted to the most considerable towns in the United States, where it will be most convenient for subscribers to call for them." It was stated furthermore that if the publisher met with sufficient encouragement, he would also issue 'Parkhurst's Hebrew Lexicon and Grammar.' To insure correctness, the proof-sheets, "after the last reading, were to be exposed in some public place near the College, and a premium of five dollars offered for the detection of an error of the press in the text."

It was thought best to omit the *Points*, for reasons which are given in the 'Proposals,' and he makes the statement that he "is very far from presuming to attempt any improvement upon the Hebrew Bibles in Common use." Van Der Hooght's edition was preferred, as it was the one with the best reputation as a standard work.

In his 'Proposals,' Day states that "at a time when an important controversy is commencing in the United States, involving on one side, the charge of idolatry, and on the other, the imputation of denying the Saviour in his essential character, an American edition of the Hebrew Bible seems peculiarly seasonable." "This will give the divine immediate access to the fountain of truth; and enable him, without the fear of being misguided by the errours or prejudice of translators, to examine and judge for himself, whether the Messiah is represented, in the Jewish Scriptures, as a created being, or a divine character." "From these advantages our clergy have been in some measure precluded, by the dearness and scarcity of Hebrew books. An apology for this deficiency in biblical learning, has also been found, in the general inattention of our countrymen to theological criticism. But the times are changing. Disputes on theological subjects are gaining ground. . . . The study of Hebrew is introduced into most of our theological schools. In a few years, an acquaintance with this language will be as essential to the reputation of a clergyman, as was a liberal education, a century ago. Our young clergy and theological students, who neglect to avail themselves of the earliest opportunity of acquiring at least a partial knowledge of Hebrew, will necessarily be subjected to the mortification of a conscious inferiority to their brethren in the ministry. In view of these considerations an edition of the Hebrew Bible has been undertaken.'' ·

Those who received the 'Proposals,' evidently did not agree in large numbers to the foregoing, nor did they subscribe to it sufficiently to enable the publisher to proceed with the printing, and the credit of having issued the first Hebrew Bible in America must go to Thomas Dobson of Philadelphia.

It seems unfortunate that Day was not given sufficient encouragement by the theologians and scholars of New England, for had his venture proved successful, it would have added further glory to that section of our country — the first to issue the Scriptures in any tongue, and according to Isaiah Thomas the birthplace of the first English printed Bible in the English colonies. It is however to the credit of Pennsylvania that not only were the first Bibles in English (unless the Kneeland and Green issue can be proved) and German, as well as the first Douay versions, issued in that Commonwealth, but that the first Hebrew Bible should have issued from a press located in its principal city.

That Dobson deserves much credit, goes without saying, but Mills Day, of New Haven, Connecticut, should at least be remembered as having been the first to attempt to issue a Hebrew Bible. That he did not succeed was due to no fault of his, but to the lack of patronage which he encountered.

The sample of type in Hebrew, which is shown in the 'Proposals' proves that, had the Bible appeared, it would have been at least a fair specimen of typography, but nothing in the 'Proposals' gives a clue as to the printer who was to do the work. The publisher states that he "flatters himself, that by employing a distinct type, rejecting the points, and comparing the proof-sheets with the large Bibles of Van-Der-Hooght and Kennicott, he will possess every advantage for giving an edition typographically correct."

He also states that "a font of type, at double the usual expence, must be procured" and that "the printer must receive a double compensation for his part of the execution." He appeals to "the friends of sacred science and the patrons of the arts in America." He also offers a copy "gratis" to any one who would obtain twelve subscriptions and become responsible for their payment, but his efforts were in vain and his "proposed" Bible must be forever classed as an unpublished book.

Mills Day was the son of Reverend Jeremiah and Abigail Day, and was born at New Preston, Connecticut, on the thirtieth day of September, 1783. He graduated from Yale in 1803, and became a tutor in that college. He died June 20, 1812, at the early age of twenty-nine, and although nearly two years elapsed from the issuing of the 'Proposals' to the date of his demise, it may be possible that that event caused the stopping of the printing of his proposed Hebrew Bible.

A TRANSLATION OF THE ROSETTA STONE

By RANDOLPH G. ADAMS

Librarian of the William L. Clements Library, University of Michigan

IN the second century B.C., Ptolemy Epiphanes sat on the throne of the Pharaohs, a descendant of that Ptolemy who took over Egypt as his share of the division of Alexander the Great's Empire. At one time in the career of this monarch, the priests at Memphis desired to do him honor and passed a set of resolutions to that purpose. These they ordered to be published in three of the languages current at the time, which was done, among other places, on that block of black stone which some French engineers unearthed at Rosetta during the Napoleonic invasion of Egypt in 1798. Bonaparte at once saw the importance of this trilingual inscription, since it contained the unknown hieroglyphic and demotic writing side by side with the Greek, by means of which the others might be deciphered. He had copies of the inscription made and dispatched to France for "the examination of the learned throughout Europe."[1] The stone itself fell into the hands of the British commander when the French troops capitulated. That a "noble general with his usual zeal for science" thus gained the treasure for the British Museum was a great disappointment to the French, but it did not deter them from undertaking the first translation.[2]

In 1802 a querulous Englishman wrote to the *Gentleman's Magazine* that a "Frenchman has undertaken the explanation of the most difficult inscription before the English literati are in possession of a single copy of the easiest."[3] From this time on the field was open to all who wished to try to resolve the hieroglyphic and demotic inscriptions with the aid of the par-

1. *Gentleman's Magazine*, LXXI, 1194.
2. *Archæologia*, XVI, 208.   3. Vol. LXXII, 725–726.

allel Greek. The first translation of these difficult texts was
probably made by the Englishman Thomas Young, whose
findings were used by the French scholar Champollion. Other
continental scholars worked over the texts with more or less
improvement before the first translation was made in the
United States.

The first Americans who undertook the task, so far as I have
ascertained, were three undergraduate students at the University of Pennsylvania. Their efforts resulted in the production of a rather remarkable volume. In the year 1855 a plaster
cast of the Rosetta Stone was presented to the Philomathean
Society of that University by Thomas K. Conrad, one of the
members of the graduating class of that year. The Philomathean is one of those literary societies that are found in pairs
in all the American colleges whose existence dates from the
eighteenth century. Primarily a debating society, it had been
accustomed from time to time to issue little publications,
mostly the text of orations delivered before it by old-fashioned
Philadelphia lawyers.

When Conrad presented the cast to the Society, he is said to
have "read a paper on the subject," but in the minutes of the
organization I have not found any evidence of this. The manuscript records of the Society are still preserved, but are disap-
pointingly silent until September 22, 1855, when we find that a
committee was appointed to haul the cast up to the rooms of
the Society. "A rosetta stone," the secretary insists on calling
it. It may still be seen in the Society's present rooms.

Three undergraduate members of the Society, Charles R.
Hale, S. Huntington Jones, and Henry Morton volunteered to
make a translation. Many years later Morton wrote down his
recollection of the beginnings of this work. Hale undertook the
translation of the Greek and demotic texts, Jones prepared an
essay on the historical significance of Ptolemy Epiphanes,
while Morton took care of the hieroglyphic inscription and

the pictorial decoration of the whole. Their contribution to Egyptology need not detain us here. Morton says, "The work progressed slowly, as it involved much study of books not readily accessible and both the present writer and Mr. Hale spent many days of more than one vacation in the Astor Library in New York, as well as in the Philadelphia Library, where only certain expensive works on Egyptology and Hieroglyphics were to be seen. Among these, one of the most important was that of 'Lepsius,' which contained a complete drawing of the inscription on the temple wall at Philæ, which proved to be another copy of the inscription covering the Rosetta Stone. This Philæ inscription was, in great part effaced, but a careful collation of what remained (made for the first time by this committee) enabled them to throw a new light on many otherwise doubtful passages of the Rosetta Stone text." [4]

On March 29, 1857, "The final Report of the Committee on the translation of the Rosetta Stone" was laid before the Society. The resolution thanking the members of the Committee for their labors indicates that Morton did the greater part of the hard work. The manuscript was elaborately illuminated and appropriately bound. But it very shortly disappeared from the Philomathean Library and for several months was supposed to be lost. When it was recovered, the prospect of another and permanent loss resulted in the following resolution: "The Society deem the Report of the Rosetta Stone Committee, including the translation, worthy of publication, and that it would be for the honor of the Society and the University." The officials at once negotiated with the translators and reported that Messrs. Hale and Morton "had a plan" for reproducing the book, which the Society accepted and returned the precious manuscript to the original committee. The trans-

4. A History of the Philomathean Society of the University of Pennsylvania (Philadelphia, 1913), p. 65.

lators requested that they be regarded as a firm of publishers and promised on their part "1st, they will lithograph the book as it now stands in fac-simile, with the following exceptions: they will omit the large plate representing the coronation ceremonies, they will insert a plate representing the temple of Phtha at Memphis, and also a plate representing the Rosetta Stone as it now stands in the British Museum, also a continuing copy of the hieroglyphics." Copies were to be sold for $2.50 to members and $2.75 to non-members.[5]

Moreover, it is recorded that a resolution of thanks was passed by the Society on the presentation of a volume on Egyptian hieroglyphics, which may still be seen, bearing the inscription "12 January, 1858, Presented to the Philomathean Society of the University of Pennsylvania by their former associate, Henry D. Gilpin." This gentleman was a well-known Philadelphia lawyer, antiquarian and bibliophile, who had been Attorney-General of the United States under Van Buren.[6]

At that time the only possible way of reproducing the hieroglyphic and demotic texts and the colored illuminations and illustrations was by chromo-lithography and the expense of preparing the necessary and numerous drawings, if done by professional artists, was prohibitive. Henry Morton set to work to acquire a new craft and engrave the stones. One of the best-known lithographers of the day was Max Rosenthal of Philadelphia. I am informed by Mr. Albert Rosenthal, the Philadelphia artist and etcher, and son of Max Rosenthal, that the plates are the work of the combined efforts of young Morton and his father. "Technically the pen work on stone and the stippling is of a character used by Max Rosenthal and first employed in lithography by him in America," Mr. Albert

5. Minutes, Dec. 11, 1857, Jan. 13, 1858, Jan. 15, 1858, and Jan. 22, 1858.

6. Précis Du Système Hiéroglyphique Des Anciens Egyptiens, par M. Champollion le Jeune, Seconde édition, Imprimé, Par Autorisation . . . A L'Imprimerie Royale, M.DCCC.XXVII; Edward Everett. The Historical Magazine with Notes and Queries, IV, 91 (1860).

Rosenthal writes me. Throughout his long life, Mr. Max Rosenthal often had occasion to discuss this book and he seems to have regarded it as one of the most remarkable pieces of work in which he had ever participated.

Every page had to be lithographed from one or more stones, and presumably the volume that finally appeared was as near like the original illuminated manuscript as was possible. Nearly every page has a highly colored border of Egyptian design, occupying in many cases as much of the area of the page as the text itself. The text is reproduced in the original handwriting of the translators and not in any type form. What became of the original manuscript, it is impossible to say.

THE FIRST EDITION

THE title of the first edition reads:

'Report | of the | Committee | appointed by the | Philoma-thean | Society | of the | University of | Pennsylvania | to trans-late the inscription on the | Rosetta Stone. |'

There is no date or place of publication on the title-page. The Preface states that it was printed "at the establishment of L. N. Rosenthal, N. W. corner of Fifth and Chestnut Sts., Phila.," and bears the date August 3, 1858. The last leaf is dated December 14. The title-page is an inserted plate, for the signatures begin with the dedication page which reads "Dedi-cated to The Hon. Henry D. Gilpin, Late Attorney General of the United States by The Authors." The book is a small quarto, 23 by 18 cm.

The pagination can be checked as follows, the bracketed number indicating unnumbered pages: Title, [1–8] 9–17 [18–19] 20–21 [22–23] 24 [25–33] 34–35 [36–37] 38–39 [40] 41–72, 81 [82–83] 84–104 [105] 106–127 [128] 113 [114–115] 116–117 [118–119] 120, 129–136. Twelve unnumbered leaves follow page 136, completing the volume. The explanation of the ap-parently missing pages from page 72 to page 81 is probably this: page 81 is where Morton's translation of the hieroglyphic text begins, and thereafter the text is in his handwriting. Up to this point the text is in Hale's handwriting. Evidently the work on these two sections proceeded simultaneously, and the translators had to guess at the pagination for the later section, which they missed by an entire signature. The same explanation fits the second inconsistency in the pagination which is seen when after page 128 the numbering of pages goes back to page 113. Two whole signatures are here taken up with Jones's essay on Ptolemy and page 129 is picked up immediately following the *second* page numbered 120. Thus half of Jones's essay is numbered correctly and half is not. The entire text consisted of twenty unmarked signatures in fours.

The first edition consisted of four hundred copies and was bound in at least two different styles of paper boards. Some were in brown with gold lettering and ornamentation, some were in maroon with black lettering and ornamentation. The designs on the binding were uniform. By the time the translators got to the binding they had evidently acquired a sufficient knowledge of hieroglyphics to compose in that writing and so the covers of the first edition bear an ingenious inscription, which, when translated back into English would run as follows: "Hieroglyphic writing, demotic writing and Greek writing on a tablet brought from Egypt, made into English by those appointed (that is, a Committee) of a wisdom-loving society (that is, the Philomathean Society) belonging to a large house where six wise men (or scribes) speak to a multitude of young men (that is, the University); together with many good words about the King of Egypt, Ptolemy." Evidently, as we can see from the Appendix, it was intended that the binding should bear an even more flowery legend in Greek, but there was not room for it and the artist never went back to correct his text. With such a cover, it is obvious that rebinding injures very much the value of any first edition.

The Second Edition

"Shortly before Christmas, 1858," relates Morton, "the first edition of this report made its appearance, and was so highly appreciated by the public that in a few days the entire edition was exhausted and many times the original price was offered by those anxious to secure them." [7]   It is not surprising then that barely four weeks after the appearance of the first edition we find work well under way for the preparation of the second edition. From that edition itself we glean only the information that "The Society at their meeting on January 21, 1859, having expressed their desire that a second edition of this report should be printed, the work was at once proceeded with by the above named committee." A few days later the Society directed that the second edition should not exceed six hundred copies and the price should not be less than five dollars a copy.[7]

But the task that faced the Committee was by no means so simple as it might seem from such brief statements in the record. Lithographing in those days was used for the reproduction of a single picture here and there in the illustration of books and periodicals. But the demand was so far from great that it could be cared for by a comparatively small number of stones. No lithographing establishment in Philadelphia, nor, is it likely, even in America at that time, kept on hand a sufficient number of stones of the required size for the production of such a volume as this, where several stones were required to print each page. When the first few pages of the first edition had been printed, Morton and Rosenthal had to hold up their work while the stones were ground down to a new surface and were ready to receive a new engraving. "Thus," says Morton "when the Society desired its Committee to print a new edition, only the stones used in the last twenty pages or so, retained any designs, and thus the printing of a new edition involved the production on stone of more than a hundred

7. Minutes, Jan. 23, 1859.

drawings. The second edition was, in its artistic portion, largely a new work." [8]

The title-page of the second edition is:

' Report | of the | Committee | appointed by the | Philoma-thean | Society | of the | University of | Pennsylvania | to trans-late the inscription on the | Rosetta Stone. | Second Edition. |'

The size is the same as the first edition. The Preface is a re-print of the first edition and so bears the same date.

The pagination of the second edition may be checked as be-fore, the bracketed figures indicating the unnumbered pages. Title, [1–8] 9–10 [11] 12–26, 26 (repeated) 32,29–31 [32–33] 34–35 [36–37] 38–39 [40] 41–57 [58–59] 60–70 [71] 72–97, 106, 99–102, 111, 104–111, 211, 121, 114–115, 124–125, 118–119 [120] 121–152. Then follow four unnumbered leaves that complete the volume. Page 27 is obviously misnumbered 26, page 28 is misnumbered 32, page 98 is misnumbered 106, page 103 is mis-numbered 111, page 112 is misnumbered 211, but the figure 2 is not reversed. Page 113 is misnumbered 121, page 116 is mis-numbered 124 and page 117 is misnumbered 125. Again the book comprises twenty unmarked signatures.

The great puzzle as to which pages of the second edition were printed from the plates of the first edition and for which pages new plates had to be engraved can be resolved only by the following table.

8. A History of the Philomathean Society, p. 68.

Page number of first edition	Corresponding page in second edition when different from first	Plates used in second edition
1	(Dedication page)	New plates with new design
2		" " " old "
3		" " " new "
4		" " " " "
5		" " " " "
6		" " " " "
7		Old plates, retouched
8		New plates with new design
9		" " " old "
10		" " " new "
11		" " " " "
12		" " " " "
13		" " " " "
14		" " " " "
15		" " " " "
16		" " " " "
17		" " " " "
18		" " " " "
19		" " " " "
20		" " " " "
21		" " " " "
22		" " " " "
23		" " " " "
24		" " " " "
25		" " " " "
26	26	" " " " "
27	26	" " " " "
28	32	" " " " "
29	29	Old plates, retouched
30	30	New plates with new design
31	31	" " " " "
32	32	" " " " "
33	33	Old plates for border, new plate for text.
34		New plates with new designs
35		" " " " "
36		Old plates
37		" "
38		New plates with new designs
39		" " " " "
40		Old plates
41		" "
42		New plates with new designs
43		New plate for text and new plate with old design for border

Page number of first edition	Corresponding page in second edition when different from first	Plates used in second edition
44		Old plates
45		" "
46		New plates with old design
47		" " " " "
48		Old plates
49		New plates with old design
50		" " " new "
51		" " " " "
52		" " " " "
53		" " " " "
54		" " " " "
55		" " " " "
56		
57		Old plates
58		New plates with old design
59		" " " " "
60		Old plates
61		" "
62		New plates with new design
63		" " " old design
64		Old plates
65		New plates with new design
66		" " " " "
67		" " " " "
68		" " " " "
70		" " " " "
71		" " " " "
72	72	" " " " "
81	73	Old plate with new lines enclosing text
82	74	" "
83	75	" "
84	76	" " with new lines enclosing text
85	77	" "
86	78	" "
87	79	" "
88	80	" "
89	81	" "
90	82	" "
91	83	" "
92	84	" "
93	85	" "
94	86	" "
95	87	" "
96	88	" "

Page number of first edition	Corresponding page in second edition when different from first	Plates used in second edition			
97	89	Old plate			
98	90	" "			
99	91	" "			
100	92	" "			
101	93	" "			
102	94	" "			
103	95	" "			
104	96	" "			
105	97	" "			
106	106	" "			
107	99	" "			
108	100	" "			
109	101	" "			
110	102	" "			
111	111	" "			
112	104	" "			
113	105	" "			
114	106	" "			
115	107	" "			
116	108	" "			
117	109	" "			
118	110	" "			
119	111	" "			
120	211	" "			
121	121	" "			
122	114	" "			
123	115	" "			
124	124	" "			
125	125	" "			
126	118	" " (text corrected)			
127	119	" "			
128	120	" " " "			
113	121	New plates with old design			
114	122	" " " " "			
115	123	" " " " "			
116	124	" " " " "			
117	125	" " " " "			
118	126	" " " " "			
119	127	" " " new "			
120	128	" " " old "			
129	129	" " " " "			
130		" " " " "			
131		" " " " "			

Page number of first edition	Corresponding page in second edition when different from first	Plates used in second edition
132		New plates for text and new plate for border, the design of which is copied from that previously on p. 133
133		New plates for text and new plate for border, the design of which is taken from that on p. 132 of the first edition
134		New plates with old design
135		" " " " "
136		" " " " "
137		Old plate
138		" "
139		New plate
140		Old plate
141		" "
142		" "
143		" "
144		" "
145		New plate
146		Old plate
147		" "
148		New plate
149		" "
150		" "
151		Old plate
152		New plate
153		" "
154		" "
155		" "
156		" "
157		" "
158		" "

The last four pages are unnumbered in both editions, and as they contain a description of the full page and other illustrations, the text is entirely different in the two volumes and so had to be printed from new plates in the second edition.

The full-page inserted illustrations may be checked by the following: The title-page has been printed from the same plates in both editions, but the plates have evidently been retouched. The reproduction of the Rosetta Stone, facing page 9 in both editions, is printed from the same plate. The image of Phtha, facing page 17 in both editions, has evidently been entirely re-drawn from the old design for the second edition. The pictures of Memphis and the Bastion de St. Julien, facing pages 43 and 57 in both editions, are printed from the same plates. The picture of Philæ, facing page 81 in the first edition and page 73 of the second edition, is printed from the same plates in both editions. The picture of Ptolemy, facing page 113 in the first edition and facing page 121 in the second edition, is printed from a new set of plates in the second edition.

A printed catalogue of the members of the Philomathean So-ciety in 1859 is bound up with copies of the second edition and at the end a small lithographed slip in Morton's handwriting is inserted, noting the copyright, which does not appear in the first edition. The original binding of the second edition was of cloth, in either red, green, or brown, with a gold sphynx stamped on the front and back covers. "The second edition," writes Morton "came out in the spring of 1859, and like its predecessor, was not very long in being exhausted. So that for over twenty years [Morton wrote in 1892] the Rosetta Stone Report has been numbered among 'scarce' publications, only to be obtained from antiquarian book dealers and at the sale of libraries."

In many copies of the second edition there will be found in-serted a letter written by Baron Alexander von Humboldt, dated March 12, 1859, conveying his congratulations to the Society upon its achievement in the translation and publica-tion and remarking:

I have received with very lively interest the Report of the Committee of the Philomathean Society at the University of Pennsylvania to translate the inscription on the Rosetta Stone. . . . The scientific analysis of the celebrated inscription of Rosetta, which despite the confusion of the hiero-glyphic style, remains a historic monument of great importance, has ap-peared to me especially worthy of praise, since it offers the first essay at independent investigation offered by the literature of the new continent.

This letter is reproduced in facsimile with an English translation in Hale's handwriting facing it. Tradition has it that similar letters were received from Washington Irving, Edward Everett, and George Grote, but I have never been able to find out what became of these.

While looking for copies of this book, I had the pleasure of examining the copy in the library of the Philadelphia bibliophile, Judge John Marshall Gest. His might be called a "large paper copy" save for the fact that it is not really printed on large sheets, but mounted on them. It measures 33 by 26 cm. Leaves taken from a copy of the second edition have been carefully mounted on the recto of the larger sheet, one page to each sheet. Thus two copies of the second edition had to be taken apart to make this one "de luxe" edition. On holding any page to the light, one can see the printing on the other side, now concealed. If Judge Gest does not possess what is technically a large paper copy, at least he has two copies in one. It is elaborately bound in black morocco, tooled, with the sphynx common to other copies of the second edition stamped in gold on both covers. This is done from the same binder's stamp as in the other copies of that edition.

In this copy there was a clipping of an editorial from a New York newspaper of 1859, which reprints the Humboldt letter and confirms the story of other and similar letters having been received from Irving, Grote, and Everett. The presence in the Harvard University Library of a copy of the first edition inscribed "Mr. Everett, with the kind regards of Mrs. Gilpin, Jany. 1st, 1859. Phila." lends additional support to the tradition.

The principal American periodical of the day, which might be expected to review a book of this sort, was the *Historical Magazine, with Notes and Queries,* and in the February issue for 1859 there is a rather enthusiastic review which the editorial writer above referred to ascribes to the pen of George Bancroft — on what authority, I do not know.[9] Another and

9. Vol. III, 62.

rather lengthy review appeared in *The Crayon* where in those days one might expect to find intelligent criticism of artistically printed books.[10] Another review appeared in the *New Englander*.[11]

Of the association copies of the book, several are worth noticing. The copy of the first edition inscribed "Library of the Philomathean Society from the authors" is preserved in the Library at the University of Pennsylvania, along with a copy of the second edition inscribed "Presented to the Philomathean Society on the occasion of its Centennial by Josiah H. Penniman" (now President of the University). Mr. Albert Rosenthal has the copy of the first edition inscribed "Max Rosenthal with the sincere regards of Henry Morton" and the Library of the University Club of Philadelphia has another bearing an inscription by Morton.

In the Appendix, Morton mentions that the book was one of the first published in Philadelphia in which the sheets had been folded by machinery, and ascribes the invention of that machine to Mr. Cyrus Chambers of Philadelphia. Mr. Chambers's copy is now in the library of a relative, Mr. John P. Croasdale, of Daylesford, Pennsylvania. In the Preface the translators express gratitude not only to Gilpin, but to William E. Whitman, and I have a copy of the second edition that Mr. Whitman presented to the Reverend G. H. Nichols, in 1860. Hale presented a copy of the second edition with appropriate inscription to the Historical Society of Pennsylvania.

Finally, collectors of this book ought to understand that they cannot be sure of having a complete set of all possible forms of the production until they possess all of the following:

The first edition bound (*a*) in maroon boards; (*b*) in brown boards. The second edition bound (*c*) in red cloth; (*d*) in brown cloth; (*e*) in green cloth; (*f*) in black morocco. The second edition with the names of the Committee not printed but actually written on page 6, bound (*g*) in red cloth; (*h*) in brown cloth; (*i*) in green cloth; (*j*) in black morocco.

10. Vol. VI, 186.   11. Vol. XXVII, 549.

The Table of Multiplication.

1	9	8	7	6	5	4	3	2	1
2	18	16	14	12	10	8	6	4	
3	27	24	21	18	15	12	9		
4	36	32	28	24	20	16			
5	45	40	35	30	25				
6	54	48	42	36					
7	63	56	49						
8	72	64							
9	81								

This Table of *Multiplication* is thus to be read, In the first Row or Column towards the left-hand, and also at the top of the Table, you have the nine Digits in bigger Figures

Bradford, 1710

The Use of the Table of Multiplication, and the Manner how it is to be read.

This Table sheweth what the sum of any two Digits multiplied one by another doth amount unto, and is thus to be read, 2 times 2 makes 4, 2 times 3 makes 6, 2 times 4 makes 8 ; Also 6 times 4 makes 24, 7 times 8 makes 56, 8 times 8 makes 64, 9 times 9 makes 81, &c.

Another Table of Multiplication.

1	9	8	7	6	5	4	3	2	1
2	18	16	14	12	10	8	6	4	
3	27	24	21	18	15	12	9		
4	36	32	28	24	20	16			
5	45	40	35	30	25				
6	54	48	42	36					
7	63	56	49						
8	72	64							
9	81								

This Table is thus to be read ; In the first Row, or Column towards the left-hand, and also at the top of the Table, you have the nine Digits in bigger Figures than the rest; the Figures in the first Column beginning with 1, and so proceeding by 2, 3, 4, &c. to 9. Those at the top of the Table, beginning with 9 towards the left-hand, and so backwards, by 8, 7, 6, &c. to 1, at the right-hand.

Leybourn, the source

---

2. The *Multiplyer*, or Sum by which you Multiply.

3. The *Product*, or Sum Produced.

But before you enter upon the Practice of *Multiplication*, it is necessary to learn the Multiplication Table by heart, which is here set in the Margin.

TO Read this Table of Multiplication, 1st, Begin at the Top, at the Figure 2, saying, 2 times 2 is 4. 2dly, 3 times 3 is 9, &c. Next, 4 times 4 is 16. Then in the last Line read, 9 times 9 is 81. The Table is so plain, that I need give you no more Directions.

Therefore I shall proceed to give you some Examples of the Practice of *Multiplication*.

1. Example. *What is the Number of 3 times 654 ?*

Answer. If you set down the Number 654, 3 times one under the other, and add them together, you will find the Number to be 1962.

But by *Multiplication* such Questions are more readily answered than by *Addition*. And therefore I set the Number in question down thus,

654 *Multiplicand*,
3 *Multiplyer*.

In order thereto, you must Observe, In Multiplication to set down the greatest Number first, and the lesser under it, and

	2 is	4
	3 is	6
	4 is	8
	5 is	10
2 Times	6 is	12
	7 is	14
	8 is	16
	9 is	18
	3 is	9
	4 is	12
	5 is	15
	6 is	18
3 Times	7 is	21
	8 is	24
	9 is	27
	4 is	16
	5 is	20
	6 is	24
4 Times	7 is	28
	8 is	32
	9 is	36
	5 is	25
	6 is	30
5 Times	7 is	35
	8 is	40
	9 is	45
	6 is	36
	7 is	42
6 Times	8 is	48
	9 is	54
	7 is	49
7 Times	8 is	56
	9 is	63
8 Times	8 is	64
	9 is	72
9 Times	9 is	81

Bradford, 1728

The YOUNG MAN's *Companion.*　141

In Multiplication observe these three Terms, *Multiplicand, Multiplier, Product.*

1. The *Multiplicand*, (generally the greater of the two Numbers) is the Number to be multiplied.

2. The *Multiplier*, (generally the lesser of the two Numbers) is the Number to multiply with.

3. The *Product*, is the Result of the Work, or the Answer to the Question. But before any Thing can be done to the Purpose, it is necessary to learn the following Table perfect by heart.

Multiplication Table.

TO read this Table of Multiplication. *First*, Begin at the Top, at the Figures 2 and 2, saying 2 Times 2 is 4. *Secondly*, Say 3 Times 3 is 9, 3 Times 4 is 12, &c. Next, 4 Times 4 is 16, &c. *Lastly*, The last Line, 9 Times 9 is 81.

12 Times		
	2 is	24
	3 —	36
	4 —	48
	5 —	60
	6 —	72
	7 —	84
	8 —	96
	9 —	108
	10 —	120
	11 —	132
	12 —	144

What is the Amount of 3 Times 654 ?

Answer, If you set the Number 654, 3 Times down on Paper, one over another, the Total will be 1962.

But such Questions are done by this Rule of Multiplication much readier, for being set down thus:

654 *Multiplicand*
3 *Multiplier*

Now to know how much 3 Times 654 is, begin thus, saying, 3 Times 4 is 12, the Figure 2 of the 12, set below the Line, and bear the 10 of the 12 in Mind, as 1 : next,

Mather, the source

COLONIAL AMERICAN ARITHMETICS

By LOUIS C. KARPINSKI

Of the University of Michigan

THE arithmetics which appeared in the New World before the Revolution reflect in large outlines the history of America. First in order come the Spanish arithmetics, published probably in small editions and based on Spanish originals. Next appears a strictly colonial product in English, a compendium of practical information modelled after English texts. Most popular up to 1800, as shown by the number of editions, are the American reprints of English originals, commonly unchanged except by the insertion of a reference to America in the title. The American texts bear witness to the fact that the English colonists made America their home; the end and goal of their ambitions was here. For nearly three centuries after Cartier no French arithmetic appears in Canada, reflecting the fact that for the great majority of the French in America Canada was only a stepping-stone to success in France and not the home of their children.

The third separate textbook on arithmetic to appear in the northern colonies was printed in New York in Dutch, a natural and typical product of New Amsterdam. The only arithmetic in German to appear in America before 1800 is dated 1786, a 'Rechenbuechlin' by Ludwig Hoecker, published at Ephrata. However, arithmetical tables in German, for traders, appeared at Germantown in 1774.

Three lists of American arithmetics have been published.[1]

---

1. Cajori, The Teaching and History of Mathematics in the United States, Washington, Bureau of Education, Circular of Information, No. 3, 1890, pp. 45–49, with the footnotes on those pages.

James M. Greenwood and Artemas Martin, Notes on the History of American Text-books on Arithmetic. Report of the Commissioner of Education for the year

Of these the most ambitious, that prepared by Greenwood and Martin, indicates only two texts before 1775. Cajori listed seven published during the period in the present United States. In the present list are included twenty-one works and also four Mexican.

The first arithmetical work printed in America appeared in Mexico in 1556. While concerned primarily with giving tables to compute the value of given quantities of silver and gold of various degrees of refinement, the author interjects a serious discussion of some twelve pages on arithmetic, and, what is more remarkable, about the same amount on strictly algebraical problems. In this work the author follows closely the procedure of sixteenth-century Spanish arithmetics, like that by Juan de Ortega, printed at Seville in 1542 and again in 1552, Of the three seventeenth-century Mexican treatises on arithmetic I have been able to locate only one, the 'Breve aritmetica' by Benito Fernandez de Belo, Mexico, 1675, which is in the John Carter Brown Library.

In English the first serious discussion of arithmetic appears in William Bradford's 'The Young Man's Companion,' of 1705 published by him in New York City. No copy is known, but Mr. Eames has established the year by the dating in problems of the 1710 edition. Bradford in 1728 states that "It is now above thirty years since I first compiled this short Manuel." The sources of the compilation are not mentioned by him. There were two principal sources: William Mather's 'A Very Useful Manual, or the Young Man's Companion,' London, 1681, and William Leybourn's 'Arithmetick, Vulgar, Decimal, Instrumental, Algebraical,' London, 1657. The fourth edition of Mather in 1695 [2] involved additions in verse by Mather's

1897-98, Washington, D. C., pp. 789–868. Report . . . for 1898–99, Washington, 1900, pp. 781–837.

W. S. Monroe, Development of Arithmetics as a School Subject, Bulletin No. 10, U. S. Bureau of Education, 1917, p. 14, with footnote and pp. 157–159.

2. Dictionary of National Biography, vol. XXXVII, pp. 31–32.

son; it is possible that some of the verses in Bradford are from this edition, to which I have not had access. The eighth edition (London, 1710) [3] bears the title in the British Museum Catalogue, 'The Young Man's Companion, or Arithmetick made easie; with plain directions for a young man to attain to read and write true English.' Twenty-four editions are said to have appeared.[4] Leybourn's treatise enjoyed at least four further editions, those of 1659, 1660, 1678, and 1700.[5] Largely the same material appeared in his compendium of mathematics of 1690.

The first twenty pages of the 1728 edition of Bradford, on Directions for Spelling, Reading and Writing True English, are practically identical, even to the italicization, with Mather. On the whole, the arithmetic (Bradford, pages 31–73, 1728 edition) was based on Leybourn's work, frequently large sections being taken verbatim. However, some sections appear to be written by Bradford, and a section on multiplication (pages 49–50) is taken verbatim from Mather. An interesting change by Bradford is in a problem given by Leybourn, "*From* London *to* Coventry *is accounted* 76 *miles. How many Yards therefore is it from* London *to* Coventry?" Bradford reads: "*From* New York *to* Philadelphia *it is accounted* 102 *Miles. How many Yards is it from* New York *to* Philadelphia?" In the edition of 1710 Bradford included also the scratch method of division. He discarded this, however, in the 1728 edition, leaving our present method as explained by Leybourn. It is possible that the earlier editions of Leybourn or Mather employed this method, but these are not available to the writer. One further division problem is included by Bradford, apparently original, in the 1728 edition; the form of the multiplication table is

3. Edition of 1728, pp. 29–30, 91, 92, et al.
4. My references are to the sixteenth (London) edition of 1741, in the University of Michigan Library.
5. My references are to the edition of 1700 in the University of Michigan Library. See also Dictionary of National Biography, vol. XXXIII, pp. 208–209.

changed from the Leybourn type to the Mather type, and some problems on the table are omitted. Aside from these changes the arithmetic in the 1728 edition is the same as in the 1710 edition.

The latter portions of Bradford's work include other material taken directly from Mather, as, for example, five letters included among fifty in Part III, on the Method of Writing Letters. The section on Bills, Deeds, Bonds, and the like does not correspond closely either to Mather or to Leybourn and includes frequently references indicating American authorship.

Of the other arithmetics listed, the American reprint of George Fisher's 'Instructor: or, Young Man's Companion,' and the reprint of Thomas Dilworth's 'Schoolmaster's Assistant' were the dominating textbooks in arithmetic in America until 1800. No other work approached these two in popularity. Fisher's work bears some resemblance to Bradford in that the author borrowed generously from Mather's work, with more verbal changes and without any acknowledgment.

ABBREVIATIONS: AAS, AMERICAN ANTIQUARIAN SOCIETY, WORCESTER, MASS.;
HSP, HISTORICAL SOCIETY OF PENNSYLVANIA; JCB, JOHN CARTER BROWN LIBRARY,
PROVIDENCE, R. I.; LC, LIBRARY OF CONGRESS; M, UNIVERSITY OF MICHIGAN;
NYHS, NEW YORK HISTORICAL SOCIETY; NYP, NEW YORK PUBLIC LIBRARY;
P, LIBRARY OF MR. GEORGE A. PLIMPTON, NEW YORK CITY.

1556. JUAN DIEZ FREYLE, Sumario Compendioso de las quentas de plata
y oro . . . Con algunas reglas tocantes al Aritmetica. Mexico.
Printed by Juan Pablos of Brescia.   (1)

1623. PEDRO PAZ, Arte para aprender todo el menor del Aritmetica, sin
Maestro. Mexico. Printed by Juan Ruyz. 2 ll. + 181 numbered
folios + 3 ll. of tables; 21 chapters.   (2)

1649. ATANASIUS REATON, Pasamonte, Arte menor de Aritmetica.
Printed by Viuda de B. Calderon. 3 ll. + 78 numbered folios; 14
chapters.   (3)

1675. BENITO FERNANDEZ DE BELO, Breve aritmetica por el mas sucinto
modo, que hasta oy se ha visto. Mexico: Viuda de B. Calderon.
4 ll. + 11 numbered folios, 1 plate.   JCB (4)

1705. WILLIAM BRADFORD, Young Man's Companion, New York. No
copy known.   (5)

1710. WILLIAM BRADFORD, The Young Man's Companion. In four parts.
Part II. Arithmetick made easie, and the Rules thereof Explained
and made familiar to the Capacity of those that desire to learn in a
little time. . . . Printed and Sold by William and Andrew Bradford,
at the Bible in New York, 1710. Two imperfect copies in private
hands; photographic copy in New York Public Library.   (6)

1719. WILLIAM BRADFORD, The Secretary's Guide, or Young Man's Companion.   (7)

1719. HODDER, BOSTON, Reprint of an English text. Printer: J. Franklin. 2 ll. + viii + 216 pp.   LC, AAS (8)

1728. WILLIAM BRADFORD, The Secretary's Guide, or, Young Man's Companion, In Four Parts. Fourth Edition. Part II, Arithmetick
made easie. New York: W. Bradford. 5 ll. + 192 pp.
JCB, LC, P (9)

1729. ISAAC GREENWOOD, Arithmetick, Vulgar and Decimal; Boston.
Printers: S. Kneeland and T. Green. First separate text by a native
of colonial America. Title, 158 pp., 4 pp. Index and 4 pp. Adv.
LC, Harvard (10)

WILLIAM BRADFORD, The Secretary's Guide, New York: Wm.
Bradford. 5 ll. + 192 pp.   LC (11)

1730. PETER VENEMA, Arithmetica of Cyffer Konst, Dutch, New York.
Printer: J. Peter Zenger. 120 pp.   NYHS (12)

1737. WM. BRADFORD, The Secretary's Guide, New York. Printer: Wm. Bradford. 5 ll. + 248 pp. NYP (13)

1738. WM. BRADFORD, The Secretary's Guide, Philadelphia: Andrew Bradford. 5 ll. + 248 pp. P (14)

1748. JONATHAN BURNHAM, Arithmetick for the use of Farmers and Country People. New London: T. Green. Advertised early in 1748 as just published (J. H. Trumbull, List of Books Printed in Connecticut, 1904). (15)

1748. GEORGE FISHER, The American Instructor; or, Young Man's Best Companion, containing Spelling, Reading, Writing, and Arithmetick, in an easier Way than any yet published. Reprint of an English work. Philadelphia. Printer: Benjamin Franklin and Hall. v + 378 pp., 5 plates. NYP (16)

1749. [Same] Boston. No copy located; Evans only authority. (17)

1753. FISHER, Young Man's Best Companion, Philadelphia. Printer: Benj. Franklin and W. Hall. v + 384 (2) pp., 6 plates. HSP (18)

1758. Conclusiones Mathematicas. . . . per *Don Fernando de Araya*, Manila. A mathematical thesis defended at the University of the Society of Jesus in Manila. M (19)

1760. GEORGE FISHER, American Instructor, 12th ed. New York: Hugh Gaine. v (1) + 378 pp. NYHS (20)

1766. FISHER, Same. New York: Hugh Gaine. (21)

1770. FISHER, American Instructor. 14th ed. v + 390 pp. New York, H. Gaine. HSP (22)
[Anon.], The Youth's Instructor . . . III Rules in Arithmetick. Boston: Mein and Fleming. 152 pp. P (23)

1770. FISHER, same, 15th ed. Philadelphia: Dunlap. v + 390 pp., port., fold. plate. AAS, NYP (24)

1773. THOMAS DILWORTH, the Schoolmaster's Assistant, being a compendium of arithmetic, both practical and theoretical. Philadelphia: J. Crukshank. (2), xiv (iv) + 192 pp., fold. leaf, portrait. Reprint of an English work. HSP (25)

1774. DANIEL FENNING, The Ready Reckoner. American edition of an English work. Germantown: Chr. Saur. 280 pp. AAS, NYP (26)
DANIEL FENNING, Der Geschwinder Rechner, Oder; des Händler's nutzlicher Gehülfe in Kauffung, etc. Germantown: Christoph Saur. 280 pp. Largely tables, but strictly arithmetical. NYP (27)

1775. Thèses de Mathematiques qui seront soutenues au Seminaires de Quebec...par MM...Panet, Perrault, Chauveaux. Quebec.
NYP (28)

1775. FISHER, Instructor or, Young Man's Best Companion. Burlington, N. J., Isaac Collins. xii + 372 pp., title, fold. plate, 15 plates. This title and date occur also as second title-page in 1787 Philadelphia edition. HSP (29)

SIXTEENTH–CENTURY MEXICAN IMPRINTS

By HENRY R. WAGNER

Of Berkeley, California

TO an American interested in the history of the New World, whether he be a North American or a South American, the early productions of the press of Mexico and Lima must always prove of fascinating interest. Like most origins, that of printing in Mexico is involved in considerable obscurity. About the only two things that we know positively are that Juan Cromberger, or Cronberger, a printer of German origin who had a large establishment in Seville, sent out a press to Mexico sometime after June, 1539, and also sent out Juan Pablos, a native of Brescia in Italy, to operate it. The other definite fact known is that Pablos printed something in December, 1540, of which the last leaf or two containing the colophon remains.

The early historians of the religious orders, writing on the provinces in Spanish America, make numerous references to the works that had been written or published by members of their own orders. Naturally these were mostly of a religious character or intended for religious instruction. Some were written in Spanish and others in the native languages.

From notices which we find scattered through the works of such writers, Antonio de Leon in 1629 managed to get together a list of some twenty-two works printed in Mexico. Of these, sixteen only are now known. Four of those which he does not say were printed have since been discovered to have been published. In no case did he give any collations, and as a rule the dates of printing are lacking. When Gonzales Barcia published a second edition of this work in 1737, he made large additions; in fact, the additions exceed in bulk the original work. Nevertheless he was not able to increase the number of sixteenth-century Mexican imprints to any appreciable extent — a sure proof that at that period very few of these works had reached Spain. From the nature of the works themselves this was what might have been expected, as most of them were locked up in the convent libraries in Mexico, and many intended for the education of the Indians had disappeared through use. Thus it is that in the early part of the nineteenth century very few of the early imprints had been described, or even seen, by European bibliographers. Henri Ternaux in his 'Bibliotèque Américaine,' 1837, lists twenty-two, of which it appears that he had actually seen only one. Beristain, who lived in Mexico and had access to the convent libraries, gives the titles of some forty-six which he presumably saw.

It was not until the suppression of the convents under the reform laws in the period between 1855 and 1860, and the consequent dispersal of many of their libraries, that these works began to appear in private hands. Several large collections were formed out of the wreck of these libraries, notably those made by José Maria Andrade, José Fernando Ramirez, Father Augustin Fischer, and last but not least, Joaquin Garcia Icazbalceta.

Icazbalceta, as he is usually called, although he should be referred to as Garcia, was the son of a Spaniard who had accumulated in Mexico a large fortune for those days. As early as 1845, when only twenty years of age, he began to devote his leisure to the collection of early manuscripts and early books. From copies in his possession and in that of Señor Ramirez he prepared a study on the early press of Mexico, which appeared in the 'Diccionario Universal' in 1855. Shortly after this, Henry Harrisse began the collection of material for his monumental work, 'Bibliotheca Americana Vetustissima,' and secured a large amount of information regarding the early imprints from Icazbalceta himself, as well as from the 'Diccionario.' In 1866 this work was published in New York, and in it will be found a description of fifteen sixteenth-century Mexican imprints and the titles of some sixty-four additional ones. From a perusal of the list it is evident that he secured his information almost entirely from Icazbalceta, as he was able to locate in the libraries of James Lenox, John Carter Brown, and S. L. M. Barlow, only eight distinct works. In 1872, in the 'Additions' which Harrisse published, appeared a notice of one more work, which at that time was in the Biblioteca Provincial de Toledo in Spain, but has since disappeared. In 1872 Harrisse's notes were translated into Spanish and published in Spain in a pamphlet entitled, 'Introduccion de la Imprenta en América.' In this list will be found a description of fifty-eight works taken from Harrisse, Icazbalceta's 'Apuntes' of 1866, and other sources, besides the bare titles of some twenty-five more.

In 1866, Icazbalceta himself published his 'Apuntes' of Mexican imprints in the native languages, embracing to a large extent the information which he had previously imparted to Mr. Harrisse; and in 1886 he published his grand work, 'Bibliografia del Siglo XVI.' By this time the libraries formed by Andrade, Ramirez, and Father Fischer had been dispersed in Leipzig and London, and large numbers of the early works had passed into the possession of American collectors, notably James Lenox, John Carter Brown, and H. H. Bancroft, who at that time was forming his library for the purpose of writing his History of California. Señor Icazbalceta described in his work one hundred and eighteen titles, of which thirteen were not known to exist; but he believed them to have been published, from what he considered reliable information derived from the early chroniclers of the religious orders or from fragments.

In 1903, Dr. Nicolás Leon, who at that time lived in Morelia, had been able to secure either copies or descriptions of a few additional sixteenth-century imprints, mostly relating to the

Tarascan language, which is spoken in that neighborhood. These additions he published in the 'Bibliografía Mexicana.' Ultimately he disposed of most of the works which he himself possessed to the John Carter Brown Library, which by this time had become very active in building up a collection of these works. Mr. Wilberforce Eames, while connected with the Lenox Library before it was merged into the New York Public Library, had been interested in the subject, and he tells me that he had considerable correspondence with Señor Icazbalceta in regard to it; and it is possible that many descriptions contained in Sabin's 'Dictionary' were obtained from him.

Finally, in 1907, José Toribio Medina, in his 'Imprenta en Mexico,' brought together all the existing information and managed to make up a list of some two hundred and thirty-four imprints. With the exception of a considerable collection of official and scholastic publications in the last decade of the century, Señor Medina was able to add very little to Señor Icazbalceta's list and Dr. Leon's additions of known works, many of his numbers being those of works supposed to have been printed.

Since the appearance of this last work no further publications, to my knowledge, have appeared on the subject, but a few hitherto undescribed works of considerable importance have since been discovered: namely, a perfect copy of the 1548 edition of the 'Doctrina Christiana,' two works of Molina printed in 1569, a 'Graduale Dominicale' of 1576, and a 'Cartilla' of 1569. Besides those now known to have been printed, as evidenced by complete or incomplete copies, there is sufficient reason to believe that at least fifty more were published of which no trace exists.

The census presented herewith can be considered as strictly up to date for the leading public libraries listed in the United States and for the British Museum. Dr. Thomas of the latter institution has only recently very kindly revised the list, and

Mr. Wilberforce Eames, Dr. George Watson Cole, Mr. Herbert Putnam, Miss Clara A. Smith, Mr. George Parker Winship, and Mr. Lawrence C. Wroth have kindly furnished me with the necessary information for the principal libraries in this country. For those in the Gates collection I have utilized the recently published sale catalogue of the American Art Association. To compile lists of these imprints in the various libraries in Spain and Spanish America I have been compelled to utilize those given by Señor Medina in his 'Imprenta en Mexico.' This embodies information of some twenty years ago, and it is a notorious fact that since that time much shifting of these copies has taken place. The Biblioteca de Fomento has been merged in the Biblioteca Nacional, and during the process a number of the books have disappeared. The Biblioteca de Ultramar, which possesses the library of Pascual de Gayangos and therefore the fragmentary numbers 2 and 3, is still in existence, but now functions as a department of the Biblioteca Nacional. The books in all three of these libraries are therefore listed under the Biblioteca Nacional.

According to the best information I could obtain while on a visit to Mexico some two years ago, the Icazbalceta collection of sixteenth-century imprints is still intact, although the library suffered some depredations during the revolution. The famous collection of José Maria Agreda, who died about four or five years ago, has been largely dispersed. I did not attempt to check up Medina's references to imprints in the Biblioteca Nacional or other public institutions in Mexico or Spain. Medina in his book also credited himself with a considerable number, but it is understood that he has disposed of some of those that he had in 1907.

It is quite likely that some of the books which were known in the last century and which have now disappeared will be found in the collection either of Sir Thomas Phillips or of Francisco de Zabalburu. This latter library, which I believe contains most of the rare works which belonged to José Sancho Rayon, has been closed for the past twenty years.

The following table shows the location of the sixteenth century Mexican imprints which have been registered. The [*] denotes that the copy is reported to be approximately complete; [†], that it is more or less fragmentary.

The numbers in the left-hand column correspond to the numbered title entries in Medina, ' La Imprenta en México,' vol. I, 1908. A brief title of some of the more common works is given in the notes at the end of the table.

ADDITIONS

Veritas domini manet in eternum. | [Large woodcut like the one on the title of the 1550 edition.] Dotrina christiana en lēgua Española y Mexicana: hecha porē los religiosos dela ord | d' sctō Domingo. [The colophon, which is on the verso of 156, will be found in Medina.]

4to, title in red and black, leaves numbered ii–clvi and two unnumbered at the end.
Preliminaries: On the verso of the title begins the *Prólogo sobre la presente obra*, which terminates on the verso of the second leaf, followed by the *Tabla*, which ends on the verso of the third leaf, followed by the *Silibario* to the end of leaf ix. The text begins on leaf x with the words *Yo pecador*, and ends on the recto of clvi. On the verso of this leaf is the colophon, and then follow two leaves, with the *Correctorio* on the recto of the first, verso blank, the last leaf being blank. Sigs.: a–v of 8 leaves each, except the last, which has 6.
Until recently this 1548 edition was known only by two imperfect copies, both lacking the title and the last two leaves; the copy belonging to Señor Icazbalceta lacked the first nine leaves and the last two, and that belonging to Señor José Maria Agreda is still more imperfect. The copy which we are describing and which is now in the Huntington Library is perhaps in the finest condition of all the examples extant of the early Mexican press.

Confessionario breue, en lengua | Mexicana y Castellana: compuesto por el muy Re | uerendo Padre Fray Alonso de Molina, de la | ordē del Seraphico padre sant Frācisco. | [Large woodcut.] Mexico, en casa de Antonio d'Espinosa Impressor. | 1569. Años. [Colophon on the verso of 18] Acabose de impri | mir este Confessionario, en | quinze de Março, de 1569. Años. |

4to, title, leaves numbered 2–18. On the verso of the title is the license of the Royal Audiencia, dated Mexico, November 24, 1564.

Confessionario ma | yor, en la lengua Mexicana y Castellana: | Compu-
esto por el muy Reuerendo padre Fray Al | onso de Molina, de la orden del
Seraphico | padre Sant Francisco: | [Large woodcut.] En Mexico | En
casa de Antonio de Espinosa Impressor. | 1569. Años. | [Colophon:]
Acabose de imprimir este Confessiona | rio, en la muy insigne y gran ciudad
de Mexico: en casa de Antonio de Espinosa impressor de libros, junto a la
yglesia | de Señor sant Augustin: a. 23 de Septiebre. Año. de. 1565. | Laus
deo. |

4to, title, leaves numbered 2–121 and 3 unnumbered at the end. In the
foliation folio 103 is misnumbered 95. On the verso of the title is the
license of the Audiencia and the *epistola nuncupatoria* to the Archbishop
Fr. Alonso de Montufar, dated Mexico, the 6th of November, 1564. The
3 unnumbered leaves at the end contain a *Tabla de las mas principales
materias*, which begins in the middle of the recto of folio 121. Sigs.: a–q
in fours, except the last, which has only two leaves.

These editions have the same collation as the editions of 1565, and apparently there is no difference between them except in the titles and in
the *Confessionario mayor* in which other differences in the first signature
would indicate that this had been reprinted. These two notable works
were at one time in the possession of Genaro Garcia, and were sold about
1916. I understand that they were bought by the Mexican government
and are therefore in the Museo Nacional or the Biblioteca Nacional.

Cartilla para ensenar a leer, nueuamente enmenda | da, y quitadas todas
las abreuiaturas que antes tenia. | [Large woodcut of San Francisco re-
ceiving the stigmata. Below this is the alphabet.] [Colophon:] Mexico en
casa de Pedro Ocharte, 1569 Años.

Small 4to, 8 unnumbered leaves.

This interesting example of what is probably the only known primer
printed in Mexico in the sixteenth century is now in the Huntington
Library. It is in three languages — Spanish, Latin, and a Mexican-
Indian dialect.

NOS DON

Hazemos saber a todos los | vezinos y moradores de todas las ciudades,
villas, y lugares de todo este obispado: assi hobres como mugeres, de cual-
quier estado, dignidad y codicio que sea . . . | que nuestro muy sancto padre
summo Romano Pontifice Pio Quinto. | . | . . ha hecho y estatudo vna
sancta constituccion y decreto en fauor del dicho sancto officio d' la In-
quisicio y sus ministros, . . . | la qual es del tenor q. se sigue. |

A broadside printed on one side only of a double folio sheet, with the
following at the bottom:

En Mexico, en casa de Pedro Ocharte: por mandado del Illustre señor
Maestro Fray Bartholome de Ledesma, Administrador | en esta Arço-
bispado por el Reuerendissimo del.

As the decree of the Pope was issued in Rome in 1569, it is the opinion of
Luis Gonzales Obregon that it was printed in Mexico sometime in 1570.
At the present time it is in the Museo Nacional.

Graduale Dominicale. [Large woodcut.] Secundum norman Misalis noui. ex decreto | Sancti Concilii Triden. nunc denuo, ex industria, studio et labore admodum Reue | rendi Bachalauri Joannis Hernandez, excussum, et innumeris mendis su perfluitacibus (quibus scaturiebat) notularum cantus repurgatum. Su | per-additis et de nouo compositis per eundem Bachalaurem, cum In | troitibus officii, cum Gradualibus, Alleluia, et Tractibus, cum demu | Ossértoris, et Communinnibus, quorum antea non fuerat vsus.| Mexici | In edibus Antonii Spinosa. | Sumtibus et expensis Petri Ocharte. | 1576. | [Colophon:] Mexici Excvdebat Antonivs Espi | nosa. 1576. |

Large folio, title, 1 unnumbered leaf, leaves numbered 1–208. Sigs.: A–Z, aa–cc. Errors in pagination: 45, 51, 120, 136, 136, for 44, 59, 115, 128, 135.

Graduale dominicale. [Large woodcut.] Secūdum normam Missalis noui: ex decreto | Sancti Concilij Triden. nunc denuo, ex industria, studio & labore admodum Reue | rendi Bachalaurei Joannis Hernandez. excusam, & in numeris mendis et su | perfluitatibus quibus scaturiebat notularum cantus repurgatum. Su | per additis et de nouo compositis per eundem Bachalaureum. cum In | troitibus officij, cum Gradualibus Alleluia, & Tractibus demum | Offertorijs, et Communionibus, quorum antea non fuerat vsus. | Mexico. | Por Pedro Ocharte. | [Colophon:] Mexici. Excudebat Petrus Ocharte. 1576.

2 p. l., 208 numb. lvs. Sigs.: A–Z aa–cc in eights. 41.7 × 25.9 cm. (Binding 42 × 27.5 cm.) Fol. 33 (E 1) missing. Errors in pagination: 36, 45, 46, 136, 113, 149, 172, 170, 125 for 39, 44, 45, 128, 131, 139, 173, 175, 205.

A comparison of the titles of these last two books and their collations would indicate that they are the same work with the exception of the title-pages and the colophons. The one first described appeared in a catalogue of Porrúa Hermanos in Mexico City in 1916. I believe it belonged to Sr. Luis Gonzales Obregon, and I have since understood that it was sold to the Mexican government. The second one described is now in the Newberry Library, Chicago, having been presented to that institution by Archbishop Plancarte in 1916. In presenting the book, the Archbishop wrote an interesting letter in which he stated that but four copies of this book were known, and that the one he had, possessed some peculiarities which made it different from the others. As I have had no opportunity to compare the two copies and do not know where the other two to which he referred are to be found, I am unable to state in what respect his copy differs from the others unless it may be in the fact that the imprints and the colophons are different. A comparison of the titles as printed here will also show some differences, mostly in spelling and in abbreviations. Whether these differences really exist or were only caused by carelessness in reproduction of the title in Porrúa's catalogue, I am unable to say.

The appearance of the book with two imprints and different colophons is not to be wondered at under the circumstances of the time. In the proceedings taken by the Inquisition against Ocharte in 1572, a full account of which will be found in 'Libros y libreros en el siglo XVI,' published in Mexico in 1914, are numerous indications that Espinosa and Ocharte were engaged in joint production of books. From the testimony produced during that trial it appears that most of the books were being printed by Espinosa at the entire or partial expense of Ocharte. It is quite possible that Espinosa had a better press and font of type than Ocharte, and therefore Ocharte had made an arrangement with Espinosa to print for a joint account the better books. There is another possible explanation of the difference. Before this book was found with the imprint of Espinosa, no work printed by him was known with a date later than 1575. It is known that Espinosa died before 1580, and it has generally been supposed that he died in 1575. Possibly what happened is that he died in 1576, shortly after printing this book, and then Ocharte put out the rest of the edition with a new title-page and a new colophon.

CORRECTION

[Tractado Breue De Chirurgia, Y Del Conocimiento Y Cvra De Algvnas Enfermedades, Q. En Esta Tierra Mas Comunmente Suelen Aver. Hecho Por El Mvy Reverendo Padre Fray Augustin Farfan, Religioso De La Orden De Sacto Augustin, Doctor En Medicina, Y Graduado En Esta Insigne Vniversidad De Mexico.]
[Colophon:] En Mexico, En casa de Antonio Ricardo. Año de 1579.

The above title is a supposititious one made from the heading of the first leaf of the text to the work; then follow 15 preliminary leaves and 274 numbered leaves, with the colophon on the recto of folio 274. On the verso of this leaf is a portrait of the author. No complete copy of this work is known, but Sr. Garcia Icazbalceta described one under No. 82, more incomplete than the one just described. He called it a 'Tratado breve de medicina,' and supposed that it was the first edition of Farfan's work, published in 1592 under the same title. This, however, is not the case. The author of the notes attached to the description of the book in Porrúa's catalogue (whom I suppose to have been Luis Gonzales Obregon) stated that Icazbalceta was entirely mistaken and that the present work was a treatise on surgery and not one on medicine. I can personally certify that this is the case, because I compared an imperfect copy in the Bancroft Library of the work just described with a copy of the 1592 'Tratado Medicina' which belonged to me, and discovered that they were entirely different works.

	José María de Agreda, Mexico City	Annmary Brown Memorial, Providence, Rhode Island	Edward E. Ayer Collection, Newberry Library, Chicago	H. H. Bancroft Collection, University of California	Biblioteca Andrade, Mexico City	Biblioteca de Guadalajara, Mexico	Biblioteca Lafragua, Mexico City	Biblioteca de Morelia, Mexico	Biblioteca Nacional, Madrid, Spain	Biblioteca Nacional, Mexico City	Biblioteca Nacional, Santiago de Chile	Biblioteca de Oaxaca, Mexico	Biblioteca Palafoxiana, Puebla, Mexico	Biblioteca Provincial, Toledo, Spain	Biblioteca de Queretaro, Mexico	Biblioteca San Isidro, Madrid, Spain	Biblioteca de Zaragoza, Spain	Bodleian Library, Oxford University	Public Library, Boston, Massachusetts	British Museum, London
1																				
2									†											
3									†											
4																				
5																				*
6		*																		*
7			*																	*
8									*					*						*
9																				
10				*																*
11																				
12																				*
13									†											
14																				
15																				
16																				
17																				†
18	*																			
19																				
20	†		†					*												
21																				*
22									*							*				
23			†													*				*
24			†						†								†			†
25																				
26		*							*											*
27																				*
28																				
29																				*
30	†																			*
31											*									*
32																				
33																				*
34	†																			†
35	†																			
36			†						*	*										
37			*		*	*														
38																				
39																				
40																				
41																				

	John Carter Brown Library, Providence, Rhode Island	Biblioteca de la Iglesia, Cartago, Costa Rica	Harvard College Library, Cambridge, Massachusetts	Museum of American Indian Heye Foundation, N. Y. C.	Hispanic-American Society, New York City	Henry E. Huntington Lib., San Gabriel, California	Joaquin Garcia Icazbalceta Collection, Mexico City	Library of Congress, Washington, D. C.	Long Island Historical Society, Brooklyn, N. Y.	José Toribio Medina, Santiago de Chile	New York Historical Society, New York City	Public Library, New York City	Newberry Library, Chicago, Illinois	W. H. Newman Collection, Buffalo, N. Y.	John Hinsdale Scheide, Titusville, Pennsylvania	Seler Collection, Berlin, Germany	Sociedad Geografica Mexicana, Mexico City	Wm. E. Gates Collection, Tulane Univ., New Orleans	Yale University Library, New Haven, Connecticut	Francisco de Zabalburu, Madrid, Spain
1																				
2																				
3																				
4																				
5	*						*					*								
6	*					*	*					*								
7	*					*	*	*				*								
8	*					*	*					*		†						
9																				
10	*					*						*			*					
11																				
12	*						*	*				*								
13						*						†								
14																				
15												*								
16	*									†										
17	†						*													
18								*												
19																				
20							†													
21							†													
22					*	*	*			*		*								
23						*	*					*								
24	*					*	†	*												
25															*					
26	*					*	*					*								
27						†														
28																				
29																				
30					*		*			*		*								
31	*				*	*	*	*		*		*								
32																				
33	*																			
34	*																			
35	†																			
36						*				*		*						†		
37	*						*	*				†						†		
38	†											*								
39																				
40												*								
41																				

	José María de Agreda, Mexico City	Annmary Brown Memorial, Providence, Rhode Island	Edward E. Ayer Collection, Newberry Library, Chicago	H. H. Bancroft Collection, University of California	Biblioteca Andrade, Mexico City	Biblioteca de Guadalajara, Mexico	Biblioteca Lafragua, Mexico City	Biblioteca de Morelia, Mexico	Biblioteca Nacional, Madrid, Spain	Biblioteca Nacional, Mexico City	Biblioteca Nacional, Santiago de Chile	Biblioteca de Oaxaca, Mexico	Biblioteca Palafoxiana, Puebla, Mexico	Biblioteca Provincial, Toledo, Spain	Biblioteca de Querétaro, Mexico	Biblioteca San Isidro, Madrid, Spain	Biblioteca de Zaragoza, Spain	Bodleian Library, Oxford University	Public Library, Boston, Massachusetts	British Museum, London
42																				†
43																				†
44																				
45																				†
46	†		*	†							†									†
47																				†
48	*		*	*																*
49	*		*	*	*															†
50			*	*																*
51					*															
52									*									*		
53																		*		
54																				†
55																				*
56																				
57																				
58																				*
59																				*
60																				
61																				
62																				
63									*											*
64	*		*																	*
65	*			†															*	*
66				†			*													
67																				
68									*											
69																				*
70																				†
71																				*
72																				*
73																				
74																				
75												*								
76																				
77																				†
78	*			†		*			*											*
79																				
80																				
81	†																			
82																				

	John Carter Brown Library, Providence, Rhode Island	Biblioteca de la Iglesia, Cartago, Costa Rica	Harvard College Library, Cambridge, Massachusetts	Museum of American Indian, Heye Foundation, N. Y. C.	Hispanic-American Society, New York City	Henry E. Huntington Lib., San Gabriel, California	Joaquin Garcia Icazbalceta Collection, Mexico City	Library of Congress, Washington, D. C.	Long Island Historical Society, Brooklyn, N. Y.	José Toribio Medina, Santiago de Chile	New York Historical Society, New York City	Public Library, New York City	Newberry Library, Chicago, Illinois	W. H. Newman Collection, Buffalo, N. Y.	John Hinsdale Scheide, Titusville, Pennsylvania	Seler Collection, Berlin, Germany	Sociedad Geografica Mexicana, Mexico City	Wm. E. Gates Collection, Tulane Univ., New Orleans	Yale University Library, New Haven, Connecticut	Francisco de Zabalburu, Madrid, Spain
42						†														
43							†					†								
44	†					*						*								
45																				
46	*		*			*	†	*				*								
47	*						†					*								
48	*																			
49	*																	*		
50	*		*			*	*	*		*		†								
51						*														
52	†																			
53						†											†			
54																				
55						†						*								
56																				
57						*											†			
58										*	*									
59	*	*				*														
60																				
61	*					*		*												
62												†								*
63			†																	
64	*					*		*				*								
65	*		*			*	*	*	*		*	*	*					*		
66							*													
67	*						*													
68	†						*	*												
69						*	*					*					†			
70							*													
71	*					*														
72	*					†	†			†										
73	*																			
74	*						*					*			*					
75																				
76							†													
77																				
78	*						*					*								
79	†																			
80												*								
81																*				
82	*																			

	José María de Agreda, Mexico City	Annmary Brown Memorial, Providence, Rhode Island	Edward E. Ayer Collection, Newberry Library, Chicago	H. H. Bancroft Collection, University of California	Biblioteca Andrade, Mexico City	Biblioteca de Guadalajara, Mexico	Biblioteca Lafragua, Mexico City	Biblioteca de Morelia, Mexico	Biblioteca Nacional, Madrid, Spain	Biblioteca Nacional, Mexico City	Biblioteca Nacional, Santiago de Chile	Biblioteca de Oaxaca, Mexico	Biblioteca Palafoxiana, Puebla, Mexico	Biblioteca Provincial, Toledo, Spain	Biblioteca de Queretaro, Mexico	Biblioteca San Isidro, Madrid, Spain	Biblioteca de Zaragoza, Spain	Bodleian Library, Oxford University	Public Library, Boston, Massachusetts	British Museum, London
83																				
84				†																
85					†															
86					†															
86²																				
87																				
88				†																
89																				
90	†																		*	**
91																				*
92																				
93																				†
94												*								
[95]									*											
96																				
97																				
98									*				*							
99									*											
100																				
101																				
102																				
103	†																			*
104				*																*
105																				*
106																				*
107																				
108																				*
109																				†
110									*											
111										**										
112										*										
113													*							
114																				
115																				
116													*							*
117										*										
118										**										
119										**										
120										*										
121																				
122						*														

	John Carter Brown Library, Providence, Rhode Island	Biblioteca de la Iglesia, Cartago, Costa Rica	Harvard College Library, Cambridge, Massachusetts	Museum of American Indian, Heye Foundation, N.Y.C.	Hispanic-American Society, New York City	Henry E. Huntington Lib., San Gabriel, California	Joaquin Garcia Icazbalceta Collection, Mexico City	Library of Congress, Washington, D.C.	Long Island Historical Society, Brooklyn, N.Y.	José Toribio Medina, Santiago de Chile	New York Historical Society, New York City	Public Library, New York City	Newberry Library, Chicago, Illinois	W. H. Newman Collection, Buffalo, N.Y.	John Hinsdale Scheide, Titusville, Pennsylvania	Seler Collection, Berlin, Germany	Sociedad Geografica Mexicana, Mexico City	Wm. E. Gates Collection, Tulane Univ., New Orleans	Yale University Library, New Haven, Connecticut	Francisco de Zabalburu, Madrid, Spain
83						*														
84	*						*													
85							*					*								
86	*						*													
86²	*					*				*		*								
87																				
88																				
89	*																			
90																				
91						*	*			*										
92						†														
93							†													
94	*					*	*			*										
95	*					*	*													
96						*														
97																				
98	*					*	*													
99							*													
100																				
101																				
102							*													
103																				
104	*					*		*		*										
105	*					*				*										
106	*					†		*		*		*								
107							†													
108												*								
109																				
110						*						†								
111																				
112	†																			
113	†					†	*													
114										*										
115										*										
116							*													
117																				
118																				
119																				
120																				
121																				
122							*													

	José María de Agreda, Mexico City	Annmary Brown Memorial, Providence, Rhode Island	Edward E. Ayer Collection, Newberry Library, Chicago	H. H. Bancroft Collection, University of California	Biblioteca Andrade, Mexico City	Biblioteca de Guadalajara, Mexico	Biblioteca Lafragua, Mexico City	Biblioteca de Morelia, Mexico	Biblioteca Nacional, Madrid, Spain	Biblioteca Nacional, Mexico City	Biblioteca Nacional, Santiago de Chile	Biblioteca de Oaxaca, Mexico	Biblioteca Palafoxiana, Puebla, Mexico	Biblioteca Provincial, Toledo, Spain	Biblioteca de Queretaro, Mexico	Biblioteca San Isidro, Madrid, Spain	Biblioteca de Zaragoza, Spain	Bodleian Library, Oxford University	Public Library, Boston, Massachusetts	British Museum, London
123															*					
124	*																			
125										*										
126																				
127																				
128																				
129										*										
130										*										*
131										*										
132										*										
133										*										
134																				
135	†		*	†		*														*
136										*										
137										*										
138																				
139										*										
140																				
141										*										
142										*										
143										*										
144										*										
145																				
146																				
147										*										
148										*										
149										*										
150										*										
151																				
152			*																	†
153										*										
154										*										
155										*										
156										*										
157										*										
158										*										
159										*										
160																				*
161										*										
162										*										
163			*	†																*

	John Carter Brown Library Providence, Rhode Island	Biblioteca de la Iglesia Cartago, Costa Rica	Harvard College Library Cambridge, Massachusetts	Museum of American Indian Heye Foundation N.Y.C.	Hispanic-American Society New York City	Henry E. Huntington Lib. San Gabriel, California	Joaquin Garcia Icazbalceta Collection, Mexico City	Library of Congress Washington, D.C.	Long Island Historical Society, Brooklyn, N.Y.	José Toribio Medina Santiago de Chile	New York Historical Society New York City	Public Library New York City	Newberry Library Chicago, Illinois	W. H. Newman Collection Buffalo, N.Y.	John Hinsdale Scheide Titusville, Pennsylvania	Seler Collection Berlin, Germany	Sociedad Geografica Mexicana Mexico City	Wm. E. Gates Collection Tulane Univ., New Orleans	Yale University Library New Haven, Connecticut	Francisco de Zabalburu Madrid, Spain
123																				
124						*														
125																				
126																				
127																				
128	*																			
129																				
130																				
131																				
132																				
133																				
134							*													
135	*						*	*				*								
136																				
137																				
138										*										
139																				
140																				
141																				
142																				
143																				
144																				
145																				
146																				
147																				
148																				
149																				
150																				
151																				
152	*					†	*			*		†							†	
153																				
154																				
155																				
156																				
157																				
158																				
159																				
160																				
161																				
162																				
163	*		*			*	*			*		*							*	

	José Maria de Agreda Mexico City	Annmary Brown Memorial Providence, Rhode Island	Edward E. Ayer Collection Newberry Library, Chicago	H. H. Bancroft Collection University of California	Biblioteca Andrade Mexico City	Biblioteca de Guadalajara, Mexico	Biblioteca Lafragua Mexico City	Biblioteca de Morelia, Mexico	Biblioteca Nacional Madrid, Spain	Biblioteca Nacional Mexico City	Biblioteca Nacional Santiago de Chile	Biblioteca de Oaxaca, Mexico	Biblioteca Palafoxiana Puebla, Mexico	Biblioteca Provincial Toledo, Spain	Biblioteca de Queretaro, Mexico	Biblioteca San Isidro Madrid, Spain	Biblioteca de Zaragoza, Spain	Bodleian Library Oxford University	Public Library Boston, Massachusetts	British Museum London
164	...	...	...	...	...	...	...	...	...	*	...	...	...	...	...	...	...	...	...	...
165	...	...	...	...	...	...	...	...	...	*	...	...	...	...	...	...	...	...	...	...
166	...	...	...	...	...	...	...	...	...	*	...	...	...	...	...	...	...	...	...	...
167	...	...	...	...	...	...	...	...	...	...	...	...	...	...	...	...	...	...	...	...
168	...	...	...	...	...	...	...	...	...	*	...	...	...	...	...	...	...	...	...	...
169	...	...	...	...	...	...	...	...	...	*	...	...	...	...	...	...	...	...	...	...
170	...	...	...	...	...	...	...	...	...	*	...	...	...	...	...	...	...	...	...	...
171	...	...	...	...	...	...	...	...	...	...	...	...	...	...	...	...	...	...	...	*
172	...	...	...	...	...	...	...	...	...	*	...	...	...	...	...	...	...	...	...	...
173	...	...	...	...	...	...	...	...	...	*	...	...	...	...	...	...	...	...	...	...
174	...	...	...	...	...	...	...	...	...	*	...	...	...	...	...	...	...	...	...	...
175	...	...	...	...	...	...	...	...	...	...	...	...	...	...	...	...	...	...	...	...
176	...	...	...	...	...	...	...	...	...	...	...	...	...	...	...	...	...	...	...	...
177	...	...	...	...	...	...	...	...	...	...	...	...	...	...	...	...	...	...	...	...
178	...	...	...	...	...	...	...	...	...	...	...	...	...	...	...	...	...	...	...	...
179	...	...	...	...	...	...	...	...	...	...	...	...	...	...	...	...	...	...	...	...
180	...	...	...	...	...	...	...	...	...	...	...	...	...	...	...	...	...	...	...	...
181	...	...	...	...	...	...	...	...	...	...	...	...	...	...	...	...	...	...	...	...
182	...	...	...	...	...	...	...	...	...	...	...	...	...	...	...	...	...	...	...	...
183	...	...	...	...	...	...	...	...	...	...	...	...	...	...	...	...	...	...	...	...
184	...	...	...	...	...	...	...	...	...	...	...	...	...	...	...	...	...	...	...	...
185	...	...	...	...	...	...	...	...	...	...	...	...	...	...	...	...	...	...	...	...
186	...	...	...	...	...	...	...	...	...	...	...	...	...	...	...	...	...	...	...	...
187	...	...	...	...	...	...	...	...	...	...	...	...	...	...	...	...	...	...	...	...
188	...	...	...	...	...	...	...	...	...	...	...	...	...	...	...	...	...	...	...	...
189	...	...	...	...	...	...	...	...	...	...	...	...	...	...	...	...	...	...	...	...
190	...	...	...	...	...	...	...	...	...	...	...	...	...	...	...	...	...	...	...	...
191	...	...	...	...	...	...	...	...	...	...	...	...	...	*	...	...	...	...	...	...
192.	...	...	...	...	...	...	...	...	...	...	...	...	...	...	...	...	...	...	...	...
193	...	...	...	...	...	...	...	...	...	...	...	...	...	...	...	...	...	...	...	...
194	...	...	...	...	...	...	...	...	...	...	...	...	...	...	...	...	...	...	...	...
195	...	...	...	...	...	...	...	...	...	...	...	...	...	...	...	...	...	...	...	...
196	...	...	...	...	...	...	...	...	...	...	...	...	...	...	...	...	...	...	...	...
197	...	...	...	...	...	...	...	...	...	...	...	...	...	...	...	...	...	...	...	...
198	†	...	...	...	...	...	...	...	...	...	...	...	...	...	...	...	...	...	...	...
199	...	...	...	...	...	...	...	...	...	...	...	...	...	...	...	...	...	...	...	...
200[e]	...	...	...	...	...	...	...	...	...	...	...	...	...	...	...	...	...	...	...	...
200[q]	...	...	...	...	...	...	...	...	...	...	...	...	...	...	...	...	...	...	...	...
200[s]	*	...	...	...	...	...	...	...	...	...	...	...	...	...	...	...	...	...	...	...
200[x]	...	...	...	...	...	...	...	...	...	...	...	...	...	...	...	...	...	...	...	...
200[b]b	..	...	...	...	...	...	...	...	*	...	...	...	...	*	...	...	...	...	...	...

	John Carter Brown Library, Providence, Rhode Island	Biblioteca de la Iglesia, Cartago, Costa Rica	Harvard College Library, Cambridge, Massachusetts	Museum of American Indian Heye Foundation, N.Y.C.	Hispanic-American Society, New York City	Henry E. Huntington Lib. San Gabriel, California	Joaquin Garcia Icazbalceta Collection, Mexico City	Library of Congress, Washington, D.C.	Long Island Historical Society, Brooklyn, N.Y.	José Toribio Medina, Santiago de Chile	New York Historical Society, New York City	Public Library, New York City	Newberry Library, Chicago, Illinois	W. H. Newman Collection, Buffalo, N.Y.	John Hinsdale Scheide, Titusville, Pennsylvania	Seler Collection, Berlin, Germany	Sociedad Geografica Mexicana, Mexico City	Wm. E. Gates Collection, Tulane Univ., New Orleans	Yale University Library, New Haven, Connecticut	Francisco de Zabalburu, Madrid, Spain
164																				
165																				
166																				
167																				
168																				
169																				
170																				
171	*						*			*		*						*		
172																				
173																				
174																				
175																				
176																				
177																				
178																				
179																				
180																				
181	*																			
182	*																			
183	†																			
184																				
185																				
186																				
187																				
188																				
189																				
190																				
191																				
192												†								
193	†																			
194																				
195																				
196																				
197																				
198						†														
199																				
200^e												*								
200^q										*										
200^s	*						*					*								
200^x										*										
200^b	b *											*								

NOTES

5-8. Tracts printed for Bishop Zumarraga, 1543–1544. Medina describes a variant issue of 8, identified by Mr. Eames; both issues are in the New York Public Library.

22. Veracruz, Recognitio, 1554.

22-23. Tracts by Fr. A. de la Veracruz, 1554.

24. Molina, Vocabulario en lengua Mexicana, 1555.

26. Constituciones del Arzobispado y Provincia, 1556. Mr. Scheide has Part II only.

30. Regula Augustini, 1556.

31. Veracruz, Speculum conjugiorum, 1556.

36. Gilberti, Dialogo en lengua de Mechuacan, 1559.

37. Gilberti, Vocabulario, 1559.

46. Puga, Cedulario, 1563.

48-49. Molina, Confessionario en lengua mexicana, 1565.

50. Ledesma, De sacramentis summarium, 1566.

64-65. Molina, Arte and Vocabulario en lengua mexicana, 1571.

78. Anunciacion, Sermonario en lengua mexicana, 1577. The Agreda collection has the last part only.

104. Estatutos, Orden de S. Francisco, 1585.

105. Constituciones Ordinis S. Augustini, 1587.

106. Garcia de Palacio, Instruccion nauthica, 1587.

110. Cardenas, Problemas y secretos de las Indias, 1591.

135. Rincon, Arte Mexicana, 1595.

163. Baptista, Advertencias para los confessores, 1600.

171. Ribera Florez, Exequias funerales del Rey Philippo II, 1600.

THE DE BRY COLLECTOR'S PAINEFULL PEREGRINATION ALONG THE PLEASANT PATHWAY TO PERFECTION

By HENRY N. STEVENS

Of London

FOR more than two hundred years the highest ambition of every great Book Collector has been to acquire a complete set of that wonderful series of illustrated Voyages and Travels edited and published by Theodore de Bry and his descendants, now familiarly termed 'De Bry.'

When it is remembered that the publication of that great work, in parts, extended over a period of no less than fifty-five years (1590 to 1644 inclusive), the extreme difficulty of securing anything like a complete Collection is readily apparent. A straight set in single editions comprises 57 Parts, viz: —

America Series in Latin 13
India Series in Latin, including the Appendix Congo 13
America Series in German 14
India Series in German, including the Appendix Congo 14
America, Part I, in English 1
America, Part I, in French 1
The "Elenchus" in Latin (or collective Title, Preface and
Table of Contents to the American Series in Latin) 1

Several private collectors and libraries possess complete sets of these fifty-seven parts in one or other of the various editions in which they were issued.

But by the time the De Bry collector has arrived at the proud and happy stage of having secured a complete straight set, he begins to realize that he has so far barely touched the fringe of the subject, and is only at the commencement of his real quest. He finds that he has merely laid the foundations, as it were, on which to build the superstructure of a really fine Collection of De Bry. It suddenly dawns on him that, if he has caught the De Bry fever, his "appetite had grown by what it fed on," and become insatiable. Having crossed the Rubicon, he must needs go on and endeavor to add to his Collection every other known edition. With renewed hopes and with his ambition fired anew, he again sets out in search of the thirty-five or forty additional parts which still have to be secured to complete a set of all editions of every part.

But if the acquisition of the original fifty-seven parts had proved an arduous task, it was nothing to the difficulties which have now to be surmounted, for they increase tenfold, nay even a hundredfold, as the set approaches nearer and nearer to completion; for each successive part that remains to be acquired is necessarily rarer and even more elusive than the last. Some editions of certain parts are so excessively rare that they are only likely to be met with once in a lifetime, though of course a great deal depends on chance.

There is an old saying that "all things come round to him who will but wait"; but in De Bry collecting one often has to wait a very long time, and perhaps may even wait in vain. So when the opportunity does occur to secure one of these super-rarities the tide must be "taken at the flood," else "the bargain passeth to thy hungry neighbour who seemeth to live but to outbid thee." It seldom happens that one has the luck to get a second chance at the same prize, but I recently had the extreme good fortune to secure some rarities which I lost about forty years ago.

In the sale of the Duke of Marlborough's Library from Blenheim Palace, at the auction rooms of Puttick and Simpson in London on December 9, 1881, Lots 2052 and 2053 consisted of a very choice collection of De Bry, amongst which were some parts of extraordinary rarity. My father was greatly excited, for with all his lengthy experience there were several pieces he had never seen before. So he determined to buy the lot if in any way possible, and we bid £700 (a record price in those days) without success, for we were outbid by the elder Quaritch at £720. We never could learn what became of that set, for Quaritch told us he was not at liberty to disclose the name of his customer. In the summer of 1922 that very same lot turned up again at Sotheby's in the sale of the library of the late Baroness Burdett-Coutts. I did not realize from the description in the Sale Catalogue that it was a reappearance of the Marlborough set, but when I went to view the lot at the sale rooms, I was overjoyed to recognize immediately my long-lost friend of forty years before. After waiting all those years without seeing or even hearing of any other copies of the super-rarities I wanted, I resolved to make a determined effort not to lose them a second time. I feared that I might be outbid by some unlimited American commission, but as the lot was not so well and fully catalogued as before, I had some faint hope that the rarities would escape the recognition of De Bry *cognoscenti*. And this actually occurred, for although my son went to the sale prepared to double our bid of forty years ago, he was fortunately able to purchase the lot at considerably less than the price realized at the Marlborough Sale. Thus was my former disappointment assuaged and my patience rewarded, for it is very seldom, in these days of continuously rising prices, that such a lucky *lapsus* occurs. The acquisition of that lot of De Bry has enabled me to describe fully, from personal inspection, many rarities which hitherto I had only been able to quote from the descriptions of previous writers.

So far I have touched only on the actual separate Parts in their various editions, but even should the collector be lucky enough to secure all these, he has still to acquire the numerous variations and different issues of certain editions. In the course of his search, the collector, as he warms to a fuller knowledge of his subject through experience, will gradually become aware of certain curious and interesting variations or discrepancies in the different editions of some of the parts. These have in many cases been identified as first, second, or even third issues of a specified edition, although the exact chronological sequence of these various issues cannot always be accurately determined. Whilst in the main the edition is the same, certain differences, alterations, or additions are noticeable which clearly indicate a separate issue. The variations occur not only in the first, but also in later editions of many of the parts, and some of them are of the very greatest rarity, for the reason that in many cases they probably formed only a very small portion of the whole impression.

The reason for these variations is not far to seek. During the interval between 1590 and 1644, whilst the whole work was current, many of the parts were reprinted several times, frequently without any indication of the fact on the title-page. Some of them were more popular than others; and when the original stock became exhausted, they were reprinted wholly or in part, sometimes with and sometimes without alterations. Many of these reprints were evidently made sheet by sheet or even leaf by leaf, as often as required to make up a shortage of certain sheets in the original stock; consequently it is a common thing to find copies in undoubted original condition which contain mixed impressions of text or plates. When the whole of the original stock was thus exhausted the part was entirely reprinted as a second edition. The same course of procedure then went on with the second edition when the stock of certain sheets was exhausted.

Then again some of the copper-plates wore out, were lost, or sustained damage, so that, when wanted for reprinting, they had to be reëngraved, and these plates are oftentimes found redrawn and reëngraved in *contre-épreuve*, that is, reversed. In some cases the original lost plate must have turned up again at a later period; for whilst a new plate occurs in an intermediate issue, the old plate is sometimes found in a later one. Hence it will be seen how the descriptions given by different bibliographers do not always agree, because the particular copies described by one were doubtless issued at different times and varied in their contents from those noted by another.

During the lengthy period in which the whole work was current, it is obvious that the contents of a later issue, even if purporting to be of the same edition, would be likely to vary somewhat from an earlier one made perhaps several years before. For instance, some leaves, maps, or plates have been added to later issues, which fact would not make the original or earlier issues imperfect. On the other hand, some maps or plates have been omitted from later issues. Thus it is that some leaves, maps, or plates are much rarer than others, and whilst called for by one bibliographical authority, are not mentioned by another; consequently there is no such thing as actual uniformity in a set of De Bry.

As time went on, the publishers appear to have issued the work in collective form, that is to say, several consecutive parts bound together in a thick volume. Alternatively some purchasers of separate parts eventually had them bound in volumes. In either case the binders seem frequently to have misplaced some of the maps. Consequently some bibliographers, being misled by a misplaced bound copy, will describe a particular map as belonging to a certain part, whereas another authority, working from another copy with the maps differently placed, will assign the same map to another part. Then a later writer, picking up information from his predecessors, will describe this map as being found in each of two parts, and so we arrive almost at a *reductio ad absurdum*, for in reality only one map is required. Discrepancies from such a cause, being merely fortuitous, are not true original variations.

Then again numerous instances occur where in some issues blank spaces are found which in other issues are filled by plates. Another fruitful source of variations is the misplacement of some of the copper-plates when printing. It frequently hap-

pens that, when reprinted, the wrong copper-plate was printed
on a certain leaf of text, and a number of copies containing the
error got into circulation before it was observed. Sometimes
the mistake was discovered and was then corrected by pasting
an impression of the correct plate over the error. These error
plates (which when corrected are usually called overlays) are
quite numerous, but, owing probably to the small number
printed at one time, they are mostly very scarce.

The question of original blank leaves is another difficult
point in connection with the correct collation of a set of
De Bry. When parts are found separately in original condition, the blank leaves necessary to complete sheets are usually
found intact. But when several parts are found together in
contemporary or later binding, some at least of the blank
leaves are generally missing. It is extremely difficult to supply
these missing blank leaves because the blanks from other parts
are not often interchangeable. The De Brys used quite a number of different papers, and it is not at all unusual to find two or
even three different sorts used in the same part. The blank
leaves are really far scarcer than the printed leaves. Of course
a copy of a part containing its proper blank leaves is more
highly esteemed by the collector than one without them; but
to the student who consults De Bry merely as a work of historical reference, the absence of the blanks is entirely negligible.

Almost every writer who has touched on the subject of
De Bry has commented on the extreme difficulty, not to say
impossibility, of making up a complete set. A hundred years
ago the great bibliographer Thomas Frognall Dibdin wrote in
his 'Library Companion,' page 382:

What a bibliographical chord am I striking, in the mention of the
Travels of De Bry! What a "Peregrination" does the possession of a copy
of his labours imply! What toil, difficulty, perplexity, anxiety, and vexa-
tion attend the collector — be he young or old — who sets his heart upon a
PERFECT DE BRY! How many have started on this pursuit, with gay

spirits and well-replenished purses, but have turned from it in despair, and abandoned it in utter hopelessness of achievement! Nor can this prize, like that of beauty, be held out as a reward for the "brave." Good fortune, good luck, accident — call it what you will — are the concomitants of such an acquisition. And what will the sceptical reader say, when I inform him, that neither the pages of De Bure nor Camus initiate him into ALL the mysteries of a perfect copy of De Bry?

Again, in 1881, my father wrote in his 'Historical Collections,' Part I, page 26:

The purchaser of this remarkably fine and sound set will have laid a solid foundation for a long life of brilliant bibliographical quiddling about the never-ending *variations*, a solace for old age that was unknown to either Cicero or Cato. No man ever yet made up his De Bry perfect, if one may count on the three great De Bry witnesses, the Rt. Hon. Thomas Grenville, the Russian Prince Sobolewski, and the American Mr. Lenox, who all went far beyond De Bure, yet fell far short of attaining all the variations they had heard of. When an earnest Collector has secured Thevenot, De Bry, and Hulsius, he possesses a never-dying pleasure that will not desert him, live as long as he may.

What was written by Dibdin a hundred years ago would be even more forceful at the present day, were it not that the great development of the study of scientific bibliography which has taken place in recent years has largely simplified matters. Numerous bibliographies and collations of special sets have appeared since Dibdin, a few of the more important being:

Weigel....................................... 1845
Brunet 1860
John Carter Brown (Bartlett) 1875
Henry Huth.................................. 1880
Lord Crawford 1884
James Lenox (Eames) 1904
E. Dwight Church (Cole) 1907
John Carter Brown Library 1919

These have thrown a flood of fresh light on the most interesting and fascinating problem, what really constitutes a perfect set of De Bry.

Even if there is a substratum of truth in what the early bibliographers have said, that actual finality may never be attained, it must be remembered that there is always the pleasure of the chase, and the recurrent joy which accrues every time when another "rarissimum" has been run to earth and added to the Collection. Every capture stimulates the pleasures of anticipation of further successes yet to come. Were finality in any form of collecting easily or absolutely attainable, one of life's main interests would be gone for ever, for the bibliophile has yet to be born who could rest content on laurels already won.

A NOTE ON THE LAWS OF THE
REPUBLIC OF VERMONT

By JAMES BENJAMIN WILBUR

Of Manchester, Vermont

VERMONT'S political independence until 1791 of the thirteen States which formed the United States makes the laws passed by its legislators, in sessions held in different parts of the wilderness comprising that State from 1778 to 1787, an interesting study. Of special interest is the story of their printing, for, when Vermont first declared her independence, the nearest presses were at Exeter and Portsmouth in New Hampshire, which was enemy country, and in Hartford, Connecticut.

The legislators met for the first time at Windsor, March 12, 1778, and adjourned March 26, to meet Thursday, June 4, in Bennington, where they sat until June 18, when they adjourned subject to the call of the Governor. Many questions were voted on but few bills or acts, so designated, were passed. An election was held and the Legislature met at Windsor, October 8, 1778. At this session, a number of townships east of the Connecticut River which had joined by union with Vermont were represented. Judah Paddock and Alden Spooner were induced to set up a press in Dresden [1] (Hanover) and as this town was then in the Republic of Vermont, the Legislature, on October 10, appointed them "printers for the General Assembly of this State." They were ready to begin printing about the date of receiving their appointment. The session adjourned October 24, after appointing a committee "to prepare the acts passed at the former sessions and likewise the present session, for the press, and get them printed." This

---

1. Harold G. Rugg, Dresden Press: *Dartmouth Alumni Magazine*, May, 1920.

vote indicated an intention to print the laws, but it is doubtful if the laws of 1778 were ever printed.

The votes at the March and June meetings show that nothing had been done beyond making manuscript copies of some of the more important acts passed. One of these manuscripts, certified to be "a copy" by Thomas Chandler, Jr., dated Windsor, March 25, 1778, is now in the possession of Mr. Matt B. Jones of Boston. Bills were presented for copying laws amounting to £48 7s. 0d. Colonel John Barrett tendered a bill to the Assembly, dated November 17, 1778, for "21 days service preparing laws for the press and going to Hanover to carry these at 36 shillings per day; to horse hire 90 miles at 1 shilling; £42 6s. 0d."

These laws were thus undoubtedly prepared for printing and delivered to Spooner to be printed. Little evidence worthy of consideration, that they were printed, is to be found. Slade ('Vermont State Papers,' p. 287) wrote, in 1823: "much exertion has been made to obtain a copy of the laws of 1778, but without effect. They were published toward the close of that year in a pamphlet form, but were never recorded in the Secretary's office." This is an assertion of an official of the State, made not more than forty-five years after the alleged fact, at a time when a number of men were living who had taken an active part in the early affairs of the State. Yet it is possible that Slade confused the printing of the Journal of 1778 with the laws of that year. Certainly no bill from the printer for printing these laws can now be found.

In a bill rendered by Spooner on June 3, 1779, which seems to include all the work he had done for the State to that time, is an item dated November 10, 1778, for printing "200 Journals of Assembly, £45–0–0." There is also a charge of £10, dated April 3, 1779, "to printing 60 votes of Assembly." This last charge may have been for printing the proceedings of October

21, 1778, as the Assembly voted to have the proceedings of that day printed.

Ira Allen, on his way home from visiting the President and Assembly of New Hampshire at Exeter, went to Dresden and from that place, November 27, 1778, issued an address of three printed pages, 'To the Inhabitants of the State of Vermont.' It detailed his negotiations with New Hampshire on dissolving the union of the sixteen New Hampshire towns with Vermont. On the bottom of the last sheet, below the printed signature of Ira Allen, is printed the following: "N.B. The laws of the state has come to hand, and will be ready for sale in a short time." This may have been an advertisement of the printer. No copy of either Journals charged for November 10, 1778, and April 3, 1779, has ever been discovered. It may be that Allen took them all and destroyed them after the union was dissolved; and that, foreseeing the dissolution, he instructed Spooner not to print the laws that had been prepared and delivered by Barrett, some days before Allen reached Dresden.

That the laws were never printed is the opinion of Mr. Wilberforce Eames, in which Mr. Matt B. Jones and I concur. That was also the opinion of Henry Hall, one of Vermont's early historians, who gave the matter some investigation. We must remember not only that they were passed as temporary laws, but that the establishment of a press had been so delayed as to make the printing of these impossible before the early part of December, and that a permanent code was to be enacted at the meeting of the Legislature early in February. What more natural than that Ira Allen, Treasurer of the State, should instruct the printers not to print the laws.

The following is believed to be the correct order of printing the laws of the Republic of Vermont from 1779 to 1791.[2]

2. Mr. Wilberforce Eames is entitled to most of the credit for the preparation of this list.

LIST OF VERMONT LAWS, 1779–1791

1. Acts and Laws, Feb., 1779, pp. (2), 12 (2), 110. Dresden, 1779.
2. " " " June, 1779, pp. 111–112. (Dresden.)
3. " " " Oct., 1779, and March, 1780, pp. (7). Hartford, 1780.
4. " " " Oct., 1780 (1st portion), pp. (6). (Westminster, 1780.)
5. " " " Oct., 1780 (2d portion), pp. 125–128. (Westminster, 1781.)
6. " " " Feb., 1781, pp. (11). Westminster, 1781.
7. " " " April, 1781 (1st portion), pp. (2). No copy can be found.
8. " " " April, 1781 (2d portion), the *money bill*, pp. (4). (Westminster.)
9. " " " June, 1781 (1st portion), pp. (12). (Westminster.)
10. " " " Oct., 1780 (3d portion), and June, 1781 (2d portion), pp. (16).
11. " " " Oct., 1781 (procuring provisions for troops), pp. 1. Westminster. No copy can be found.
12. " " " Oct., 1781 (money tax bill), pp. (1). Westminster.
13. " " " Oct., 1781, pp. (4). (Westminster.)
14. " " " Feb., June, and Oct., 1782, and Feb., 1783, pp. 12. Windsor, 1783.
15. " " " June and Oct., 1782 (Revised Laws), pp. 38. (Bennington, 1783.)
16. " " " Feb., 1783, pp. (6).
17. " " " Feb., 1783, pp. (3). Bennington, 1783.
18. " " " Oct., 1783, pp. 10. Windsor, 1784.
19. " " " Oct., 1783, pp. 39–47. Windsor, 1784.
20. " " " Feb. and March, 1784, pp. 15. Windsor, 1784.
21. " " " March, 1784, pp. 49–54. Windsor, 1784.
22. " " " Oct., 1784, pp. 12. Windsor, 1785.
23. " " " June, 1785, pp. 7. Windsor, 1785.
24. " " " Oct., 1785, pp. 9. (Windsor.)
25. " " " Oct., 1786, pp. 20. (Windsor.)
26. " " " Oct., 1786, pp. (12). Bennington, 1786.
27. Statutes, Feb. and March, 1787, pp. (4), 5–18, 171. Windsor, 1787.
28. Acts and Laws, Oct., 1787, pp. 16. (Windsor.)
29. " " " Oct., 1788, pp. 28. (Windsor.)
30. " " " Oct., 1789, pp. 19. (Windsor.)
31. " " " Oct., 1790, pp. 11. (Windsor.)
32. " " " Jan., 1791, pp. 28. Bennington.

THE PROMOTION LITERATURE OF GEORGIA

By VERNER W. CRANE

Assistant Professor of American History, Brown University

GEORGIA, the last successful enterprise of English colonization in North America, was also one of the first notable achievements of modern philanthropy. Thus a double interest attaches to the crop of pamphlets and of journalistic and poetical effusions which the activities of Oglethorpe and his associates called forth.

Most of these Georgia items have long been commonplaces of Americana — described by Rich, Sabin, Winsor, the De Renne catalogue; reprinted, several of them, by Peter Force and in the Georgia Historical Society 'Collections.' But there are other titles, especially for the neglected pre-settlement period, which should find place in the Georgia bibliography. There are questions, too, of provenience and of authorship that can be illumined from documentary sources, or by applying a more rigorous criticism to the accepted canon. Moreover, in one great library of American history there are undescribed copies of several Georgia tracts that possess unique association interest. And it remains to place the early Georgia literature fairly in its setting — as the product of a remarkable publicity campaign, designed to "sell" Georgia to Parliament, to charitable folk, and to intending colonists. To a marked degree, the extraordinary vogue that Georgia enjoyed in those first years was the consequence of efficient "booming" by its promoters, and by their literary and journalistic friends. Promotion literature was, of course, no new *genre*, but the Trustees perfected its technique. A modern press agent would have little, perhaps, to teach those Parliamentarians and clergymen of two centuries ago, who, at their first meeting as a Common Council, adopted the following resolution:

That Measures be taken to prevent the Publishing in the News Papers anything relating to this Society that shall be disadvantageous to their Designs; And that Mr. Oglethorpe be desired to take the said Measures & to cause such Paragraphs to be Published in the said News Papers as may be proper for the promoting of the said Designs.[1]

When the Georgia press campaign was thus launched, a royal charter had just been obtained, after three years of planning and negotiation. During those years — which should no longer be the "unknown period" of Georgia history, now that the 'Diary of Viscount Percival afterwards First Earl of Egmont'[2] has been published — there were merged two movements, one strategic, the other philanthropic, to produce the Georgia enterprise. Each has its literature. The pamphlets relating to earlier colonization attempts upon the southern frontier (Azilia, the Golden Islands, Carolana, Purry's first enterprise) are better known, no doubt, than the literature of the charitable movement. Elsewhere[3] I have told briefly how a little charitable society organized about 1724 by Dr. Thomas Bray to administer a legacy for the education of negroes in the colonies, and to carry on his own philanthropy in the founding of parochial libraries, was enlarged in membership in 1730 to include the Parliamentary prison reformers, and widened in function to embrace within its scope the establishment of debtor colonies in America. The bibliography of the Associates of the late Reverend Dr. Bray — now revealed as the parent organization of the Georgia Trust — includes, notably, [Samuel Smith]: 'Publick Spirit, illustrated in the Life and Designs of Thomas Bray' ... London. MDCCXLVI; second edi-

1. Colonial Records of the State of Georgia, II, 3.

2. Historical Manuscripts Commission, Manuscripts of the Earl of Egmont. . . . Vol. I. 1730–1733. 1920. Vol. II. 1734–1738. 1923. A third volume will complete this notable diary. On its importance for the early history of Georgia, see Ulrich B. Phillips, "New Light Upon the Founding of Georgia," in Georgia Historical Quarterly, VI, 5–12.

3. "The Philanthropists and the Genesis of Georgia," in American Historical Review, XXVII, 63–69.

tion, 1808.[4] It includes also the so-called Georgia sermons —
anniversary sermons which were preached before Trustees and
Associates in joint meetings long after the trusts had been
legally separated.[5] In the British Museum is another pertinent
Bray item: 'Missionalia: or, a Collection of Missionary Pieces
relating to the Conversion of the Heathen; both the African Negroes and American Indians.' London. 1727.[6] These
tracts reveal Bray intensely concerned for the conversion of
the American Indians, but opposed to the famous scheme of
Berkeley for a college in Bermuda, which had captured the
imagination of one of Bray's Associates, Lord Percival. Instead, Bray advocated settling "artisan-missionaries" on the
borders of the colonies to convert and civilize the natives; thus
a barrier would be built up against Indian barbarism, and
English territory would be strengthened and extended. The
seriousness with which the Georgia Trustees approached their
responsibility for the Indians was, perhaps, part of their inheritance from Bray.

4. See *Ibid.*, p. 63 (note 3) for a discussion of the authorship of this tract.

5. The series of Georgia sermons begins with the sermons of Samuel Smith and
John Burton, preached February 23, 1731, and February 24, 1732, before the Associates of Dr. Bray, as "anniversary sermons," on a fund left, apparently, in Bray's
will. Percival, Diary, I, 223–225. When they were published, in 1733, the title-
pages indicated that they were preached before *Trustees* and Associates; but of
course the two bodies had not yet been separated, nor indeed did the Georgia Trust
yet exist. There was a mistake, also, in the date of Burton's sermon. From 1733
until at least 1750, with the exception, possibly, of one or two years, these sermons
were preached before Trustees and Associates on the occasion of the annual meeting
of the former in March. There is evidence that the preachers were suggested by the
Associates, and that the fund was theirs. However, the publication of the sermons
was part of the elaborate Georgia publicity. For the peculiar origins of the Rundle
sermon (1734) see Diary, II, 23, 25, 26. The John Carter Brown Library possesses a
nearly complete collection of these sermons from 1731 to 1750.

6. Several separately printed tracts are bound together in one volume with the
above printed title-page. Some unrelated pamphlets are also bound in, and the
volume does not contain Part II as indicated in the table of contents. For the later
history of the Associates, see An Account of the Designs of the Associates of the
late Dr. Bray; with an Abstract of their Proceedings. London. MDCCLXII. (Later
editions, 1764, 1769, 1772, etc.)

The earlier colonization pamphlets, from Montgomery's
'Discourse' of 1717 to Purry's 'Memorial' of 1724,[7] had no
discoverable direct relation to the founding of Georgia; but
they all advertised Carolina, and the need of frontier defense
in the South, at a time when the colonial authorities were just
awakening to the danger of French "encirclement." In 1729,
when the surrender of the Carolina charter to the Crown was
pending, there was printed in London the first edition of
Joshua Gee's 'The Trade and Navigation of Great Britain
Considered,'[8] one of the most widely read of the commercial
tracts of the century. Repeatedly Gee insisted upon the value
of the southern colonies: of Virginia, and especially of South
Carolina — "the most improveable, in my Apprehension, of
any of our Colonies" — and made suggestions for transporting
the poor thither which were strikingly paralleled, a little later,
in Oglethorpe's first exposition of his charitable colony scheme.
The most significant passages are in Chapter XXVII, in which
Gee suggested that not only convicts, but the unemployed,
who "cannot find Methods of Subsistence at home," should be
transported and settled upon tracts of a hundred acres on the
borders of the southern colonies, their quit-rents to be payable
later in hemp or flax. Such colonists, marrying young, would
multiply rapidly, "by which Means those vast Tracts of Land
now waste will be planted, and secured from the Danger we
apprehend of the French over-running them." Silk, as well as
hemp and flax, Gee expected from those "inviting Places."
Now when Oglethorpe, in February, 1730, unfolded his plan
to Lord Percival — for a dozen years thereafter his chief collaborator — one might imagine he had just come from reading Gee's pamphlet. "The scheme," recorded Percival in his

7. I owe to Mr. Wilberforce Eames the information that the British Museum
possesses a copy of a contemporary edition of the Purry Memoire of 1724 printed in
English, probably by the same printer.

8. Later editions appeared in rapid sequence, 1730, 1731, 1738, 1750, 1760, 1767.
The quotations are from pp. 23, 44, 60–61, of the first edition.

faithful 'Diary,'[9] "is to procure a quantity of acres either from the Government or by gift or purchase in the West Indies [that is, America], and to plant thereon a hundred miserable wretches who being let out of gaol by the last year's Act, are now starving about the town for want of employment; ... that in time they with their families would increase so fast as to become a security and defence of our possessions against the French and Indians of those parts; that they should be employed in cultivating flax and hemp, which being allowed to make into yarn, would be returned to England and Ireland, and greatly promote our manufactures. All which I approved." Silk culture was another hopeful prospect. Though Gee hardly suggested a new colony, under separate government, in other respects the resemblances between his ideas and Oglethorpe's were so close as to raise the presumption, not of coincidence, but of derivation. That Oglethorpe knew the pamphlet we have no external proof; but that a deputy-governor of the Royal African Company should not have known it is difficult to believe.

Though Oglethorpe apparently envisaged his first modest scheme of a charitable colony in the terms of Gee's recent suggestions,[10] his practical incentive came, of course, from his own noble labors as the chairman of the Parliamentary gaols committee of 1729. The work of that committee had been hailed in verse by the Reverend Samuel Wesley in "The Prisons Opened"; [11] and by James Thomson in the more famous apostrophe to the "generous band" of prison reformers which he interpolated in his poem 'Winter' in 1730. "Ye sons of mercy! yet resume the search" — the exact occasion for this poetical appeal is revealed in Oglethorpe's long colloquy with Percival of February 13, 1730.

9. Vol. 1, 44–46, February 13, 1729–30.
10. Of course it is possible that Gee derived his notions from contact with Oglethorpe: or both men from a common source.
11. Nichols: Literary Anecdotes of the Eighteenth Century (1812 ed.), 1, 405.

A tantalizing clue to a "first" Georgia pamphlet not now, apparently, extant, is furnished by a note in the second edition of 'Publick Spirit' (1808). The editor, H. J. Todd, had access to the lost early journals of the Associates, and perhaps to other perished sources. To Samuel Smith's statement that "a design was formed of establishing a Colony in America," Todd furnished this note:

Proposals, with a view to this object, had been published by John Norris. They were dedicated to the Members of Parliament. The author endeavours to point out "in this removal to America" the certain and sure method of lessening the great number of poor throughout this kingdom, to the great advantage of them and their families, the future ease of parish charges, the increase of trade, an addition to the crown revenue, and profit to the kingdom in general.[12]

It is just possible that Norris was the "late author" of a scheme for settlement in Carolina, to whom reference was made in the 'Political State of Great Britain,' April, 1730.[13]

Of the Georgia press campaign it is impossible here to write at length. Besides undisguised advertisements, numerous flattering references to Georgia appeared in the monthly magazines and in the daily sheets, the inspiration of which is suggested both by their contents and by the items in the general accounts of the Trustees for 1733 and 1734, of charges for "publishing Articles and Advertisements in the Publick News Papers."[14]

Of similar official origin were practically all the Georgia pamphlets of the first dozen years, with the obvious exception of the printed "libels" of the "malcontents." In some years

12. Note [E] on p. 57, referring to p. 50. There was a Sir John Norris who was a Member of Parliament, and on the gaols committee. In 1712 there had been printed an interesting tract designed to promote emigration to Port Royal, called Profitable Advice for Rich and Poor. In a Dialogue, or Discourse between James Freeman, a Carolina Planter, and Simon Question, a West-Country Farmer. This is commonly ascribed to a John Norris of Charles Town.

13. Vol. xxxix, 345.

14. The General Account of all Monies and Effects Received and Expended by the Trustees for Establishing the Colony of Georgia in America. (June 9, 1732–June 9, 1733), [1733], p. 10; Colonial Records of Georgia, iii, 52.

the Trustees were at considerable expense for propaganda, to win subscriptions from the public, and when that resource proved disappointing, to secure subsidies from Parliament. Thus in the first year £133 9s. 10d. was expended on stationery and printing; in 1735–36, £113 3s. 8½d.; in 1740–41, £153 1s. 8½d.; in 1741–42, for printing of books and pamphlets alone, £131 1s. 8d.[15] Several of the pamphlets were issued in de luxe editions, from the best presses of England; some were illustrated with maps and engravings. Georgia publicity was not merely persistent, but of high grade. It was probably no accident that, among several candidates, an author was selected as Secretary for the Trust. Benjamin Martyn, to be sure, offered his services without immediate compensation, but a salary was afterwards paid him, and meanwhile the patronage of so distinguished a society as the Georgia Trust was not to be despised by a struggling Government clerk and scribbler. Of his selection Percival wrote that "he is a very ingenious young man, and writ a tragedy ['Timoleon'] last year, which had great success on the stage."[16] Martyn readily turned his hand to pamphleteering, and was the author or compiler of most of the Georgia tracts — including, it is probable, the well-known pamphlet usually attributed to Oglethorpe.

It was Martyn, Percival reveals,[17] who prepared that first rare and beautiful prospectus of the new philanthropy, for the use of collectors of subscriptions: 'Some Account of the Designs of the Trustees for Establishing the Colony of Georgia in America.' London. MDCCXXXII. There were two folio editions,[18] one of them enriched with engravings: a head-piece,

15. Colonial Records of Georgia, III, 16, 113, 225, 239.

16. Diary, I, 286; also 412. Colonial Records of Georgia, II, 3, 5, 105, 514. Dictionary of National Biography, XXXVI, 314–315.

17. Diary, I, 289.

18. It is probable that of these two editions the pamphlet embellished by Pine is the later. The other edition which bears a headpiece of the conventional sort (Ceres, horns of plenty and the like), is composed of two leaves without title-page, and has in the JCB and BM copies the lower half of page 4 blank. This we may

with a characteristically Utopian scene of colonial pioneering, and a tailpiece, both engraved by J. Pine.[19] It had also a map, the so-called "first map of Georgia." The source of the map is readily identified as the Nairne inset in Edward Crisp's 'Compleat Description of Carolina' [1711].[20] A special interest attaches to the John Carter Brown copy of the illustrated folio. On a blank sheet at the end is a contemporary certified copy of the commission issued to the collectors of benefactions.[21] The name inserted was that of an enthusiastic friend of the colony, and one of its poetical choir — the Reverend Samuel Wesley, father of John and Charles. Here, apparently, is the copy of 'Some Account' which Wesley exhibited to prospective donors, with convenient evidence of his authority attached in the attested copy of his commission.

In 1732 was also published the first edition of perhaps the most famous of all the Georgia pamphlets — especially famous because it has commonly been ascribed to the founder himself:

speak of as edition "A." Mr. Leonard L. Mackall has called my attention to the fact that in the De Renne copy of this edition, the blank space is occupied by an impression of the map which appears in the Pine edition, in the Smith "Sermon" and in all three issues of Martyn's "Reasons," with the difference that the De Renne map bears an inscription on Florida which obviously has been erased from the plate as it was printed in the three works here specified. The appearance of an earlier state of this map in a single known variant issue of edition ".A" seems to indicate the priority of edition "A" over the Pine edition, containing a state of the map with erasures. (L. C. W.)

19. John Pine (1690–1756), engraver of the celebrated edition of Horace. Bryan's Dictionary of Painters and Engravers, 1904, IV, 121.

20. Copy in Library of Congress. Thomas Nairne was the first Indian agent of South Carolina, and a notable advocate of English expansion. The original manuscript map, sent home in 1708, has disappeared; but the tradition appears in several manuscript and engraved maps of the period. The plate as engraved for the Georgia map evidently followed its prototype, the Crisp-Nairne map, more closely than the final impressions show; these reveal erasures which can be identified with legends on the Carolina map. The De Renne copy, as Mr. Mackall points out in Georgia Historical Quarterly, II, 76, is an "earlier state," before the erasures were completed.

21. The commission is dated November 16, 1732; the attestation, November 27. The former is identical with the British Museum copy of a blank engraved commission (bound in with the two folios of Some Account) except that, of course, the Pine head-piece does not appear as in the engraved commission.

'A New and Accurate Account of the Provinces of South-Carolina and Georgia,' printed for J. Worrall and "sold by J. Roberts near the Oxford-Arms in Warwick Lane." [22] The first two chapters contained an optimistic description of the country, based upon Archdale and upon J. P. Purry's 'Description Abrégée,' Neufchatel [1730].[23] Two following chapters argued the advantages to England, from the mercantilist as well as the charitable view, of sending the poor to Georgia, where they "may be happy . . . , and profitable to England."

The sole basis for the attribution of this pamphlet to Oglethorpe by Rich and others is a statement in John Nichols: 'Literary Anecdotes of the Eighteenth Century.' [24] From the Bowyer list of imprints for 1732 Nichols cited 'An Account of the Colony in Georgia'; and also (this apparently has been overlooked), 'An Essay on Plantations; or Tracts relating to the Colonies' — both of 'which, Nichols asserted, "were the production of James-Edward Oglethorpe, Esq." But the first title fits Martyn's 'Some Account' as well as 'A New and Accurate Account'; and in any case it is probable that Bowyer's accounts showed only that Oglethorpe paid for the printing.

That Oglethorpe was responsible for launching a collection of colonial tracts is itself a matter of considerable interest. The collection in question was undoubtedly the undated compilation: 'Select Tracts relating to Colonies,'[25] in which the first selection was 'An Essay on Plantations. By Sir Francis

22. A second edition, altered only in the title-page, was issued in 1733. I have not seen this. Books relating to the History of Georgia in the Library of Wymberley Jones De Renne. 1911. P. 22.

23. On the De Renne Library acquisition of the "only known copy" of this Purry pamphlet, see the article by L. L. Mackall, in Georgia Historical Quarterly, II, 76.

24. (1812 edition), II, 17.

25. Like A New and Accurate Account, this was "printed for J. Roberts at the Oxford-Arms in Warwick Lane." The British Museum catalogue suggests 1700 as the date of Select Tracts; but the date is clearly established by an entry in the Gentleman's Magazine, II, 1087: "A Register of Books publish'd in November, 1732" includes both Select Tracts and A New and Accurate Account.

Bacon.' The fourth and fifth chapters comprised 'The Benefit of Plantations or Colonies. By William Penn'; and 'A Discourse concerning Plantations. By Sir Josiah Child.' The Introduction began:

> Nothing so much improves the Mind, and directs the Judgement to right Determinations as Experience and the Opinions of wise Men. As new Colonies are now so much talked of, it may be agreeable to the Publick, to see what has been writ upon that Subject by Philosophers, Statesmen, and Merchants, Men of different Professions, living in different Ages and Countreys, who could have no Common View in deceiving.

Compiled in 1732 by one of the Georgia group (perhaps by Oglethorpe), the 'Select Tracts' takes an important place in the Georgia propaganda. The pamphlet in its selections, especially from Child, fairly met the most serious objection which could arise against the Georgia project — the current prejudice against draining population away from the mother country.

There are difficulties in assuming Oglethorpe's authorship of 'A New and Accurate Account' which do not apply to Secretary Martyn. The Preface concludes with a fulsome tribute to the Trustees which would have come with better grace from a servant of the Society than from the principal member. The style is rhetorical; at the same time the author was a rather scholarly fellow, given to the pedantries of footnotes and bibliographical prefaces! These were characteristics, by the way, of Martyn — witness the 'Reasons' of 1733 and 'An Impartial Enquiry' of 1741. Not merely in general traits of style, but also in specific rhetorical devices the pamphlet is stamped with the mannerisms of Martyn.[26] Moreover, in content his pam-

---

26. A few striking parallels follow. They are the more impressive since in several instances they appear in discussions of slightly different topics.

New and Accurate Account	*Reasons* (First edition)
Page 30. ". . . the Multitude of unfortunate People . . .: Some undone by Guardians, some by Law-Suits, some by Accidents in Commerce, some by Stocks and Bubbles, and some by Suretyship."	Page 19. "The Ways that lead to a Man's Ruin are various. Some are undone by Over-trading, others by Want of Trade, many by being responsible for others."

phlet of the next year was an amplification of Chapters III and IV of 'A New and Accurate Account':[27] here, and in other of his writings, he cited some of the same sources. Of particular interest is this reference in the preface of 'A New and Accurate Account':

Since the following chapters were prepared for the press, I have read a curious pamphlet, entitled, Select Tracts relating to the Colonies &c. sold by Mr. Roberts, the publisher of this essay.

After praising the style and manner of the introduction to that compilation, the author congratulates himself that his own arguments are confirmed on so high authority. Now in Martyn's 'Reasons' are several specific references to just these colonial writings of Penn and Child; the latter's argument, especially, that population is not a direct evidence of national wealth, is considerably developed. Bacon's essay, moreover, was frequently cited in Martyn's later 'Impartial Enquiry.'

In 1733 the Georgia propaganda was continued by the printing of Martyn's 'Reasons for Establishing the Colony of Georgia, with Regard to the Trade of Great Britain.' ... Six hundred copies were ordered by the Trustees in March; in April, when a petition for funds was preparing, six hundred more, "one of them to be deliver'd to Every Member of Both Houses of Parliament." Besides these two issues (the second including some additional matter), a second edition with further additions and changes, and with the author's name on

Page 31. "I have heard it said (and 't is easy to say so) let them learn to work . . ."	Page 19. "I have heard it said, that our Prisons are the properest Places for those who are thrown into them . . ."
Page 33. "It may be asked, if they can't get Bread here for their Labour, how will their Condition be mended in Georgia? The Answer is easy . . ."	Page 17. "If it should be ask'd here, How will these People, who cannot work at the Plough at home, be able to go thro' the same Labour abroad? The Answer is obvious. . . ."

27. Compare the discussion of silk culture in A New and Accurate Account, pp. 55–59, with that in Reasons, pp. 5–11; and the references to Roman colonization, p. 52 of the former and pp. 21–22 of the latter.

the title-page, was also issued in the same year.[28] By charter
the Trustees were required to lay an annual report of receipts
and expenditures before the Lord Chancellor and Master of
the Rolls; in 1733 the first report, with its interesting list of
benefactions, was ordered printed "to send to some of our
principal subscribers." This fair folio was itself a benefaction,
for the stationers Mount and Page donated the paper and
printing of two hundred and fifty copies, "stich'd in blew
Paper." [29] An abridgement of the account was annexed to
John Burton's anniversary sermon of 1732, printed this year
at the request of the Trustees, as was also Samuel Smith's sermon of 1731. The latter was accompanied by the reprinted
'Some Account,' and by a statement of the designs of Bray's
Associates — now legally separated from the Georgia Trust,
but for long after closely linked in personnel.

Between 1733 and 1740 Georgia publicity declined in volume. Peter Gordon's 'A View of Savanah as it Stood the 29th
of March, 1734' (dedicated to the Trustees), as engraved by P.
Fourdrinier,[30] was apparently an official issue; a thousand copies of each of the three laws enacted by the Trustees were

28. For issues and editions, see De Renne, pp. 16–17. The provenience of the
pamphlet is revealed in Percival, Diary, 1, 367, and Colonial Records of Georgia, 11,
21, 29. A French translation was included in the ninth volume of Recueil de Voiages
au Nord, Amsterdam. 1738. For Kramer's proposals to translate the tract into
"High Dutch," see Colonial Records of Georgia, 11, 193. Curiously, an advertisement facing the title-page of Martyn's Impartial Enquiry (1741) announced the
second edition as "Lately Published."

29. Colonial Records of Georgia, 1, 131. There seems to have been some confusion as to the extent of the stationers' offer, Adam Anderson first reporting that
they had offered to give paper and printing "for any Books to be printed for the Use
of the Colony." Ibid., p. 118. On the other hand, Percival noted that Mount offered
"to give the paper if we let him have the printing such things as we publish."
Diary, 1, 387. Besides the General Account, Mount and Page this year issued the
printed sermons.

30. Colonial Records of Georgia, 11, 65 (Common Council Journal, April 6,
1734): "Order'd That sixteen Guineas be paid to Mr. Peter Gordon as a Consideration for his Draught of Savannah." Winsor, Narrative and Critical History, v,
368, has a reproduction of a later version (1741).

ordered;[31] annual accounts were issued;[32] newspaper paragraphs continued. But the only pamphlet of the period was apparently not printed at the Society's expense.[33]

Meanwhile, Georgia continued to be an object of piquant interest to men of letters — from Pope and Savage and Thomson to nonentities like "one Williams, a poor man," wrote Percival, "and as poor a poet."[34] Several poets apparently stood close to the circle of the Trustees. The Reverend Samuel Wesley has been credited with the poems which were published together in a fine folio of 1736: 'Georgia, a Poem. Tomachachi, an Ode. A Copy of Verses on Mr. Oglethorpe's Second Voyage to Georgia.' The first is among many contemporary eulogies of Oglethorpe — "Stranger to Repose" — and of the Trustees — "Lovers of Virtue, Friends of Human Kind." The second is one of the most striking expressions in eighteenth-century English literature of that enthusiasm for the "noble savage" which was voiced by so many European writers from the sixteenth century to the nineteenth. James Thomson has been named "the first important humanitarian poet in English";[35] it is suggestive that the three philanthropies that he praised were Oglethorpe's prison reforms, the founding of Georgia, and the erection of the Foundling Hospital by Thomas Coram, an Associate and a Trustee. Possibly Aaron Hill's own earlier connection with the Azilia project prompted his epigram on the naming of the colony of Georgia.[36] Much minor Georgia poetry appeared in the Gentleman's Magazine; the proprietor, Cave, was a continuous benefactor of the enterprise, and in 1735 offered a medal bearing the head of Oglethorpe, and

31. Colonial Records of Georgia, II, 97.

32. *Ibid.*, p. 138.

33. A New Voyage to Georgia. By a Young Gentleman ... London. MDCCXXXV.

34. Diary, II, 198.

35. By C. A. Moore, in Modern Language Association Publications, 1916, pp. 281–282.

36. Aaron Hill, Works. 1753, IV, 152. D. Brewster, Aaron Hill: Poet, Dramatist, Projector. New York, 1913, p. 58.

other prizes for poems in honor of "The Christian Hero." Of the poems submitted in competition, several lauded Georgia's founder.[37] No other American colony, surely, had so good a press, or so musical a chorus!

The second period of active Georgia propaganda covered the years from 1740 to 1744. The Trustees were then seeking to secure Parliamentary support for Georgia on a regular annual basis, to relieve them from the necessity of depending so completely upon the uncertain favor of Sir Robert Walpole. They were anxious, therefore, that Parliament should undertake an investigation of the colony. On the other hand, those were the years when a formidable faction of the colonists, aggrieved at the prohibition of slaves and rum, and at the system of land tenures, dissatisfied with Oglethorpe and other officials in Georgia, were assailing the Trustees in printed "libels" and through their agent in England, Thomas Stephens — the son of that Secretary William Stephens who was the Trustees' most loyal servant in the colony. There was friction also with South Carolina, and criticism of Oglethorpe's conduct of the St. Augustine expedition. All of these controversies produced pamphlets: of these, only a few can be mentioned.

The opening shot in the Trustees' campaign for a Parliamentary investigation was the tract printed in December, 1740 (it bore date 1741) entitled, 'An Impartial Enquiry into the State and Utility of the Province of Georgia.'[38] Martyn was the author, but the pamphlet was read and amended by a committee of the Common Council before a thousand copies were ordered printed. Those distributed among the members of

37. On this competition see Gentleman's Magazine, v, 778; vi, 99, 414–415; viii, 58. For other poetry see Ibid., ii, 94; iii, 209; iv, 501, 505; xiv, 501, 558.

38. In the De Renne catalogue this is ascribed to Egmont. However, Martyn's authorship is clearly established by Egmont's Journal, in Colonial Records of Georgia, v, 410, which also reveals a very interesting political division among the Trustees. Of this pamphlet the John Carter Brown Library has two copies, differing only in the addition, on the title-page of copy 2, of "[Price one shilling and Six Pence]."

Parliament "disposed many," the Trustees believed, "to be friends to the Colony, who were not so before." Egmont and his son personally presented three copies at Court, to the King, the Duke of Cumberland, and the Prince of Wales.[39] Further in anticipation of an inquiry, the Trustees in June, 1741, ordered the Secretary [40] to prepare the well-known folio, 'An Account shewing the Progress of the Colony of Georgia in America from its First Establishment'; and at the same time a map of the coast and settlements from Carolina to St. Augustine was ordered engraved.[41] This pamphlet was even more carefully revised by the Trustees than its predecessor. Thomas Stephens was now in England attacking the Trustees by pamphlet [42] and in the lobbies. From Charles Town had come copies of that caustic indictment of the management of Georgia, written by the leaders of the "malcontents," Patrick Tailfer, Hugh Anderson, and David Douglas: 'A True and Historical Narrative of the Colony of Georgia, in America.' [43] Not, apparently, without difficulty, in view of the possibly libellous nature of the tract, Stephens found an English bookseller, Crokatt, to bring out a reprint in London in December, 1741.[44] Already the contents were known to Egmont, who on his own initiative ordered printed as "an antidote," "to put in the hands of members of Parliament," 'A State of the Province of Georgia, attested upon Oath in the Court of Savannah, November 10, 1740.' [45] Although some of his colleagues be-

39. *Ibid.*, pp. 416, 430.   40. *Ibid.*, p. 438.

41. One of the two copies of this pamphlet in the John Carter Brown Library contains the map. Winsor, Narrative and Critical History, v, 379, reproduces a German copy of this map, slightly altered, which appeared in Samuel Urlsperger: Ausführliche Nachricht. XIII. Dreyzehenten Continuation . . . Erster Theil. Halle und Augsburg. MDCCXLVII. At the bottom of the German engraving, in the Urlsperger tract, is a view of the mills at Ebenezer.

42. Egmont's Journal, in Colonial Records of Georgia, v, 422–427, 440, 617.

43. On the Charles Town editions, see Church Catalogue, IV, No. 940. It is there incorrectly stated that the London edition appeared in the *following* year.

44. Colonial Records of Georgia, v, 471, 578–579.

45. *Ibid.*, p. 578. This document had been transmitted by Colonel Stephens in November, 1740. *Ibid.*, p. 406.

lieved that 'A True and Historical Narrative' was so scandalous as to defeat its own ends, Egmont was aroused, and led the counter-attack, denouncing the libel in interviews with the Lord Chancellor and the Lord President.[46] Another move, apparently, in the defense of their administration, was the publication in three volumes for the use of the Trust of William Stephens's 'A Journal of the Proceedings in Georgia, beginning October 20, 1737'; in a separate pamphlet was printed the brief 'Journal received February 4, 1741' which also makes part of Vol. III of the larger 'Journal.'[47] When Thomas Stephens, although meantime he had been censured by the House of Commons for libelling the Trustees, returned to the assault in 1743 with 'A Brief Account of the Causes that have retarded the Progress of the Colony of Georgia,' it was Egmont who replied in further defense of the policy of which he had been, in England, the outstanding proponent.[48] Already, however, this original policy of the Trustees, who had viewed Georgia as peculiarly a barrier colony, and had so stubbornly opposed the efforts of the colonists to develop a planting society like that of South Carolina, was undergoing transformation. The first concessions were in land tenures; on this head was published a folio containing 'The Resolutions of the Trustees for Establishing the Colony of Georgia in America (8 March 1741/2) relating to the Grants and Tenure of Lands within the said Colony.' [1742].

In conclusion, it is the pleasant task of the writer, who in this essay has drawn largely upon the riches of the John Carter Brown Library, to direct attention to certain unique Georgia treasures which that collection possesses. Wesley's copy of 'Some Account' is one of them; the Egmont copy, with bookplate, of the Stephens 'Journal' (including the rare third

46. Colonial Records of Georgia, v, 583, 585.

47. For description of these rarities, see De Renne catalogue, p. 21.

48. Georgia Historical Society Collections, II, 88 note; De Renne, p. 260. I have not seen the Egmont reply.

volume) is another, long known to bibliographers. On the same shelf are to be found three copies of the English reprint of 'A True and Historical Narrative' (besides the original Charles Town edition), two of which are elaborately annotated by way of a running refutation of the impeachment of the Trustees' policy and management. There is also a copy of 'A Brief Account' of 1743, with comments written in the same clear, small hand— including a note on the title-page that this tract was "publish'd by Tho. Stephens, who on his knees rec'd at the Bar of the H. of Commons the censure of being a false scandalous and malicious fellow." It is evident that the commentator found the margins of 'A True and Historical Narrative' too narrow for full expression of his dissent, for one of the copies was interleaved and rebound, to give fuller scope for his scornful rebuttal. A sample is the following comment upon Anderson's reference to the "hundred hackney Muses" who had conspired to paint Georgia a paradise: "The Hyperboles of Poetry should not influence so great an author as this pamphleteer, bred to books at an University, the meanest school boy makes allowances in these flights." Among the notes are numerous citations from the Stephens journals, from letters, and from conversations, which supply sufficient internal evidence of authorship — though this, apparently, has not hitherto been determined. One proof among several must suffice. Opposite p. xii appears this note: "Mr. Beaufain Collector of Charlestown in Carolina informed me, that Patrick Graham a freeholder of Savannah made 59 £ last year (1741) only by selling his mulberry plants to the Inhabitants." Compare the following record of the identical conversation:[49]

Jany 15.[1742] Mr Bofin acquainted me with the following particulars: ... He ... read part of a letter he lately received from America, informing him that Patrick Graham Surgeon at Savannah (a most industrious

49. Colonial Records of Georgia, v, 587. Since this was written, I have received a confirmation of Egmont's authorship of these notes from Mr. J. A. Roberts, editor of the Percival Diary, based upon comparison of handwriting.

Planter) had made this year 50£ by mulberry seeds which he collected at Purysburg, and . . . sold them to his Neighbours at a penny a plant.

The latter quotation is from the 'Journal of the Earl of Egmont.' Like the John Carter Brown copy of the Stephens 'Journal,' these pamphlets were once part of the library of Oglethorpe's earliest and ablest collaborator, that generous philanthropist, and veracious diarist of the Age of Walpole — John Lord Percival, first Earl of Egmont.

BOOKS ON ARCHITECTURE PRINTED IN AMERICA, 1775–1830

By ALEXANDER J. WALL

Librarian of the New York Historical Society

THE earliest printed work on the subject of architecture is that of Leone Battista Alberti, printed at Florence in 1485. But the work of Vitruvius, dating back approximately to 25 B.C., stands preëminent as the fountain of all written knowledge on this subject. The earliest printed book of Vitruvius was issued at Rome about 1486; the first illustrated edition appeared at Venice in 1511. Countless volumes on architecture have been issued since that time by many authors the world over, but this contribution toward a bibliography will be confined to the books printed in America prior to 1831.

The American colonies produced no original work on architecture, and the earliest books printed here were popular English works republished here. Thus, Abraham Swan's 'British Architect,' first printed at London in 1745, and in 1775 reprinted in Philadelphia, was the first book on architecture published in America. About this year, 1775, there was in preparation a twelvemo volume which did not receive a title-page. This, which is in the possession of Mr. R. T. Haines Halsey of New York, appears to be a made-up volume, containing a bookplate of the Carpenters' Company of Philadelphia, with the name of Thomas Savery, a prominent carpenter of Philadelphia, who was born in 1751 and died in 1818. It has thirty-six plates and a leaf of text containing a price-list. The plates are arranged thus: first, a ground-floor plan and a front elevation of Carpenters' Hall at Philadelphia; then, plates of upright construction, roofs, windows, sills and joints, stairs, cornices, mantels, gates, doorways, and pillars. It is believed that these plates were engraved in America.

In 1786 John Norman, an Englishman by birth, published in Boston a work on architecture, entitled, 'The Town and Country Builder.' Other popular English books reprinted here and used extensively in the United States were the works of William Pain and B. & T. Langley. These authors opened the great stores of architectural design and building to the everyday carpenters by placing at their disposal simplified works which made it possible for the average joiner to construct beautiful houses.

It was not until 1797 that the first distinctly American work appeared in the United States, entitled 'The Country Builder's Assistant,' by Asher Benjamin. It was first printed at Greenfield, Massachusetts, and contained engraved plates designed by the author.

The preface to 'The American Builder's Companion,' the second work by Asher Benjamin, issued in 1806, states that two thirds of the contents of foreign publications on architecture was unsuited to buildings in America. Hence Benjamin designed his books to answer the needs of carpenter-builders in constructing houses, churches, and public buildings throughout the rural districts of the country. His publications were so simple that a carpenter could follow the plan of construction without difficulty; and it is to be remembered that the structures of colonial design that we admire to-day in almost every locality, which were built in the decade immediately following the Revolutionary War, are largely due to these architectural books, which circulated in the United States and simplified the larger technical works of the earlier masters of design.

An examination of these volumes, and a comparison with existing architectural features of houses and churches of the locality where the compilers practised the vocation of architect and builder, will leave little doubt as to the practical use these publications were put to. Some of the houses built by

Asher Benjamin are referred to in 'The Georgian Period,' 1902 (volume 3, page 105), Kimball's 'Domestic Architecture of the American Colonies,' 1922, and Wardner's 'Old South Meeting House,' Windsor, Vermont, 1923 (pages 18 and 19).

When we read the introductions to the early architectural books printed in America, we learn that they were all at one in the purpose to bring to the American carpenter-builder practical publications to guide effective construction with real merit. So these books ranged in size from the folio to a handy pocket-size book. That they were much used is proved by their comparative scarcity to-day, and by the many houses still standing whose construction follows their designs.

While a number of copies of the books listed have been located in various libraries and private collections, it was a matter of surprise to the compiler to find in the sixty-odd libraries inquired of, that not one had a comprehensive collection of these books. In fact the greater number had none, or not more than one or two, on the subject, issued before 1830. Of the twenty-one titles and thirty-five editions listed, the American Antiquarian Society has fourteen, Mr. W. Gedney Beatty thirteen, the New York Historical Society ten, the New York Public Library and Library of Congress, each nine, the Boston Public Library eight, the New York Society Library and Yale University Library, each six.

There being but eleven compilers of these architectural books prior to 1820, I have arranged the following titles under the author or compiler, giving some biographical data for each and a short title of the books and various editions. After each title I have mentioned the copies found.

ABRAHAM SWAN

is called a "Carpenter" on the title-page of the 1745 London edition of 'The British Architect,' which was issued at thirteen shillings. Later he styled himself "Architect." His books were the first published in America on architecture, and were sponsored by John Norman, who came to America as early as 1774.

The British Architect: or, the Builders Treasury of Stair-Cases. . . . One Hundred Designs and Examples, curiously engraved on Sixty Folio Copper-Plates. By Abraham Swan, Architect. Philadelphia. Printed by R. Bell, Bookseller, . . . For John Norman, Architect Engraver, . . . M,DCC,LXXV. Folio.

    Copies: HSP, FI, WGB, CU, LC, RTHH, CC, AAS, NYHS.

The British Architect: or, the Builder's Treasury of Stair-Cases. . . . One Hundred Designs and examples, curiously engraved on Sixty Folio Copperplates. Boston: Printed Typographically by John W. Folsom, for John Norman, Engraver, No. 75, Newberry Street, M,DCC,XCIV. Folio.

    The second American edition of this book, with same text and plates. Copies: AAS, BPL.

A Collection of Designs in Architecture, containing New Plans and Elevations of Houses, for General Use. . . . In two volumes. Each containing Sixty Plates, curiously engraved on copper. Designed, by Abraham Swan, Architect: and Engraved, by John Norman. Vol. I. Philadelphia: Printed by R. Bell, Bookseller, . . . M,DCC,LXXV. Folio.

    This book, the second of Swan's works republished in Philadelphia by John Norman, was never completed, so far as known. The 'Proposals,' dated Philadelphia, June 26, 1775, were announced in the first edition of 'The British Architect,' which stated the intention of printing it by subscription, in numbers to be published monthly. One number, dedicated to John Hancock, containing four pages of text with ten plates, was published with the above title-page, which is from the only known copy in The New York Public Library. It is presumed that the war interfered with the completion of the book. The complete work was printed in London, 1757.

JOHN NORMAN

was an Englishman who first appears in this country at Philadelphia, advertising in the *Pennsylvania Journal* of May 11, 1774, as an Architect and Landscape Engraver, from London. The same year he was a member of the firm of Norman and Ward, Engravers and Drawing Masters. In 1780 Norman removed to Boston and issued the first number of the *Boston Magazine* in 1783, and the first Boston Directory in 1789. Stauffer's 'American Engravers' says that he was the first to attempt a portrait of George Washington, which he engraved about 1779. It was this John

Norman who was sponsor for the publication of the books by Abraham Swan and the first book of William Pain in 1792. He died intestate in Boston, June 8, 1817, aged 69 years. His widow, Alice Norman, petitioned on June 23, 1817, to have James Fullick appointed to administer the estate, which according to inventory amounted to $620.47.

The Town and Country Builder's Assistant: . . . illustrated by upwards of 200 Examples, Engraved on 60 folio Copper-plates. By a Lover of Architect. Boston: N. E. Engraved Printed and Sold by J. Norman.
This work, a compilation from English sources, contains the same frontispiece that appeared in Isaac Ware's 'The Complete Body of Architecture,' London 1756. Folio.
Copies: MHS, WGB, LC, BPL, RTHH, MMA, OC.

WILLIAM PAIN

architect and carpenter, according to the London *Architects' Journal* of March 5, 1919, was the author of seven volumes. Of his antecedents nothing is definitely known and he died no one knows when. He had a son, James, who became a builder and surveyor. In 1763 he published at London 'The Builder's Pocket Treasure or Palladio Delineated and Explained,' which thus made easy for the village joiners the doctrines of Palladio.

The Practical Builder, or Workman's General Assistant: . . . The Fourth Edition, Revised and Corrected by the Author William Pain, Architect and Joiner. Engraved on eighty-three plates. Boston: Printed and sold by John Norman, No. 75 Newbury-street. M,DCC,XCII. 4to.
First American edition of Pain's books.
Copies: NYPL, YU, BPL, NYHS, EI, WGB.

The Builder's Pocket-Treasure . . . correctly engraved on fifty-five plates. . . . A New Edition, London Printed: Boston Reprinted, and sold by William Norman, at his shop No. 75, Newbury-street. MDCCXCIV. 12mo.
Copy: BPL.

The Practical House Carpenter; or, Youth's Instructor: . . . The whole illustrated, and made perfectly easy, by 148 Copper Plates, . . . The First American from the Fifth London Edition, with Additions. Boston: Printed and sold by William Norman, Bookseller and Stationer, No. 75, Newbury-Street. 1796. 4to.
Copies: BPL, AAS, EI, HCL.

[Same.] The sixth Edition, with additions. Philadelphia: Printed by Thomas Dobson . . . 1797. 4to.
    Copies: NYPL, HSP, UP, RTHH, LC, CC, WGB.

The Carpenter's Pocket Directory; . . . Engraved on Twenty-four plates, . . . Philadelphia: Published by J. H. Dobelbower, and J. Thackara. 1797. 8vo.
    Copy: NYPL (lacks two plates).

ASHER BENJAMIN

of whom little has been known, issued the first original work on architecture produced in America. He was a carpenter-architect working in Greenfield, Deerfield, and surrounding Massachusetts towns. He was born in Greenfield, Mass., June 15, 1773, perhaps the son of Caleb who lived in Montague, Mass., and who married, first, November 30, 1797, Achsah Hitchcock, born in Brookfield March 16, 1773, and second, in August, 1805, Nancy Bryant, born January 16, 1787.

In his book on the ' Practice of Architecture,' 1833, he says: "In the year 1795 I made the drawings and superintended the erection of a circular staircase in the State House at Hartford, Conn., which I believe was the first circular rail that was ever made in New England." It was invented by Peter Nicholson of England and published in 1792. Wardner in his ' Old South Meeting House,' Windsor, Vermont, says that Asher Benjamin proposed starting a school of architecture in Windsor, where he owned a dwelling, in 1802, and that his influence was felt and followed in much of the building in the Connecticut Valley. In 1803 his name appears in the Boston Directory and there he continued to live until his death in 1845. His will, dated November, 1844, was probated September 8, 1845. He owned two dwelling-houses on the east side of West Cedar Street, Boston, between Mt. Vernon and Pinckney Streets, and bequeathed them to his two daughters, Sarah Smith Benjamin and Elizabeth Augusta Bliss. His two sons, James and John Bryant Benjamin, both died without issue. The family burial-place was at Mount Auburn. His daughter, Elizabeth A., was born January 4, 1800, and died at Springfield, Mass., June 22, 1877. She was the wife of William Bliss, a graduate of Harvard in 1818. Their grandson is Chester W. Bliss, now of New London, Conn. Asher Benjamin published a number of books, editions of which continued after his death. A composite reprint of his books was issued in 1917 by Aymar Embury II. Those issued to 1830 are as follows:

The Country Builder's Assistant: containing a Collection of New Designs of Carpentry and Architecture; . . . correctly engraved on thirty copper plates: . . . Printed at Greenfield, (Massachusetts). By Thomas Dickman. M,DCC,XCVII. 8vo.

> Mr. G. C. Gardner in 'The Georgian Period,' vol. 3, p. 105, refers to a 1796 edition of this work, which is incorrect, as 1797 is the earliest date of publication.
> Copies: AAS, GCG.

The Country Builder's Assistant . . . thirty-seven copperplates. . . . Boston: Printed by Spotswood and Etheridge, for the Author, sold by him, and by Alexander Thomas, Worcester, 1798. 8vo.

> Copies: NYHS, YU, NYSL, LC, EJ, HCL, CE, WGB, ELE.

The Builder's Assistant; . . . thirty-seven Copperplates. . . Third Edition. Greenfield: Printed by Thomas Dickman. 1800. 8vo.

> Copy: AAS.

The Country Builder's Assistant: . . . thirty-seven copperplates. . . . Greenfield, Mass. Printed by John Denio. 1805. 8vo.

> Copies: NYPL, AE.

The American Builder's Companion; or, a new system of Architecture: particularly adapted to the present style of building in the United States of America. Containing, forty-four engravings, . . . By Asher Benjamin, Architect and Carpenter, and Daniel Raynerd, Architect and Stucco Worker. Boston: Published by Etheridge and Bliss, Proprietors of the Work. S. Etheridge, Printer, Charlestown. 1806. 4to.

> Copies: NYHS, LC, BPL, WGB, HCL, AAS, HSP, WL, AE.

The American Builder's Companion; . . . fifty-nine copperplate engravings. Second Edition, corrected and enlarged. . . . Charlestown. Printed by Samuel Etheridge, Junr. 1811. 4to.

> Copies: BA, OC.

The American Builder's Companion . . . fifty-nine copperplate engravings. Third Edition, corrected and enlarged. . . . Boston: Published by R. P. & C. Williams, for the author. Printed by Thomas G. Bangs. April 1816. 4to.

> Copies: NYPL, AAS, RTHH, WGB, GSM & T.

The American Builder's Companion; . . . sixty-one copperplate engravings. Fourth Edition, corrected and enlarged. . . . Boston: Published by R. P. & C. Williams, Cornhill Square; (Between No. 58 and 59
Cornhill, opposite the Old State House.) 1820. 4to.
Copies: NYHS, AAS, NJHS, UP.

The American Builder's Companion; . . . Sixty-Three Copperplate Engravings, Fifth Edition, Corrected and Enlarged. . . . Boston: Published by R. P. & C. Williams, Cornhill Square, . . . 1826. 4to.
Copy: MMA.

The American Builder's Companion; . . . seventy Copperplate Engravings. Sixth Edition. Corrected and Enlarged. . . . Boston: Published
by R. P. & C. Williams. Cornhill Square; . . . Dutton & Wentworth,
Printers. 1827. 4to.
Copy: WGB.

The Rudiments of Architecture: being a treatise on practical geometry,
on Grecian and Roman Mouldings; . . . thirty-two copperplates. Boston, Printed for the Author, by Munroe and Francis, No. 4, Cornhill.
1814. 8vo.
Copies: NYPL, PU, NYSL, BPL, AAS, WGB, MMA, AE, NYHS.

The Rudiments of Architecture: . . . thirty-four copperplates. Second
Edition, . . . Boston: Published by R. P. & C. Williams, Cornhill-
Square, . . . 1820. 8vo.
Copies: AAS, GCG, WGB.

The Practical House Carpenter. Being a complete development of the
Grecian Orders of Architecture, . . . sixty-four large quarto copper
plates. . . . Boston: Published by the Author, R. P. & C. Williams,
and Annin & Smith. 1830. 4to.
Copies: BA, YU, LC, AAS, EI, OC, GCG.

WILLIAM NORMAN

a bookseller and stationer of Boston, issued one book which
in all probability he compiled. Little is known concerning
him, but that he was related to John Norman (perhaps his
brother) seems apparent from the fact that in the Boston
Directories from 1798 to 1805 his address was the same as
that of John Norman. He published Pain's ' Builder's Pocket
Treasure' at Boston in 1794 and Pain's 'Practical House
Carpenter,' Boston, 1796.

The Builder's Easy Guide, or Young Carpenter's Assistant: containing
a great variety of useful designs in carpentry and architecture; . . . To
which is added, a list of the price of Carpenter's Work, in the Town of
Boston . . . forty-eight copper plates, . . . Boston: Printed and Sold
by William Norman, Book and Chart-Seller. Oct. 1803. 4to.

The list of carpenter's prices referred to in the title is lacking in the
only known copy of this book, which is in the New York Society
Library.

BATTY LANGLEY

the son of Daniel and Elizabeth Langley, was born at Twick-
enham, England, in 1696, and died at Soho, March 3, 1751.
He issued a number of books in England and had a considerable following. A sketch of his life with a reproduction of his
portrait is contained in Chancellor's 'The Lives of the British
Architects,' London, 1911. Only one of his books was republished in America prior to 1830.

The Builder's Jewel; or the Youth's Instructor, and Workman's Remem-
brancer . . . 200 Examples, engraved on 100 Copper Plates. By B. and
T. Langley. The First American Edition. Charlestown: Printed by
S. Etheridge, For Samuel Hill, Engraver, No. 2, Cornhill, Boston. 16mo.

This is a pocket-size volume, issued without date; an advertisement
in the *Salem Gazette* of March 7, 1800, announces that it had just been
published. The printer Etheridge began printing at Charlestown in
1799. The engraver's name, Hill, is an error for Samuel Hall.
Copies: AAS, HCL, WGB, CE.

OWEN BIDDLE

the son of Owen and Sarah Parke Biddle, was born in Philadelphia, April 28, 1774 and died May 25, 1806. An architect
and builder, he built the old bridge over the Schuylkill River
at Market Street, which was opened in 1804. He married
Elizabeth Rowan, May 2, 1798. He taught the rudiments of
architecture, and published one book, which went through
four editions before 1830, three of them after his death.

The Young Carpenter's Assistant; or, a system of Architecture, adapted
to the style of Building in the United States. By Owen Biddle, House
Carpenter, and teacher of architectural drawing, . . . Philadelphia:
Printed and Sold by Benjamin Johnson, No. 31, Market-Street. 1805.
4to, 44 plates.

Copies: LCP, AAS, HCL, NYHS, WGB, CC.

The Young Carpenter's Assistant; . . . Published by Johnson and Warner, . . . Philadelphia. . . . Printed by Robert and William Carr. 1810. 4to, 44 plates.
Copies: AAS, BPL, NYHS.

The Young Carpenter's Assistant; . . . Published by Johnson and Warner, Philadelphia . . . William Brown, Printer, . . . 1815. 4to, 44 plates.
Copy: YU.

The Young Carpenter's Assistant; . . . Published by Benjamin Warner, . . . Philadelphia. . . . William Dickson, Printer, Lancaster, Pa. December, 1817. 4to, 44 plates.
Copies: NYSL, WGB, RTHH.

PETER NICHOLSON

was born at Prestonkirk, East Lothian, England, July 20, 1765, and died at Carlisle, England, June 18, 1844. He was a writer on practical architectural subjects and published a number of books listed in the 'Dictionary of National Biography,' London, 1895, which gives a good sketch of his life. He did not come to America, but one of his books was republished here.

The Carpenter's New Guide: being a complete book of lines for carpentry and joinery . . . eighty-four copper-plates: . . . The eighth edition, from the sixth London edition. Philadelphia: Printed and Published by M. Carey & Son, No. 126, Chesnut Street, June, 1818. Griggs & Co. Printers. 4to.
(Editions of this book were printed after 1830.)
Copies: NYSL, GSM & T.

STEPHEN WILLIAM JOHNSON

was associated with three others in a brewery business in New Brunswick, New Jersey; they borrowed their capital in 1796 from John Jacob Astor. Johnson was connected by marriage with Jacob Klady, the potter, who deeded land in trust for Johnson's wife Mariah and his brother Thomas Johnson, druggist, of London. This land was clay land for the pottery.

Rural Economy: containing a treatise on Pisé Buildings; . . . on the Culture of the Vine; and on turnpike roads. With [8] plates. New Brunswick, N. J. Printed by William Elliot. For I. Riley & Co. No. 1, City-Hotel, Broadway, New-York. 1806. 8vo.
Copies: NYHS, NYPL, BA, SHSW, PU, LC, HEH, NJHS, LCP, RCL, NYSL.

MINARD LAFEVER

was born near Morristown, New Jersey, in 1797 and died at Williamsburg, Long Island, September 26, 1854. He worked as a carpenter, and later became an architect and the author of several books on architecture, all but one published after 1830. He erected a large number of private and public buildings in New York, New Jersey, New England, and Upper Canada, and nearly forty sacred edifices, a number of which are in Brooklyn, New York. He is buried in Cypress Hills Cemetery.

The Young Builder's General Instructor; containing the five orders of architecture, . . . sixty-six elegant copper-plate engravings. By Minard Lafever, Architect, and Practical Builder in the City of New York. Newark, N. J. Printed by W. Tuttle & Co. 1829. 4to.
Copies: NYPL, YU, LC.

JOHN HAVILAND

born near Taunton, England, December 15, 1792; died in Philadelphia, March 28, 1852. He came to the United States in 1816 and became noted as a designer of prison buildings, planning the Halls of Justice, New York City, the United States Mint, and the Eastern Penitentiary in Philadelphia.

The Builder's Assistant, containing the five orders of Architecture . . . 150 copperplates. By John Haviland, Architect, and engraved by Hugh Bridport, Artist. Vol. I [II & III]. Philadelphia: Published by John Bioren. . . . 1818–1824. 8vo.
Copies: LCP, FI, GSM & T, CC.

A Description of Haviland's Design for the New Penitentiary, now erecting near Philadelphia . . . Philadelphia: Published by Robert Desilver, No. 110, Walnut Street . . . 1821. 8vo.
Copy: LCP.

The Practical Builder's Assistant; . . . 150 engravings. Second Edition. Baltimore, F. Lucas Jr., [1830]. 8vo, 4 vols.
Copies: YU, LC.

A Description of Tremont House, with Architectural Illustrations. . . . Boston: Published by Gray and Bowen. M,DCCC,XXX. 4to, 31 plates.
Copy: NYHS.

This book, published without an author's name, is included in the list although no general search for other copies was made. Other books of a related interest are the House Carpenters' Books of Prices, and Cabinet-Makers' Price Books. A few of these came to the attention of the compiler and they indicate that the principal cities, New York, Boston, and Philadelphia, had each its society of tradesmen, which published 'Rules of Work' that specified the amount to be charged for all construction work. Of these books I have met with two published in Boston in 1774 and 1800, four in Philadelphia, in 1786, 1801, 1808, 1827, one in Carlisle, Pennsylvania, in 1795, and one in New York, in 1817.

The above list may not be complete. It is possible that some books and authors may yet come to light, that are not mentioned in this article. The newspapers covering the period are still to be examined for possible publication announcements, and further search may reveal other copies. It is the intention of the compiler to continue this work and eventually to reprint it in a more complete form, with additional bibliographical details. I wish to acknowledge my indebtedness to the collectors and librarians who so kindly responded and assisted in this work. In particular I am indebted to Mr. R. T. Haines Halsey for the loan of his books, and to Mr. W. Gedney Beatty of New York for his kindness and generosity in placing at my disposal not only his books but many notes upon this subject, which formed the foundation on which I built.

List of Abbreviations

AE.	Aymar Embury, New York.
AAS.	American Antiquarian Society.
BA.	Boston Athenæum.
BPL.	Boston Public Library.
CC.	Carpenter's Company, Philadelphia.
CE.	Charles Ewing, New York.
CU.	Columbia University (Avery Library).
EI.	Essex Institute.
ELE.	Edmund L. Ellis, New York.
FI.	Franklin Institute, Philadelphia.
GCG.	George C. Gardner, Springfield, Mass.
GSM & T.	General Society Mechanics and Tradesmen.
HCL.	Harvard College Library.
HEH.	Henry E. Huntington Library.
HSP.	Historical Society of Pennsylvania.
LC.	Library of Congress.
LCP.	Library Company of Philadelphia (Ridgeway Branch).
MHS.	Massachusetts Historical Society.
MMA.	Metropolitan Museum of Art. (See OC.)
NJHS.	New Jersey Historical Society.
NYHS.	New York Historical Society.
NYPL.	New York Public Library.
NYSL.	New York Society Library.
OC.	Ogden Codman Library in the Metropolitan Museum of Art.
PU.	Princeton University Library.
RCL.	Rutgers College Library.
RTHH.	R. T. Haines Halsey, New York.
SHSW.	State Historical Society of Wisconsin.
UP.	University of Pennsylvania Library.
WGB.	W. Gedney Beatty, New York.
WL.	Watkinson Library.
YU.	Yale University Library.

ISAAC EDDY, PRINTER–ENGRAVER

By HAROLD GODDARD RUGG

Assistant Librarian, Dartmouth College Library

THE history of printing in Vermont is both interesting and unusual. The first press in the State was the famous Dresden Press of 1778 and 1779, located at Dresden, now Hanover, New Hampshire, when that town with sixteen others east of the Connecticut River was a part of Vermont.

The Daye Press on which were printed the Dresden items was located successively in three or four Vermont villages: Windsor, probably Westminster, Weathersfield, and finally Woodstock. In 1814 Alden Spooner sold the press to Isaac Eddy "by whom it was repaired, and again put in use, after enjoying a respite from labour for many years. By Mr. Eddy it was transferred to David Watson of Woodstock."[1] Later it was rescued from oblivion and is now in the collection of the Vermont Historical Society at Montpelier. From some of the smaller Vermont towns, now scarcely known except for their interest to collectors of Americana, came very interesting imprints. Such places as Fair Haven, the home of the famous Matthew Lyon, Barnard, Danville, Peacham (now well known as the birthplace of the Honorable George Harvey), and Weathersfield were the homes of printing presses, the output of which was small in number. Gilman in his 'Bibliography of Vermont' credits Weathersfield with six imprints. Five additional titles (including one not printed by Eddy) have been discovered. An examination of the copyright records of the State of Vermont reveals no further imprints of this town.[2]

1. Vermont Journal, May 22, 1826.
2. These valuable records are available in the office of the clerk of the District Court of the United States, District of Vermont, at Burlington, Vermont.

Weathersfield, named from Weathersfield, Connecticut, is situated in the Connecticut River Valley north of Bellows Falls and just south of Windsor, a veritable center of early printing. The town was chartered in 1761 and in 1810 had a population of 2115. The little hamlet of Greenbush where Isaac Eddy engaged in printing is located in the western part of the town near the Cavendish line. In 1815 it boasted of a tavern, and in 1818 of a store. In 1820 a post-office was established there.[3] To-day it is a hamlet of not over a dozen houses.[4]

Although Isaac Eddy has many descendants living to-day, little authentic biographical data regarding him is to be found. He was born in Weathersfield, Vermont, February 17, 1777, and died at Waterford, New York, July 25, 1847. He apparently lived in Weathersfield until 1826 when he moved to Troy, New York, and later to Waterford. He married first Lucy Tarbell, who died March 8, 1828, and second Susannah Foster, who died in 1855. He was the father of thirteen children. One printed account refers to him as a portrait painter [5] in early life; another as an engineer.[6]

"The History of Windsor County, Vermont" by Aldrich and Holmes mentions the hamlet Greenbush, and states that "Isaac Eddy, an inventor, about this time (1815) erected a building where he experimented with perpetual motion. He afterward converted it into a printing and copper-plate engraving establishment publishing wall maps. This building in 1838 was made into a church." The statement that Eddy made wall maps is probably incorrect. Some confusion may have arisen from the fact that in this little village wall maps of

3. Aldrich, L. C., and Holmes, F. R., The History of Windsor County, Vermont. Syracuse, N. Y., 1891.

4. An early industry of the town of Weathersfield possibly located at Greenbush was "a printing ink establishment where is manufactured a very superior quality of engraving ink." — Zadock Thompson, History of Vermont, Natural, Civil and Statistical. Burlington, 1842.

5. Genealogy of Eddy Family, by Charles Eddy. Brooklyn, 1881.

6. The Eddy Genealogy, Boston, 1884.

New Hampshire and Vermont were made at a later period by George White. Further confusion, also, may have developed from the fact that Lewis Robinson of Reading lived for a while in Greenbush, later moving to South Reading where he engaged in making maps and Biblical wall pictures in colors. As will be seen later, Robinson and Eddy had business dealings with each other. Then too there is extant a folio wall map of New Hampshire with an inset view of Bellows Falls, Vermont, signed O. T. Eddy, Walpole, New Hampshire. This O. T. Eddy was Oliver T. Eddy, the oldest son of Isaac. According to an old newspaper clipping (date unknown) he was associated with his father in Vermont "in a printing office, the son doing the engraving." This clipping makes the erroneous statement that Oliver made the first copper-plate map of Vermont and New Hampshire. Later in life he was a portrait painter and invented the "Typographer." Mr. E. W. Butterfield of Concord, New Hampshire, a native of Weathersfield, has in his possession the sales book of Castor Cowles of Weathersfield Centre for the years 1816–17. In this are some interesting records of Isaac Eddy. On May 29, 1816, there was charged against him "Garden seeds 3 cents, one pair suspenders, 5 cents and one roll of Black Boll, 13 cents." On April 26, 1817, Eddy bought one half mug of sling for thirteen cents, and one meal of bread and cheese for seventeen cents.

Eddy must have been considered a man of learning and importance, for we find that in 1805 when only twenty-eight years old he delivered an oration in his native town, "An | Oration, | Delivered At Weathersfield, | In February 1805.| On Fatality And Predestination, | Or the Predeterminate and Irrevocable decrees of God, | Relative To The Dispensation | Of All Events And Terminating Results | Incident To The Several States Of Our Existence, To Which In Poetry, | Adapted To The Preceding Subject, | Is Added, | A Solitary Meditation | On The | Starry Heavens | The Infinity Of God,

And The Blindness | And Frailty Of Man; | Also, | On The
Almighty Power, | And | Supreme Dignity Of God |. This
was "printed for the subscribers," by Nahum Mower, Windsor, 1805. This item unknown to Gilman bears the following
"Prefatory Address, to The Brethren And Audience", which
gives us a measure of his intellectual ability.

Worthy and Respectable Brethren, and Audience,

Deeply affected and impressed as I feel at this time, having a serious,
awful and solemn sense of the Almighty power and infinite wisdom of God,
marvellously displayed, and in splendid brilliancy discovered to us, in the
stupendous and wonderful works of Creation and Providence, and in cope-
ous effusions to us more recently revealed in the regular succession, continuation, and preservation of all things, being, and life; and having also a
fresh view of the shortsightedness and frailty of man — It is therefore, that
I now appear in public to reveal in a thetorical manner, a few faint ideas I
have arranged on the subject of Fatality and Predistination, or the Pre-
determinate decrees of God, relative to the dispensation of all occurences,
all events, and terminating results in both our mortal and immortal states
of existence, and to the means of the original apostacy of the human family
and the plan of Redemption, in the gospel, represented to us through Jesus
Christ our Lord.

It may appear singular, however, that one in my humble condition, and
of my rank, should presume even the most distant attempt to engage in a
work of so vast importance.

Literature, you are sufficiently apprised, all common and even the most
ordinary privileges of which to obtain, I have ever been deprived, — and to
display this science could not have been the stimulating motive — pride
nor ambition, it seems, could not have excited it.

But, my friends, fate has ordained and prompted me to move in that
elevated sphere.

Of the ten known Eddy Weathersfield imprints, five of
which are local in character, three bear the imprint Isaac Eddy
and the others that of Eddy and Patrick. The Eddy and
Patrick imprints were printed in the years 1814 and 1815.
Apparently sometime in 1815 the partnership was dissolved.
Two items issued in this year were printed by Eddy alone.
The latest known imprint bears the date 1816. Patrick, who
was Eddy's partner in the years 1814–15, was probably Samuel Patrick, Jr., either a resident of Windsor at one time, or
possibly a journeyman printer. References relating to him are
also found in the Cowles Account Book.

The Eddy and Patrick imprints are as follows: 1. Abell's Almanac for 1815. 2. Dutton's 'Thoughts on God.' 3. Peck's 'A Short Poem,' etc. 4. 'A Plain Answer.' 5. 'History of Water Birds.' 6. Merritt's 'Discourse on the War.' 7. Cottin's 'Elizabeth.' The imprints by Eddy alone are: 1. Winchester's 'An Elegy.' 2. Translation of Secundus. 3. Roberson's 'Dialogues.' The circumstances of the printing of each of these items is given below with as much detailed information as it has been possible to gather.

The issue of Spooner's *Vermont Journal* (Windsor) for October 24, 1814, contains the following advertisement:

Doct. Abell's New-England Farmer's Almanac for 1815 is out of the Press, and will be ready for Sale in a few days by the Thousand, Gross, Dozen, or Single, by most of the Printers, Booksellers and Merchants, in New-Hampshire and Vermont. . . . Weathersfield, Oct. 21, 1814.

No printer's name, however, is given. Abell's Almanac for the next year, 1816, was printed in Windsor.

Another imprint for 1814 is 'Thoughts on God, Relative to His Moral Character, in Comparison with the Character, which Reputed Divines Have Given Him.' The author, Salmon Dutton, was one of the leading citizens of the bordering town of Cavendish and was the author of other works. As a preface this book has an "advertisement by another hand" signed S. C. L. [Samuel C. Loveland.]

The rarest Weathersfield imprint is 'A Short Poem Containing a Descant on the Universal Plan. By John Peck. Also, The Wrestler, who found an Evil Beast, contended with him, and threw him, being an answer to Peck's Poem on the Universal Plan. By Samuel C. Loveland.' This is the title given in Richard Eddy's 'Universalism in America.' Gilman has entries for this pamphlet under Loveland and Peck, but his titles do not exactly correspond to that given by Richard Eddy. Then, too, the title found in the newspaper advertisement varies somewhat from that given by Eddy. No copy of this pamphlet has been located in any collection of Americana.

Another rare title is 'A Plain Answer to "A Sermon Delivered at Rutland West-Parish in the year 1805"; entitled, "Universal Salvation: A Very Ancient Doctrine: With Some Accounts Of The Life, And Character Of Its Author. By Lemuel Haynes, A.M." In Prose And Poetry Composition.' Gilman attributes this to S. C. Loveland, whereas Richard Eddy attributes it to Hosea Ballou. From evidence in the preface it is probable that Ballou was not the author.

The author of these rare pamphlets was likewise a local man of repute. The Reverend Samuel C. Loveland, ordained in 1814, resided for a while in the neighboring town of Reading, Vermont. He was the author of several other pamphlets, and of 'A Greek Lexicon adapted to the New Testament with English Definitions' Woodstock, 1828, and was editor of the *Christian Repository*, an important Universalist magazine in its day. In the *Vermont Republican* for February 18, 1815, appeared an advertisement:

Just Published, price fifteen cents single, and for sale at the Book-Store of Jesse Cochran, in Windsor. The Famous Poem of John Peck, On the universal plan; — also The Wrestler, Who Found an evil beast, contended with him, and threw him; being an answer to Peck's Poem on the Universal Plan; both in one book. By Samuel C. Loveland. Likewise A Plain Answer to a sermon delivered at Rutland, West Parish, in the year 1805 entitled, Universal Salvation, a very ancient doctrine, with some accounts of the life and character of its author, by Lemuel Haynes, A.M., in prose and poetic composition. . . . The Author of the Plain Answer, is called a preacher of the Universalian Order; yet was never willing to own the devil as father or brother in his ministry, but always denied him, and has now written publicly against him.

Those of all denominations of christians, who feel opposed to that old, cunning, laborious and very presumptuous preacher, the devil and have fourteen cents to spare, are solicited by the author to call and purchase one of the above mentioned books.

PRADICATUR UNIVERSALIS

'A History of Water Birds' (cover title), a child's book not mentioned by Gilman, contains crude woodcuts "copied precisely from Bewick's celebrated birds." These may have been engraved by Isaac Eddy.

It is impossible to account for the publication in Weathersfield of Timothy Merritt's 'Discourse on The War With England Delivered in Hallowell, On Public Fast, April 7, 1814,' printed in 1815. There was a press in Hallowell, Maine, at this time, and in these days of infrequent mails it is difficult to determine why this local Maine item should have been printed in an obscure Vermont hamlet. Merritt was a Universalist minister and author of several publications.

'Elizabeth, or the Exiles of Siberia' by Madame Cottin was apparently a popular book of the day. It is interesting to note that this book, although printed by Eddy and Patrick, was published by P. Merrifield of Windsor.

Of the items printed by Eddy alone there is 'An Elegy Upon Messrs. John and Charles Wesley, George Whitefield, and John de la Fletcher, eminent ministers of the Gospel, written by Mr. Elhanan Winchester.' Winchester was a well-known Universalist divine and author who died in 1797. Possibly Mr. Loveland was instrumental in having this item printed. An engraving of Mr. Winchester, made in 1831, has also been attributed to Eddy.

It is likewise impossible to account for the publication of 'The Portal to the Cabinet of Love; consisting of the Basia of Johannes Secundus.' It would be interesting to know who made this translation of the first American edition of Secundus. This book bears the imprint, "Printed and Published by Isaac Eddy." It is the only item naming Eddy alone as both printer and publisher.

The last of the Eddy imprints is 'Select And Original Dialogues, Orations And Single Pieces Designed For The Use Of Schools,' by Lewis Roberson, "published by the author." Lewis Roberson was Lewis Robinson of the neighboring town of Reading. He was born August 19, 1793. In a sketch of him by his son Calvin [7] we find the following: "Soon after he came

7. Centennial Celebration, together with an historical sketch of Reading, Windsor County, Vt., by Gilbert A. Davis, Bellows Falls, 1874.

of age and began the world for himself, he engaged in the business of book publishing, establishing a printing office at Greenbush. He published a number of works there, mostly educational, which were well up to the times in merit, and style and finish. But he soon after went into the copper-plate printing and the publication of maps and scriptural paintings, at South Reading, which proved much more remunerative." Of the works published by Robinson there has been located only this volume and one other, a child's book 'The | Robber, | or | Sons of Night: | a True story. | Weathersfield: | Published by L. Roberson. | A. D. Pier, Printer. | 1816.' | Wyman Spooner, son of Alden, states that Eddy sold his press to David Watson of Woodstock. So it is difficult to account for this one item printed by A. D. Pier. No reference is made to this book in Gilman, nor is any other Pier imprint known. It is possibly the only Pier imprint and may have been printed on the Eddy press before it was moved to Woodstock.

As an engraver Isaac Eddy is best known by the extremely crude engravings on copper which he made for the first edition of the Vermont Bible. Stauffer [8] states that Isaac Eddy made "several exceedingly crude line engravings" for the first Vermont Bible, but lists only one 'Elijah and the Widow's Son.' He also credits to him and to James Wilson an engraving 'The Epochs of History.' In Fielding [9] we find six additional engravings attributed to Eddy: a portrait of Eliza Wharton, a portrait of Elhanan Winchester, a view of the Vermont State Prison, and three Bible engravings, The Holy Family, St. John, and St. Matthew. O'Callaghan [10] gives a very careful detailed description of this Bible listing seven engravings, omitting the St. Matthew. Gilman likewise lists only seven engravings. Perfect copies of this Bible contain seven engrav-

8. Stauffer, American Engravers on Copper and Steel. New York, 1907.
9. Fielding, American Engravings on Copper and Steel. Philadelphia, 1917.
10. O'Callaghan, A List of Editions of the Holy Scriptures and parts thereof printed in America previous to 1860. Albany, 1861.

ings by Eddy and one by James Hill. The engravings in the various copies seen are not always opposite the same pages. They vary slightly in size but are approximately $7\frac{1}{2} \times 6$ inches. In the revised edition of Dunlap [11] brief mention is made of Eddy and his engravings "which are the crudest specimens of engraving we have seen."

Each of these Bible plates with the exception of 'Jesus of Nazareth which was crucified' [The Resurrection] which is by James Hill, and the St. Matthew are surmounted with the words "First Vermont Edition." These two, strange to say, are surmounted by the words "Vermont First Edition." At the bottom of the plates are the words "Isaac Eddy sculpt. Weathersfield Vt. Windsor Published by Merfield [sic] and Cochran, 1812." The word "Vt." is omitted from the Elijah engraving.

In the *Washingtonian* for October 22, 1810, we find the following proposals for publishing this first Vermont Bible.

VERMONT BIBLE
PROPOSALS
BY MERRIFIELD AND COCHRAN
FOR PUBLISHING
AN ELEGANT QUARTO EDITION
OF THE
HOLY BIBLE

. . . It is but a few years, since a Bible was printed in America — it has never before been attempted in Vermont. In commencing this great and interesting work, the Publishers will spare neither pains nor expense to have the Vermont Bible of good materials, and made perfectly correct; and to have the execution in a style of decency and elegance. . . . In short, it is believed, that every Family, in this state, will feel an ambition to be furnished with a copy of the first Bible printed in Vermont.

---

11. Dunlap, A History of the Rise and Progress of the Art of Design. A new edition illustrated and edited with additions by F. W. Bayley and C. E. Goodspeed. Boston, 1918.

CONDITIONS

1. It will be printed on good paper and a new type.

2. The price to Subscribers, neatly bound and lettered, will be Five Dollars.

3. Those who subscribe and become accountable for ten copies, shall have an eleventh gratis.

4. As a liberal subscription is anticipated, the work will be put to press immediately, and forwarded with all possible speed.

WINDSOR, VT., *Oct.* 1810.

Subscriptions received at the Washingtonian Office.

The next information regarding the Bible is found fourteen months later in the issue of the *Washingtonian* for January 6, 1812:

Gentlemen holding subscriptions for the Vermont Bible are requested to turn them in to the publishers, for the first of March, 1812.

In the issues of the *Washingtonian* for August 17 and following dates we find the final notice as follows:

BIBLES

SUBSCRIBERS TO THE

VERMONT BIBLES

are requested to call and receive their books. For the accomodation of those who have not had an opportunity to subscribe for this work, the Publishers have concluded to sell them to companies of ten or over, at the subscription price, viz.

Without PLATES,	$5.00
With 8 plates	5.50
— 8 plates & MAP	5.75

The price to non subscribers, will be enhanced fifty cents.

MERRIFIELD AND COCHRAN

WINDSOR, *Aug.* 1812.

Heretofore there has been dispute as to the first edition of this Bible, some making the claim that the issue with plates was the first. This notice proves that both variants were issued simultaneously.

In the same year 1812, Eddy also made an engraving for John Russell's 'An Authentic History of the Vermont State Prison.' This engraving appears as a folding frontispiece, thirteen by five and one-half inches in size and bears above the picture the caption 'An Oblique Front View of the Vermont State Prison' and below the words "Isaac Eddy sc. Weathersfield, Vt." Of the eight copies of this book which have been examined, only three contain the frontispiece. John Russell, the author, was born in Cavendish, Vermont, a town bordering on Weathersfield, July 31, 1793, and was only nineteen years old at this time. His proposals for publishing this history are found in the *Washingtonian* for June 29, 1812, and in the two following issues:

AN AUTHENTIC HISTORY
OF THE
VERMONT STATE PRISON

From the Passing of the Law for its erection in 1807 to July, 1812. . . .

BY JOHN RUSSELL, JUN.
CONDITIONS:

This work will contain nearly 150 duodecimo pages, and shall be printed on good paper and a fair type, and neatly bound and lettered.

It will contain an elegant Copper-plate engraving of the State's Prison. Price to subscribers 50 cents — non-subscribers, 75. Subscriptions received at this office. The work will be put to press immediately. Windsor (Vt.), July 27, 1812.

In the Apology to this work the author states in part:

It was not the unpardonable vanity of becoming an AUTHOR, but "necessity the mother of invention," that produced the present work.

The only motive for writing the History of the Vermont State Prison was, the aid that the sale of the copyright would afford the author in obtaining a collegial education. . . .

It is said that with the sales of this book and his 'History of the War between the United States and Great Britain,' the author paid his expenses at Middlebury College.

One of the most interesting of the signed Eddy engravings is a large folio engraving issued in two sections with the caption 'Chronology Delineated to illustrate the History of Monarchial Revolutions.' Stauffer lists this under James Wilson as 'The Epochs of History.' [12] Apparently he had

12. Stauffer, No. 3400.

never seen the upper section of this engraving which bears the caption mentioned above. Although the engraving is signed 1813, the earliest newspaper reference to it is found in the *Washingtonian* for May 23, 1814. Likewise in the clerk's records at Burlington, Vermont, we find "Be it remembered that on the third day of February in the thirty-eighth year of the Independence of the United States of America Isaac Eddy of the said district hath deposited in this office the title of a Chart . . . chronology delineated . . ." The prospectus is as follows:

CHRONOLOGY DELINEATED
To illustrate the History of Monarchial Revolutions.

Isaac Eddy, Engraver and Copper Plate Printer, Weathersfield, Vermont, has just published, and offers for sale, by the Hundred, Dozen, or Single a CHRONOLOGICAL CHART, to illustrate the History of Monarchical Revolutions. This Chart is the work of an eminent French Historian and Chronologer, and was first published at Paris. The encouragement it has met with among men of genius and learning is no small proof of its general utility. Since its first publication it has passed through twelve large editions in France, besides several in Great Britain. It is engraved on a copper plate, upward of three feet in length, and about two feet in width, and the work much finer than usual in works of this size. . . .

It is represented by a Tree at the root of which is a Frontispiece, representing about 30 Beasts, Birds, etc. and the first man Adam giving names to them, as represented in the Book of Genesis. This has never been inserted in any European edition, and is executed in an excellent manner. . . .

In short, it is the most concise and accurate system of chronology ever published, and intelligible to every person capable of reading. Nothing in the power of the Publisher, has been wanting to render the present edition accurate, and the impression elegant. Without arrogating too much to himself, he thinks he can safely affirm, that, in point of elegance, this edition is vastly superior to any before published, and, in this affirmation, he is supported by the opinion of Engravers of the first eminence.

To the Patrons of the Fine Arts, this work is addressed, — and since Literature in general is encouraged, and the fine arts are patronized; since the present is the *first American edition*, of a work so justly celebrated in Europe; and since it is at once useful, amusing and ornamental; the Publisher hopes to secure their approbation, and meet with liberal encouragement in this attempt to disseminate useful knowledge.

Gentlemen holding Subscription Papers, are desired to call or send, and receive their Copies, within three months, otherwise the Publisher will not consider himself holden to deliver them at the subscription price.
Weathersfield, May 9, 1814.

The upper section, inside the borders, is twenty-one inches in width by eighteen and three-fourths in height; the lower, twenty-one inches in width by seventeen inches in height. The plate impression in the bottom half makes it appear like a complete engraving, but in the upper half the plate impression runs off the lower edge so that the sheet may be pasted together making an engraving thirty-six by twenty-one inches.

An unsigned folio engraving entitled 'Maria,' sixteen inches in height by twenty-one inches in width, has been attributed by some to Eddy. This crude engraving represents the forlorn Maria seated beside the trunk of a large tree. In the distant background to the left is a high mountain, to the right a small village. Below the engraving proper is a poem of six stanzas. Several years ago, Mr. Frank W. Coburn of Lexington discovered in a Vermont farmhouse several fresh copies of this engraving together with several fresh copies of the 'Chronology.' From the association of these remainders it has been assumed by some that the 'Maria' is the work of Eddy.

The above are all the known engravings signed by Isaac Eddy. The Eliza Wharton portrait is signed "Engraved and printed at Pendletons. Eddy"; and the Elhanan Winchester "Eddy sc. . . 1831." Both were published in Boston. Another engraving signed Eddy is found as a vignette on the title-page of Jacob Abbott's 'The Young Christian.' These engravings, both of a later period, are so far superior in workmanship to the Bible and other known engravings of Isaac Eddy that we are forced to conclude that they must have been by another hand. By some they have been attributed to James Eddy, an engraver of portraits who is known to have worked in Boston. The name of Isaac Eddy does not appear in the Boston directories for the years 1818 to 1847, during which years these engravings were made. The name "James Eddy, engraver and lithographer, 1 Graphic Court," does however appear at various intervals in the directories for these years. This evidence would seem to prove that the engravings signed "Eddy sc. . . . Boston" are the work of James Eddy.

It has become more or less customary for the compilers of auction catalogues and others to attribute to Isaac Eddy any and all unsigned engravings published in Windsor and Woodstock. It is probable that Eddy did more work than we know of, and quite possible that he illustrated some of the many chapbooks published in these places, but care should be taken not to attribute to him all Vermont engravings of this period.

In the town of Weathersfield there is a tradition concerning Eddy and his work which has been traced to the 'History of Reading, Windsor County, Vermont,' volume 2, bv Gilbert A. Davis. Mr. Davis reprints an unsigned article from the April 1900 issue of the *Interstate Journal* (White River Junction, Vt.) regarding Hank White, a famous New England Minstrel Singer. "His parents were of more than ordinary intelligence, his father George White working in his younger days with the Eddys, who resided in Weathersfield, and were among the early printers of Vermont. They printed the entire Bible with engravings in which the Apostles are depicted in modern garb, with stovepipe hats. Mr. White was afterwards an engraver and printer of maps." No evidence can be found that a Bible was ever printed in Weathersfield. The reference is no doubt to the Windsor Bible that Eddy illustrated, although there we find no Apostles with stove pipe hats.

Abner Reed of Connecticut and James Hill of Boston made engravings for books published in Windsor. The engraving by James Hill for the Vermont Bible is as crude as any work done by Eddy. Since various children's books printed in Woodstock and Windsor contain identical cuts, it is possible that the original woodblocks passed from one printing press to another. Then too the name E. Hutchinson is signed to a few old maps and to an early Masonic engraving. Hutchinson was Ebenezer Hutchinson, a publisher, of Woodstock and Hartford, Vermont. In Abell's 'New England Farmers' Diary and Almanac for 1823' Hutchinson advertises: "He likewise gives notice that Copperplate Engraving is still carried on at his factory in Queechee Village, Hartford, Vermont, by Mr. Moody M. Peabody. Also the Copper Plate Printing and Comb Making Business, in their various branches — where are also kept for sale Maps of various sizes." Peabody's crude engraving 'The Unjust Sentence of the Jews Against Jesus Christ, the Saviour of the World'[13] published in 1823 was either engraved by Peabody in Queechee, Vermont, or more probably in Reading at which place he was residing April 28, 1823.[14]

In this article, which the author realizes is incomplete, an attempt has been made to collect all the published legends and facts regarding Isaac Eddy and to add to this knowledge some new facts, but only a beginning has been made. Several problems remain unsolved for future bibliographers to undertake.

BIBLIOGRAPHY OF EDDY PUBLICATIONS

Copies of all except numbers three and four, owned by the author; no copy of number three located; a copy of number four in Tufts College Library.

ABELL, TRUMAN. The | New-England Farmer's | Diary, | And |Almanac, | For The Year Of The Creation, According To Sacred | Writ, 5777, And The Christian Era, | 1815. | Being the third after Bissextile or Leap Year, and the thirty | ninth of American Independence. | Containing, | Besides the usual Astronomical Calculations, a great variety | of Matter that's Curious, Useful and | Entertaining. | Fitted to the Latitude and Longitude of the town of Windsor, | (Vt.) but will serve for any of the adjacent States without | sensible variation. | By Truman Abell. | [Woodcut.] [Poem of six lines.] Weathersfield, Vt. | Printed by Eddy and Patrick. | Price, 7¼ Dolls. per gross — 75 cts. per doz. — and 10 Cts. single. | 211 × 127 mm. 48 pp. (unnumbered), wrappers.   (1)

DUTTON, SALMON. Thoughts | On God, | Relative To His Moral Character, | In Comparison With The Charac- | ter, Which Refuted Divines | Have Given Him. | To Which Is Added A Short Supplement. | On The | Doctrine of Free Agency; | Also, A Few Observations On | Prayer. | By Salmon Dutton, Esq. | Printed By Eddy And Patrick, | Weathersfield, Vt. | 1814. | 163 × 105 mm. 102 pp., boards.   (2)

13. Stauffer, No. 2422.   14. Vermont Journal, April 28, 1823.

LOVELAND, SAMUEL C. A short poem, containing a Descant on the Universal Plan. By John Peck. Also, The Wrestler, who found an Evil Beast, contended with him and threw him, being an answer to Peck's Poem on the Universal Plan. By Samuel C. Loveland. Weathersfield, Vt. 16mo. 16 pp., 16. [Title taken from Richard Eddy's "Universalism in America," p. 497.] (3)

[LOVELAND, SAMUEL C.] Attributed by Richard Eddy to Hosea Ballou. A | Plain Answer | To | "A Sermon, | *Delivered at Rutland West-Parish,* | *in the year* 1805"; | Entitled, | "Universal Salvation: | A Very Ancient Doctrine; With | Some Accounts Of The Life, And | Character Of Its | Author, | By Lemuel Haynes, A.M." | In Prose And Poetic Composition. | [Biblical quotation] | Weathersfield, Vt. | Printed by Eddy and Patrick. | 1815. | 203 × 124 mm. 27 pp., wrappers. (4)

A | History, | And Description Of | Water Birds; | Consisting chiefly of the most rare | and singular kinds; with accu- | rate drawings and engravings of | each; copied precisely from *Be-* | *wick's* celebrated Birds. | [Woodcut.] Weathersfield, Vt. | Printed And Sold By | Eddy And Patrick. | 1815. 165 × 100 mm. 24 pp., wrappers. Printing on cover reads History | Of Water Birds. | [Cuts.] (5)

MERRITT, TIMOTHY. A | Discourse | On | The War With England. | Delivered | In | Hallowell, | On | Public Fast, | April 7, 1814. | By Timothy Merritt. | Weathersfield, Vt. | Printed By Eddy And Patrick. | 1815. | 180 × 108 mm. 22 pp., wrappers. (6)

COTTIN, MADAME. Elizabeth; | Or, The | Exiles Of Siberia: | A Tale Founded Upon Facts. | *From the French of Madame Cottin.* | Windsor: Published by P. Merrifield. | *Eddy and Patrick, Printers* | 1815. | 102 × 76 mm. 174 pp., boards. (7)

WINCHESTER, ELHANAN. An | Elegy Upon | *Messrs. John and Charles Wesley, George Whitefield,* | *and John de la Fletcher, eminent Ministers of* | *the Gospel,* | Written | By Mr. Elhanan Winchester. | [Two Biblical quotations.] | Weathersfield, Vt. | Printed by Isaac Eddy. | 1815. | 200 × 121 mm. 11 pp., wrappers. (8)

SECUNDUS. The | Portal | to the | Cabinet Of Love; | consisting of the | Basia of Johannes Secundus, | *newly translated into english verse.* | with the | Epithalamium. | Also, | Fragments . . . Being Some Poetical | Pieces On the Kiss, | &c. | Weathersfield, Vt. | Printed And Published By Isaac Eddy. | 1815. | 148 × 90 mm. 98 pp., boards. (9)

ROBERSON, LEWIS. Select | And Original | Dialogues, | Orations | And | Single Pieces, | Designed For The Use Of Schools, | By Lewis Roberson. | [Quotation.] | Weathersfield, Vt. | Published by the Author. | Isaac Eddy, Printer. | 1816. | 166 × 100 mm. 180 pp., boards. (10)

The following seven engravings more fully described in the text, are from the Holy Bible, first Vermont edition, Windsor, 1812. The copy described is in the Library of the American Antiquarian Society.

Elijah Raising the Widow's Son.   Opposite p. 260.
Holy Family.   Opposite title-page of New Testament.
St. Matthew.   Opposite page 765.
St. Mark.   Opposite page 789.
St. Luke.   Opposite page 806.
St. John the Evangelist.   Opposite page 832.
St. Paul.   Opposite page 877.

An oblique Front View of the Vermont State Prison, folding frontispiece to "A History of the Vermont State Prison . . ." by John Russell Jr. Windsor. 1812.

Chronology Delineated to illustrate the History of Monarchial Revolutions, published by Isaac Eddy. Weathersfield, Vermont 1813. *With the privilege of copyright. Engraved by James Wilson, Bradford and by Isaac Eddy, Weathersfield, Vermont.* Large folio engraved sheet. [Vt. Hist. Soc. & H. G. R.]

LAWS

FOR THE

BETTER GOVERNMENT OF CALIFORNIA

"THE PRESERVATION OF ORDER,

AND THE

Protection of the Rights of the Inhabitants,"

DURING THE MILITARY OCCUPATION OF THE
COUNTRY BY THE FORCES OF THE
UNITED STATES.

BY AUTHORITY OF R. B. MASON,
Col. 1st U. S. Drags. & Governor.

San Francisco:
PUBLISHED BY S. BRANNAN

1848.

THE FIRST CALIFORNIA LAWS PRINTED IN ENGLISH

By CHESTER MARCH CATE

Assistant Librarian of the Henry E. Huntington Library, San Marino, California

IN discussing the confusion in legal procedure that prevailed in California during the period immediately subsequent to the conquest of that country by the United States, one writer says: "Before the end of the war Mexican laws not incompatible with United States laws were by international law supposed to be in force; but nobody knew what they were, and the uncertainties of vague and variable alcalde jurisdictions were increased when Americans began to be alcaldes and grafted English common-law principles, like the jury, on Californian practice. Never was a population more in need of clear laws than the motley Californian people of 1848–1849." [1]

The attitude of the people, the press, and the Governor, with reference to this situation, makes an interesting study. At the beginning of 1848, Governor Richard B. Mason found himself in a position of much uncertainty as to events in the immediate future. Mexico and the United States were still at war. Separated as he was by a matter of months from information from Washington and Mexico, he knew at the beginning of April nothing of the peace treaty of Guadalupe Hidalgo of February 2d. The 'Supplement' of the *California Star*, however, contained on April 1st news from Mazatlan as late as February 1st mentioning rumors of a speedy prospect of peace, and there was a general feeling that the war with Mexico would soon terminate in favor of the United States. In the event of peace, Mason, a military governor, had every right to suppose that he would cease to function as such, that his rule would be succeeded by a civil administration, and that laws similar to

1. Encyc. Brit., vol. v (1910), p. 19.

those in the United States would come into force. In the anticipation of such a sequence of events he no doubt felt that the labor of preparing and putting into operation a civil code — for which the necessity might pass even before its completion — was a work of supererogation.

That pressure of public opinion was eventually sufficient to induce Governor Mason to prepare a code of civil laws, and that these laws were actually printed, was until recently unknown. From the sale of the library of William H. Winters, a former librarian of the New York Law Institute, in March of 1923, the Henry E. Huntington Library came into possession of what is believed to be the only known copy of these laws. Notices of the discovery of this volume which appeared at the time of the sale were generally erroneous; in one the place of publication was given as Monterey; in another it was described as "the first book printed in San Francisco"; and even in the sale catalogue the inscription on the title-page was wrongly interpreted. The title-page is shown herewith in facsimile. The collation is A–H ⁴, I ²; and the correct reading of the inscription is: | Not published in consequence of | the news of peace | J. L. Folsom |. Mr. Folsom was the Collector of Customs at San Francisco.

Apparently Governor Mason made no secret that he was at work on these laws. Brannan, in an editorial in the *California Star* of April 22d, says:

Governor Mason, we are credibly informed, has commenced the judicial organization so long talked of, and so absolutely required. We sincerely hope that the new system, whatever it may be, may soon be developed. A judiciary system, and a judicious code of laws, adapted to the peculiar wants and interests of our people, are all that California now requires to insure her present happiness and future prosperity as a territory, and her ultimate power, magnificence and grandeur as a state.

The *Californian*, in the issue of April 26th, has an editorial to the same effect:

Civil Code of Laws. — Some time ago we received an intimation from a valuable correspondent at Monterey that Governor Mason would probably soon commence the judicial organization so much needed in this territory, and from time to time, we have heard the same rumor repeated; but we have refrained from giving it publicity until we could be more positively informed on the subject. We are now enabled to state on good authority, that the organization spoken of has actually commenced. This properly executed, and California may be considered as fairly set out on the road to prosperity and greatness.

Between April 26th and May 3d something seems to have occurred which caused Mason to reconsider the advisability of continuing his work, for on the latter date the *Californian* has this comment:

The Civil Organization. — We have been credibly informed that Gov. Mason has relinquished the project of a civil organization which we mentioned last week as being in process, as he is in daily expectation of a communication from Washington, probably appointing a governor and furnishing a pattern code of laws.

This news seems to have brought forth considerable protest. The *Californian* of May 17th devotes a column and a half to a discussion of the situation. The editor says that the amount of space at his disposal is not sufficient to publish all the complaints he has received on this subject; "the proper course to be pursued by the people undoubtedly is to address their petitions directly to the Governor"; even if the two governments have commenced negotiations for peace, he cannot believe, in view of the long time which must necessarily elapse before a territorial government can be established, that the Governor has again changed his views upon this subject. In conclusion he repeats his former request that the people should "forward their petitions to the Governor, fully representing their necessities and asking His Excellency's immediate action in reference to the matter"

Even more drastic criticism is voiced by Brannan in the *California Star* of May 20th:

If there is, as is feared, a disposition to delay this long-talked-of organization, on the part of Gov. Mason, in expectation of a relief from the discharge of what is viewed, apparently, as a responsible and hazardous piece of service, we are of the opinion the day is hastening on that will demand the prompt administration of active and efficient laws, for the security of person and property, and the most stringent measures become advisable, that, had a code of laws been seasonably framed, and their mild and persuasive influence earlier felt, might have been avoided. What hope is held out — what well based and reasonable belief can there exist that California will, within the next three years, enjoy the beneficent result of the introduction of laws from the seat of the U. S. Government?

Does the Governor fear to overstep his authority?

Gen. Kearny, it appears, came here with abundant authority conferred upon him to establish any system of laws which he believed the state of the country would require. . . . Undoubtedly the powers, assumed by his successor, are the same at this time. We can express astonishment, therefore, that to this time no movement has been made towards executing the will of our government. We trust its accomplishment will receive the attention of our present governor before unpleasant consequences arise from past neglect. The people of this territory are now awaiting the promised administration of decisive law. — They require it — they expect it, and to it they are entitled.

Such criticism, together with the numerous petitions that must have come to him personally, seems to have had an immediate effect on Governor Mason. By this time his compilation must have been completed and his 'Laws' ready for the press, for on May 21st we have a letter from him to Captain Folsom in which he says:

Sir:

I send Mr. Hartnell, the government interpreter, to San Francisco, to attend to the correctly printing of the Spanish translation of some laws, &c., that I intend to publish. The Spanish printing heretofore done in San Francisco has generally been so full of errors that it is important that Mr. Hartnell should attend to the proof sheet of this himself. I desire that you will have a number of copies, both in Spanish and English, struck off and stitched together, so that they can be distributed in that way together. Send me, if it be possible, one or more copies so as to reach me before the arrival of the *Anita*, and an English copy without the Spanish, if the latter will cause any delay. I hope, by the printer using his utmost exertions, that he may get this printing done before the sailing of the *Anita*. I wish the manuscript copy returned to me, and not a copy of the printing retained in the printer's office, or be suffered to go abroad. . . .

On the 1st of June the Governor evidently supposed that Folsom and Hartnell were busy in San Francisco carrying out his instructions. In a letter of that date to John Townsend, with reference to the settlement of the Leidesdorff estate, he says:

> ... There are now in process of printing some laws touching the settlement of estates, &c.; and therefore the bond ... should be in accordance with such laws as are now, or may be hereafter, applicable to such accountability and settlement.

Just at this time, however, printing in San Francisco was, owing to the general exodus to the gold fields, nearly at a standstill. On the 2d of June the editor of the *Californian*, in the "triple character of editor, printer and devil," suspended publication with a broadside announcing the signing of the treaty of Guadalupe Hidalgo just four months previous. And on the 14th of June the *California Star* appeared "before the remnant of a reading community" for the last time. Under such circumstances it is not surprising to find that by August 1st the 'Laws' seem still not to have been printed, — at least no copy had reached Governor Mason, — for we have a letter of that date from H. W. Halleck, Secretary of State, to James A. Hardie, in which Halleck says:

> SIR:
>
> In reply to your letter of July 28th, relative to the settlement of the estate of the late William A. Leidesdorff, I am directed to inform you that as soon as the printing of the laws can be completed, a court will be organized which can take cognizance of this matter.... The governor wishes you to hurry the printing as much as possible....

Five days later, however, occurred an event of major importance in its bearing on Mason's Code. On the 6th of August Mason was officially notified of the existence of peace, and on the 7th he issued his proclamation conveying the news to the people of California. Work on the laws must have been stopped at once for on the 12th Hartnell seems to have returned to Monterey.

What became of the printed laws? The fact that from the date of their printing up to the present time only the copy which belonged to Captain Folsom has been brought to light, makes it seem likely that most of the impression was destroyed.

Probably not many copies were printed; and it is possible that the copy here described is the only survivor. If this is the "English copy without the Spanish" which Governor Mason on May 21st requested Folsom to send him, it must have come again into Folsom's hands and have been inscribed by him at a later date, for there seems no reason for his inscribing on a copy intended for the Governor a note recording a fact with which the Governor was already familiar. It seems more likely that this is a copy which Folsom kept for his own and annotated for future reference or for the information of someone other than Governor Mason. If this is true, a second copy may be still in existence.

Writing later in the year to L. W. Hastings, under date of October 24th, Mason says,

> ... I had prepared a code of laws, and a judicial organization; and, although they were sent to the press in due season, I did not succeed in getting them printed before I received official notification of the ratification of the treaty of peace between the two republics, owing to the stopping of the presses upon the discovery of the gold mines, &c.

How much clearer this letter would have been had Mason substituted for "before" the words "until after"! Worded as it is, it certainly gives the impression that his code of laws was not printed at all; and, in the absence of any copy, this no doubt seemed a logical conclusion.

The analysis of the subject-matter of these laws will be left to the legal historian who must from now on consider Mason's Code a fundamental document among his printed sources.

NOTE: Quotations for which special authority has not been given are from the Executive Documents of the Senate or House of Representatives, 31st Congress, 1st Session.

ANN FRANKLIN OF NEWPORT, PRINTER,
1736–1763

By HOWARD MILLAR CHAPIN

Librarian of the Rhode Island Historical Society

THE entrance of women into business and politics has been so marked and so extensive in this twentieth century that we are prone to think of it as something novel and to forget that in colonial days there were women shopkeepers, women brewers, women printers and even women pirates. Ann Franklin, the subject of this paper, was one of that group of colonial women, often skilled practical printers, who by the operation of presses contributed signally to the enrichment of the literary, political, and economic life of the country.

Ann or Anna Smith, the daughter of Samuel Smith and Anna his wife, was born in Boston on October 2, 1696. As a child she played about Boston town, saw its rapid growth, attended church and helped with the household duties, picking up what scanty education the period and the circumstances of her life permitted. Boston was a small town when Ann Smith was a child. Her earliest recollections of it must have been of the thrilling days of Queen Anne's War. It was in 1707, when Ann was eleven years old, that the soldiers returning from the unsuccessful attempt on Port Royal were derided, mocked, and insulted by the women of Boston, as they marched crestfallen through the streets. She must also have remembered the jubilation three years later when Port Royal finally fell. In 1711 the huge English fleet of warships and transports, gathered for the Quebec expedition, anchored for many days in Boston harbor and thrilled the inhabitants with what Judge Sewall tells us was "a goodly charming prospect." In 1721 the terrible scourge of smallpox visited Boston, infecting nearly six thousand persons and causing nearly a thousand deaths.

Of more personal interest to her, however, must have been the trouble between James Franklin, publisher of the *New England Courant*, and the local authorities. In June, 1722, the energetic young printer was imprisoned, and in the following January he was forbidden to publish his paper, except after submitting its issues to the censorship of the authorities. To circumvent this order the paper appeared after February 11, 1722–23 in the name of his brother and apprentice, Benjamin. On February 4, 1723, one week before this device which deceived nobody was put into effect, Ann Smith and James Franklin were married,[1] and for several months at least the young wife had the privilege of living in the same house with one of the great men of his age. In view of Benjamin's dissatisfaction with his brother's treatment of him during these months, it is doubtful whether she found him an agreeable companion, but it may be that in these first days of her wedded life she began to learn the details of a craft in which later she became proficient.

Boston was not a particularly good place for James Franklin to do business. He never recovered entirely from the effects of his clash with the authorities, and upon the invitation and advice of his brother John and of some other inhabitants of Newport he decided to remove to a town where he would be free both from competition in his trade and from the enemies whom he had made among the Massachusetts officials. The exact date of the removal of the Franklins from Boston to Newport is not known. Franklin certainly printed at Boston in 1726 and at Newport in 1727, and in the latter town, with the practical help of his wife, he continued to practise his craft for the next eight years.

1. By the Reverend John Webb, pastor of the New North Church, Boston. Their children were five in number: James; Ann, who died Nov. 2, 1730, aged 2 years and 8 months; Abiah; Elizabeth (called Sarah by Benjamin, but Elizabeth in the Newport records), and Mary.

The most difficult piece of type-setting done by the Franklins at Newport was the "Perpetual Almanac," a broadside that was printed about 1730. It is impossible not to associate Ann's nimble fingers with the intricate detail of this work. In 1732 they started the first Rhode Island newspaper, the *Rhode Island Gazette*, which was not financially a success and was soon discontinued.

February 4 was a fateful day in James Franklin's existence, for on that day he was born and married and on that day he died. He passed to his rest in 1735, leaving his young family and his printing establishment to the care of his widow. Ann Franklin took up the burden of her responsibilities with characteristic resolution and determination. She involuntarily became the first New England woman printer, and quite naturally during the first year of her widowhood confined herself mostly to commercial job printing.

The record of only one item printed by Ann Franklin in 1735 has come down to us, but that is not strange for we have knowledge of only three items printed by James Franklin in the preceding year, although it is certain that these did not represent his entire output. The 1735 item was a piece of early American poetry entitled 'A Brief Essay on the Number Seven. A Poem. By a Well-wisher to Truth.' In his 'Bibliography of Newport' (1887), Hammett mentions this poem and describes it as a duodecimo, but neglects to say whether it is a broadside or a pamphlet. The printing of this fugitive piece, which has since disappeared, was probably paid for by its anonymous author.

The Widow Franklin became "colony printer" and in 1736 printed at least one proclamation for the colony. The earliest work still extant [2] that bears her imprint is 'The Rhode Island Almanack for the Year 1737.' The Franklins had printed a

2. Beaven's Essay listed as 1736 in Rhode Island Imprints and by Evans was "Re-Printed by James Franklin" and the year date 1736 erroneously ascribed to it was doubtless based on the note in Hammett's Bibliography.

Rhode Island Almanac annually from 1728 to 1735. James Franklin's death broke up the series and no almanac was issued in 1736. These Almanacs seem to have been profitable, so that as soon as Ann Franklin had made herself at home in the business that had been thrust upon her, she decided to continue the series. She employed Joseph Stafford to prepare the Almanac for her and printed it in the early days of 1737. The imprint reads "Newport: Printed and sold by the Widow Franklin at the Town School-House. 1737." [3] It is a leaflet of sixteen pages and contains items of local interest as well as poetry and astronomical calculations.

The Widow Franklin's printing establishment was in the basement of the town schoolhouse on the north of the Parade, now Washington Square, Newport. A picture of the building can be seen in Newell's 'View of Newport.'

As colony printer, the Widow Franklin printed the Supplementary Pages to the Digest of 1730, pages 245 to 283, covering the period 1732 to 1736–37. The arms of the colony, a woodcut owned by the Franklins, appears at the head of this publication. 'Instructions for Right Spelling,' a pamphlet by G. Fox, has been described as a Newport, 1737, imprint, but the writer rather doubts this, as some of the type ornaments are not found in any other Franklin imprints. Another Stafford Almanac was issued by the Widow Franklin for the year 1738.

Basing our deductions on extant examples, a procedure of course not particularly accurate, it would appear that in 1738 the Widow Franklin went more extensively into book printing as a speculation. Religious discussion was perhaps the leading topic of the day, so we are not surprised to find religious books bearing her imprint. 'The Christian's Daily Exercise' a poem of 12 pages by the Reverend Mordecai Matthews, and the Reverend Ebenezer Parkman's 'Zebulon Advised' were issued

3. This item is placed under 1736 instead of 1737 in Rhode Island Imprints.

and sold by her during this year. The latter was the most extensive work (as far as we know) that she had attempted up to this time. It is a sixteenmo of 92 pages. The introduction is by the popular Newport Congregational preacher, the Reverend Nathaniel Clap.

In putting in type the writings of Newport's leading citizens, clergymen, governors, and literary lights, the widow Ann must have come into personal contact with them and have been inspired and stimulated by the association. The contact between the writer and the type-setter in those days was more direct than now and hence gave the latter somewhat the feelings and advantages of a professional man, raising the work, particularly in a small establishment, from that of a trade to something approaching a profession.

Stafford prepared an almanac for Boston for 1739, leaving Ann Franklin the alternative of not issuing one for Rhode Island or of preparing it herself. Undaunted, she chose the latter alternative and so became one of the earliest women almanac-writers. Her husband had published some six almanacs under the pseudonym of "Poor Robin" and the Widow decided to revive "Poor Robin" for her almanac, as it would come with better grace as a pseudonymous publication than under her own name. She had doubtless helped her husband with his "Poor Robins" and so could turn her former experience to her present necessity. She continued this series of almanacs for at least three years, perhaps longer.

In 1741 she printed as a broadside a curious poem by William Chandler, who surveyed the colony's boundary. It is a metrical 'Journal' of his work in this survey. Most of the known works from her press have been listed in 'Rhode Island Imprints' and in Evans, and so need not be recounted here. She printed the writings of such local celebrities as the Reverend James MacSparran, the Reverend John Callender, Governor Richard Ward and Governor William Greene.

In addition to the books and broadsides listed, we know that she printed many legal forms, though few of these have come down to our day. The examples which have been located are a mortgage deed (1741), a commission (1746), a custom-house permit (1744), a ship's registration (1742), a warrant (1742) and a power of attorney (1744). Ann Franklin also printed the earliest extant Rhode Island "prox," as the printed ballots were called in those days. This was used in the election of 1744.

The most extensive piece of printing that Ann Franklin issued is the 'Acts and Laws' of Rhode Island, a folio of over 300 pages, printed in 1744. These were the stirring days of King George's War, when Newport was a bustling seaport, crowded with privateersmen and sailors engaged in illicit trade. Ann must have seen these brave adventurers sail out the harbor, later to return laden with the rich spoils of war. She must have seen the troops embark that participated in the capture of Louisbourg, one of the world's strong fortresses, and she must have often heard the drummers beating up for volunteers, when the colony sloop *Tartar* or impressed privateers were sent forth on the emergency of an expected raid by enemy vessels.

James Franklin the younger returned from an apprenticeship with his uncle Benjamin at Philadelphia and took up the burden of the Newport printing establishment in 1748. The Widow Ann then retired from the management, leaving the business in the hands of her son.

It is hard to imagine such an able woman suddenly giving up all participation in a business that had been her livelihood for more than a decade, and we must picture her rather as advising and assisting her son with the experience that she had gained in those laborious years. Indeed we find bills made out in the name of a partnership, "Ann & James Franklin," in 1758, although we do not find this partnership name appearing on any extant imprints.

They printed the colony's currency and in 1758 established a weekly newspaper which is still issued, *The Newport Mercury*. It had always been the hope of James Franklin, Sr., to establish a successful newspaper at Newport. His widow carried on his hopes and ambitions, and according to Thomas she made some attempts to revive the *Gazette*. Over twenty years after his death she achieved this ambition of her departed husband.

The Franklins attended Dr. Ezra Stiles's church and the death of James Franklin, Jr., is recorded by Stiles as April 21, 1762, in the thirtieth year of his age. This corrects Thomas, who gave his death as August 22. By James Franklin's death the responsibilities of the printing establishment were again thrust upon the Widow Franklin's shoulders. She carried on the business under the name of Ann Franklin, this imprint appearing on the *Newport Mercury* for May 11, 1762. She now became a full-fledged newspaper publisher and editor and successfully carried on the *Mercury*. She was also colony printer, printing the acts and resolves at the end of each session, as well as printing books and various forms and blanks.

The Widow Franklin, now in her sixty-seventh year, found the printing business much more arduous than it had been twenty years earlier. She took Samuel Hall [4] into partnership and the imprint of "A. Franklin and S. Hall" appears on the *Mercury* for August 17, 1762, and so continued until April 18, 1763. It is rather curious that at this very time there was in existence in Philadelphia another printing firm of Franklin and Hall, a more celebrated partnership, of which Benjamin Franklin was the senior member.

Ann Franklin passed to her rest on April 19, 1763, and the following obituary appeared in the next issue of the *Mercury*:

4. Mason, in Reminiscences of Newport, p. 84, erroneously states that Ann Franklin married Samuel Hall, her partner.

THE 19th Instant departed this Life, Mrs. ANN FRANKLIN, in the 68th Year of her Life. She had a fine Constitution, firm and strong; — was never sick, nor ailing, scarcely in the whole Course of her Life, 'till a few Months before her Dissolution; nor did she ever take any sort of Medicine in all that long Space of Time, 'till that Sickness seized her, which brought her down to the Grave. When she reflected, in Health, on the Goodness of her Constitution, she was at a Loss to guess what Part would be attack'd by Sickness in order to bring on her Dissolution — But in her we see an Instance of the Truth of that Word, "The strong Men shall bow themselves" — She was a Widow about 29 Years — And tho' she had little to depend upon for a Living, yet by her Oeconomy and Industry in carrying on the Printing Business, supported herself and Family, and brought up her Children in a genteel manner; — all of whom she bury'd sometime before her Death. — She was a Woman of great Integrity and Uprightness in her Station and Conversation, and was well beloved in the Town. She was a faithful Friend, and a compassionate Benefactor to the Poor, (beyond many of great Estates) and often reliev'd them in the Extremity of Winter. — And, she was a constant and seasonable Attendant on public Worship, and would not suffer herself to be detain'd by trivial Family-Concerns: *Herein she excell'd most of her Sex.*

She enter'd into the Christian Life in her early Youth, and has, ever since, adorn'd her Profession by an exemplary Conversation. And, under all the varying Scenes of Life, and some shocking Trials laid on her in the Wisdom of Divine Providence, she maintain'd a noble Fortitude of Mind, mixt with Patience and Submission to the Will of God; though not without Imperfection.

For several Weeks before her Death she was in great Darkness and Distress of Mind; but it pleased God, a few Days before her Departure, to shine in upon her Soul, and lift up the Light of his Countenance upon her, and thereby to give her *that Peace of God, which passeth all Understanding.*

And so she pass'd from Time to Eternity in the lively View and Prospect of eternal Life, through Faith in the Son of God, who gave his Life a Ransom for Sinners; that they, and they only, who believe on Him, and obey Him, might have and enjoy a glorious happy Life without End, in the open vision, and full Fruition of the Author of their Being and Blessedness. "The Memory of the Just is blessed."

Her Remains were interr'd on Thursday last.

Isaiah Thomas wrote of her:

She was aided in her printing by her two daughters and afterward by her son when he attained to a competent age. Her daughters were correct and quick compositors at case; and were instructed by their father whom they assisted. A gentleman, who was acquainted with Ann Franklin and her family, informed me that he had often seen her daughters at work in the printing house, and that they were sensible and amiable women.

The press which Ann Franklin used is still preserved and is on exhibition at Mechanics Hall, Boston.

THE WORK OF HARTFORD'S FIRST PRINTER

By ALBERT CARLOS BATES, M.A.

Librarian of the Connecticut Historical Society

HARTFORD, the capital of the State, was the third town in Connecticut in which a printing office was established. The first was New London, where a press was set up in 1709 by Thomas Short, who was succeeded three years later by Timothy Green of Boston, son of Samuel the second printer at Cambridge, Massachusetts. The second town was New Haven where printing was established in 1755 by James Parker, the imprint changing during the year to James Parker & Company. Parker himself remained in New York, where he conducted a printing office, and the firm was represented in New Haven by his partner, John Holt. When Holt returned to New York in 1760 to aid Parker in the work there, the press in New Haven was left in charge of Thomas Green, who had probably been employed in the office for two or three years previous to that time.

Thomas Green, grandson of the senior Timothy Green of New London and son of Samuel of the same place, was born in that town August 25, 1735. He was bred to the trade of a printer, and doubtless received practical experience in the editing and publishing of a newspaper while working as a young man in the office of his grandfather. When left in charge of Parker's printing office in New Haven, his duties included not only a general printing and publishing business but the editing and issuing weekly of Parker's newspaper, *The Connecticut Gazette*, then beginning its sixth year, and also serving in Holt's place in the capacity of postmaster of the town. Four years later the publication of the *Gazette* was discontinued with the issue of April 17, 1764, and Parker "resigned the business," as Isaiah Thomas expresses it, of his printing office to Benjamin Mecom, a printer by trade, whom his uncle Benjamin Franklin had appointed postmaster at New Haven.

Thus thrown upon his own resources, Thomas Green removed with his wife and two children to Hartford and there set up a printing office, probably late in the summer of 1764. It seems a reasonable assumption that he bought the whole or a part of the furnishings of the New Haven office. Presses, types, and paper were alike difficult to procure at this time and to have ordered these from England would have caused many months delay.

Having established himself in business in Hartford, Green appears to have diligently pursued his chosen work of a printer. He first issued an almanac, an article desired by almost every household. Next he established a newspaper, which he edited and published. This was *The Connecticut Courant*, a paper whose owners to-day are proud of its distinction as the oldest paper in this country continuously published under the same name in the same town. This newspaper must have taken much of Green's time; but in addition he found time to issue almanacs, election, funeral and other sermons, religious and political tracts, an agricultural tract, a petition to the king, official proclamations, poetical broadsides and pamphlets, a prophecy, perhaps an Indian captivity, and a politico-religious volume of above 250 pages.

After laboring at his trade in Hartford for three years, Thomas Green in 1767 entered into partnership in New Haven with his brother Samuel Green, who had opened a printing office there the previous year. In October they issued the first number of *The Connecticut Journal and New Haven Post-Boy*, "Printed by Thomas and Samuel Green, at the Printing Office in the Old State-House."

Early in 1768 Green removed his family from Hartford to New Haven, and on April 18 his name appears for the last time on the *Courant* as its sole printer or publisher. After that the imprint became Green & Watson, although Green states that his "Connections with the Printing Business there [in Hartford], in some Measure, still subsists." This connection was probably only a financial one, and after three years Green's name disappears from the *Courant* and Ebenezer Watson, who is said to have been taught the printer's trade by Green, became its sole proprietor. Green continued in the printing business in New Haven until January 1809, when he retired from the firm, which for ten years had been Thomas Green & Son, leaving his son and namesake to carry on the work. He died in New Haven three years later, in May 1812.[1]

No effort has heretofore been made to compile a careful bibliographical list of Thomas Green's Hartford imprints. It is not expected that the list is absolutely complete or perfect, and perhaps a few items in it should have been omitted; but it will at least serve as a basis for future work. The fact that a majority of the imprints which make up the list are credited to the Connecticut Historical Society (CHS) should not be taken as indicating that these are the only copies known; but only that the collations were made from copies in the library of that Society. The collations of other imprints are from copies in the Library of Congress (LC), the New York Historical Society (NYHS), the Vermont State Library (VSL), the Watkinson Library of Reference in Hartford (WLR), and the Library of Yale University (YUL).

1. A more extended sketch of Thomas Green may be seen in the Papers of the New Haven Colony Historical Society, vol. VIII.

LIST OF THOMAS GREEN'S HARTFORD IMPRINTS, 1764–1768

1764

AMES, NATHANIEL. An Astronomical Diary: Or, | Almanack | For the Year of our Lord Christ, | 1765. | Being the first after Bissextile or Leap-Year. | Calculated for the Meridian of Boston, New- | England, Lat. 42. Deg. 25 Min. North. | Containing, | Eclipses; Ephemeris; Aspects; Spring-Tides; Judg- | ment of the Weather; Feasts and Fasts of the Church; | Courts in Massachusetts-Bay, New-Hampshire, Con- | necticut, and Rhode-Island; Sun and Moon's Rising | and Setting; Time of High-Water; Roads, with | the best Stages or Houses to put up at.' — An Elegy on | the Death of the late Dr. Ames. — Some practical | Rules for Husbandry.| By Nathaniel Ames. | [Twelve lines of verse.]

Hartford: | Re-printed and Sold by Thomas Green, at | the Heart and Crown, near the North- | Meeting-House. | 12mo, in 4s: signatures [A], B, C; 12 ff.   CHS (1)

In the *Courant* of December 3, 1764, appears the advertisement: "Ames's Almanack, for 1765. To be sold by the Printer hereof, by Wholesale and Retail, on the most reasonable Terms."

CONNECTICUT COURANT. The Connecticut Courant. | Monday, October 29, 1764. (Number ∞.) | [— Dec. 31, 1764.]

Hartford: | Printed by Thomas Green, at the Heart and Crown, | near the North-Meeting-House. | Folio; 2 ff.   CHS (2)

This "Specimen" issue was followed, probably four weeks later on Monday, November 26, by number 1, no copy of which is known to exist. Number 2 bears date Monday, December 3, and the other numbers follow in regular succession; seven issues appearing during the year.

ELLSWORTH, SAMUEL. An Astronomical Diary: | or, an | Almanack | For the Year of our Lord Christ | 1765. | Being the first after Bissextile or Leap-Year. | Calculated for the Meridian of Hartford, in New- | England, Lat. 41 Deg. 56 Min. North, 72 Deg. | 48 Min. West Long. | Wherein is contained, the Rising and Setting of the Sun | and Moon, Eclipses, Judgment of the Weather, Time | of High Water, Aspects, Observable Days, Courts in | New England, Roads, &c. | By Samuel Ellsworth | Of Simsbury.

> Oft have I view'd in Admiration lost,|
> Heav'ns sumptuous Canopy, and starry Host, |
> With levell'd Tube, and astronomic Eye, |
> Pursu'd the Planets whirling thro' the Sky. |

Hartford: Printed by Thomas Green, at the Heart | and Crown, near the North-Meeting-House. | 12mo, in 8s; 8 ff.   YUL (3)

So far as is known this almanac is the first thing printed in Hartford. In the preliminary issue of *The Connecticut Courant* (Number ∞.) dated October 29, 1764, it is advertised as follows: "Just Published, and to be sold by the Printer hereof, Ellsworth's Almanack for the Year 1765. Calculated for the Meridian of Hartford."

1765

AMES, NATHANIEL. An | Astronomical Diary; | Or, | Almanack | For the Year of Our Lord Christ | 1766; | Being the Second after Bissextile or Leap-Year. | Calculated for the Meridian of Boston, | New-England, Lat. 42 Deg. 25 Min. North. | Containing, | Aspects; Spring tides; Judgments of the Weather; Feasts | and Fasts of the Church; Courts in Massachusetts-Bay, | New-Hampshire, Connecticut and Rhode-Island, Sun and| Moon's Rising and setting; Moon's Place; Time of | high water; Public Roads, with the best Stages or | Houses to put up at; Eclipses, with a Representation of | the solar Eclipse. | By Nathaniel Ames. | [Ten lines of verse.]

Hartford: | Printed and sold by Thomas Green. | 12mo, in 4s: signatures unmarked; 12 ff. CHS (4)

This issue was printed from the same forms as the edition printed and sold by Timothy Green at New London, with change of imprint only; and notwithstanding its imprint it was no doubt printed at New London. It differs in general style from the other almanacs that bear the imprint of Thomas Green, and certain of the astronomical signs differ slightly from those used by him.

CHURCH, BENJAMIN. Liberty and Property vindicated, | and the St–pm–n burnt. | A Discourse | Occasionally made, | On burning the Effigy of the | St–pm–n, in New-London, in | the Colony of Connecticut. | By a Friend to the Liberty of this Country. |

Published by the desire of some of the Hearers, | in the Year 1765. | Small 4to, in 2s: signatures [A], B, C: collation; title, 1 p.; The Epistle Dedicatory, 1 p.; text, pp. 3–11; 1 p. blank. WLR (5)

The authorship of this publication is credited to Benjamin Church. The Stampman was Jared Ingersoll. Trumbull's 'List of Books Printed in Connecticut' gives New London as the place of printing, while Evans' 'American Bibliography' credits it to Thomas Green of Hartford. The rather elaborate head piece and type ornaments appearing on page 3 have not been observed elsewhere, and 'are not found on any publication known to have been issued in Hartford. It seems extremely doubtful if this was printed by Thomas Green. A reprint was issued in Boston in 1766.

CONNECTICUT COURANT. The Connecticut [Cut] Courant. | Tuesday, January 8, 1765. (Number 7.) | [— Dec. 30, 1765.]

Hartford: Printed by Thomas Green, at the Sign of | the Heart and Crown, near the North Meeting-House. | Folio, 2 ff. CHS (6)

This number appeared a day later than the regular time of publication; but the later issues, so far as they are known, appeared on Monday. The issues of August 5, no. 37; August 19, no. 39 (probably); September 23, no. 44; October 14, no. 47 (probably) were of one leaf only. No copies are known of January 28, no. 10; February 4, no. 11; 11, no. 12; 18, no. 13; 25, no. 14; March 18, no. 17; April 8, no. 20; 15, no. 21; 22, no. 22; or of nos. 48, 49, 50, 51, 52. A skip of five weeks was made between no. 47 on October 14 and no. 53 on December 30. It is reasonable to presume that it was caused by inability to procure paper. The imprint varies with different issues and in that of May 13 first shows the new location of the printing office that had removed "to the Store of Mr. James Church, opposite the Court-House, and next Door to Mr. Bull's Tavern."

DORR, EDWARD. The Duty of Civil Rulers, | to be nursing Fathers to the | Church of Christ. | A | Sermon | Preached before the | General Assembly, | Of the Colony of | Connecticut, | At Hartford; | on the day of the | Anniversary Election; | May ix^th, 1765. | By Edward Dorr, A. M. | Pastor of the first Church in Hartford.

Hartford: | Printed by Thomas Green, at the Heart and | Crown, opposite the State-House. | 8vo, in 4s and 2s: signatures [A⁴], B–D⁴, E²: collation; half title, 1 f.; title, 1 p.; request for copy for printing, 1 p.; text, pp. 5–34; 1 f. blank.   CHS (7)

This is the first election sermon printed in Hartford. The number printed is not known; but the usual edition at this period was 300 copies.

DORR, EDWARD. A Discourse, | Occasioned by the | Much lamented Death, | of the honorable | Daniel Edwards, Esq; | of Hartford; | A Member of His Majesty's | Council, for the Colony of Connecticut; And One | of the Assistant Judges of the Honorable, the | Superior Court, for said Colony. | Who departed this Life, | (at New-Haven); | September 6th, 1765. | In the lxv^th Year of his Age. | Delivered soon after his Decease. | By Edward Dorr, A. M. | Pastor of the First Church in Hartford. |

Hartford: | Printed by Thomas Green. | Small 4to, in 2s: signatures [A], B–F: collation; half title, 1 f.; title, 1 p.; dedication, 1 p.; text, pp. 5–23; 1 p. blank.   CHS (8)

ELLSWORTH, SAMUEL. An Astronomical Diary, | or | Almanack, | For the Year of our Lord Christ | 1766. | Being the Second after Bissextile or Leap-Year. | Calculated for the Meridian of Hartford, Lat. | 41 Deg. 56 Min. North, 42 Deg. 48 Mi. West Long. | Wherein is Contained, | The Rising and Setting of the Sun and Moon, | Eclipses, Judgment of the Weather, Time of High- | Water, Aspects, Observable Days, Courts, &c. | By Samuel Ellsworth. | [Six lines from Pope.]

Hartford; | Printed and sold by Thomas Green, at the | Heart and Crown, opposite the State- | House, and next Door to Mr. Bull's Tavern. | 12mo, in 4s: signatures, [A], B, C; 12 ff.   CHS (9)

FITCH, THOMAS. An | Explanation | of | Say-Brook Platform; | or, | the principles of the consociated churches | in the colony of Connecticut: | collected from their plan of union. | By One that heartily desires the Order, Peace and Purity of these | Churches. |

Hartford: | Printed by Thomas Green, at the Heart and Crown, 1765. | Small 4to, in 2s: signatures [A] (first and last ff., placed outside of the others), B–I, K: collation; title, 1 f.; text, pp. 3–39; 1 p. blank.   CHS (10)

The authorship of this pamphlet is accredited without question to Governor Thomas Fitch. It is advertised in the *Courant* of May 27 as "Lately Published, and to be sold at the Printing Office."

HOLLY, ISRAEL. A Word in Zion's Behalf; | or, | Two Mites cast into the Church's | Treasury. | Being | A Short Discourse | Upon Matthew XXIII 9. | Wherein is briefly shewn, | The Right and Duty of private | Judgment, without Controul from Human Autho- | rity, in Matters of Religion, as founded on the | Authority of Christ; commanding us to call no | Man Father upon Earth: With the necessary Con- | sequence thereof, considered, in the Rise, Formation, | Privileges and Power of Particular Christian Churches. | With some | Remarks on Mr. Beckwith's Letter; | In Which he asserts, That he has proved, that no Or-|daining Power was ever given to the Church by | Jesus Christ. | By Israel Holly, | Pastor of a Congregational Church in Suffield. | [Five lines of scripture.]

Printed at the Heart and Crown, in Hartford. | Small 8vo, in 4s and 2s: signatures, A–H⁴, I²: collation; title, 1 p.; To the Reader, 1 p.; text, pp. 3–68. CHS (11)

The pamphlet by Reverend George Beckwith on 'The Invalidity, or Unwarrantableness of Lay Ordination,' to which this was an answer, was printed in 1763; and this 'Word' was answered by Beckwith in 'A Second Letter,' printed in 1766. This pamphlet is assigned to 1765 by Henry M. Dexter in his 'Congregationalism as seen in its Literature.'

METHOD of Raising | Hemp, | In Lancaster County, | Pennsilvania. | Hartford, | Printed and Sold at the Heart and Crown | 1765. | Small 8vo; 8 pp. YUL (12)

It is advertised in the *Courant* of April 29, 1765, thus, "Just Published, And to be sold at the Heart and Crown, in Hartford. (Price 4 Pence.) Some short, and plain Directions for the raising of Hemp."

WHITAKER, NATHANIEL. A | Sermon | Preached at the | Ordination | Of the Reverend | Mr. Isaac Foster, | At Stafford Second Society, | In the Colony of Connecticut; | On the 31st Day of October, 1764. | By the Reverend | Nathaniel Whitaker, A.M. | Pastor of the Church of Christ at Chelsey, in Norwich. | [Nine lines from Saint Paul.]

Hartford: | Printed by T. Green. MDCCLXV. | 16mo, in 4s: signatures, A–G+: collation; title 1 p.; request for copy to print, 1 p.; text, pp. 3–56+.

Private collection (13)

Probably only signature H, which may have consisted of only four pages, is wanting.

1766

AMES, NATHANIEL. An | Astronomical Diary; | or, | Almanack | For the Year of our Lord Christ | 1767; | Being the Third after Bissextile, or Leap-Year. | Calculated for the Meridian of Boston, | New-England, Lat. 42° 25′ North. | Containing, | Aspects; Spring-tides; Judgment of the Weather; | Feasts and Fasts of the Church; Courts in Massa- | chusets-bay, New-

Hampshire, Connecticut and Rhode- | Island; Sun and Moon's rising and setting; Moon's | Place; Time of High Water; Public Roads, with | the best Stages or Houses to put up at; Eclipses; | Quaker's Meetings; an Account of the supreme | executive Courts that are held in England, &c. &c. | By Nathaniel Ames. | [Ten lines of verse.]

Connecticut: | Printed and sold by Thomas Green, in Hartford; | Timothy Green, in New-London; And, | Samuel Green, in New-Haven. | 12mo, in 8s and 4s: signatures unmarked; 12 ff.   CHS (14)

The work is issued in the style of Thomas Green's printing and he was no doubt the printer of it. A note on the last page requests those who incline to encourage paper manufacture to save their old cotton and linen rags "for which they may have a good Price, at the Paper Mill at Norwich, or the Printing-Office in Hartford." It is advertised in the *Courant* of December 15, 1766.

CONNECTICUT COURANT. The Connecticut Courant. | Monday, January 6, 1766. No. 54. | [— Dec. 29, 1766.]

[Hartford: Thomas Green.] Folio, 2 ff.   CHS (15)

The first imprint of this year is on the issue of May 2: "Hartford; Printed by Thomas Green." It was regularly issued each Monday. The issues for March 17, no. 64 (probably); April 21, no. 69 (probably); September 29, no. 92 were of one leaf only. A supplement of one leaf was added to the issue of September 15, no. 90. No copies are known of June 9, no. 76; July 7, no. 80; 21, no. 82; August 25, no. 87; October 27, no. 96; November 17, no. 99; 24, no. 100.

DAVIES, SAMUEL. Little Children | Invited to | Jesus Christ. | A Sermon, | Preached in Hanover County, Virginia, | M ay 8, 1758. | With | An Account of the late remarkable | religious Impressions among the | Students in the College of | New-Jersey. | By Samuel Davies, A. M. | The Fifth Edition. |

Hartford: | Printed and sold by T. Green, at the Heart | & Crown, opposite the Court-House, 1766. | (Price Six Coppers.) | 16mo, in 6s: signatures A, B: collation; title, 1 f.; text, pp. 3–24.   CHS (16)

Advertised in the *Courant* of October 6, 1766. "Price 4d." A sixth edition, Boston, 1770, was "Printed for Knight Sexton at Hartford."

DAVIES, SAMUEL. Little Children | Invited to | Jesus Christ. | A Sermon, | Preached in Hanover County, Virginia, | May 8, 1758. | With | An Account of the late remarkable | religious Impressions among the | Students in the College of | New-Jersey. | By Samuel Davies, A. M. | The Fifth Edition. |

Hartford: | Printed for, and sold by Shem Chapin, of | Springfield, 1766. | (Price Six Coppers.) | 16mo, in 6s: signatures A, B: collation; title, 1 f.; text, pp. 3–24.   CHS (17)

This was printed from the same forms as the other issue of the fifth edition, with change of imprint only.

DELL, WILLIAM. The Trial |of | Spirits, | both in | Teachers and Hearers. | Wherein is held forth | The clear Discovery, and certain Downfal, | of the Carnal and Anti-christian Clergy | of these Nations. | Testified from the

Word of God, to the University | Congregations in Cambridge. | [By] William Dell, Minister of the | Gospel, and Master of Gonvil and Caius | College·in Cambridge. |

[London: First printed in the Year 1666.] 12mo, in 4s: signatures, A–H: collation; title, 1 f.; text, pp. 3–62+. CHS (18)

Advertised in the *Courant* of September 15, 1766, as "Just Re-Printed, and to be sold by Thomas Green, at the Printing-Office, in Hartford." The imperfect copy described above is no doubt one of the issue advertised by Thomas Green in 1766, and was no doubt printed by him at Hartford. The printer's blocks at the top of page 3 are of a form much used by him at this time, and the book contains the autographs of two Windsor people. Unfortunately the lower part of the title, containing the imprint, is missing from the copy seen. The original imprint has been added in brackets from the advertisement, in the belief that it appeared on this issue. Comparison with a copy of another edition shows that the missing portion of the text at the end would occupy only one printed page (63), and so that only the fourth folio of signature H is missing. Whether this issue bore Green's imprint is not known.

DEVOTION, JOHN. The Necessity of a constant Rea- | diness for Death. | A Discourse, | Preached at Hartford North-Meeting-House, | May 25ᵗʰ, 1766. | Occasioned by that | Alarming Providence, | The sudden | Demolition of the School- | House, by Gun-Powder; | Whereby about Thirty Persons were wounded, | Six of whom are since dead. | By the Reverend | John Devotion, A.M. | Of Say-Brook; providentially present. | [Five lines of quotations.]

Hartford: | Printed and Sold by Thomas Green, at the | Heart and Crown, opposite the State-House. | 12mo, in 4s and 2s: signatures, A⁴, B², C⁴, D²: collation; title, 1 p.; author's acknowledgments, 1 p.; Preface signed by E. Dorr, pp. 3, 4; text, pp. 5–24. CHS (19)

Advertised in the *Courant* of September 29, 1766.

EDWARDS, JONATHAN. Ruth's Resolution: | A | Discourse, | Delivered | By the late Reverend | Jonathan Edwards, | Of Northampton. |

Hartford: | Re-printed by Thomas Green, at the Heart and | Crown, opposite the Court-House. | 12mo, in 8s: collation; title, 1 p.; text, pp. 2–16. CHS (20)

Probably issued in 1766 or 1767.

ELLSWORTH, SAMUEL. An Astronomical Diary; | or, | Almanack, | for the | Year of our Lord, 1767. | Being the Third after Bissextile, or Leap-Year. | Calculated for the Meridian of Hartford, | in Connecticut. | Wherein is contained, | The Rising and Setting of the Sun and | Moon; Eclipses; Judgment of the Weather; | Time of High Water; Aspects; observable Days; | Courts, Roads, &c. | By Samuel Ellsworth. | [Ten lines from Young.]

Hartford: | Printed and Sold by Thomas Green. | 12mo, in 8s; 8 ff. CHS (21)

Advertised in the *Courant* of October 13, 1766.

FARRAND, DANIEL. Redemption From Death; Or, | Christ triumphing over the Grave. | A | Sermon, | Delivered at the | Funeral, | of | Mrs. Sarah Gold, | late wife of the | Rev. Hezekiah Gold, | Of Cornwall. | August 30, 1766. | By Daniel Farrand, A.M. | Pastor of the Church at Canaan. | [Scripture quotations, three lines.]

Hartford; Printed by Thomas Green. | 12mo, in 2s, 4s and 6s: signatures [A²], B⁴, C⁶: collation; title, 1 f.; To the People of Cornwall, 1 f.; text, 18 pp.; probably 1 f. blank, wanting. CHS (22)

FITCH, THOMAS. Some Reasons | that influenced | The Governor | to take, and | The Councillors | to administer | The Oath, | Required by the Act of Parliament; commonly | called the Stamp-Act. | Humbly submitted to the Consideration of the Publick. | MDCCLXVI.

Hartford; | Printed and sold by Thomas Green. | Small 8vo, in 4s: signatures A, B: collation; title, 1 f.; text, pp. 3–14; 1 f. blank. CHS (23)

Advertised in the *Courant* of March 17, 1766.

The author of these "Reasons" was Governor Thomas Fitch.

HOOKER, NATHANIEL. The religious Improve- | ment of Harvest. | A| Sermon, | Preached, July 27ᵗʰ, | 1766. | By Nathaniel Hooker, A. M. | Pastor of a Church in Hartford. | [Three lines of quotation.]

Hartford: | Printed by Thomas Green, MDCCLXVI. | Small 8vo, in 6s: signatures, A, B: collation; title, 1 p.; To the Reader, 1 p.; text, pp. 3–24. CHS (24)

Advertised, "In a few Days will be Published," in the *Courant* of September 1, 1766.

A PETITION | to | His Majesty King George the Third. | Small 4to, probably in 4s (two sheets) and 2s; signatures unmarked: collation; title, 1 f.; Petition, pp. 1–5; 9 pp. blank; Power of Attorney, 1 p.; 3 pp. blank. VSL (25)

Both the Petition and the Power of Attorney are dated at the end "New-England, November, 1766." The petition ends about midway on page 5. The remainder of that page and the four blank pages next following contain autograph signatures. The three blank pages following the Power of Attorney also contain autograph signatures. All of the known copies of this petition are bound together into one volume. Three of them lack the last four pages, containing the Power of Attorney and the blank pages following it. This brings up the query whether or not the Power of Attorney should be considered as a separate publication from the Petition. There seems, however, to be no sufficient reason for considering it a separate publication. The type ornaments at the beginning of the petition are the same as those used by Thomas Green and the manner of their arrangement is in his style. There would seem to be no question that this Petition was printed at Hartford by Thomas Green in 1766.

PROCLAMATION. By the Honorable | William Pitkin, Esq; | Governor of His Majesty's English Colony of Connecticut, in New-England, | in America. | A Proclamation. | [Appointing June 26, 1766, as a day of public thanksgiving.]

Printed by Thomas Green, at the Heart and Crown, opposite the State-House, in Hartford. | Broadside; print 9 × 15¾ inches.   YUL (26)

REMINGTON, E. [Cut] | A Short Account | of Three Men that were kill'd by | Lightning, at Suffield, May 20, | 1766, Viz. | Samuel Remington, | James Bagg, | Jonathan Bagg. |

Broadside; print 7 × 11⅜ inches.   Private collection (27)

Below the cut and title are 41 numbered verses of four lines each arranged in two columns, the last verse followed by the date and author's name — "August 26, 1766. E. Remington." The cut, which is at the left of the seven lines of the title, shows Death, Gabriel and a vault containing three coffins. This cut had been used by Timothy Green, uncle of Thomas, in a juvenile issued by him in New London in 1762, and had previously been used in Boston at least as early as 1749. As Suffield is less than twenty miles from Hartford, it seems extremely probable that this is a Hartford publication.

SALTER, RICHARD. The gospel-ministry a warfare, with the | manner in which it is to be managed, | and the motives the gospel sug- | gests to influence thereto: | represented in a | Sermon, | preached at the | Ordination | Of the Reverend | Eleazer Storrs, | at | Sandisfield, | February 26th, A.D. 1766. | By Richard Salter, A. M. | Pastor of the first Church of Christ in Mansfield. | [Four lines of scripture.]

Printed for, and Sold by Lieut. John Stil- | man, of Sandisfield. | 12mo, in 4s and 2s: signatures [A⁴], B², C⁴, D²: collation; title, 1 f.; text, pp. 3-24.   CHS (28)

Lieut. John Stilman removed from Wethersfield, which is adjacent to Hartford, to Sandisfield, Mass., as early as 1754.

The type ornaments and the general style of the printing indicate that this is the work of Thomas Green.

WATTS, ISAAC. A Wonderful Dream. By Doct. Watts.

Sold at the Printing office in Hartford. 12mo: 12 pp. No title page. (29). Advertised in the *Courant* of Feb. 24, 1766, as follows:

"Just published, and to be sold at the Printing-Office in Hartford. A wonderful Dream or Vision, concerning America. 'Your Old Men shall dream Dreams.'" Possibly printed in New London, as an edition "Printed and sold in New London" was advertised in the *New London Gazette* of Feb. 7, 1766. The title, imprint and collation given above are from Trumbull's 'List of Books printed in Connecticut.' No copy of this edition is known. Evans' 'American Bibliography' describes a 12mo, 12 page edition of this work printed at New London in 1770 as a poem of 68 stanzas.

1767

AMES, NATHANIEL. An Astronomical diary; or, Almanack for the year of our Lord Christ 1768 . . . by Nathaniel Ames . . .

Hartford: Printed and sold by Thomas Green. 12mo. (30)

This entry is copied from Evans' 'American Bibliography.' No copy is known; it is not advertised in the *Courant*, and it seems very doubtful if there was such an issue.

BARTHOLOMEW, ANDREW. A Proof and Explanation of | the Decree of God: | A | Sermon, | Delivered before | The Association | Of | Litchfield-County, | In Goshen, | October 2ᵈ, 1766. | And now made Public at the Desire and Cost of | Some of the Hearers. | By Andrew Bartholomew, M. A. | Pastor of the Church of Christ in Harwinton. |

Hartford; | Printed and Sold by T. Green, at the Heart | and Crown, 1767. | 12mo, in 4s: signatures [A], B–D: collation; title, 1 f.; text, pp. 3–32. CHS (31)

Advertised in the *Courant* of July 27, 1767.

BATES, WILLIAM. Christ in the Clouds, | Coming to | Judgment; | or, the | Dissolution of all Things. | Wherein is plainly set forth, | The Second Coming of Christ | to Judgment. | As also, the Arraignment, Trial, Condemnation, | and most dreadful Sentence that shall be past | upon all impenitent Sinners. | With the happy and glorious Condition of those that have | repented, believed, and preferred Christ above All. | Being the Substance of a Sermon preached | by that Reverend Divine | Dr. Bates. |

Hartford: | Printed and sold by Thomas Green, at the | Heart and Crown. | 12mo, in 8s: collation; title 1 p.; text, pp. 2–16. LC (32)

Advertised in the *Courant* of August 10, 1767, as "Just Re-printed," price 4*d*.

CONNECTICUT COURANT. The | Connecticut Courant; | and the | Weekly Advertiser. | Monday, January 5, 1767. Numb. 106. | [— Dec. 28, 1767.]

Printed by Thomas Green, at the Printing-Office, opposite the State-House, in Hartford. | Folio, 1 f. (?2 ff.) CHS (33)

A cut of the heart and crown design separates the two words in each of the three lines of the title. In the last issue of the year a cut of the Royal Arms takes the place of the former cut. It was regularly issued each Monday. The issues of January 5, no. 106 (perhaps); January 19, no. 108 were of one leaf only. A supplement of one leaf was added to the issues of March 30, no. 118; April 6, no. 119; April 20, no. 121; June |, no. 127. No copies are known of July 6, no. 132; December 7, no. 154.

EELLS, EDWARD. Christ, the Foundation of the Salvation | of Sinners, and of civil and ecclesiasti- | cal Government; | illustrated in a | Sermon, | preached before the | General Assembly | of the Colony of | Connecticut, | on the Day of the | Anniversary Election, | May 14ᵗʰ, 1767. | By Edward Eells, M. A. | Pastor of the Second Church in Middletown. | [Scripture quotations, six lines.]

Hartford: | Printed by Thomas Green, at the Heart & Crown, | opposite the Court-House. | 12mo, in 4s: signatures [A], B–D: collation; title, 1 p.; official request for copy to print, 1 p.; text, pp. 3–30; 1 f. blank.   CHS (34)

ELLSWORTH, SAMUEL. An Astronomical diary; or Almanack, for the year of our Lord 1768 ... by Samuel Ellsworth ...

Hartford: Printed and sold by Thomas Green. 16mo.   (35)
This entry is copied from Evans' 'American Bibliography.' No copy is known; it is not advertised in the *Courant*, and it seems very doubtful if there was such an issue.

FROTHINGHAM, EBENEZER. A Key, | To unlock the Door, | That leads in, to take a | Fair View | of the | Religious Constitution, | Established by Law, in the Colony of | Connecticut. | With a short Remark upon Mr. Bartlet's | Sermon, on Galatians iii. i. | Also, A Remark upon Mr. Ross, against | the Separates and Others. | With a short Observation upon the Expla- | nation of Say-Brook-Plan; and Mr. Ho- | bart's Attempt to estab-lish the same Plan. | By Ebenezer Frothingham. | [Scripture quotations, eleven lines.]

Printed in the Year 1767. | 12mo, in 4s and 2s: signatures, A–I, K–N⁴, O², P⁴, Q², R⁴, S², T⁴, V², X⁴, Y², Z⁴, Aa², Bb⁴, Cc², Dd⁴, Ee², Ff⁴, Gg², Hh⁴, Ii², Kk⁴, Ll², Mm⁴, Nn², Oo⁴, Pp²: collation; title, 1 f.; "Preface," pp. 3–8; "The Author's Apology," pp. 9–42; "Some Remarks, upon the | Religious Constitution, of | the Colony of Connecti- | cut, established by Law, | &c. |," pp. 43–252; "Errors, to be corrected," 1 f.   CHS (36)
The first signature is printed on different and poorer paper than the rest of the book. Page 64 is followed by page 67. A design, surrounding a capital letter, made up of 32 type ornaments irregularly arranged in a pattern, on page 43, is identical with a design appearing in the *Courant* of September 7, 1767, and also with one in Bartholomew's sermon printed by Green in 1767. The three are printed from the same set up of type ornaments. This apparently proves that the volume was printed in Hartford by Thomas Green, and refutes the commonly accepted state-ment that Bernard Romans' *Annals of the Troubles in the Netherlands*, vol. 1, 1778, was the first book of more than one hundred pages printed in Hartford.

GAY, EBENEZER. The Sovereignty of God, in de- | termining Man's Day's, or the | Time & Manner of his Death; | Illustrated and Improved, | in a | Sermon, | Preached at Suffield, May 22ᵈ 1766. | At the Funeral of | Three Young Men, | Who were killed by Lightning, | May 20ᵗʰ, 1766. | By Ebenezer Gay, A.M. | Pastor of a Church in Suffield. | [Four lines of scripture.]

Hartford: | Printed by Thomas Green, at the Heart and | Crown, oppo-site the Court-House, | M,DCC,LXVII. | 8vo, in 4s; signatures, [A], B, C; collation; half-title 1 p.; author's reason for printing, 1 p.; title, 1 f.; text, pp. 5–24.   Private collection (37)
This is probably the first edition.

GAY, EBENEZER. The Sovereignty of God, in deter- | mining Man's Days, or the Time | and Manner of his Death: | Illustrated and improved, | in a | Sermon, | Preached at Suffield, May 22ᵈ, 1766, | At the Funeral of | Three Young Men, | Who were killed by Lightning, | May 20ᵗʰ, 1766. | By Ebenezer Gay, A.M. | Pastor of a Church in Suffield. | [Three lines of scripture.]

    Hartford: | Printed by Thomas Green, at the Heart and Crown, | opposite the Court-House, 1767. | 8vo, in 4s; signatures, [A], B: collation; title, 1 p.; author's reason for printing, 1 p.; text, pp. 3–16.   CHS (38)

    Advertised in the *Courant* of July 27, 1767; but which edition is there advertised cannot be told.

HOLLISTER, ISAAC. A brief narration of the captivity of Isaac Hollister who was taken by the Indians Anno Domini 1763. Written by himself.

    Hartford: Printed by Thomas Green. [1767.]   (39)

    The above entry is copied from Evans' 'American Bibliography,' where also is given an edition with the imprint "New-London: Printed by Timothy Green." [1767.] Apparently neither of these issues was seen by Mr. Evans, as he gives no collations of them. Evans also notes the following edition:

    A brief | Narration | of the | Captivity | of | Isaac Hollister, | Who was taken by the | Indians, | Anno Domini, 1763. | Written by himself. |

    Hartford. | Printed for, and Sold by Knight Sexton. | 12mo, in 4s: collation; title, 1 p.; text, pp. 2–8.

    As the only copy of this Sexton edition seen by Evans (CHS) has an owner's name with the date 1770, he assigns the issue to that year. In the *Courant* of April 17, 1769, Knight Sexton of Hartford has an advertisement giving a long list of books for sale by him, among which is the "Brief Narration of the Captivity of Isaac Hollister." This brings up a number of questions. Was the edition advertised by Sexton the one "Printed for, and Sold by" him? If so, was it then just printed, or had it been printed a year or more before the date of the advertisement, making it the work of Thomas Green rather than of Green and Watson? If printed previous to the middle of April, 1768, was the edition printed for Sexton identical with the unseen edition credited by Evans to Thomas Green in 1767? The style and the printer's ornaments appearing in the Knight Sexton edition indicate that it is the production of the press in Hartford.

HOLLY, ISRAEL. The Substance of a discourse delivered on the day of the funeral of three young men who were killed by lightning at Suffield, May 20, 1766.

    Hartford: Printed by Thomas Green, 1767. 12mo.   (40)

    This entry is taken from Evans' 'American Bibliography.'

    No evidence is found as to the date of issue of any of the five editions with the exception of the fourth, which is dated 1767. It seems not improbable that one or more of the earlier editions were issued in 1766, and the fifth edition may have been issued in 1768.

HOLLY, ISRAEL. The Substance of a discourse delivered on the day of the funeral of three young men who were killed by lightning at Suffield, May 20, 1766. The second edition.

Hartford: Printed by Thomas Green, 1767. 12mo; 27 pp. (41)
The above from Evans' 'American Bibliography.'
An imperfect copy of perhaps this edition in CHS lacks probably the first and last folios. It is (now) in signatures [A]³, B², C⁴. D³. It begins on p. III in the midst of an introduction which ends in the middle of p. IV and is signed I. H. The text begins with the heading "Youth liable to sudden Death" on p. 5 (and has the same words for running headline) and ends with a row of printer's blocks near the bottom of p. 26. Both the fourth and fifth editions have a hymn by Isaac Watts following the discourse. It is probable that the hymn appeared on the recto of the missing leaf at the end of signature D, and that the verso of the leaf was blank.

HOLLY, ISRAEL. The Substance of a discourse delivered on the day of the funeral of three young men who were killed by lightning at Suffield, May 20, 1766. The third edition.

Hartford: Printed by Thomas Green, 1767. 12mo. (42)
This entry is taken from Evans' 'American Bibliography.'

HOLLY, ISRAEL. Youth liable to sudden Death; | Excited seriously to consider thereof, and speedily | to prepare therefor. | The Substance of a | Discourse, | Delivered on the Day of the | Funeral of three Young Men, | Who were killed by Lightning, at Suffield, | May 20, 1766. | Published at the Request of Many. | By Israel Holly. | Preacher of the Gospel in Suffield. | [Scripture quotations, six lines.] The Fourth Edition. |

Hartford: | Printed by Thomas Green, 1767. | 12mo, in 4s: signatures, [A], B, C: collation; title, 1 f.; text, pp. 3–24. CHS (43)

HOLLY, ISRAEL. Youth liable to sudden Death; | Excited seriously to consider thereof, and speedily to | prepare therefore. | The substance of a | Discourse, | Delivered on the Day of the | Funeral of Three Young Men, | who were | Killed by Lightning, | At Suffield, May 20, 1766. | By Israel Holly, | Preacher of the Gospel in Suffield. | [Scripture quotations, six lines.] The Fifth Edition. |

Hartford: | Printed by Thomas Green. | 8vo, 1 f., followed by two unmarked signatures in 4s: collation; title, 1 f.; text, pp. 3–18. Probably lacks either a half-title or a blank leaf at the end in the same signature as the title. CHS (43)

LIBERTY IN SLAVERY: | Or, | The Idolatrous Christian. | Some | Poetical Thoughts, | Occasioned by the late | Public Rejoicings | at Hartford, | On the News of the Repeal of the | Stamp-Act. |

Tall 16°, in 4s: collation; title, 1 leaf; text, pp. 3–8. NYHS (45)
Heading of text reads "Some Poetical Thoughts, &c." Contains 38 numbered verses of four lines each, followed by the word Finis. The

form and style of arrangement of the printers' ornaments on the title page, above the heading of the text and after Finis are characteristic of Thomas Green's work.

PERRY, JOSEPH. The Character of Moses illustrated and | improved: | in a | Discourse, | Occasioned by the Death of the Honorable | Roger Wolcott, Esq; | of Windsor, who, for several Years, was | Governor of the Colony of Connecticut; | And died May 17, 1767, | In the 89th Year of his Age. | Preached the first Opportunity after his Funeral. | By Joseph Perry, A.M. | Pastor of the Second Church of Christ in Windsor. | [Scripture quotations, seven lines.]

Hartford; Printed by Thomas Green. | Small 4to, in 2s: signatures [A], B–G; collation; title, 1 f.; text, pp. 3–28.   CHS (46)

PROCLAMATION. By the Honorable | William Pitkin, Esquire. | Governor of His Majesty's English Colony of Connecticut, in | New-England, in America. | A Proclamation. |

Hartford: Printed by Thomas Green. | Broadside; print 10½ × 16¼ inches.   YUL (47)

Appointing April 8, 1767, as a day of fasting and prayer.

SMITH, COTTON MATHER. Jesus Christ, a Comforter to | humble Mourners: | A | Discourse, | Delivered at Sharon, | On Account of the | Much lamented Death of | Mrs. Sarah Day, | Late Consort of | Mr. Jeremiah Day. | Who died of a | Child-Bed Fever, | On the 25th of August, 1767. | Published at the earnest Request of the Friends | By Cotton-Mather Smith, A.M. | Pastor of the Church in Sharon. | [Scripture quotation, one line.]

Hartford; | Printed by Thomas Green, at the Heart & | Crown, 1767. | 12mo, in 4s: signatures, A–C: collation; title, 1 f.; text, pp. 3–24.
                      CHS (impf.) (48)

THOMPSON, J. The lost and undone | Son of Perdition; | or, the | Birth, Life and Character | of | Judas Iscariot, | Faithfully collected from several ancient Authors of | undoubted Credit. | By J. Thompson. | [Small cut.] |

Hartford; Printed and Sold at the | Heart and Crown. | 12mo, in 4s: signatures [A], B; collation; title, 1 f.; text, pp. 3–15; 1 p. blank.
                      CHS (48)

Evans' 'American Bibliography' notes a New London edition of 1767, and it is thought probable that this edition was printed during the same year.

1768

CONNECTICUT COURANT. The | Connecticut [*Royal Arms*] Courant. | Monday, Jan. 4, 1768. (Numb. 158.) | [— Dec. 26, 1768.]
     Hartford: Printed by T. Green. | Folio, 2 ff.   (50)
     It was regularly issued each Monday by Green to and including April 18, no. 173. After that the imprint became Green and Watson to and including March 12, 1771, after which Green's name is dropped and Ebenezer Watson continues alone as the printer. A supplement of one leaf was added to the issue of March 21, no. 169. No copies are known of March 28, no. 170; April 4, no. 171. Some copies of no. 165, February 22, were by error dated February 29. The subscription price is given in the issue of May 2 as six shillings lawful money per year.

PROCLAMATION. [*Royal Arms*] | By the Honorable | William Pitkin, Esq; | Governor of His Majesty's English Colony of Connecticut, in New-England, | in America. | A Proclamation. | [Appointing April 6, 1768, as a day of fasting and prayer.]
     Hartford; Printed by Thomas Green, at the Heart and Crown, opposite the Court-House. | Broadside; print 8⅞ × 12⅔ inches.
                           Private collection (51)

WRITINGS OF REV. JOHN COTTON

By JULIUS H. TUTTLE

Librarian of the Massachusetts Historical Society

CHIEF among the guiding spirits of the first generation of the Massachusetts Bay Colony in New England was the Reverend John Cotton, teacher of the First Church in Boston. While vicar of St. Botolph's Church in Boston, England, he gave warm encouragement to the adventurers who were courageously and surely shaping the affairs of the Bay Company in London. This was during the long months of their preparation before Governor John Winthrop and his associates set sail in March, 1630, for the new plantation bringing with them their Royal Charter.

Cotton was then in middle age, with a quarter of a century of service in that pulpit behind him; and his heart and soul were with the faithful ones who were taking their all into the wilderness of New England. His sermon, preached in 1630 to this Company on their leaving Southampton, was their farewell on leaving for the New World; and it gave valid reasons, drawn from Gospel sources, for their entering into their great enterprise and their rights in the settlement.

Cotton followed the large tide of emigration from their English homes to the New World, and reached Boston on September 4, 1630, having taken passage on the ship Griffin, with Hooker, and Stone, Mr. Peirce, Mr. Haynes (a gentleman of large estate), and others, who, according to Governor Winthrop, in his Journal, "gat out of England with much difficulty, all places being belaid to have taken Mr. Cotton and Mr. Hooker, who had been long sought for to have been brought into the high commission."

He brought with him his library which "was vast, and vast was his acquaintance with it; but although amongst his readings he had given a special room unto the fathers, and unto the school-men, yet at last he preferred one Calvin above them all." He was immediately ordained as Teacher of the First Church in Boston, and continued in this service until his death on December 23, 1652. An enduring memorial of the "Patriarch of the Massachusetts Theocracy," in the form of a life-size recumbent portrait statue by the late Bela Lyon Pratt, was placed in a recess in the south wall of the nave in the First Church, by some of his descendants in 1906. The marble base incloses tracery from the walls of St. Botolph's Church, Boston, England where he was vicar from 1612 to 1633.

Cotton Mather in his 'Magnalia' (I, 280; 1853) says of his grandfather, that "his printed works, whereof there are many, that praise him in the gates, though few of them were printed with his own knowledge or consent."

An effort has been made to list some of the copies of each of these titles.

[1630.] Gods | Promise | to his | Plantation. | . . . || London, | Printed by William Jones for John Bellamy, and | are to be solde at the three Golden Lyons by the | Royall Exchange. 1630.   (1)
   Sig.: A⁴ (first leaf, probably blank, wanting), B⁴, C⁴, D². (1), (4), 20 p. Title, v. blank; 4 p. To the Christian Reader, signed I. H. (probably John Humphrey); 1–20, text, 2 Sam. 7.10. *Copies:* BM; HC; MHS; Y; JCB.
   Joshua Scottow in his Narrative of the Planting of the Massachusetts Colony Anno 1628 (Boston, 1694), says "Some of their choice Friends, as the Reverend Mr. Cotton, and others, went along with them from Boston in Lincolnshire to Southampton, where they parted, and he Preacht his Farewel Sermon." John Rous in his Diary (Camden Society, 1856, 66: 53) records on June 7, 1630, that "some little while since the company went to New England under Mr. Wintrop. Mr. Cotton, of Boston in Lincolnshire, went to theire departure about Gravesend, and preached to them, as we heare, out of 2 Samuel, VII, 10." Samuel Fuller's entry in his letter of June 28, 1630, relating to this incident, reads: "Here is a gentleman, one Mr. Cottington, a Boston man, who told me, that Mr. Cotton's charge at Hampton was, that they should take advice of them at Plymouth." [1]

[1] Reprinted in 1 Coll. Mass. Hist. Soc., III, 75. Entered in the Stationers' Register, July 3, 1630.

The writer of the Preface says that "many may either not know, or doe not consider upon how full a ground and warrant out of the word of God that undertaking (which was the occasion of this Sermon) hath hitherto proceeded," and that leave to print was obtained "with some difficulty" from "the Reverend Authour," also that "Erelong (if God will) thou shalt see a larger declaration of the first rise and ends of this enterprise." Coddington in his 'Demonstration of True Love,' 1674, says that this sermon and the "Planter's Plea" were printed by John Humphrey, their Agent.

[1630–1634.] Gods | Promise | to his | Plantations | . . . || [same to] . . . sold . . . 1634. (2)

Sig.: A², B², C⁴, D⁴. (1), (2), 20 p. Title, v. blank; 2 p. To the Christian Reader; [continues same]. *Copies:* BP; C; HC; Y.

[1630–1686.] God's | Promise | [same to] . . . 1634. | Reprinted at Boston in New-England, by Samuel Green; and | are to be sold by John Usher. Anno. 1686. (3)

Sig.: A⁴–C⁴ (last leaf, probably blank, missing). Title, v. blank; 1–20, text (continues same). *Copies:* AAS; BA; BP; MHS; Y.

[Before 1633.] A short discourse . . . touching the time when the Lordes day beginneth whether at the Eveninge or in the Morninge. *Manuscript.* (4)

A photograph of the first page of this manuscript, of which no printed copy has been found, was exhibited by Dean Chester N. Greenough at the meeting of the Colonial Society of Massachusetts, on April 17, 1917.[1] The original is at Emmanuel College, Cambridge, England. Dean Greenough called attention to Cotton Mather's statement in the 'Magnalia' that "The sabbath he [John Cotton] began the evening before: for which keeping of the Sabbath from Evening to Evening, he wrote arguments before his coming to New England: and I suppose, 'twas from his reason and practice, that the Christians of New England have generally done so too."

[1634.] [Election sermon, Mass. Gen. Court.] (5)

No copy of this first Massachusetts Election sermon is known to be extant.

[1634–1713.] A | Treatise | I. Of Faith. | II. Twelve Fundamental Articles | of | Christian Religion. | III. A Doctrinal Conclusion. | IV. Questions and answers upon | Church-Government | — | Taken from Written Copies long since de- | livered by the late Reverend Mr. John | Cotton, . . . || Printed in the Year 1713. (6)

Sig.: A⁴–C⁴, D². 28 p. *Copies:* BP; Y.

The "Questions" bear date "25. 11m. 1634," and were the first preparation of what appeared in 'The True Constitution,' and in 'The Doctrine of the Church,' 1642. These are the "first of a long and valuable series of statements and discussions from his pen touching the general

[1] Published, Col. Soc. Mass., 19:366.

question of Church life and Order," according to the Reverend Henry M. Dexter in his manuscript copy made on April 5, 1866, now in Yale University Library.

[1634–1642.] The True | Constitvtion | Of | A particular visible Church, proved by Scripture. | . . . || London: | Printed for Samuel Satterthwaite, at the Signe of the black Bull | in Budge Rowe, neare to Saint Antholines | Church. 1642. (7)
  Sig.: A⁴, B⁴. (1), 13 p. Title, v. blank; 1–13, text. *Copies:* JCB; BM; B; BP; C; HC; MHS.
  The Thomason copy is dated July 18.

[1634–1642.] The | Doctrine | of the Church, . . . |— || London: | Printed for Samuel Satterthwaite, at the signe of the | black Bull in Budge Row. 1642. (8)
  Sig. same as in "The True Constitution," and collation.
  Same; pages after 6 missing.
  Copy: B.
  In the heading of the text the word "Constitution" is crossed out with a pen, and the word "Doctrine" written above it. This heading in the next imprint is changed to "The | Doctrine | of the | Church, | And in | Government."

[1634–1643.] The | Doctrine | of the | Church, | To which are committed the Keys of the | Kingdome of Heaven. | . . . | — |The Second Edition: | Printed according to a more exact copy; the Marginall | proofes in the former Edition misplaced, being herein placed more | directly; . . . || London, | Printed for Ben: Allen & Sam: Satterthwaite, and are to be sold in Popes- | head Alley and Budge-row. 1643. (9)
  Sig.: A⁴–B⁴. (1), 13 p. Title, v. blank; 1–13, text; last page blank.
  Copies: JCB; BM; MHS; Y.

[1634–1644.] [Same to] . . . | To which is committed . . . | The Third Edition. More exactly corrected, the Marginall proofes in | the former Edition misplaced, being herein placed | more directly; and many other faults both in the | Line and Margent are here corrected. | — || London, Printed for Ben: Allen, and are to be sold in Popes-head Alley. 1644. (10)
  Sig.: A⁴, B⁴. (1), 14 p. Title, v. blank; 1–14, text. *Copies:* JCB; C; HC; MHS; Y.

[1636–1713.] Sermon | . . . Deliver'd at Salem, 1636. | . . . || Boston: Printed in the year, 1713. (11)
  Sig.: 1l., and A⁴–E⁴. (1), 40 p. Title, v. blank; 1–40, text, "By the Reverend, Old Mr. John Cotton, | At Salem, June, 1636." *Copies:* BP; MHS.

[1640–1655.] An | Exposition | upon | The Thirteenth Chapter | of the | Revelation. | . . . Taken from his mouth in Short-writing, and some | part of it corrected by Himselfe soon after the Prea- | ching thereof, . . . but nothing of the sense al- | tered. | — || London, | Printed by M. S. for Livewel Chapman, at the Crown | in Popes-head Alley, 1655. (12)

Sig.: [A]⁴ (first leaf blank) — Ll⁴ (last leaf blank), Mm⁴ (last leaf blank). (1), (4), 262, (6) p. Title, v. blank; 4 p. To | the Reader, signed Thomas Allen, at Norwich, | the 1. day of | the 1. month, 1654-5; 1–262, text, An | Exposition | . . . ; 2 p. blank; 6 p. A Table, ending with Errata in twelve lines. Mr. Allen states that "(having lived in that American wildernesse about 13. or 14. yeares in the Towne next adjoyning to Boston, and so had thereby the happy priviledg of enjoying the benefit of the precious labours of Mr. Cottons, in his Lecture upon every fifth day in the week) I say I do here declare and testifie unto the world that these Sermons . . . were published by . . . Mr. John Cotton, about the 11. and 12. moneths (if I mistake not) of the year, 1639, and the first and second of the yeare 1640. upon his weekly Lecture at Boston"; and that "the publisher of this Exposition, who having the pen of a ready Writer, did take those Notes from the Mouth of the Preacher." *Copies:* BM; BP; MHS; Y.

Thomason copy is dated June 19.

[1640–1656.] [Same to] . . . and | some part of it Corrected by himself soon after the | Preaching thereof, . . . but nothing of the | Sense altered. | — || London, | Printed for Tim. Smart, at the Hand and Bible in | the Old-Bayly. 1656. (13)

Sig.: [1st in ⁴, first leaf missing]; *⁎* in 2; B⁴–Ll⁴ (last leaf blank); Mm⁴ (last leaf missing) [same to] 1654-5; 2 p. The Analysis of the 13. Chapter; 2 p. The Reader is desired to correct with his pen these faults | (amongst others) which Through precipitance of the | Press have fallen to the prejudice of the sence; [continues same.] *Copies:* JCB; BP; HC.

[1641.] An | Abstract | or the | Lawes | of | New England, | as they are now established. | — | [Printer's device] || London, | Printed for F. Cowles, and W. Ley at Paules Chain, | 1641. (14)

Sig.: A⁴, B⁴, C². (1), 15, (2) p. Title, v. blank; 1–15, text; 2 p. The Table; last page blank. *Copies:* BP; MHS; JCB; HC.

This was offered to the General Court, but never adopted.

[1641–1655.] An | Abstract | of | Laws | and Government. | . . . | — | Collected and digested into the ensuing Method, by | . . . John | Cotton, . . . | — | And now published after his death, by | William Aspinwall. . . . || London, | Printed by M. S. for Livewel Chapman, and are to be sold | at the Crown in Popes-head Alley, 1655. (15)

Sig.: A⁴–E⁴, F⁴ (last leaf blank). (1), (5), 35. Title, v. blank; 5 p. To the Reader, signed Will. Aspinwall; v. blank; 1–35, text; v. blank; 1 p. An Analysis of Lawes and Government accommodated to New-England; 1 p. These are the principall faults which have es- | caped the Presse, sixteen lines. *Copies:* JCB; HC; MHS; Y.

[1641.] A | Coppy | of | A Letter | of Mʳ. Cotton of | Boston, . . . || Printed in the yeare 1641. (16)

Sig.: A⁴. (1), 6 p. Title, v. blank; 1–4, text, signed John Cotton; 5, 6, Questions put to such as are admitted to | the Church-Fellowship. *Copies:* B; JCB; BM; HC; MHS; Y.

[1641.] Gods | Mercie | Mixed with his | Ivstice, | . . . || London, | Printed by G. M. for Edward Brewster, and Henry | Hood at the Bible on Fleet-Bridge, and in | S. Dunstanes Church-yard, 1641. (17)

    Sig.: A⁴–S⁴. (1), (6), 135 p. Title, v. blank; 6 p. To the Christian Reader, signed by Mat. Svvallovve, From my Study in London, | May 20, 1641.; 1–26, Gods | Mercy in his | Peoples deliverance.; 27–49, The | Saints | Deliverance | ; v. blank; 51–72, Gods | Mercie Ma- | nifest in his | Ivstice.; 73–135, The Wickeds | Craft; v. blank. *Copies:* JCB; BP; C; HC; MHS; BM.

    Entered in the Stationers' Register, March 5.

[1641–1658.] The | Saints | Support & Comfort, | . . . [Printer's device] || London, | Printed and are to be sold by Thomas Basset in | Sᵗ. Dunstans Church-yard in Fleet-street. 1658. (18)

    Sig.: 1l., and B⁴–S⁴. (1), 135 p. Title, v. blank; 1–26. Gods | Mercy . . . [continues same to end]. *Copies:* BM; HC; Y.

[1641.] The way of Life. | . . . || London, | Printed by M. F. for L. Fawne, and S. Gellibrand, at the Brasen | Serpent in Pauls Church-yard. 1641. (19)

    Sig.: *A*⁴, B⁸–Gg⁸, Hh⁴. (1), (6), 481 p. Title, v. blank; 6 p. To the Reader, signed, William Morton; 1–122, The Povring ovt | of | the Spirit; 123–197. Sinnes | deadly VVound; v. blank; 199–253, The | Christians | Charge; v. blank; 255–481, The | Life of | Faith; v. blank. *Copies:* B; JCB; BM; BP; C; HC; MHS; Y.

    Entered in the Stationers' Register, December 14, 1640.

[1642.] A Brief | Exposition | Of the Whole Book of | Canticles, | or, | Song of Solomon; | . . . || London, | Printed for Philip Nevil, at the signe of | the Gun in Ivie-Lane, 1642. (20)

    Sig.: 1l., and B⁸–R⁸, S⁴. (1), 264 p. Title, v. blank; 1–264, text. *Copies:* JCB; BP; HC; Y.

[1642–1648.] A Briefe [same to] . . . Solomon: | . . . ||London, | Printed by J. Young for Charles Green, and are to be | sold at the Signe of the Gun in Ivie-Lane. 1648. (21)

    Sig.: A⁸–Q⁸. (1), 256 p. Title, v. blank; 1–256, text, The | Canticles, | or | Song of Songs | opened and explained [continues in headings for each of eight chapters.] *Copies:* BP; C; HC; MHS.

[1642.] The | Churches Resurrection, | . . . || London: | Printed by R. O. & G. D. for Henry Overton, | and are to be sold at his Shop in Popes-head-Alley, | 1642. (22)

    Sig.: A⁴–D⁴ (last leaf blank) 30 p. Title, v. blank; 3–30, text. *Copies:* B; JCB; BA; BM; BP; C; HC; MHS; Y.

[1642.] A Modest and Cleare | Answer | to | Mʳ. Balls Discourse of | set formes of Prayer. | . . . || London, | Printed by R. O. and G. D. for Henry Overton, | in Popes head-Alley, 1642. (23)

    Sig.: A⁴–G⁴. (1), (2), 49, (1) p. Title, v. blank; 2 p. To the courteous Reader; 1 p., Advertisements | Vpon the Discourse; followed by 1–49, text; v. blank; 1 p. Courteous Reader, I intreat thee take paines to | correct these faults escaped: sixteen lines; v. blank. *Copies:* JCB; BM; B; C; HC; MHS; Y.

[1642–1642?] A | Modest | and | Cleer Ansvver | to | Mr. Ball's Discourse | of | Set Formes | of | Prayer. | . . . || London; Printed for H. Overton in | Popes-Head Alley. [1642?] (24)

Sig.: A⁸–E⁸, F⁸ (last two leaves, probably blank, missing). 90 p. Title, v. blank; 2 p. To the Courteous Reader; [5], 6, Advertisements | upon | The Discourse; followed by 6–90, text. *Copies:* BP; JCB.

[1642.] The | Powrring | ovt of the | Seven Vials: | . . . || London, | Printed for R. S,¹ and are to be sold at Henry Overtons shop | in Popes-head Alley. 1642. (25)

Sig.: A², B⁴–E⁴, F²; A⁴–C⁴; A⁴–C⁴; A⁴–E⁴, F²; A⁴, B⁴, Bb⁴ [2d leaf Aa2], Cc⁴ [2d leaf Bb2, last leaf blank]; Aaa⁴, Bbb⁴, Ccc² [last p. blank]. (1), (2), 35, 24, 24, 43, 16, 14, 19 p. Title, v. blank; 2 p. To the Christian Reader, signed I. H. (probably John Humphrey); 1–16, Viall I; 17–35, The Second | Viall; 1–24. The Third | Vial; 1–24, The Fourth | Vial; 1–13, The Fift Viall; 14–26, The Sixth Viall; 27–43, The second part of the sixth Viall, 1–16, The Third Sermon; 1–14, The Fourth Part; 1–13, The | Seventh and | Last Viall | opened, last p. blank. *Copies:* AAS; B; JCB; BM; BP; C; HC; MHS; Y.

The Preface speaks of this as "a taste of the ordinary Weeke-daies exercise, . . . taken from his owne mouth, whose Pen would have more fully answered thy greatest expectations could his time (drunke up with continuall waighty, and various imployments) afforded him more liberty and leisure, to have fyled over his owne notions: . . . which was not intended, when first delivered, for any more publike use, then of his owne private Auditorie."

The Thomason copy is dated April.

[1642–1645.] The | Powring | Out of the Seven | Vials: | . . . || London, | Printed for R. S. and are to be sold at Henry Overtons | Shop in Popes-head Alley. 1645. (26)

Sig.: A⁴–V⁴ (1), (2), 156 p. Title, v. blank; 2 pp. To the Christian Reader, signed I. H.; 1–156, text. *Copies:* BM; BP; JCB; C; HC; MHS; Y.

[1643.] A | Letter | of | Mʳ. John Cottons | . . . | to | Mʳ. Williams a Preacher there. | . . . | — | Imprimatur, John Bachiler | — || Printed at London for Benjamin Allen. 1643. (27)

Sig.: A⁴, B⁴. Title, v. blank; 1–13, text; v. blank. *Copies:* BM; BP; HC.

[1644.] The | Keyes | Of the Kingdom of | Heaven, | . . . || London, Printed by M. Simmons for Henry Overton, and are to be sold at his | Shop entring into Popes-head Alley, out of Lumbard-street, 1644. (28)

Sig.: A⁴, a², B⁴–H⁴, I². (1), (10), 59 p. Title, v. blank; 10 p. To the Reader, signed, Tho: Goodwin. | Philip Nye; 1–59, text, Of the Keys,

¹ Perhaps Ralph Smith.

followed on page 59 by This is licensed and entred according to Order. *Copy:* BM.

Thomason copy dated 14 June.

[1644.] The | Keyes | [same] | || London, Printed by M. Simmons for Henry Overton, at his Shop | entring into Popes-head Alley out of Lumbard-street. 1644.   (29)

Sig.: A⁴, A², B⁴–H⁴, I². (1), (10), 59 p. Collation same. *Copies:* BP; HC; MHS.

[1644.] The | Keyes | . . . || London, | Printed by M. Simmons for Henry Overton, and are to be | sold at his Shop in Popes-head-Alley, 1644.   (30)

Collation and pagination same. *Copies:* BA; HC; MHS.

[1644.] The | Keyes | . . . [continues same].   (31)

Copies: B; JCB; C; HC; Y.

According to a note by Dr. Dexter in the Yale copy, the British Museum copy is exactly like the Yale copy with the exception that on page 7 a marginal reference to Heb. 4.3 appears in the former. The John Carter Brown Library has two issues, corresponding apparently to the Yale and BM copies. In addition to the variation observed by Dr. Dexter, the following are noted in the JCB copy of the BM variant:

In the Yale copy, the second paragraph on page 6 has ten lines; in the BM copy it has eleven lines. In the BM copy, on page 7, in lines 14, 15, 16, 17, and 36, several words have been italicized which in the Yale copy are in roman type. These additions to text and typographical improvements seem to indicate that the Yale issue is the earlier. There was no resetting of type even of the pages in which variations occur. The JCB copy corresponding to the BM or second issue is a BM duplicate.

[1644–1843.] The | Keyes | . . . 1644 | — || Boston: Reprinted by Tappan and Dennet, | 1843.   (32)

Sig.: 2l., 1ᵃ–9⁶. iv, 108 p. Title, v. blank; (iii), iv, Preface | to | the American Edition, signed The Editor, Boston, May 24, 1843; 1–18, To the Reader, signed Tho: Goodwin, | Philip Nye; 19–108, text. *Copies:* MHS; and other libraries.

[1644.] The | Keyes | . . . [same to] Discipline. | — | The second time Imprinted. |— | [six lines quotations] — | — | Published | by Tho. Goodwin, |Philip Nye. | — || London printed by M. Simmons for Henry Overton, and are to be | sold at his shop in Popes-head-Alley. 1644.   (33)

Collation and pagination the same, but set up anew. *Copy:* Y.

[1644.] The | Keyes | . . . [same to] Discipline | — | The second time Imprinted. | — | . . . || London, | Printed by M. Simmons for Henry Overton, at his Shop | entring into Popes-head Alley, out of Lumbard-street, 1644.

Collation and pagination same. *Copy:* MHS.   (34)

[1644.] Sixteene | Questions | of Seriovs and | Necessary Consequence, | Propounded unto Mr. John Cotton . . . | Printed according to Order. | — | [Printer's device] | — || London: | Printed by E. P. for Edward Blackmore at the signe of | the Angel in Pauls Church-yard. 1644.   (35)

Sig.: A⁴, B⁴. (1), 14 p. Title, v. blank; 1 p. Deare and Reverend Sir; v. blank; 3–14, text, Certain | Questions |. *Copies:* B; JCB; BM; BP; Y.

Entered in the Stationers' Register September 11. Thomason copy dated September 13.

[1644–1647.] Severall | Questions | . . . || London, | Printed for Thomas Banks, and are to bee sold in Black- | Friers on the top of Bride-well Staires, and in West- | minster Hall, at the signe of the Seale. 1647. (36)

Sig.: A⁴, B². (1), 10 p. Title, v. blank; 1–10, text. *Copies:* JCB; BM; B; BP; MHS.

The Thomason copy is dated Feb. 22, 1646–7.

The date in the British Museum Copy has been changed by pen to 1646. The copy in the Massachusetts Historical Society is bound in contemporary binding with fifty-four leaves added on which some contemporary hand has written as follows on the leaf following the title: Reverend & Beloved Brethren | For an Answer to your (Interrogatories shall I call them or) | Questions, . . . | I have here (by the help of Christ) sent you (according to your | desire) a plain & homely Answer to each particular. | . . . | The printed Part I corrected by yᵉ MSS. Original; 11–25, The Elders Reply; 26–97. Mʳ: Cottons Rejoynder; 98–116, Mʳ: Cottons Revisall.

[1645.] The | Covenant | of | Gods free Grace, | . . . | Whereunto is added, A Profession of Faith, made | by the Reverend Divine, Mʳ. John Davenport, in | New-England, at his admission into one of | the Churches there. | — | Imprimatur, John Downame. | — || London, | Printed by M. S. for Iohn Hancock, and are to be sold | at his Shop in Popes-head Alley, 1645.
(37)

Sig.: [A]², B⁴–E⁴. (1), (2), 40 p. Title, v. blank; 2 p. To all who have Interest in the | Covenant of Grace; 1–33, text; 34–40, A Profession of Faith. *Copies:* BM; JCB; HC.

The Preface says that "These comfortable Notes being in the hands of a friend to the Authour, who commending the worth and excellence of them, thought not good to smother them by burying them in oblivion."

Entered in the Stationers' Register September 22. Thomason copy dated September 23.

[1645.] The | Way of the Churches | of Christ | in New-England. | . . . || London, | Printed by Matthew Simmons in Aldersgate-streete. | 1645. (38)

Sig.: A⁴–Q⁴. Title, v. blank; 5 p. The Epistle to the Reader, | signed by N. H. | I. H; v. blank; 1–116, text; 3 p. An Alphabeticall Table; v. blank. *Copies:* B; BA; JCB; BM; C; HC; MHS; Y.

The writers of the Epistle state that "The unwillingnesse of Licencers to licence our tracts, and the earnest endeavours of some, to move complaints two or three of our most moderate books, that with hard travell gat a convoy of Licences, to cut through the Presses, are not dumb witnesses how much our way is barred, and our hands tyed short. And for Plaintiffs to burne records, or to lock up records, and then to importune the Defendants to produce those records, are two things that cannot in our apprehension be said to hold no analogie. Yet with much sweat, and wiles, some messengers have got through that Court of Guard, to anticipate, or satisfie (if it might be) those clamourers for a larger Narration. ... If all things in this Treatise, as now printed, doe not answer punctually word for word, to the first written Copie, let the reverend Authour, and the candid Reader pardon us, because we had not the fairest Copie, nor knew wee, till the Book was neer done, that there was a better to be had, nor to this day yet ever saw it ... Diverse Objections formerly laid against the Printing of this Book (to the sadding of the Authour). Some whereof are now answered by the late season of printing it. Others, by the necessitie of them, that conscientiously and candidly cry out for information. Others, by the fore-printing of the Keyes, to open the full minde and whole sphere of the Authors Judgment in this. Others, by that putting forth in print of an answer to this Book, before this was mid-wifed by the Presse into the world." In John Owen's Defence of John Cotton (1658), it says that this manuscript was written several years before he wrote the "Keyes" (1644), carried to England and printed there without the author's privity, and to his regret.

[1645.] The | Way of the Churches | ... [continues same].   (39)
Collation and pagination same; but set up anew. *Copy:* MHS.

[164–.] In Domini Nortoni Librum, ad Lectorem | Prefatis Apologetica.
Sig.: C⁵⁻⁸, D¹⁻⁴.   41–56 p.   (40)
A part of 'Massachusetts | or | The first Planters of New-England,' | ... signed on page 56, Johannes Cotton | in Ecclesia Bostoniensi | Presbyter docens. *Copies:* BP; HC; MHS.

[1646.] A | Conference | Mʳ. John Cotton | held at | Boston | With the Elders of | New-England, | ... | — | Written by Francis Cornwell, | ... ||
London, Printed by J. Dawson, and are to be sold | by Fr. Eglesfield, at the signe of the Mary-gold | in Pauls Church-yard. 1646.   (41)
Sig.: A⁸, a⁴, B⁸–D⁸. (1), (16), (5), 48 p. Title, v. blank; 16 p. To the | Honovrable | and | True-hearted lover of | his Countrey, Sir Henry | Vane Junior, Knight, sometimes | Governour of New-England; ... signed Fran. Cornwell, Orpington, in Kent, | the ninth Month, | 1645; 5 p. To all the Churches ... signed Fran. Cornwell; v. blank; 1–48, A | Conference that Mʳ. | Iohn Cotton had | with the Elders ... | touching three Questions | that are here dis- | cussed on: *Copies:* BP; HC.
The copy at the Boston Public Library has a second title, as follows, and contains the handwriting of "Samuel Sewall; Febr: 9. 1712/13."

[1646.] Gospel | Conversion: | ... | — | Opened | By John Cotton, at a Conference in | New-England | — | Together, | With some Reasons against | stinted Formes of praising God | in Psalmes, be | Now published for the generall good, | Francis Cornwell, | Minister of the Gospel | — || London, Printed by J. Dawson. | 1646.   (42)
Signatures and pagination, same. *Copies:* BP; HC.
This title is pasted on the stub of the preceding title, 'A Conference,' in the HC copy, which apparently makes this a second issue. It follows "Twelve Reasons" and "A Description" by Cornwell.

[1646.] The | Controversie | Concerning | Liberty of Conscience | in |
Matters of Religion, | . . . | — || London, Printed by Thomas Banks, and
are to be sold at | his shop in Black-Fryers on the top of Bride-well |
Staires. 1646.   (43)
    Sig.: A⁴, B⁴. (1), 14 p. Title, v. blank; 1–14, text, Scriptures and Rea-
sons written long since by a . . . | close prisoner in Newgate, . . . sent
some while since to Mr. Cotton, by a friend; signed John Cotton. *Copies:*
B; JCB; BP; BM; HC; MHS; Y.
    The Thomason copy is dated Oct. 9.

[1646–1649.] [same] . . . | — || London: Printed by Robert Austin, for
Thomas Banks, and | are to be sold at Mrs. Breaches Shop in West- |
minster-Hall. 1649.   (44)
    Sig.: A⁴, B⁴. (1), 14 p. Title, v. blank; [continues same]. *Copies:* BM;
B; JCB; HEH; NYP.

[1646.] Milk | For | Babes. | Drawn | Out of the Breasts of both | Testa-
ments. | Chiefly, for the spirituall nourishment | of Boston Babes in either
England: | But may be of like use for any | Children. | . . . || London |
Printed by J. Coe, for Henry Overton, | and are to be sold at his Shop, in |
Popes-head Alley. | 1646.   (45)
    Sig.: A⁸ (1), 13 p. Title, v. blank; 1–13 text. *Copies:* BM; HEH.

[1646–1648.] Milk for Babes . . . London . . . 1648.   (46)
    Copy: BM.
    Mr. Eames mentions this title in his 'Early New England Catechisms,'
page 24.

[1646–1656.] Spiritual | Milk | for | Boston Babes | In either England . . . ||
Cambridg: Printed by S[amuel] G[reen] for Hezekiah Vsher at Boston in
New England. | 1656.   (47)
    (1), 13 p. *Copy:* NYP (Livermore copy).
    On the back of the title this copy bears the signature of Jno. Hull,
master of the Mint and member of the First Church, in 1648, which
Mr. Eames has noted in his 'Catechisms,' page 24.

1646–1665.] Spiritual Milk for Babes.   (48)
    Mr. Eames has reasoned from the entry "Corrected in Quotations by
L. H. 1665" in the title-page of the 1672 edition that there probably was
an edition printed this year (page 25 of his 'Catechisms').

[1646–1668.] Spiritual | Milk | for | Babes, | . . . ||London: | Printed for
Peter Parker, near | Cree-Church. 1668.   (49)
    (1), 13 p. *Copy:* BP.

[1646–1672.] Spiritual | Milk | for | Babes | . . . || London: | Printed for
Peter Parker, in | Popes-head-Alley. | 1672.   (50)
    Copy: LCP.
    Mr. Eames's 'Catechisms,' page 25.

[1646–1690?] Milk for Babes . . . [Boston: Printed by Samuel Green] (51)
14 p.

Thomas Prince in his manuscript catalogue says "Mr. Bartholomew Green says — It was wrote by Mr. Cotton Mather & Printed by Mr. Samuel Green."

[1646–1691.] Spiritual Milk for Babes. (52)
This appeared with Grindal Rawson's Indian Catechism, 'Nashauanit-tue Meninnunk,' Cambridge, 1691. *Copies:* AAS; NYP.

[1646–1720.] Spiritual Milk for Babes. (53)
This appeared in the 'Indiane Primer,' Boston, 1720, at pages 30–46, with Grindal Rawson's translation into Indian language. Noted by Mr. Eames, page 65. *Copies:* AAS; NYP; BP.

[1646–1747.] [Same.] (54)
In the same, Boston, 1747. Noted by Mr. Eames, page 66. *Copies:* AAS; NL; NYP.

[1647.] The | Bloudy Tenent, | washed, | . . . | Whereunto is added a Reply to Mr. Williams | Answer, to Mr. Cottons Letter. | — || London, | Printed by Matthew Symmons for Hannah Allen, at the Crowne in | Popes Head-Alley. 1647. (55)
Sig.: 1l., B⁴–Z⁴, Aa⁴, Bb⁴, Cc²; Aa⁴–Ss⁴. (1), 195, 144 p. Title, v. blank; 1–195, text, The | Bloody Tenet | 1–144, text, A Reply to | Mʳ. Williams his | Examination; | And Answer of the Letters sent | to him by John Cotton. *Copies:* B; JCB; BP; BM; C; HC; MHS; Y.
The copy in the Massachusetts Historical Society belonged to Rev. Peter Bulkeley, October 26, 1647, given him then by Mr. Cotton; and was later owned by Rev. Ezra Stiles; by the Edwards Church Ministerial Library at Northampton; and by Samuel Wells, Northampton.
The Thomason copy is dated May 15.

[1647.] The | Grovnds and Ends | of the | Baptisme | of the | Children of the Faithfull. | . . . || London, | Printed by R. C. for Andrew Crooke at the Sign of the | Green Dragon in Pauls-churchyard, 1647. (56)
Sig.: A⁴ (first leaf, probably blank, wanting), b², B⁴–Z⁴, Aa⁴, Bb⁴. Title, v. blank; 3 p. To the Reader, signed by John Cotton; 4 p. To the Reader, signed by Tho. Goodwin; 1 p. The Grounds, heading reset on p. 1 following and text corrected on p. 2. 1–4, The Grounds; 5–196, text. *Copies:* B; JCB; BM; BP; C; HC; MHS; Y.
Cotton says in To the Reader that this discourse was compiled by him in answer to a printed book, "The Author I forbeare to name . . . reputed one of the chiefest note of that way, for moderation and freedome, from the leaven of other corrupt opinions, which are wont to accompany the denyall of Infants Baptisme . . . a young Scholar, (but of pregnant gifts and parts) Mr. Benjamin Woodbridge, dwelling in my house, seeing me solicitous for the young man [a son of one of his 'Graceous Saints in Lincolnshire,' now a member of a neighbouring Church and standing 'aloofe to the Baptisme of Children'], undertooke the answer of the Booke," which was "speedily and acutely" done. As this was "so full of Scholarship and termes of Art" that the young men "could not well

understand it," Cotton decided that he must answer it himself in "such a familiar language, as might best suite with his capacity."

The Thomason copy is dated Oct. 10, 1646.

[1647.] Singing | Of | Psalmes | A Gospel-Ordinance. | . . . || London; | Printed by M. S. for Hannah Allen, at the Crowne | in Popes-Head Alley: and John Rothwell at the | Sunne and Fountaine in Pauls-Church-yard. | 1647. (57)
Sig.: 1l., B⁴ (stub between between 2 and 3) to K⁴. (1), 72 p. Title, v. blank; 1–72, text, Of the | Singing | of Psalmes. *Copies:* HC; MHS; JCB.

On a copy at Harvard College Library is written Thomas Shepard's name, 1655, and William Brattle's book, March 23, 1704/5; and the latter wrote "My Hᵈ Grand Father Mʳ Thomas ·Shepard Pastʳ of Cambr: as my Fathʳ told me Mʳ Cotton acknowledged it wⁿ it came forth: also; Mʳ Edward Bulkley pastor of yᵉ cʰ of Xᵗ in Concord told me Sept. 20. 1674, that wⁿ he boarded at Mʳ Cotton's house at yᵉ 1st coming forth of this book of singing of psalmes, Mʳ Cotton told him that my Father Shepard had the chief hand in yᵉ composing of it and yʳfore Mʳ Cotton said: I am troubled that my bro. Shepard's name is not prefixed to it."

Dean Chester N. Greenough of Harvard University in his valuable article on this work in the Publications of the Colonial Society of Massachusetts (20:239) says in conclusion: "It thus seems fairly evident that we should hesitate to give way to the impression that John Cotton was at fault for having failed to make sure that Thomas Shepard, if he was the principal author . . . received credit therefor on the title-page." The two copies, here indicated, have a list of errata, apparently in the hand of Cotton, written on the back of the title-page. The copy in the Massachusetts Historical Society was given by Cotton to Richard Mather. Dean Greenough calls attention to the fact that only one of the list of errata was corrected in the second edition of 1650.

The Thomason copy is dated March 28.

[1647–1650.] Singing | of | Psalmes | . . . || London, | Printed by J. R. at the Sunne and Fountaine in Pauls- | Church-yard: and H. A. at the Crowne in Popes- | Head-Alley. 1650. (58)
Sig.: leaf, B⁴–K⁴. (1), 72 p. Title, v. blank; 1–72, text, [continues same]. *Copies:* JCB; C.

[1648.] The Way of | Congregational | Churches | Cleared: | . . . || London, Printed by Matthew Simmons, for John Bellamie, | at the signe of the three Golden Lions, | in Cornhill. 1648. (59)
Sig.: A⁴, a², B⁴–O⁴, Aa⁴–Ee⁴, Ff². (1), (9), 104, 44 p. Title, v. blank; 6 p. An Epistle Pacificatory, | . . . signed by Nathanael Holmes, below which on the last page is a short paragraph, and Imprimatur | January 1, 1647. John Bachiler; 3 p. The Contents, followed on the third page with five lines of Errata; 1 p. blank; 1–104, text, Treatise I; 1–44, The second Part (being Doctrinal, and Controversial | Concerning Congregational

Churches and their | Government. *Copies:* JCB; BM; BP; C; HC; B; MHS; Y.

Entered in the Stationers' Register, Jan. 12. The Thomason copy is dated Feb. 9.

The John Carter Brown Library Catalogue describes copies with different words at the end of leaf 4a; "vi-bipending" and "re-viling."

[165 -1658.] A | Defence | Of | Mr. John Cotton | From the imputation of | Selfe Contradiction, | charged on him by | Mr. Dan: Cavvdrey | Written by himselfe not long | before his death. | — |. By John Owen: D:D: . . . | — || Oxford, | Printed by H: Hall: for T. Robinson. 1658. (60) 100, 83 p. Title, v. blank; 3-100, Christian Reader, by John Owen; followed by 1-3, The Preface; 3-83, text. *Copies:* JCB; BP; BM; HC; B.

[1650.] Of the | Holinesse | of | Church-Members. | . . . || London: Printed by F. N. for Hanna Allen, and are to be sold at | the Crown in Popes-head Alley. 1650. (61) Sig.: A², B⁴-P⁴. (1), (2), 95 [103] p. Title, v. blank; 2 p. To my Honored, Worshipfull, | and worthy Friends, . . . with the | whole Congregation and Church at Boston: | signed John Cotton; 1-95, text, Quest: I. . . . | Chap. I | . . . Sect. I. [to Sect. XVII]; 1 p. blank. Pages 89-95 are misnumbered for 97-103. *Copies:* JCB; BM; BP; C; HC; B; MHS; Y.

The Thomason copy is dated April 20.

[1650.] Some Treasure Fetched out of Rubbish.
Copies: BM; Y. (62)

[1650-1660.] Some | Treasure | Fetched out of | Rubbish: | . . . concerning the Imposition and | Use of | Significant Ceremonies in the Worship of God. viz. | I. A Discourse upon I Cor. 14.40. . . . | II. An Enquiry, . . . | III. Three Arguments, . . . || London, Printed in the year, 1660. (63) Sig.: A², B⁴-K⁴, L². (1), (2), 75 p. Title, v. blank; 2 p. To the Reader; 1-8, text; 9-52, May not the Church; 52-75, Of the Surplice; 1 p., v., blank. It is stated in the preface that "Mr. John Cotton, that faithful Servant of Christ, (famous in both Englands) was the known Author of the first Discourse, and (as it is verily believed) of the second also," and that "Mr. Robert Nichols studiously composed the third." Also that "These ensuing Treatises were found laid by the Walls, and covered with dust, in the study of an old Non-Conformist, (there being diverse Copies of each, under several unknown hands:) " *Copies:* BM; HC; MHS.

The copy in the Massachusetts Historical Society was owned by Thomas Shepard in 1660, who wrote after part I, "sᵈ to be Mʳ J. Cotton's B.D." The Thomason copy is dated Oct. 8, 1660.

[1651.] Christ | The | Fountaine of Life: | . . . | Published according to Order. | — || London | Printed by Robert Ibbitson. | MDCLI. (64)

Sig.: A⁴–Kk⁴. (1), (4), 256 p. Title, v. blank; 4 p. The Contents; 1–256, text. *Copies:* JCB; BP; C; HC.

Advertised in the *Perfect Diurnall,* May 12, 1651, noted by Roger P. McCutcheon, in Pub. Col. Soc. Mass. 20:88.

Entered in the Stationers' Register, by Samuel Mann, March 24. The Thomason copy is dated June 4.

[1651.] [Same] . . . || London, | Printed by Robert Ibbitson, and are to be sold by | George Calvert at the signe of the half Moone in Watling Street, near Pauls Stump. | MDCLI. (65)
Sig.: A⁴–Kk⁴. Title, v. blank; 4 p. The Contents; 2 p. Books Printed for George Calvert; [continues same]. *Copies:* JCB; HC.

[1654.] A Briefe | Exposition | . . . | of | Ecclesiastes | . . . | Published by Anthony Tuckney, D.D. | Master of St. Johns Colledge in Cambridge. | — || London, | Printed by T. C. for Ralph Smith at the Bible | in Corn-hill. 1654. (66)
Sig.: [A]⁴, B⁸–S⁸, T⁴ (last leaf, probably blank, wanting). (1), (6), 277, (1), (1) p. Title, v. blank; 6 p. To the Right Worshipfull, | Mr. George Caborn, Mayor; | . . . and . . . | friends of Boston in Lincolnshire, signed Anthony Tuckney, From St. Johns Colledge | in Cambridge | July 7, 1654; 1–277, text, A Briefe | Exposition | . . . ; 1 p. Books printed for Ralph Smith; 1 p. Mr. Cotton on Ecclesiastes (line down middle of page); 1 p. blank. *Copies:* B; BA; JCB; BP; BM; HC; MHS; Y.

Publication noted in the *Perfect Diurnall* of July 24, 1654. See Pub. Col. Soc. Mass. 20:91, noted by Roger P. McCutcheon. Entered in the Stationers' Registers, Jan. 24.

[1654–1657.] A Briefe | Exposition | . . . [same to] Cambridge. | The Second Impression, Corrected | — || London, Printed by W. W. for Ralph Smith at the Bible | in Cornhill. 1657. (67)
Sig.: A⁸–R⁸. (1), 6, 258, (1), (1) p. Title, v. blank; 6 p. [Same], dated From S. Johns Col | ledge in Cambridge, | July 7, 1654; 1–258, text, A Briefe Exposition upon | Ecclesiastes; 1 p. Books printed for Ralph Smith, v. blank; 1 p. Mʳ. Cotton on Ecclesiastes, down the middle of the page; 1 p. blank. *Copies:* JCB; BM; BP; C; HC; MHS.

[1654.] The New | Covenant, | . . . | — | Being the substance of sundry Sermons | Preached by | Mʳ Cotton | At Boston in New-England, some years since, | and corrected by his owne hand, not | long before his death | — || London: Printed by M. S. for Francis Egles- | field, & John Allen, at the Marigold, and Ri- | sing Sun in Pauls Church-yard. 1654. (68)
Sig.: B⁸–O⁴, in 'The Covenant of Grace,' London, 1655. (1), 198 p. Title, v. blank; 1–198, text. *Copies:* B; JCB; BM; BP; HC; MHS; Y.

This was "delivered back" by Mr. Cotton after correcting the notes taken, "into the hands of a Gentleman, (one of the Church in Boston then) who coming over hither, and being about to return, left it with me to take order for the Printing of it," as noted by Thomas Allen in his address To the Reader in the 'Covenant of Grace.'

[1654–1655.] Certain | Queries | . . . | Published by a Friend to whom | the Author himselfe sent them | over not long before his Death. | — || London | Printed by M. S. for John Allen | and Francis Eglesfield in Pauls | Church-yard. 1654. (69)

Sigs. O [5–8], P8, in 'The Covenant of Grace,' London, 1655. (1), 22 p. Title, v. blank; 1–22, text. *Copies:* JCB; BM; BP; HC; MHS; Y.

Thomas Allen says in To the Reader: "That of the Queries I had from the Reverend Author himself (my most Honoured friend) in a letter from him, with liberty (if it might be thought meet) of publishing of it: At my coming over from that Country (which was about a year before his death) he delivered unto me the same in substance, but in another Form, viz. in 12 Propositions, and therefore did then express his un-willingness to yield to the impression of them (being moved thereunto by a Reverend Elder then present with us) by reason (as he said) they were set down by way of Propositions; but afterward the Lord having directed him to mould them into another model (turning the twelve Propositions into eleven Queries) he was pleased to send them over unto me as here they are presented . . . unto which (may it be without offence) I shall be bold to add one more to make up the number even and round." This 12th Query runs from page 15 to the end.

[1654.] The Result | of a | Synod | at | Cambridge | in | New-England, | Anno. 1646. | . . . | — || London | Printed by M. S. for John Allen | and Francis Eglesfield in Pauls | Church-yard. 1654. (70)

Sig.: Q8 to end, in 'The Covenant of Grace,' London, 1655. (1), 75, (1), p. Title, v. blank; 1–47; text, The Result of the Disputati- | ons of the Synod, or Assembly, | at Cambridge in New-England, | Begun upon the first day of the 7th Month, An. | Dom. 1646; 48–75, The | Nature & Power | of | Synods; | 1 p. Courteous Reader, as to faults in the press, signed, Vale. *Copies:* B; JCB; BM; BP; HC; MHS; Y.

[1655.] The | Covenant | of | Grace | . . . || London: Printed by M. S. for Francis | Eglesfield and John Allen, at the Marigold, and | Rising Sun in Pauls Church-yard. 1655. (71)

Sig.: A8, a8, B8–U8. (1), (7), (8), (2), (9), (2), (1), 198, (1), 22, (1), 75, (1). Title, v. blank; 7 p. To the | Truly Vertuous and | Religious . . . Mris Catharine Hodson, signed W. Retchforde; 1 p. blank; 8 p. To the Reader, signed Tho: Allen; 2 p. Books | Sould by John Allen | at the Rising Sun in | Pauls Church-yard; 9 p. The Contents of the Treatise | concerning the Covenant; 2 p. Some Faults to be Corrected | by the Reader; 1 p. blank; (1), 198, The New | Covenant, | . . . 1654; (1), 22, Certain | Queries | . . . 1654; (1), 75, The Result | of a | Synod | at | Cambridge | . . . 1646. | . . . 1654; 1 p. Courteous Reader; | By reason of the Death of the | Reverend Author, and the far | distance of his loving Friend | (the Publisher of this Booke) | some faults may have escaped the | Presse, for the which the Printer | desireth excuse. | Vale; 1 p. blank. *Copies:* B; BM; BP; HC; MHS; Y.

[1655-1659.] A | Treatise | of the | Covenant | of | Grace, | . . . | — | The second Edition, by a Copy far larger then the | former; and Corrected also by the Authors | own hand.| This Copy was fitted for the Press, by Mr. Tho. | Allen Minister in Norwich. | — || London, | Printed by Ja. Cottrel, for John Allen, at the | Rising-Sun in Pauls Church-yard. | 1659.   (72)
Sig.: A⁸, B⁴, B⁸-Q⁸, R⁶. 1 p. blank, v. "The 13. of the third Moneth," the reasons of this Publication, signed by Joseph Caryl, in which he writes, "The Name of Cotton is an oyntment poured out: nor needs there more to commend a Book to any godly acceptation than to say, 'tis his"; title, v. blank; 2 p.   The | Stationer | to the | Reader, signed J. A. [John Allen], who says that he received the Treatise "from a neer Friend and Relation, one of the reverend Elders" of Mr. Cotton's Church in Boston, which is a third part larger than the first edition. The reason for this "enlargement, is not from any addition by any other hand, but (as may easily be conceived) from the diversity of the Amanuenses, who did take the Notes of his Sermons, some writing the same more largely and exactly then others, and several Copies so taken being presented to the reverend Author to correct, He, as he had leisure (willing and ready to gratifie the desire of his Friends) did peruse and rectifie the sense with his pen, as he went cursorily over the same"; 16 p.   A | Table of the Contents; 1 p. an erratum, v. blank; 1-250, text; 2 p. Books sold by John | Allen, at the Sun-rising | in Pauls Church-yard. *Copies:* BP; MHS.
This was advertised in the *Mercurius Politicus*, on May 26, 1659, as noted by Roger P. McCutcheon in Pub. Col. Soc. Mass. 20:94. The Thomason copy is also dated May 26, 1659.

[1655-1671.] A | Treatise | of the | Covenant | of | Grace, | . . . The Third Edition, Corrected, and very much | Enlarged by the Authors own Hand | — || London, | Printed for Peter Parker, in Popes-head-Ally, | next Corn-hill, 1671.   (73)
Sig.: A⁸-P⁸. (1), (1), (14), 223 p. Title, v. To the Reader signed by Joseph Caryl; 14 p. A | Table of the Contents; 1-223, text. *Copies:* C; HC; MHS.

[1655.] A Brief | Exposition | . . . of | Canticles. | Never before Printed [— | . . . | Published by Anthony Tuckney D.D. Master | of Saint Johns Colledge in Cambridge. | — || London, | Printed by T. R. & E M. for Ralph Smith | at the Signe of the Bible in Cornhill, neere | the Royall Exchange. 1655.   (74)
Sig.: A⁸-Q⁸ (last two leaves blank). (1), (1), (1), (10), 238 p. 1 p. Cotton on the Canticles, down the middle of the page; v. blank; 1 p. blank; v. Imprimatur, | Joseph Caryl. | Jan. 23, 1653; title, v. blank; 10 p. To the Reader, signed by Anthony Tuckney, Cambridge July 24, 1655; 1-238, text. *Copies:* JCB; BM; BP; HC; MHS.
Advertised in the *Perfect Diurnall*, Sept. 17, 1655, noted by Roger P. McCutcheon in Pub. Col. Soc. Mass. 20:92.

[1656.] A | Practical Commentary, | . . . | upon | The First Epistle Generall of | John. | . . . || London, | Printed by R. I. and E. C. for Thomas Parkhurst, and are to be | sold at his shop at the Three Crownes over against the | Great Conduit, at the lower end of Cheapside, | M.DC.LVI. (75)
 Sig.: [A]⌐Iii⁴. (1), (4), (1), (1), 431, (1) p. Title, v. blank; 4 p. To the Reader, signed Chr. Scott. From my Study in | Muchwakering | in Essex, Octob. | 15, 1655; 1 p. "It is sufficiently evident by the preceding | Epistle, and by many other arguments, that the | ensuing sermons were preached by Mr. John | Cotton, whose name is so deservedly precious | among the Saints of God, that it cannot but in- | courage them to read them, and hath invited me to | allow them to be printed for the publick good. | Edmund Calamy"; 1 p. Books printed for, and sold by Thomas Parkhurst; 1–431, text, with three lines, "Errata" at foot of last page; 1 p. v. blank. Copies: JCB; BP; C; HC; MHS.
 Mr. Scott speaks of Cotton as "a burning and shining light, famously eminent abroad and at home," and says that the Notes fell by providence into his hands and that he wishes to make them "usefull for the Publick."
 Entered in the Stationers' Register on May 23. The Thomason copy is dated Aug. 26.

[1656–1658.] A | Practical Commentary, | [continues same] . . . | The second Edition . . . || London, | Printed by M. S. for Thomas Parkhurst, and are to be sold at | his shop at the Three Crownes over against the Great | Conduit at the lower end of Cheapside, | M.DC.LVIII.　　　　　(76)
 Sig.: 1 l, A⌐Kkk⁴ (last leaf blank). (2), (6), 431, (6) p. 1 p. blank, v. Reader, signed by Roger Drake, Feb. 26, 1657; title, v. blank; 3 p. To the Reader, signed, Chr. Scott. From my Study in | Muchwakering |; 2 p. Books lately printed for Thomas Parkhurst [this by mistake of binder precedes the part, To the Reader]; 1 p. continues same to "Edmund Calamy; 1–431, text; 1 p. v. blank; 6 p. The Table. Copies: JCB; BP; HC; MHS.

[1663.] A | Discourse | about | Civil Government | in a | New Plantation | Whose Design is | Religion. | Written many Years since . . . || Cambridge: Printed by Samuel Green and Marmaduke Johnson. | MDCLXIII.　　(77)
 Sig.: A⌐C⁴. 24 p. Copies: BP; HC; MHS.
 Cotton Mather in his Magnalia (Book III, 56) says that "the name of Mr. Cotton, is, by a mistake, put for that of Mr. Davenport."

SOME NOTES ON THE USE OF HEBREW TYPE IN NON–HEBREW BOOKS, 1475–1520

By ALEXANDER MARX

Librarian of the Jewish Theological Seminary, New York

THE history of Hebrew printing is a fascinating subject. Like the history of the Jews, it takes us to almost every country in the world. It is in consequence a very difficult task to trace its development and follow its migrations from country to country. The fundamental essay by Cassel and Steinschneider published in 1851 [1] is, of course, out of date. The summary of this article given in the Jewish Encyclopedia [2] does not even try to go beyond it and to utilize the many corrections found in Steinschneider's later works and the numerous recent discoveries, which have greatly enriched our knowledge of early Hebrew printing and, naturally, have added many new puzzles.

If my friend, Professor Freimann,[3] were right in his conjecture that the first edition of *Bahya's [4] commentary on the Pentateuch s. l. 1491, now found in the library of the Jewish Theological Seminary, was printed in the East this book would precede the Cettinje Bible and could claim to be the first product of the Balkans. But to me this edition looks distinctly like a Spanish incunabulum and I cannot admit the validity of Freimann's proof.

Another Hebrew book, slightly later in date than the edition of Bahya just mentioned, may on stronger grounds dispute the title of the Cettinje Bible to priority in the peninsula. There is an edition of *Jacob ben Asher's code Tur, which in express words, not in figures, states that it was printed in Constantinople on Friday, Tebet 4,5454 (= 1493).[5] We know fifteen books by the same printer from 1505 to 1511 and it is therefore generally assumed that this book really appeared in 1503 and was erroneously dated ten years earlier. Such mistakes in date are not uncommon in Latin incunabula where it is the omission of an X which is responsible for the error.[6] Here, however, such an explanation is impossible and it seems a little hazardous to assume that the printer should spell out fifty for sixty. The day of the week and date curiously fit both years, 1493 and 1503. If we consider that the Spanish Jews took their types and illuminations with them to Constantinople, where we meet them in the sixteenth century, we may wonder why they waited so long before they made their first trial in printing in their new home. In spite of the difficulties of readjustment a single effort may have been made to establish a printing press in Constantinople in 1493 which for some reason or other was perhaps not repeated by the same printer till twelve years later. Nor is it impossible that a few more books were printed in the course of these years which have not reached us yet. After all, of five copies of this code now known only those in Oxford, and the British Museum (?), have the colophon with the date.

The Lisbon presses were transferred by their owners to Fez, as we now know from two copies of the ritual work of *Abudrahim printed in 1516.[7] Whether some of the other books showing the same type were printed in Fez at an earlier date we cannot determine as long as only fragments and no complete volumes came to light. It is interesting in this connection to refer to the discussion by Richard Garnett,[8] as to the first book printed in Africa. Speaking of the doubts about the existence of a book said to be printed in Funchal, Madeira, 1637, and one supposed to have appeared in Loanda on the West coast of Africa in 1641, he adds: "I need not say that the first African book would be a treasure almost rivalling the volume with which Mexico initiated American typography in 1539." I wonder how many students of the history of printing are aware of the discovery of a printing press in Fez well over a hundred years earlier.

There is here as in many other subjects an unfortunate lack of coöperation between the specialists in Hebrew studies and those of other branches. I strongly realized this when I became interested in the subject of these notes and came across a great many incorrect statements or insufficient references. I am therefore woefully aware of the incompleteness of my own material, which I have put together only in order that it might instigate others to correct and complete it and to publish such additional material as they know of or may come across. Working in a highly specialized library, I may have overlooked some general bibliographical helps which might have lightened my task and made it more complete. I shall be thankful for any additional bit of information.

The subject referred to in the preceding paragraph is the use of Hebrew letters, words or passages in non-Hebrew books, mostly cut and printed by Christians. This subject is only an episode of the history of early Hebrew printing, which deserves a monograph in the style of Proctor's volume on the printing of Greek in the fifteenth century. In no instance during the fifteenth century was movable type employed even where it might easily have been obtained from Jewish printers. We cannot conclude from this fact that there existed no relationship between the two for we find cases of illuminated borders being used both for Hebrew and Latin books. One such example, the beautiful border occurring in Tuppo's Aesop, 1485, and again in the Soncino Bible of 1488 was pointed out by Lippmann.[9] My brother, Moses Marx, recently drew my attention to another instance he came across in the preparation of the 'Thesaurus Typographiae Hebraicae Saeculi XV.' The borders used in the 'Manuale Caesaraugustanum' attributed by Haebler[10] to Ixar about 1486 or 1487 occur again, as he noticed, in the *Lisbon Abudrahim of November 25, 1489. They occur already in the first book printed in Lisbon, *Nachmanides' 'Commentary on the Pentateuch' (July 15, 1489)[11]

and, what is much more interesting, in an undated Ixar Pentateuch [12] generally placed 1490–95 (!). Undoubtedly we may
assume that this book was printed before the borders were
transferred to Lisbon, i. e. 1486–89. On the other hand, the
fact that these borders were used in Ixar in a Hebrew book
greatly strengthens Haebler's theory of the origin of the Manuale in that city. His main proof is that the printer Alfonso
Fernandez de Cordova whose type he recognizes in the volume
was associated with the Jewish printer Solomon Zalmati in
Valencia, 1484–85. We meet Zalmati again at Ixar in 1490
and therefore Haebler assumes that de Cordova also went
there. It may be of interest to add that we find the same borders again in Constantinople in 1505 [13] seq.

1475–1499

It is characteristic of the economic and cultural state of the
Jews of Germany that in the country of Gutenberg they did
not practise printing till the end of the third decade of the
sixteenth century.[14] On the other hand, we find the first Hebrew words in Germany in a Latin text as early as 1475, the
same year in which the first dated Hebrew books appeared almost simultaneously in the South and the North of Italy,
Rashi on the Pentateuch in Reggio di Calabria [15] and *Jacob
ben Asher's code in Pieve di Sacco [15a]. [1] Petrus Nigri (Peter
Schwarz) in his *'Tractatus contra perfidos Judeos de con-
ditionibus veri messie,' the account of a disputation held in the
preceding year at Regensburg between the author and some
Jews, published June 6, 1475, in Esslingen by Conrad Feyner,
gives several Hebrew and Aramaic texts in transcription. He
adds at the end a Hebrew alphabet and on fol. 10 of the volume
three words in Hebrew which were reproduced by Dibdin and
others. [2] Two years later in 1477 he added a short primer
of Hebrew to his larger work, * 'stern des Meschiah,' published at the same press. Nestle [16] has reprinted this primer
and some extracts of the Latin treatise.

It is rather curious to read Nestle's praise of the beauty of the Hebrew characters employed by Feyner; a closer inspection at once reveals their unevenness as well as their clumsy and unsightly form. The British Museum Catalogue of fifteenth-century books (II, 514) has for the Latin volume the statement "woodcut Hebrew letters," but for the German volume it states "Hebrew 180." Yet in this volume the Hebrew is undoubtedly cut in wood and the one page which has 14 lines of Hebrew and from which the measure, 180, has been taken clearly reveals itself as printed from one block since the lines are not entirely straight and are not at exactly equal distances from one another. The German text in the parallel column is clearly printed independently.[17]

Nestle states, page 8, that these two are the only books printed in Germany before 1500 which include Hebrew letters. This is not entirely correct, though the other instances are of no real importance. [3-4] Breydenbach added a Hebrew alphabet (with names of the letters written above them) to his travels to the Holy Land, Mayence, 1486, Lyons, 1488, and Speyer, 1502,[18] these being the first cases in which Hebrew letters occur in France. The original blocks of the first edition were repeatedly used for new issues in different places.

In Philip Culmacher's [5] 'Regimen wider die Pestilenz,' [Leipzig, Martin Landsberg, after 1492] we find a few Hebrew letters on the back of the title-page. Sudhoff,[19] rightly remarks that the word Ananzipata which serves as the center for a blessing against the pestilence 'auch in schauerlichen hebräischen Schriftzeichen vergeführt wird."

The first words of Genesis in Hebrew (as well as Greek and Latin) are found in [6] Dürer's woodcut of Jerome in Hieronymi Epistolae, Basle, Nicolas Kessler, 1497.[20]

In Louvain we find a few lines of Hebrew texts inserted in [7] Paulus of Middleburg's Epistola Apologetica printed by John of Westfalia ca. 1488 (Campbell, 1364).[21] I have before

me three of these pages with Hebrew photographed from the
copy in The Hague, which clearly show that the inserted texts
are not printed from movable type but that the passages, consisting of one, two, three, or four lines, are always cut on a
wood block. Therefore the lines are not quite straight and the
single letters look a little different in every case. The same
applies to all the books mentioned so far.

In Italy I find a few Hebrew letters and words used in
[8] *Pico della Mirandola, Opera II, Bologna, B. Hector, 1495,
on two pages near the end of his treatise Heptaplus on the
Creation, while elsewhere in many places blanks are left for
Hebrew texts as they are in the Venice edition of 1498.[22] The
letters are not well cut but not as clumsy as in the German
volumes. In Bologna some beautiful Hebrew volumes had
previously been printed by Jews.

Aldus used a few Hebrew words in his edition of [9] Po-
liphilo, Venice, 1499, fol. 68 (h 8) recto in the illustration together with Arabic, Greek, and Latin.[23] Here also he did not
employ movable type as is evident from the difference in the
characters.

This is all I have found about Hebrew words or letters used
in non-Hebrew texts in the fifteenth century. I have no doubt
that more books include such words but unfortunately the
bibliographers have paid very little attention to this point and
even Proctor omits to mention the fact.

1500–1520
A. ITALY

As we finished the fifteenth century with Aldus we now begin the sixteenth with him. [10] A specimen page of a polyglot
Pentateuch, 1501, reproduced by Renouard[24] still shows great
unevenness in the letters and does not come up to the general
standard of Aldus.

It is different with the little primer which was repeatedly
published by the author. This unique small duodecimo en-

titled [11] 'Introductio *utilissima* hebraice discere cupientibus' in the Johns Rylands Library [25] was fully described by
Panizzi.[26] It is printed on 8 leaves from right to left like a
Hebrew book, in red and black type, and uses a larger unvocalized and a smaller vocalized font of Hebrew elegantly
cut by Francesco da Bologna after the type of Soncino.

[12–16] This 'Introductio *perbrevis* ad hebraicam linguam'
as he called it later, Aldus reprinted in 4 quarto pages from
left to right without use of red as an appendix to his Latin
grammar in 1501 and again to the undated *Lascaris, 1501–
03. It was again reprinted from the same type in the Latin
grammar of 1508; it was reset in the *Lascaris of 1512 [26a] and
the Latin grammar of *1514 and 1523 according to Renouard.

In the sale catalogue of G. Manzoni's library [27] an edition of
[17] Aldus's 'Introductio,' 4 leaves, 8vo, is mentioned and
ascribed to the year 1501. Our Library has an undated duodecimo of the sort marked as an unknown Aldine edition with
the book plate of Carolus Jacobus Stuart Baronettus. Here in
opposition to the previously mentioned editions only one
small font of Hebrew is used. I cannot judge whether it is
really from the Aldine press, but must refer to a remark of
Manzoni [28] that very many editions of the four leaves of this
Introductio exist, of which those in octavo are certainly not
printed by Aldus. Otherwise Aldus does not seem to have
made use of his Hebrew type.

Two of the works from the press of the famous Jewish
printer Gerson (Hieronymus) Soncino in his beautiful type
fall within the scope of this paper; the printer's own [18] 'Introductio ad literas hebraicas,' Pesaro, 1510,[29] of which Manzoni possessed a unique copy which he showed to be the source
of Aldus's primer and [19] *Petrus Galatinus, 'Opus de ar-
canis catholicae veritatis,' Ortona, 1518 [30] (Feb. 18).

The primer of Aldus was very frequently reprinted in the
early part of the sixteenth century. Thus the [20–21] Florence

editions of *Lascaris, the one dated 1515, the other undated but from about the same time, have this appendix in fairly well-cut characters.[31] We shall meet it again in Germany.

On July 8, 1513, there appeared at Fossombrone [22] *Paulus of Middleburg, 'Paulina de recta Paschae celebratione et de die passionis domini nostri Jesu Christi' which has some Hebrew type (in the eighth book, sig. M 2b one word, M 4b two lines, N 2a–5b a column of two to three letters for the dates of the Hebrew years). In the sixteenth book (Z 1a and 4a) we find the Tetragrammaton in large characters, while all other passages are in a small heavy and fairly good type, which occurs again at the end of the volume in the concluding formula.

From the same year 1513 (after August 1) we have a little volume [23] *Augustinus Justinianus, 'Precatio pietatis plena ad deum omnipotentem composita ex duobus et septuaginta nominibus divinis Hebraicis et latinis una cum interprete commentariolo,' Venice (?), 12mo, which, fol. 11a, has nine lines of vocalized Hebrew from the Pentateuch, and on 11b a few unvocalized Hebrew words on the margin besides two in the text which are repeated on 12a. These passages are evidently not printed from movable type, but from ugly woodcuts partly almost unreadable.

In November, 1516, the same scholar edited in Genoa the [24] *Polyglot Psalter with the well-known reference to Columbus on the margin of chapter XIX. The Hebrew and Aramaic texts have vowels and accents, a Hebrew and Aramaic introduction is unvocalized; smaller type is used for the large quotations in the marginal notes. In order to fill the lines extended letters are employed and illuminated initials occur at the beginning of the introductions and in the text. The type is much inferior to that of Basle and rather awkward.

In Rome three small works of Elijah Levita [32] were printed in 1518 in the house of Juan Giacomo Fagiot di Montecchio by Jewish printers with special permission of Pope Leo X

(1513–21). Without having seen the book, Steinschneider[33] ascribes to Rome [25] Agathius Guidacerius, 'Grammatica Hebraica' including Isaiah chapter LII–LIII in Hebrew and Latin which is dedicated to the same Pope. De Rossi,[34] who owned a copy, says nothing about the printing place; Schwab (no. 155) recording the copy of the Bibliothèque Nationale repeats Steinschneider's suggestion and (no. 222) mentions [26] another (?) [35] grammar by the same author, likewise found in the Bibliothèque Nationale, without the texts from Isaiah and without printing place, which he dates ca. 1518. A comparison between these grammars and Levita's books would show whether both come from the same press, as Rieger [35a] takes for granted.

In 1520 Hebrew letters were omitted in [27] Benedictus de Falco 'de origine hebraicarum, graecarum et latinarum literarum,' printed in Naples; they were written in by hand in the Paris copy.[36] Between 1486 and 1492 some of the most beautiful Hebrew incunabula had been printed in this city.

Although there probably were many more instances of the use of Hebrew type in Italy in the beginning of the sixteenth century, I have not come across any others.

B. GERMANY [37]

Turning to Germany we have the inestimable advantage of being able to refer to Proctor's Index of the early printed books in the British Museum II, 1, which generally records the occurrence of Hebrew type and in many instances also mentions where a printer employed woodcut type. Proctor did not go far enough in this respect but I must gratefully acknowledge my indebtedness to his masterly book which greatly enriched the following lists. Important and exact information on some books which I have not seen is found in two papers by Professor Gustav Bauch, 'Wolfgang Schenck und Nicolaus Marschalk'[38] and 'Einführung des Hebräischen in Wittenberg.'[39] To the latter essay Bauch appends an Index Bibliographicus[40] with the exact titles of a number of books discussed hereafter and also a record of copies in a dozen German libraries. I thought it advisable to add wherever possible the numbers of this Index (quoted as B) as well as those of Proctor and, for the books falling within its scope, also those of Boecking's bibliography of the Reuchlin-Pfefferkorn controversy in the second volume of his great edition of the 'Epistolae obscurorum virorum' [41] from which some additions were gathered for my list. About half of them are found in the Library of the Jewish Theological Seminary and could therefore be examined and compared at leisure.[41a] Many of these form part of the recently acquired E. N. Adler Library, most of the others of the Sulzberger Collection.

In general these books exhibit very poor specimens of Hebrew character. The Rabbinical type used by Thomas Anshelm and also that of Erhard Oeglin being far better than their square characters. Of the latter Anshelm's are distinctly superior to those of all the other printers with the exception of Froben, the only printer of Hebrew whose work during our period deserves mention besides that of the Soncinos and Daniel Bomberg or the Prague printers. Movable type for Hebrew was distinctly not yet the rule; we find many instances of specially cut larger or smaller wood blocks which were mostly discarded after they had once served their purpose. Only Marschalk seems to have preserved them, for a line of his Erfurt edition of Aldus's primer occurs a few years later at Wittenberg and perhaps he used his blocks again in Rostock. The forms of most of the Hebrew letters of the German printers are extremely clumsy. It therefore seems to me that even where movable type was used it was not of the same character as the Latin or German type. It seems that the letters were cut in wood or soft metal and not cast. It is hard to say what model the printer wished to imitate; I am inclined to believe that it was a kind of Hebrew character written by German

Jewish converts to Christianity. The Rabbinical type of Oeglin in Boeschenstein's grammar indeed shows remarkable similarity with Boeschenstein's handwriting in our copy of Reuchlin's 'septem Psalmi.'

1. Erfurt

In Germany we meet with Hebrew characters in the sixteenth century for the first time in [28] a reprint of Aldus's 'Introductio Utilissima' which was published in Erfurt in 1501 or 1502 through Nic. Marshalk, Pr. 11232, B 41,[42] Steinschneider whom I follow first described the volume.[43] Like the first edition of the primer with which it shares the title 'Introductio *utilissima*' and the size the booklet is printed from right to left. Like its predecessor also the Hebrew and a great part of the Latin is printed in red. Letters, syllables, and words, according to Steinschneider are printed not from movable type but "from woodcuts which look like caricatures of the Aldine letters cut by Francesco da Bologna."[44] Proctor also remarks "woodcut Hebrew letters." The same characterization applies to the next Erfurt volume containing Hebrew I know. *Boeschenstein's 'Vil guter Ermanungen,' 1523, in which two lines of woodcut Hebrew are found above and one below the German title. These are repeated two and three times respectively in the course of the booklet. But this leads us beyond the period of the present paper.

2. Speyer

[29] 1502, Breydenbach travels appeared in Speyer with new cuts including the Hebrew alphabet according to Davies; see above.

3. Freiburg

A woodcut alphabet is found in the first edition of [30] *Greg. Reysch, 'Margarita philosophica,' Freiburg, Joh. Schott, July, 1503, Pr. 11717 (without reference to Hebr.).

4. Strassburg [45]

Of much greater interest for our subject are the editions of Reysch's work published by Joh. Grüninger at Strassburg.

[31] *1504 (Feb. 23), Pr. 9891, including the Hebrew grammar by Pellican. In the beginning of the volume we find an alphabet as in the preceding edition but not as well cut. After the Latin grammar the Hebrew one is inserted sig. F IX–F XXVIII including five pages of Hebrew texts. Four of them are excerpta Ysaiae, the first in one, the others in two columns, followed by two chapters of Psalms with Latin translation in parallel column; the first word of Isaiah is in very large letters (the third of them a misprint). Then follows a dictionary, the first word of which is larger than the rest. (Proctor only notes two sizes of the letters); the letters are very uneven and a little different from the alphabet at the be-

ginning of the volume; the lines are not quite straight; the little work undoubtedly was reproduced from woodcut blocks, not from movable type.
The grammar which is shown by the letter on fol. F XVIIIa to be written
by Conrad Pellican in Basle, 1503,[46] has been reproduced in facsimile by
Nestle.[47]

The Hebrew texts do not appear again in Grüninger's later editions.
The blocks were probably destroyed and it was considered not worth while
or it was too difficult to have them cut again; or the printer may have become aware of the incredibly poor character of his work.

[32] The next edition [48] of 1508 (March 31), is Pr. 9907, which has a
shortened grammar; according to Nestle it gives the reproduction of Pellican up to fol. F XVIb of the preceding edition and then follow some Hebrew texts in Latin transcription.

[33] In the *third edition of Grüninger, 1512 (May 31), Pr. 9924, the
Hebrew grammar is placed in the 'Matheseos in Margaritham philosophi-
cam,' sig. B, 1–6, C, 1–2, stopping fol. XIIIIa of ed. 1504. It is preceded by
5 pages of a general introduction already extant in ed. 1508.

[34] Ed. 1515 (Jan. 24) seems to repeat the appendix although Pr. 9935
has no reference to Hebrew. The alphabet in the beginning of the text is
found in all the editions. It is not identical with that of 1504.

5. COLOGNE

In Cologne Hebrew printing occurs late in our period but woodcuts of
Hebrew characters occur earlier and not rarely.

[35–36a] 1503, 1504 and 1506 (Quentell's sons), Jacobus Gaudensis,
'textus dominicae passionis,' Pr. 10383 A (p. 14) and 10406 states that these
contain woodcut Hebrew. The first edition, 1503, which I saw in Frankfurt
and Berlin and that of 1504 contain on the title-page the sentence Jesus
Nazarenus Rex Judaeorum in Hebrew, Greek and Latin, the Greek showing the most curious superabundance of breathings and accents over almost
every vowel, except the article. This sentence occurs most frequently in
our period, e. g. at the end of Aldus's primer, in verses 40 and 45 etc.

[36b] *A recently acquired book of 28 ll. 4to lacking title-page and
last leaf, evidently printed by Quentell at Cologne in our period, has fol.
4h the heading 'Textus parrianis dominice ex quatuor evangelistio per
Magdalium Gaudeniem collectres.' The text is quite different from the
preceding booklet of our author and contains fol. 7b, 8a, 20a, 21a, 22a,
23, 25, 26a Hebrew words or short passages. Each word was separately
cut in wood as can be seen, e. g. 20a, 23a, 26a.

[37] 1508, March 13 (Johann von Landen), Pfefferkorn, Hebrew translation of the Lord's Prayer, Ave Maria, and Credo; a single leaf 4to printed on
one side only. The text is printed from left to right with the transcription
placed under each Hebrew word and the translation above it.[49]

[38] 1509, Jan. 3, Id. *'wie die blinden Juden yr Ostern Halten,' Böck
VI, has on fol. 9a and 9b–10a two passages of Exodus without vowel-points
but with Raphe signs, with transcription over the line. Instead of printing
the text from right to left the transcription goes from left to right and the

Hebrew words are placed in inverse order under this transcription offering a very curious appearance.

[39] Same date, Id. 'der Juden veindt' Boeck. VI, 1, with Hebrew on title-page and text vocalized, again printed from left to right with transcription.

[40] 1509, Feb. (Heinrich of Neuss), Id. *'quomodo ceci illi iudei suum pascha servent,' Pr. 10561, Boeck. V, contains on fol. 9a–b the same texts as 38) but vocalized and printed properly from right to left, the transcription being printed over every word.

[41] 1509, March (Heinrich of Neuss), Id. *'Hostis Judaeorum,' Pr. 10562, Boeck. VI contains on 2a–b words and phrases preceded by transcription, 3b and 4a pieces from the prayer-book, 9–10 passages from the Prophets; printed from right to left vocalized, with transcription above the lines.

[42] 1510 (Heinrich of Neuss), Id. 'In lob und eer dem . . . Maximilian' Boeck. VII, 1.

[43] 1510 (March) (Heinrich of Neuss), Id. *'In laudem et honorem . . . Maximiliani,' Pr. 10564, Boeck. VII contains fol. 8b–9a list of the Biblical books in Hebrew unvocalized, from right to left. Latin names above and transcriptions underneath.

The difference in the appearance of the various letters in each of these volumes proves that the lines were always cut in wood or soft metal and that this printer had no movable type.

[44] Boecking, pp. 73–74 prints from a Wolfenbüttel MS. a circular of Pfefferkorn which, he thinks, was also published as a broadside. At the end it contains some lines of Hebrew, or rather German written in Hebrew characters, also from left to right, as in 37–39, a fact which favors Boecking's hypothesis; I therefore include it here. Perhaps it ought to be placed before [40] on account of the arrangement of the Hebrew. Looking at the original, MS. Wolfenbüttel 757. 1 Nov., I noticed that the four lines of Hebrew characters together with the transcription are actually printed and pasted at the end of the copy of the German text.

[45] ca. 1510 (Johann of Landen). *Victor von Carben, 'Propugnaculum fidei Christiane,' Pr. 10496 does not mention Hebrew. On back of title the Ave Maria transcribed into Hebrew characters, translation of Jesus Nazarenus rex Judaeorum similar to that found on the title of the Juden veindt of Pfefferkorn, square and cursive Hebrew alphabet, and in the latter character, transcription of 'Victor sacerdos olim Judaeus.' On the back of the last page there are four sentences and three words with transcription and translation above them. On the margin we find as a heading printed across from the third to the ninth line 'Vera hebrea verba.' In an inserted cutting from a catalogue of Wilfred de Voynich from whom the copy was bought it is correctly stated that both pages are printed from full-page woodcut blocks.

[46] 1517 (Eucharius Cervicornus), *Josephus, 'de imperatrice e ratione,' Erasmus's paraphrase, Pr. 10580, contains on fol. 3b one word in Hebrew.

[47] 1517 (August 7), Aldus's 'Introductio perbrevis,' appendix to 'de literis graecis,' Pr. 10581.[50]

[48] 1518 (June 11), *Johann Heil 'Bsalterium in quatuor linguis exaratum,' *viz.* Hebrew, Greek, Chaldean (i. e. Ethiopic) and Latin ed. Johannes Potken, Pr. 10598. In a medium-sized square type with vowels and one accent in the middle of each verse (ethnahta). The first letter of the text is a nice initial in a cut. The 'introductiuncula in tres linguas externas' includes practically Aldus's primer with change of reading matter which mainly follows Adrian's Hebrew translations so often reprinted in these early primers.[51]

6. Pforzheim, Tübingen, and Hagenau

The first German printer who used movable type for Hebrew was Thomas Anshelm who in his second printers mark used in Pforzheim since July, 1507, and in Tübingen as well as in a later one used in Hagenau[52] employs the Tetragrammaton with the letter shin inserted. In 1505 he employed a neat Rabbinic type cut after Spanish MSS. and in the following year added a large square type somewhat bulky, with vowels. Smaller type was added several years later.

He printed first at *Pforzheim* [49], 1505, Reuchlin, 'tuetsch missive warumb die Juden so lang im ellend sind,' Pr. 11753, Boeck. I[53] using the Rabbinic type in the longer or shorter passages occurring on every page.

[50] *1506 (March 27),[54] Id. Rudimenta Hebraica; uses the large vocalized type which is out of proportion to the Latin and compels the printer to lead the lines all along wherever Hebrew is used. On the last page of the text we find two lines of a quotation from the Talmud in Rabbinic characters.

[51] Henrichmannus, 'grammaticae institutiones'; Pr. 11764, mentions use of the large Hebrew type in the edition of 1508 and 11709a in that of Hagenau, 1520. No Hebrew is recorded in the editions of other printers, Leipzig, 1510, Pr. 11341; Hagenau, Heinrich Gran, 1512 and 1514, Pr. 11655 and 11659. According to Steiff,[55] Anshelm published twelve more editions of this grammar. Does it include a Hebrew primer?[56] In the 1508 edition and the one at Hagenau a Hebrew word occurs on fol. 12a and 13a respectively.

In Tübingen we find Anshelm using a smaller font of Hebrew with vowels. It occurs for the first time in [52].

[51b] 1511 (August),* Reuchlin, Augenspiegel Pr. 11722, Steiff 22, Boeck. IX contains a few separate words in the Rabbinic type on sigs. B 4b, C 1. Proctor does not mention the Hebrew.

[52] 1512 (March), *Reuchlin's Latin translation of Joseph Hussopaeus, 'lanx argentea,' Pr. 11726, Steiff 30, containing one line on fol. 3b near the end of the introduction.

[53] 1512 (July), *Aldus 'de literis graecis' with the Hebrew primer at the end, Pr. 11729, Steif 32. On the first page of this appendix the alphabet is given in the old large type, otherwise only the smaller type occurs.

[54] 1512 (August), *Reuchlin, 'septem psalmi poenitentiales,' Steiff 33, contains nine pages of Hebrew text printed from right to left with Reuch-

lin's Latin translation on the opposite page. The explanation printed from left to right contains many Hebrew passages, occasionally unvocalized. This is the first real Hebrew text printed in Germany and by far the best in our period outside of those printed in Basle. The small type used is far superior to the larger one used by Anshelm in other books. Our copy has on the title several MS. lines in clear German Rabbinic characters including the name 'Johann Böschenstein, priest of the uncircumcised,' who evidently owned the copy.

[55] 1513 (January), * Matthaeus Adrian, 'Libellus Hora faciendi,' Steiff 40, against Pfefferkorn's leaflet mentioned above no. 44. This pamphlet is printed in the oriental way from right to left and contains Adrian's translations with Latin above and transcription underneath. It uses the large type with vowels.

[56] 1513 (March), *Reuchlin, Defensio contra calumniatores suos colonienses (Steiff 42, Boecking XIII, 1) contains towards the end of the book (sigs. i, 2–4) several Hebrew passages in the small type with or without vowels.

[57] 1514 (March), *'Clarorum virorum epistolae ad Joh. Reuchlinum,' Pr. 11737, Boeck. XV, Steiff 54; contains on fol. 45a–b, two letters in Hebrew in the large type unvocalized. On this account the lines are not as heavily leaded as usual and the upper part of the lamed, the only Hebrew letter to go above the line, has no place between the lines and is therefore mostly pushed down spoiling the appearance of the page.

[58] 1514, Reuchlin, Defensio, a reprint of 56 (Steiff 65; Boecking XIII, 2).

[58a] 1515 (August), *Athanasius in librum Psalmorum translated by Reuchlin Pr. 11742, Steiff 78, Boeck. XX contains a passage in Hebrew in the small font unvocalized in sig. B 2a. Proctor has no reference to Hebrew.

In HAGENAU Anshelm printed

[59] 1517 (March), *Reuchlin, 'de arte Cabbalistica,' Pr. 11685, Boeck. XXIV, using the large Hebrew type unvocalized in the numerous Hebrew quotations all through the book. The lamed here reaches into the line above, whether Latin or Hebrew, so that the ugly appearance which marred the Hebrew pages of the preceding number is avoided. Proctor makes no reference to use of Hebrew.

[60] 1518, February, *Reuchlin, 'De accentibus et orthographia linguae Hebraicae,' Pr. 11690, uses the large type with and without vowels and accents; the Hebrew again is out of proportion to the Latin. At the end of the volume he gives the accents with their Hebrew names and with musical notes while on the preceding pages the names of the accents are printed in red with some specimen word bearing the respective accent in black type underneath.

[61] 1518, *Joh. Cellarius, 'Isagogicon in Hebraeas literas,' B 24; uses the large type with and without vowels.

[61a] 1518 (May), Phil. Melanchthon, Institutiones graecae grammaticae has sig. h4b 3 words in the large type showing the author's ignorance of Hebrew.

[62] 1519 (Jan.),[57] *Moses Kimhi 'in introductorio grammaticae,' Pr. 11697; Introduction in a smaller Hebrew font unvocalized, text vocalized, colophon without vowels, in the larger type. Except for title and dedicatory letter this little volume is entirely Hebrew.

[63] 1519 (March), Athanasius, 'de variis quaestionibus,' Latin translation by Reuchlin, Pr. 11698, Boeck. XXXIIII uses the large type without vowels in many Hebrew passages quoted in the 'aduatationer.'

[64] 1519 (May), 'Illustrium virorum epistolae, Hebraicae, Graecae et Latinae ad Joh. Reuchlin,' Pr. 11702, Boeck. XXXVIII, uses large type without vowels in the two letters reprinted from [57] sig. m1 and in the Hebrew statement of Reuchlin printed sig. E on 7 pages from right to left. The texts are sufficiently spaced to avoid the ugly appearance referred to under [57]. Hebrew words occur also in a few other places.

[65] 1519, *Aldus, 'De literis Graecis' with the Hebrew primer 12mo,[58] uses the large type.

[66] About Henrichmannus 1520, see above.

7. WITTENBERG

In Wittenberg the first Hebrew characters according to Bauch 23, Centralblatt, 390, were used by Joh. Gronenberg.

[67] 1508 (Dec.), Andreas Carlstadt, 'Distinctiones Thomistarum.' Bauch informs us (l.c. and Monatsschrift, p. 146) that the last page of this book contains some specially cut childishly imperfect Hebrew lines which he reprints, but unfortunately not in facsimile. They are in large square characters vocalized with Latin translation underneath and are not worse than many others.

[68] 1509 (Sept. 6), Thiloninus Philymnus, 'Comoedia Teratologia,' B 55, Centralblatt, p. 391, Monatsschrift, p. 147. Bauch states that this volume contains one woodcut line from Marschalk's edition of Aldus's primer (see above, Erfurt [28]).

[69] 1518, Philipp Melanchthon 'sermo de corrigendis adolescentiae studiis,' Pr. 11844 B. 45; according to Pr. woodcut Hebrew; according to Bauch, Centralblatt, p. 398, there are two Hebrew passages, fol. 6b. One is in square, the other in German Rabbinic character, both incredibly poor woodcuts.

[70] 1518 (Dec.), *Joh. Boeschenstain, Hebraicae grammaticae institutiones, Pr.11837, Bauch 14. Steinschneider, Handbuch, quotes an old description by Hirt according to which the first alphabet is printed, the rest including the whole of pp. 11–12 is written in red ink. Bauch, p. 214, makes the same statement, but Pr. remarks all Hebrew written in. In our copy I have the impression that the first alphabet was first printed from a woodcut block, the lines not being straight and large spaces being left between the names printed above the letters in Latin characters. They are afterwards traced over with ink which shines through the opposite page. But I am not entirely sure. The rest of the Hebrew text is filled in, in our copy, in red ink also, evidently by the hand of the author.

Bauch claims that movable Hebrew type was first used in Wittenberg by Joseph Klug in Aurigallus, 'Compendium hebraicae grammaticae' October, 1523, and that the first Hebrew text printed was Melanchthon's editions of Lamentations, January, 1524. But the proofs Bauch gives [59] that these books were printed by Klug seem very flimsy. He does not mention the edition of Obadiah printed by Johannes Grunenberg in large type, 1521,[60] probably edited by Aurigallus.

8. AUGSBURG [61]

In Augsburg several of Pfefferkorn's German pamphlets were reprinted, but here the printer seems to have used movable type. The appearance of the Hebrew is still very uncouth but the same type appears again in 1514 and as conclusive proof that the text is set up I found in our copy of the 'Judenfeind' (formerly Kloss) a letter (mem) printed upside down.

[71] 1509 (Erhard Oeglin) *Pfefferkorn, 'der Juden veindt,' Pr. 10706, Böck. VI, 2. Same texts as mentioned under Cologne 12, but printed from left to right; has a Hebrew line with translation above and transcription below on title.

[72] same date (Erh. Oeglin) Id. 'wie die blinden juden yr Ostern halten,' Pr. 10707, Böck. V.

[73] 1510 (Erhard Oeglin) Id. 'Zu lob und Ere des . . . Maximilian,' Pr. 10708, Boecking VII, 2 has fol. 7b–8a the same texts as [42] (Böcking VII, 3 has still another edition s. l. e. a.).

[74] 1514 (May) (Erhard Oeglin) *Joh. Boeschenstein,[62] 'Elementale introductorium in hebreas literas,' Pr. 10715. Has the same square characters with and without vowels as the previous number, and besides on the title-page three words and on 3b an alphabet in cursive characters which are very similar to Boeschenstein's handwriting as mentioned above, no. [54]. Includes the Ten Commandments, Lord's prayer, Ave Maria, Credo, Magnificat, etc., in Hebrew, Latin, and German in parallel columns.

[75] 1515 (April 28) (Joh. Miller) Joh. Foeniseca, Opera, Pr. 10827; on verso of title and fol. 2a is a short Hebrew grammar with the first two verses of the Psalms in Hebrew. I saw the book some years ago but my notes contain no further details.

[76]* 1516 (June 9) (Joh. Miller),*Paulus Ricius, 'Porta lucis,' Pr. 10835; uses Oeglin's type on title-page and in various places of text where one or two Hebrew words are inserted. They are handled much less skillfully than in Oeglin's books, the words sometimes being quite crooked and spoiling the appearance of the page.

[77] 1520, May (Grimm and Wirsung), *Moses Kimhi, 'Rudimenta Hebraica,' ed. Joh. Boeschenstein, Pr. 16916; uses a new type somewhat larger but quite crude; text vocalized, but not editor's introduction; a few large initial letters.

[78] 1520, April (Grimm and Wirsung),*'Septem Psalmi poenitentiales' with Latin and German translation by Boeschenstein, Pr. 10917. Type a little smaller and less heavy than the previous. First word of each psalm with very large type. At the end two lines in Rabbinic type.

[79] 1520 (Grimm and Wirsung), *Aldus, 'Introductio utilissima Hebraice discere cupientibus' corrected by Boeschenstein with Adrian's

translations, reprint of Basel 1518 ed. with Froben's preface (see [96]); same type as [77].

9. OTTBEUREN

In Ottbeuren Proctor mentions Hebrew type with vowels but rough as being used in

[80] Oct. 10, 1511, in 'Passio septem fratrum' 11954. Three words from Psalms occur, fol. 17b, in the 'Translatio sancti Alexandri,' in square characters probably woodcuts.

10. FRANKFURT

In Frankfurt Beatus Murner printed three books containing a few words in Hebrew vocalized in a large woodcut type which is better than most of these productions. The books are most carefully described by M. Sondheim,[63]

[81] *1512, Thomas Murner, 'Ritus et phase celebratio judeorum,' Pr. 11958, Sondheim 3; two words on title and one at bottom of fol. 5b, Pr. here and in the following does not mention the Hebrew characters.

[82] 1512 *Id. 'Benedicite iudeorum,' Pr. 11959, Sondheim 4. Three Hebrew words on two lines on the title-page, same size as in [52].

[83] 1512 Id. 'der iuden benedicite,' same as previous in German, Pr. 11960, Sondheim 5; contains according to Sondheim the same words on the title while a reprint of the same year, Sondh. 7, omits the Hebrew lines.

11. LEIPZIG

[84] In Leipzig Melchior Letter in 1516 printed the Hebrew grammar of Bartholomaeus Caesar, 'Elementale Hebraicum,' B. 21, in which as Bauch informs us [63a] blanks are left for all the Hebrew which is written in the only known copy in the Library of the Deutsche Morgenlaendische Gesellschaft. This booklet really does not come within the compass of my paper as these are probably more books with blanks for Hebrew type. It is included like [27] to give as complete a list as possible of Hebrew grammars up to 1520.

Hebrew printed from woodblocks is recorded by Proctor for two other Leipzig printers in 1520: (Valentin Schuman), [85] Philip Novenianus, *'Elementale Hebraicum,' Pr. 11548, B. 53. Three sizes of square characters, two very large, occur besides a cursive alphabet (notula curreno), all very uneven and awkward, and

(Wolfgang Stoeckel), [86] Aug. Alveld, 'tractatus de communione sub utraque specie,' Pr. 11502. Fol. 2b we find the Tetragrammaton, the letter Ibin and, three times, the combination of both, very clumsy and uneven woodcuts.

12. ROSTOCK

In Rostock Nicolaus Marschalk, who was responsible for the first Hebrew characters used in the sixteenth century in Germany printed three little books of his in 1516:

[87] April 1, 'Rudimenta prima linguae Hebraicae,' B. 42.
[88] April 5, 'Orationes hymni,' etc., B. 43
[89] May 1, 'Compendium grammatices hebraice,' B. 44.

Nestle [64] first drew attention to these booklets of 4, 4 and 12 leaves respectively. Neither Bauch nor Nestle gives information about the Hebrew characters he used. Do we have here a repetition of his old woodcuts from Erfurt? According to Bauch, Centralblatt für Bibliothekswesen, 405-6, he had bought back his old Erfurt type from Gronenberg of Wittenberg.

C. SWITZERLAND

In Basle [65] Hebrew printing began late but it quickly superseded all the other presses mentioned before. Hebrew alphabets occur in the new editions of [90-91] Reysch's Margaritha philosophica, 1508 and *1517; the latter is much superior to those of the earlier editions. The fame of Hebrew printing in Basle is due to Johann Froben.

After September 1, 1516, there appeared from his press as an appendix to the edition of Jerome's works [92] *'Psalterium quadruplex' in fol. containing the Hebrew, Latin, and Greek text with translation into Latin. Froben employed a medium-sized vocalized type with one accent in the middle of the verse; headings of the pages and numbers of the chapters in neat Rabbinical type; and a large alphabet on the last page in C. P[ellican]'s one page Institutiuncula. The printer frequently used extended letters to fill the lines.

(After 1516 Nov.), there followed another purely Hebrew edition of the [93] *Psalms in 32mo with a short Hebrew preface by Pellican and, beginning on the left side of the volume, *Wolfgang Faber (Capito)s 'institutiuncula in Hebraeam linguam' which is missing in some copies. The type is similar to the preceding but blacker and therefore heavier looking; no Rabbinic type but large letters for title and first word of each Psalm.

[94] 1516 Aldus, 'Alphabetum Hebraicum' as appendix to Theodor Gaza's Greek grammar.[66]

[95] 1518 (Jan.), Capito 'Institutionum Hebraicarum libri duo,' a larger grammar.[67]

[96] 1518 (March 15), *Aldus, 'Introductio utilissima Hebraice discere cupientibus' with Mat. Adrianus's [68] oratio dominica, etc., in the same neat type B. 2.

[97] 1520 (February), this book was reprinted again, with the omission of a sentence of Froben's preface. B. 3.

[98] 1520 (August), 'Proverbia Salomonis, Praefatio Fratris Conradi pelicani. Epitome hebraicae grammaticae. Fratris Sebastiani munsteri.' [69]

[99] To our period probably also belongs:[70] 'Praecationes quaedam' and 'Cantica videliceo Oratio dominica Symbolum Apostolorum,' etc. 8vo, Hebrew and Latin in an anonymous translation.

These Basle editions are, except for the Complutensian Polygot, the first real Hebrew books printed at a Christian press, for that of Bomberg, although owned by a Christian, was actually run by Jewish scholars. Froben's type shows a curious slant to the left which has some similarity with the Bologna Psalms of 1477 and the prayer book according to the German rite, ca. 1490, and occurs again in some of the other books printed later in the South of Germany, e.g. in Thiengen and Freiburg.

D. LOW COUNTRIES

In the Low Countries we have according to Schwab [71] Pagninus 'Institutiones Hebraice' Leyden (Lugdunum Batavorum) 1520; but Pagninus was printed in Lyons (Lugdunum) and, as Porges[72] rightly pointed out, a 1520 edition never existed but is due to a mistake caused by the fact that MDXX is printed on one line and VI on the next.

In Louvain Thierry Martens published, ca. 1520, [100] *'Dictionarium Hebraicum,'[73] an abridged Hebrew dictionary excerpted from that of Reuchlin with a short grammar at the end. He uses a rather poor large alphabet at the beginning of the Grammar and as headings in the dictionary and a neat small type without vowels in the dictionary, with vowels in the grammar.

E. FRANCE

In France we find Hebrew type in our period only in a few books published in Paris by Gilles de Gourmont.

[101] 1508 *Franciscus Tissard's Hebrew grammar. The curiously cut Hebrew characters, as Porges [74] rightly remarks, remind us more of the Spanish hand than of the German which we noticed in most of the preceding books. But the letters are so uneven and sometimes crooked that I

cannot escape the impression that they also were not printed from movable type but from woodcut blocks. We can therefore easily understand that in the last part of the grammar we get the paradigms of the verb from the second conjugation onward only in transcription and no more in Hebrew type.

[102] Schwab mentions a reprint from the preceding volume, of the alphabet, the Lord's prayer, etc., found in the Bibliothèque Nationale.

In 1520 the same printer published two books under the supervision of Augustinus Giustiniani, whom we met already as editor of the Genoa Psalter; see [23], [24].

[103] Feb. 28, Moses Kimhi's grammar vocalized with specially cut new type, the preparation of which took 18 months.[75] The Bibliothèque Nationale and the John Rylands Library have copies on vellum.

[104] June 4, Ruth and Lamentations with an appendix containing the part of Joseph Sarco's grammar on numerals [76] with dedication of the corrector Petrus de Soublefour. Neither of these volumes is accessible to me, but the type is undoubtedly the same as used by Gourmont in 1523 in *Johannes Cheradamus Hypocrates 'Rudimenta quaedam Hebraicae grammaticae' 4to, which is still very primitive, though much superior to that used for Tissard. A further improvement of Gourmont's Hebrew type is noticeable in *Joannes Cheradamus, 'Alphabetum Linguae Sanctae, mystico intellectu refertum,' 1532, 12mo. The characters found here mean a great advance over the previous characters, but they are by no means pleasing and have many imperfections. They remind us more of German models and have the slant characteristic for this class in all its reproductions in Germany.

Reed [77] mentions also two editions of an 'Alphabetum Hebraicum et Graecum,' 1507 and 1517, both as printed by Gourmont. The former may be due to a confusion with the reprint from Tissard's grammar of 1508. The latter probably refers to the Basle edition of this year which Steinschneider originally ascribed to Paris, an error which he later rectified but which was repeated by Schwab.

[105] According to Chevillier [78] a few verses or lines of Hebrew occur in 'Annotationes doctorum Virorum in Grammaticos, Oratores, Poetas, Philosophos, Theologos & leges' printed by Jodocus Badius Ascensius, August 15, 1511. I find no reference to Hebrew type in P. M. Renouard's Bibliographie, Paris, 1908, II, pp. 38–39, or id., I, pp. 66–69 in the chapter on the characters used by Badius.

F. SPAIN

We conclude with the most important and largest publication which falls within the scope of the present paper, the great [106] *Polyglot, Complutum, 1514–17.[79] The letters of this Bible naturally are cast after a Spanish model, though they are not identical with any of the Incunabula printed in

Spain.[80] Two fonts of letters are used, large ones for the text and smaller ones for the marginal notes and in the first volume also for the Targum. The first letter of each book of the text of the Pentateuch is in especially large size. The text is vocalized. In the early pages the printer is frequently troubled by blank spaces at the end of the line which he later adjusted by improving the spacing of the words. We therefore find in the beginning of the book a large number of special signs similar in form to a yod in order to make the Hebrew column even. On some pages these signs occur on almost every line in groups of 2, 3, 4, and even 5. Later on, however, as the printer acquires more skill, they almost entirely disappear. While the work does not reach the perfection of Bomberg's editions, it is certainly a most creditable piece of work. The same type, as far as I know, was only used once more in 1526 in the reprint of Alfonso de Zamora's [81] Hebrew grammar, the first edition of which is found in the sixth volume of the Polyglot. The colophon of the 1526 edition mentions as typesetter Roderigo della Torre, like the author probably a Maranno. Besides Alfonso de Zamora, two other converts coöperated in the work of the Polyglot, another Alfonso and Paul Coronel. But they were probably all concerned with establishing the Hebrew text.

We have now reached the end of our survey. Looking over our lists we notice that the greater part of the publications we have recorded are Hebrew grammars. In Germany the Reuchlin-Pfefferkorn controversy about the books of the Jews with its large pamphlet literature is responsible for a considerable proportion of our list; of the couple of dozen items which date from the first decade of the sixteenth century almost half belong to this group. In several instances Hebrew passages are brought in merely for show without inner connection with the subject of the booklets. Half the items from Germany and almost all those from Italy and France are grammars and the editions of Biblical books mostly show by their additions that they were to serve as text-books for studying Hebrew; only the polyglots might perhaps be excluded. The only other Hebrew texts we meet are translations from the New Testament which also occur as reading exercises in the little grammars and various editions of Moses Kimhi's compendious Hebrew grammar. Thus our list offers a certain record of the serious efforts made during these decades to further the study of Hebrew in order to bring about a better understanding of the Bible. Most of these efforts, though, were extremely feeble and only at the end of our period we find a few grammars which consist of more than a few leaves, Reuchlin's great works of 1506 forming the exception. It is astonishing how often the slight primer of Aldus was reprinted or sometimes recast.

Another obvious fact is the gradual increase in the number of publications which altogether amount to about a hundred. While we enumerated nine for the twenty-five years, 1475–1500, there are four or five in Italy and six in Germany from 1500–05; two in Italy and France, one in Switzerland, and twenty in Germany (all but eight due to the above-mentioned controversy), 1505–10; six in Italy, one in France, and over a dozen in Germany, 1511–15; four in Italy, two in France, one in Belgium, nine in Switzerland, and twenty-three in Germany, besides the Polyglot in Spain, 1515–20. The three polyglot Psalters and the smaller Biblical books all appeared during this last half-decade, while the Hebrew passages in the books prior to 1510 on the average were considerably shorter than in the following period.

While at first we meet mostly with woodcut Hebrew letters, cast type becomes the rule towards the end of our period. Still even after 1520 woodcut Hebrew letters do not entirely disappear. In the first book containing Hebrew letters which appeared in England, Wakefield's 'Oratio de utilitate trium linguarum,' London, Wynkyn de Worde, 1524, of which the

Harvard Library has a copy, a few words appear rudely cut on wood, as Reed [82] informs us. The author also complains that he had to omit a part of his book for lack of type.

Again in our own country we find a few words in Hebrew printed from blocks, not from movable type, in the "Bay Psalm Book," Cambridge, 1640, which was made accessible in a facsimile reprint [83] by the eminent bibliographer in whose honor this volume is published.[84]

NOTES

1. Ersch und Gruber, Allgemeine Encyklopaedie, Section II, vol. 28, pp. 21–94.

2. XII, pp. 295–335.

3. *Zeitschrift für Hebräische Bibliographie*, IX, 184–185, XXIII, 28–29.

4. I designate with a star in this article those books which are found in the Library of the Jewish Theological Seminary.

5. Steinschneider, Cat. Bodl., p. 1182, gives an abstract of the colophon and following De Rossi, Annales Hebraeo-Typographici, Sec. XV, Parma, 1795, p. 106, suspects the date. This volume is printed by David ibn Nahmias and his *brother* Samuel, while the later Constantinople editions mention David and his *son* Samuel. This is an additional reason to permit a longer space of time between the Tur and the other publications of these printers.

6. Pollard, An Essay on Colophons, pp. 45–47, mentions five instances of such mistakes, four from the year 1478.

7. Freimann, l. c., XIV, 1910, 79–80, cf. 127; XV, 1911, cf. 180–181. The next press in Africa was established at Cairo. Our Library has a fragment of an otherwise unknown book, Refuot Ha-Talmud, Cairo, 1562, printed by one Gerson, son of Eliezer Soncino; cf. Freimann, l. c., XII, 15.

8. Essays in Librarianship and Bibliography, New York, 1899, pp. 123–124.

9. The Art of Wood Engraving in the Fifteenth Century, London, 1888, p. 15, note, cf. *Jewish Quarterly Review*, New Series, XI, 113–114.

10. Bibliografica Iberica, II, p. 114. Geschichte des spanisches Frühdrucks im Stammbäumen, Leipzig, 1923, pp. 36–46, where the borders of the Manuale (p. 37) and the Abudraham (p. 42) are reproduced. Haebler assumes that these borders were originally cut by Alfonso de Cordova, who was a goldsmith, to serve with Hebrew type, and that it is only due to a chance that we first meet with them in a Christian liturgical work.

11. In the first page, missing in our copy. It is reproduced in I. M. Hillesum, Bibliotheca Rosenthaliana. En Keur uit de handschriften en boeken, Amsterdam, 1919, p. 9, and C. P. Burger, De incunabelen . . . in de Bibliothek der Universiteit van Amsterdam, The Hague, 1923, p. 8.

12. Reproduced in Wachstein, Bibliothek der Israelitischen Kultusgemeinde, II, Wien, 1914, p. 29.

13. In the Pentateuch of 1505, the first dated Constantinople book of the sixteenth century, and the six books enumerated by Freimann, *Zeitschrift für Hebräische Bibliographie*, XXI, 1918, p. 28.

14. In Oels, Silesia, 1530, and in Augsburg, 1534. In Prague, Hebrew printing was practised from 1512.

15. The unique copy of this book, of which our library has parts of two leaves, is in Parma. The colophon is reproduced in the Jewish Encyclopedia, x, 329, a page in A. S. Onderwijzer Raschie's Leven en werken, Amsterdam, 1901. De Rossi expressly states that his copy is defective in the beginning. In spite of this, curiously, the beginning of the text is reproduced in facsimile by Faulmann, Illustrierte Geschichte der Buchdruckerkunst, Vienna, 1882, p. 217, and repeated by Marzi, La Bibliofilia, II, 1900, p. 131, and Fumagalli, Lexicon Typographicum Italiae, Florence, 1905, p. 323, as a specimen of the earliest Hebrew book. While the book is printed in Rabbinical characters, these lines show square characters and are evidently from a manuscript supplement of the missing pages. Faulmann discusses the type and color of ink, etc., without noticing this. He states "nur sind die gross gedruckten Anfangsworte näher zum Text gerückt als im Original." Marzi and Fumagalli, who evidently copy Faulmann's facsimile, fail to repeat this statement!

15a. For convenience of reference I number the books which form the subject of this paper.

16. Nigri, Boehm und Pellican, Tuebingen, 1893.

17. See e. g., the reproduction in Olschki's catalogue, 1909, p. 42.

18. H. W. Davies, Bernhard von Breydenbach and his Journey to the Holy Land, 1483–1484, London, 1911, exhaustively deals with the reprints of the plates and alphabets from the same blocks in the different editions and reproduces the Hebrew alphabet from the first edition which I have seen in the New York Public Library. He states on p. xix that the edition of Haarlem, 1486, recorded in the 'Census' from the Boston Athenaeum is really the Pilgrimage of Human Life by G. de Deguilville. No mention is made in the text of reprints from the same blocks.

19. Deutsche medicinische Inkunabeln, Leipzig, 1908, no. 201, p. 177. My attention was first drawn to this volume by Dr. G. P. Winship; Prof. C. P. Fisher had the page photostated for me from the copy in the Library of the College of Physicians at Philadelphia.

20. I learned of this fact through the reproduction in Jos. Baer & Co., Incunabula xylographica et typographica, Supplementum, II (Lager Katalog 585), p. 435.

21. My attention was first drawn to this volume by T. B. Reed, A History of the Old English Letter Foundries, London, 1887, p. 63. I do not know whether the Hebrew letters also occur in the earlier edition, Louvain, 1484 (Campbell, 1362).

22. According to L. Geiger, Johann Reuchlin, Leipzig, 1871, pp. 167–168, note 3.

23. I was not aware of this fact when dealing with Aldus's use of Hebrew type in Papers of the Bibliographical Society of America, XIII, Chicago, 1919, pp. 64–67.

24. Annales des Aldes, 2d ed., III.

25. It is placed in the year 1500 in the Catalogue of this library, 1899, p. 921, and therefore perhaps ought to have been mentioned in the previous paragraph. Schwab, Incunables Orientaux, Paris, 1883, no. 93, says vers 1501.

26. Chi era Francisco da Bologna?, London, 1858, p. 11, seq. Four pages of the little volume are reproduced by Panizzi in appendix 7.

26a. Our library has two copies of this edition in which the Hebrew primers show marked differences; e. g. in one the few lines of the last page are printed to the right, in the other to the left as in the other issues we have.

27. Bibliotheca Manzoniana, II, Citta di Castello, 1893, p. 242, no. 4186 bis. An

Aldus s. d. in 8vo, in the Bibliothèque des Chartres is recorded in Répertoire des ouvrages pedagogiques du xvi siècle, Paris, 1886, p. 3.

28. Annali Tipographici dei Soncino, ii, Bologna, 1883, p. 261, note.

29. See his full description, l. c., no. 59, pp. 256–265 and the catalogue of his library, l. c., no. 4186.

30. Manzoni, l. c., no. 108, pp. 464–470.

31. The Latin is printed in italics throughout in the undated edition except for the headings; in the dated edition in our library mostly roman type is used. In one of the two copies of the dated edition the appendix agrees exactly with that of the Lascaris, Venice (Melchior de Sessa and Petrus de Ravanis), 1521; it is probably taken from this edition.

32. Sefer ha-Harkabah, August, 1518, Sefer ha-Bahur and Luah ha-Binyanim, September, 1518, Steinschneider, Cat. Bodl., p. 836, no. 13, 935, no. 6, 2800, no. 5561, De Rossi, Annales Hebraeo-Typographici ab an. M.D.I. ad M.D.X.L, Parma, 1799, p. 17, nos. 81–82.

33. Bibliographisches Handbuch über die Literatur der hebräischen Sprachkunde, Leipzig, 1859, p. 56, no. 757, 1.

34. L. c., p. 48, no. 40.

35. The Répertoire (see note 27), p. 344, says s. l. e. a. and records only one edition.

35a. Vogelstein und Rieger, Geschichte der Juden in Rom, ii, Berlin, 1895, p. 115.

36. M. Schwab, l. c., no., 263.

37. Cf. Freimann, Über die ersten hebräischen Drucke in Deutschland (1512–1519), Israelitische Monatsschrift (Wissenschaftliche Beilage zur Jüd. Presse), 1899, no. 8, pp. 45–46.

38. Centralblatt für Bibliothekswesen, xii, 1895, pp. 353–409.

39. Monatsschrift für Geschichte und Wissenschaft des Judentums, xlviii, 1904.

40. Pp. 478–490.

41. Leipzig, 1869, pp. 55–115.

41a. While the paper was in proof I could see a few of the other books of the list in Wolfenbüttel, Frankfurt, and Leipzig, and add a few notes. I wish to thank the officials of these libraries, especially my friends Prof. A. Freimann and Prof. Gotthold Weil for their great courtesy.

42. Cf. Centralblatt, pp. 371–372.

43. Hebraeische Bibliographie, i, 129, ' Bibliographisches Handbuch,' p. 13.

44. Cf. Proctor's judgment on the first Greek type which appeared in Erfurt shortly before in 1500 (The Printing of Greek in the Fifteenth Century, Oxford, 1900, pp. 138–139). "It is an exceedingly rude type . . . it is so barbarous as to defy conjecture as to the model on which it is based."

45. In Torrentinus, Elucidarius carminum, Strassburg, 1505, and often elsewhere the Hebrew words are given in Latin characters; see Steinschneider, Handbuch, p. 140, no. 2015, and cf. Schwab, no. 115.

46. The date of this letter, Basle, 1503, is the source of the mistake of the older bibliographers who mention a Basle edition of 1503. In spite of Nestle's decisive rectification the Basle edition still figures in Schwab, no. 97, and hence in E. N. Adler, Gazetteer of Hebrew Printing, London, 1917, p. 8.

47. Conradi Pellicani, de modo legendi et intelligendi Hebraeum durch Licht-druck neu herausgegeben, Tübingen, 1877; the facsimiles were given again in the book mentioned in note 16.

48. On this and the other editions see Nestle in the introduction to the 1877 publication and Kautzsch, *Theologische Literaturzeitung*, III, 1878, pp. 457–458.

49. Wolf, Bibliotheca Hebraea, III, Hamburg, 1727, p. 940; L. Geiger, *Serapeum*, 1868, p. 196, and *Jahrbücher für deutsche Theologie*, XXI, Gotha, 1876, p. 197.

50. Johann Peringius, Exhortatio studiosae juventutis ad linguam hebraeam, Cologne, Eucharius Cervicornus, 1517 (*Centralblatt für Bibliothekswesen*, XIV, 568), according to a communication of Professor Porges does not contain any Hebrew.

51. Porges in Simonsen-Festschrift, Copenhagen, 1923, p. 185, note, quotes an edition of Böschenstein, Hebr. Grammaticae institutiones, Cologne, 1520, in which blank space is left for many of the Hebrew words. As he informs me, the date is misprinted and it is the edition mentioned by Steinschneider, Handbuch, p. 24, no. 252, 2 from Maittaire and Panzer as printed by Joh. Soter, October, 1521.

52. Schwab, pp. 63–65; Steiff, pp. 18–20; *Revue des Études Juives*, XI, 317.

53. Cf. L. Geiger, Johann Reuchlin, Leipzig, 1871, p. 206, note 1.

54. In the copy of the Bibliothèque Nationale the last leaf seems to be missing, which caused some difficulty to Schwab, no. 109.

55. Der erste Buchdruck in Tübingen, 1881, p. 38.

56. Steinschneider does not refer to Heinrichmannus either in his Handbuch or in his Zusaetze und Berichtigungen, Leipzig, 1896.

57. Besides the Latin date we find a Hebrew colophon stating that the book was finished December 17, 1518. According to Steinschneider, Handbuch, p. 74, no. 1051, 3, Cat. Bodl., p. 1840, the Bodleian has two copies, one merely with Hebrew title and colophon, the other like the one before me.

58. Our copy lacks the title and introduction of Aldus to De literis Graecis; at the end it states formulis Thomae Anshelmi Badensis with the printer's first device. It is undoubtedly the edition quoted by Steinschneider, Handbuch, p. 12, no. 110, 5, from Panzer which Joh. Secerius excudit formulis Th. Anselmi.

59. *Centralblatt*, 409.

60. Le Long-Masch, I, p. 82; Steinschneider, Cat. Bodl., no. 39a.

61. Cf. Steinschneider, Hebraeische Drucke in Deutschland, *Zeitschrift für Geschichte der Juden in Deutschland*, I, Braunschweig, 1887, pp. 282 ff., who only mentions nos. 45, 48–50.

62. Our Library has a contemporary print of Böschenstein's picture signed J. H. with an ornament in the form of a small tree between the two letters. Underneath we find three lines of Hebrew containing Psalms 7, 18, and 119, 75. The letters are very large and show German character.

63. Die aeltesten Frankfurter Drucke, Frankfurt, a. M., 1885.

63a. *Monatsschrift*, p. 284.

64. *Centralblatt für Bibliothekswesen*, XVI, 1899, p. 231.

65. Cf. above note 46.

66. Steinschneider, Cat. Bodl., p. 2810, no. 6710, corrects Handbuch, where Paris is given as printing place. Schwab, no. 185 quoting him, still ascribes the book to Paris.

67. Steinschneider, Handbuch, p. 32, no. 344.

68. Bauch, 2–3, ascribes the whole booklet to Adrian. The printer expressly states in the preface that he uses Aldus and only replaces his Hebrew translations by those of Adrian; see above no. 28.

69. Steinschneider, Cat. Bodl., no. 38, L. Geiger, *Jahrbücher* (as in note 49) p. 215, note 1.

70. L. Geiger, ib., 197, note 4.

71. No. 262, repeated in Adler's Gazetteer; Reed, pp. 63–64, probably also refers to this book.

72. *Centralblatt für Bibliothekswesen*, XIV, 568.

73. Cf. F. L. Hoffmann in *Hebraeische Bibliographie*, I, 1858, pp. 107–108.

74. Simonsen-Festschrift, Copenhagen, 1923, p. 184. Porges gives, pp. 172–187, a full account of this rare grammar.

75. Wolf, I, 893, note f; Chevillier, L'origine de l'imprimerie de Paris, Paris, 1694, pp. 292–293, and from him Wolf, II, 950, reprints the editor's preface.

76. Cat. Bodl., pp. 8–9, no. 35, Handbuch, p. 123, no. 1763.

77. L. c., pp. 62–63.

78. L. c., p. 291, repeated by Wolf, III, 949.

79. James P. R. Lyell, Cardinal Ximenes, London, 1917, pp. 24–52, Ginsburg, Introduction to the Massoretico-Critical edition of the Bible, London, 1894, pp. 906–925, who proves that the Hebrew text is based on the Lisbon Pentateuch, the Naples Bible, and a Madrid manuscript.

80. Lyell, l. c., p. 46.

81. About him see Neubauer, *Jewish Quarterly Review*, VII, 398–417.

82. L. c., p. 64.

83. The Bay Psalm Book being a Facsimile Reprint of the First Edition with an Introduction by Wilberforce Eames, New York, 1905; see also W. Eames, A List of Editions of the Bay Psalm Book, New York, 1885, p. 6.

84. Even in much later times Hebrew letters were cut in wood occasionally. Thus Mr. Voynich once showed me a book printed at Lisbon in 1724 which had some very oddly shaped Hebrew characters, Francisco Manuel de Mello, Tratado de sciencia cabala.

THE FASCICULUS TEMPORUM

A GENEALOGICAL SURVEY OF EDITIONS
BEFORE 1480

By MARGARET BINGHAM STILLWELL

Librarian of the Annmary Brown Memorial, Providence, R. I.

THE 'Fasciculus Temporum' was unquestionably the most popular chronicle of its time. It recorded the world's history to date, from the Creation to 1474, the year of its official publication — with supplementary paragraphs in later editions giving the news of the hour. In a sense, it was both encyclopædia and newspaper. Judging from the number of editions issued between 1474 and 1500, it must have been one of the most widely read books of its century.

From their shelves in The Annmary Brown Memorial twenty-four editions look down upon me, interesting in sub-ject-matter, fascinating in their peculiar typographical setting. It was the lure of the twenty-four which led me, one fine autumn day, to set out upon a comparative survey of editions in the effort to see what might be learned from their curious construction. And it was the multiple complexities of the twenty-four that forced me presently to take shelter at that frequent resting-place, 1480. It happens that this date is not illogical as a temporary stopping-place, for the eight editions issued prior to 1480 comprise practically a third of those on record as issued in Latin before the end of the fifteenth century.

Allowing the possible estimate of two hundred copies for each of the thirty-three editions on record, over six thousand copies of this chronicle of the world's history must have been published simultaneously and successively in several languages and in several countries. By the same reckoning, of the five signed editions issued at Cologne before 1480, and the single editions issued respectively at Louvain, Speier, and Venice during the same period, well over fifteen hundred copies may have been upon the market during the first six, or seven, years after the chronicle appeared in printed form. With index, introduction, and text, its usual form is a folio volume of approximately a hundred and fifty pages — the exact number varying with the edition. And each edition presents individual characteristics as well as certain inherited features.

Werner Rolewinck, the author of the chronicle and a prolific writer, is said to have died of the plague in 1502, after having spent fifty-five years in devoted study at the Carthusian monastery in Cologne. In 1495, Johann Tritheim, a fifteenth-century booklover and writer, went to see Rolewinck who was then in his seventieth year. Apparently in the course of the visit he obtained the titles of thirty of Rolewinck's writings — "hec sunt que se scripsisse mihi nuper confessus est." These he proceeded to list under Rolewinck in his 'Cathalogus Illustrium Virorum (Mainz, *circa* 1495), correctly entering the chronicle as comprising the world's history from the Creation to Pope Sixtus IV; or, to quote the entry from the Memorial's copy of the 'Cathalogus,' "Fasciculus temporum cum circulis ab exordio mundi usque ad tempora sixti pape quarti." Rolewinck he says was a man "in divinis scripturis studiosissimus, et valde eruditus, ingenio subtilis, vita et conversatione devotus. Scripsit multa praeclara volumina." Thus it is that the anonymous author and his chronicle are described to us by one of his contemporaries.

Rolewinck himself was editor of the official edition of the chronicle printed at Cologne by Arnold Ther Hoernen in 1474 which, in its various issues, is the forefather of all the editions within the present survey — with the single exception of the so-called "spurious" undated edition printed at Cologne, in 1473–74, by Nikolaus Götz.

Around this Götz edition there still hangs a veil of mystery. The author's usual printer was the printer of the official edition. According to Voulliéme, Ther Hoernen issued fully eighteen editions of Rolewinck's works. The colophon in his printing of the chronicle proves it to be unmistakably an authorized edition. Yet at approximately the same time, and in the same town, there appeared an edition by Nikolaus Götz. The first impulse is to call the Götz edition pirated, and it has long been a point of discussion which of the two was the earlier. It has been variously maintained that the Götz edition of the chronicle may have been on the press at the time the authorized edition was in process; that it may even have been issued toward the end of 1473; and that in any event it must have appeared before 1477, since by that time Götz was presumably at work upon his [1478] edition — in which, however, he deserted his first format completely and adopted the superior arrangement of the Ther Hoernen edition and its successors.

A recent study of the copy in the Pierpont Morgan Library, the only copy of Götz's first edition on record in America, occasions the present suggestion that this first edition was experimental and may well have been done with the author's knowledge. Or, if one insists upon believing it stolen property, it must be that Götz secured an early draught of the author's manuscript and with that in hand raced the official edition in the printing. Considering the fact that author and printers lived in the same small community, it seems more kindly to accept Götz's first edition as an experiment in which, as one reads it page by page, one can see possibly the author and printer feeling their way along together in the effort to systematize the author's notes and to transcribe into printed form the miscellany of facts comprising the chronologies which, in clumsy fashion, struggle to run parallel throughout the text.

In the first portion of the Götz, from the Creation to the birth of Christ, the arrangement of the text is almost unintelligible — at least it can be followed only by effort. Gradually system begins to take command of chaos until, by the time one approaches the end of the volume, its arrangement becomes nearly as orderly as that which prevails throughout the edition of Ther Hoernen.

Likewise in the first portion of the Götz index, the subject-entries — often inserted at irrelevant places — completely overthrow the alphabetical order which the index is seeking to maintain. For instance, in the *A* section below the Assyrian kings there are listed the kings of Babylonia and of Persia. After which interruption the index proceeds with its references to Assyria, Astrology, etc. And quaintly enough under both Babylonia and Persia in their proper places, one is cross-referenced to Assyria for the list of kings. Also one finds such naïve subjects as "Boni homines in veteri testamento," beneath which are sixty-nine names in the order of pagination, to the utter confusion of the alphabet. But the idea of indenting the subject-entries evidently occurred by the time the typesetter had reached section *E* and the index from that point onward becomes more usable. In the Ther Hoernen edition these bungling subject-entries were wisely omitted, and the index is as clearly arranged and as workable as any book need have.

Does it not seem that the Götz edition was at first the literal copy of notes intelligible enough to the author, not developed for general use, but gradually worked into systematic form while on the press; and that in the Ther Hoernen edition, logical in its arrangement from beginning to end, both author and printer approached their problem from the point of view of the reading and purchasing public? The colophon of the Hoernen edition states that it has been printed "just as it is edited by its author" and that it follows "the first copy which the venerable author arranged with his own hands." This, therefore, proves the latter half of the thesis to have been true, that for this edition copy was prepared deliberately with a view to publication; and it offers nothing to prove that the first half may not also have been the case.

Just how far Ther Hoernen may have been responsible in developing the superior system of the authorized edition is a question. As he was a most capable printer, it is probable that he had much to do with it. Yet, even if he only followed page for page the manuscript as arranged by the author, much credit is due him — for he transcribed written notes into printed notes and he maintained throughout so consistent a scheme that subsequent printers followed his type-setting with precision. Even now, and in spite of the highly abbreviated Latin in which the text is given, it is possible to find one's way unerringly through his pages.

The text of the chronicle comprises a series of disjointed paragraphs for the most part of a biographical nature but with occasional sections recording events of historical importance — earthquakes, comets, the founding or the capture and destruction of cities, the invention of printing, etc.

The book in fact is a chronological 'Who's Who.' Its typographical arrangement, however, is infinitely more complicated than any modern printer would care to undertake. Its interest to fifteenth-century readers was purely historical. It was the history of their world to date. But since its tabulation of Biblical events antedated "higher criticism" by some centuries and since its knowledge of legendary days was also prior to the age of "scientific comparative mythology," its historical interest to present readers has become quaint and antiquarian. It is in its curious typographical construction, and in the contribution that its study adds to our knowledge of fifteenth-century methods of printing and editing, that its present interest lies.

Through the centre of each page of text there runs a wide band or ribbon set off from the text by double rules. Along the top of this band there runs at frequent intervals a chronology by "Anno Mundi" which places the Creation at the year I, gives the birth of Christ as 5199 and the last date in the book as 6673. At the base of the band, and at similar intervals, there appear the corresponding years according to Christian chronology. This system starts on the twenty-fourth folio of the text at the birth of Christ and runs by decades to the end of the volume, to A.D. 1474, the year of publication. The B.C. dates run backward from Christ's birth to the Creation and they are placed upside down, a device which is of immense help to the reader of the book — by the merest glance at a page you can tell exactly where you are, A.D. or B.C.

Between these parallel chronologies is a series of circles each representing, in the years before Christ, His ancestors from Adam down; and, beginning with Peter at A.D. 34, His ecclesiastical descendants, the Popes. Large squares and in some of the subsequent editions large-sized circles are used in this centre band to indicate the six eras in Biblical history: the Creation, and the periods beginning with Noah, Abraham, David, the Babylonish captivity, and the birth of Christ. Similar distinction is accorded Joseph and Mary. During the time of the Great Western Schism half-circles are used to represent the popes and antipopes, and in connection with popery it is interesting to note that Joanne, "Papa mulier," who appears in the index of Götz's first edition, is carefully omitted in the Ther Hoernen and succeeding editions — although not infrequently supplied in contemporary hand, under A.D. 860.

Above and below the centre band, which runs page for page throughout the chronicle, are the biographical and historical paragraphs whose typography is most curious of all. Instead of running continuously as do the paragraphs of the introduction, those in the text are spaced off and interwoven around one another so as to accompany the circles which, interspersed throughout the text, give prestige to certain persons important in Biblical history, in mythology, or among the rulers of the world. Frequently these circles are joined by horizontal lines, so that in some instances the "Reges ytalie, Reges assiriorum, Pontifices, Reges israhel" and "Reges syrie" go marching through the pages of the book on parallel lines and in accord with the periods designated in the centre band. Each page therefore represents the events of a given period and, according to the number of important personages honored by the circles, each presents to the eye a different geometric pattern.

The biographical paragraphs are always placed as near as possible to the circle representing the person described. The historic paragraphs seem to occupy whatever space may have been available in their proper period. When space proves insufficient the last word is followed by a symbol, at the reappearance of which, on the following page, the text of the incomplete paragraph continues. Although the text generally follows that of the original, word for word, the spelling is variant in all editions. It seems hardly probable that the compositor made up his text from dictation; he could not then have followed the interwoven paragraph spacing which reappears edition after edition from 1474 up to 1479, when the disjointed paragraphs show a tendency to assume more continuous setting. It seems more probable that the compositor in these early editions read the copy himself line by line and carried each succeeding phrase in mind while he set his type, spelling the words himself and introducing such abbreviations as he needed to make each line or paragraph come out right at the end.

The woodcuts, which in the early editions are fairly numerous in the first portion of the book, are often more decorative than illustrative. In two instances, however, actual cities are portrayed. The picture of Cologne as it appears in the Ther Hoernen edition is a most interesting representation of the cathedral in process of construction. The engraving of Venice, which appears in the edition printed by Georg Walch in 1479, shows the Piazzetta approached from the water, but with the Palace of the Doge and the columns of the Winged Lion and of St. Theodore reversed in position. Although the reversing of position is usually taken to mean that a picture has been traced from some other drawing, in this instance the one in the Venetian edition of the 'Fasciculus' is the first engraving of Venice as yet recorded.

From a decorative point of view, the conventional woodcuts used for Nineveh, Trèves, Rome, Jerusalem, etc., vary considerably in artistic merit. In some editions, the cuts are extremely crude. In others they have a quaint charm, those in the Louvain edition being in technique the most attractive and finished. In the Ther Hoernen edition the typesetting is superior in effect to the cuts. In the Louvain, the gray of the woodcuts is superior in quality to that of the type blocks. Apparently when the chronicle was first issued, certain intended illustrations were not ready. In later issues these appear and in succeeding editions the various printers selected new points for illustration which, in turn, were repeated by their successors.

Considerable confusion has resulted in the description of these woodcuts owing to the fact that some writers have used the term "new cuts" to mean new points illustrated, and other writers to mean new drawings for the usual points of illustration. In the sense in which a modern newspaper editor "features" certain items of interest, it may be said that the several points featured in Ther Hoernen's edition are for the most part featured in succeeding editions; or, that the additional points featured in the Louvain edition are repeated in the Venetian. The cuts themselves, however, are invariably new drawings from new designs.

The only instances in the present survey where drawings are copied or borrowed occur in the Winters and [1478] Götz editions and in the case of the Tower of Babel in the Speier edition which, although newly drawn, is closely modelled upon that in the Ther Hoernen. Both towers are square, according to tradition, with the base made of "sun-dried bricks," and with two of the eight towers described by Herodotus as placed one upon the other. In both, the upper section is incomplete. That in the Ther Hoernen leaves one in doubt as to whether the tower was in process of building, or whether the artist had in mind its early destruction by "earthquake and thunder." Since the chasm is tidy in outline, the tower is presumably going up rather than coming down. But the Speier artist removes all doubt by adding a carefully constructed crane with pulley and tongs. His tower is going up. One may playfully read much into these little pictures of olden times, but the fact remains that each artist as he set out to make a sketch, however crude the result, had something in mind that he sought to represent. By the reversal of imagination and with his finished product as a guide, one need not be far wrong in one's conclusions.

Even in this small group of fifteenth-century books there are a number of interesting "firsts" — the picture of Cologne and its Cathedral, so Mr. Murray believes, is the first drawing of an actual place to appear in a printed book; and, to quote Mr. Pollard, illustration properly so called began in the Low Countries with Veldener's edition of the 'Fasciculus'; the Walch edition is the first illustrated Venetian book; the first Götz and the Ther Hoernen editions together mark the beginning of book illustration in Cologne. The Götz, moreover, is one of the early books in which an attempt was made to number the leaves in type. Ther Hoernen, who has the distinction of being the first printer to have used leaf-numbers, — and that in a sermon of Rolewinck's printed in 1470, — left his edition of the chronicle entirely without printed foliation. It was intended, however, that the numbering should be supplied by hand, for in the index of the Ther Hoernen edition and so with its successors the leaf-numbers are given — with a dot before or after the number to indicate the recto or verso.

It is here that one comes to the parting of the way, for the Ther Hoernen index was issued in two forms, one occupying eight leaves and the other nine. It is this which occasions the terms "eight-leaf-index issue" and "nine-leaf-index issue" in the tables that accompany this introduction. Each of these issues also contains variations in the text and illustrations, and each has lineal descendants among the editions produced by subsequent printers. In the collation of the editions issued before 1480, the appearance of these inherited and repeated characteristics divides·the editions into three distinct series — the Louvain-Venice, the Cologne, and the Speier Series.

The first Louvain edition printed by Veldener, for instance, may be rated as a full-blooded and direct descendant of the eight-leaf-index issue — with the single exception of a continued sentence. The Harvard copy of this issue (the only copy on record in America) lacks the continued section of a paragraph beginning on folio 23a. In the memorial's copy of the nine-leaf-index issue, the complete paragraph appears (folio 23a–b). The paragraph likewise appears in full in the Louvain edition. Mr. Murray, in his valuable study of the Ther Hoernen edition,[1] divides the eight-leaf-index issue into two sub-

1. The Edition of the Fasciculus Temporum printed by Arnold Ther Hoernen in 1474, by A. G. W. Murray (The Library, 1913, 3d series, vol. IV, 57–71), in which the author discusses the priority of the eight-leaf-index issue over the nine-leaf-index issue and divides each into the following sub-issues:

    I. The eight-leaf-index issue without Cologne and Crucifixion.
   II. "   "   "   "   " with   "   "   "
  III. The nine-leaf-index issue "   "   "   "
  IV. "   "   "   "   "   " supplementary matter.

No copies of II and IV are as yet recorded in this country. Recent correspondence with Mr. Charles Martel shows the Thacher Library-of-Congress copy of the Ther Hoernen 1474 edition to be a third sub-issue of the nine-leaf-issue index — without Cologne and the Crucifixion, and also without the continued half-sentence on folio 23b. Since these omissions occur on three consecutive folios, it seems very possible that a gathering was inserted from some left-over stock of Mr. Murray's I. With the exception of the omissions in this gathering, the Thacher LC copy seems to correspond to the nine-leaf-index issue as collated in the Cologne series of the accompanying tables, and the make-up of the copy as described by Mr. Martel indicates that it is in original state.

issues — one without and one with the illustrations of Cologne and of the Crucifixion. In the Harvard copy the leaves on which these cuts should appear, as well as part of the mutilated paragraph, are lacking.

One wonders, therefore, whether the lacking half-sentence appeared in the second of the sub-issues, its omission having been caught and corrected at the time the woodcuts were inserted; whether for his text Veldener changed to a nine-leaf-index issue, in which the full paragraph appears; whether copies of the eight-leaf-index were ever bound with copies of what in the present collation is the nine-leaf-index text; or, whether Veldener finding a sentence ending in mid-air, with a continuation sign but no continuation, searched a friend's copy and chanced upon one containing the desired portion. The collation of all existing copies of the Ther Hoernen may some day prove the first or third supposition to have been true.

No additions to the index appear in the Louvain edition. Five instances have been noticed, however, in which the reference numbers of the index are misprinted. But the text shows improvements. Twenty new paragraphs have been added by Veldener, and six illustrations. These points become of interest in connection with the edition issued in 1479 by Georg Walch at Venice. The five misprints noticed in the Louvain index are not reproduced, but nineteen of the twenty paragraphs added in the Louvain appear in the Venetian edition — thus indicating that Walch must have set his index and the first few pages of his text direct from the eight-leaf-index issue of Ther Hoernen; that at the eleventh folio something attracted his attention to the additional matter of the Louvain edition, which from that point he followed page for page (making occasional variations of his own and inserting the woodcut of Venice — all of which features a peep into a future collation shows to be reproduced in Ratolt's edition of the following year).

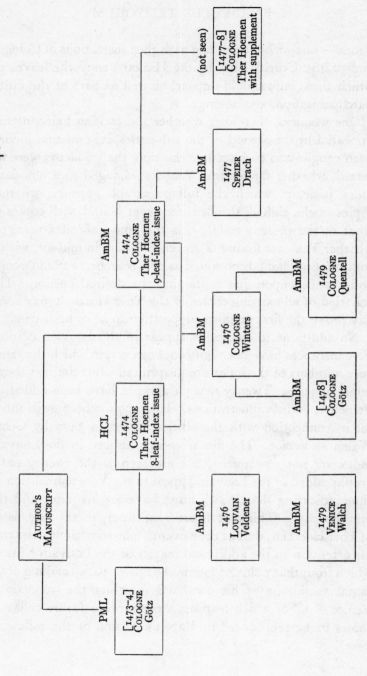

TABLE A. THE FASCICULUS TEMPORUM BEFORE 1480

AUTHOR'S
MANUSCRIPT

[1473-4]
COLOGNE
Götz

1474
COLOGNE
Ther Hoernen
8-leaf-index issue

1474
COLOGNE
Ther Hoernen
9-leaf-index issue

[1477-8]
COLOGNE
Ther Hoernen
with supplement
(not seen)

1477
SPEIER
Drach

1476
COLOGNE
Winters

1476
LOUVAIN
Veldener

1479
COLOGNE
Quentell

[1478]
COLOGNE
Götz

1479
VENICE
Walch

PML

HCL

AmBM

AmBM

AmBM

AmBM

AmBM

AmBM

A study of the Cologne edition issued by Conrad Winters in 1476 indicates that apparently he used the eight-leaf and nine-leaf-index issues interchangeably. Since the extra size of his paper made the setting of type for his index quite different from that in either of the Ther Hoernen issues, he may even have been unconscious of the fact that the copies which he had at hand varied in make-up. In fact he must have followed the entries rather unintelligently because his introduction, on larger paper than the Ther Hoernen, occupies fewer pages and in consequence the text following folio 3a varies one page from Ther Hoernen's typesetting. Yet Winters blindly copied the Ther Hoernen index, numbers and all, leaving it for his readers to discover that they must subtract one if they would find the references in his text.

This same blunder is repeated by Götz in his second edition, in which he follows Winters throughout — with a few misprints of his own and the addition of eleven new paragraphs at the end. His edition is so clumsily printed that it rather exonerates the author's manuscript from undue responsibility for the lack of style in Götz's first edition. A printer who could not follow neatly printed text with good effect could not be expected to have done much with an author's manuscript — whether he stole it or was given it by the author for publication. It seems that Quentell may have felt the clumsiness of the Götz edition for, although he followed the index of Götz's second edition, he changed to the Winters edition for his text, adding as his contribution signatures and a charming little cut representing the Adoration of the Magi.

It is probably because of the popularity of the chronicle and the consequent number of volumes in circulation that its printers so frequently made use of more than one edition in building up their copy. A most interesting variation of this method occurs in the edition issued by Peter Drach at Speier in 1477. Evidently he set his type by the eight-leaf-index issue of the Ther Hoernen and then, becoming aware of improvements, revised his setting by the nine-leaf-index issue. In the text he gives the troublesome half-sentence lacking in the eight-leaf, and in the index sixteen out of the seventeen entries peculiar to the nine-leaf index but lacking in the eight-leaf. Four of these entries are out of alphabet in the Speier edition, at the end of sections, as if added after the type had been set; and one of them, "Heraclites," is inserted in the place which alphabetically belongs to "Hester" — the one which is omitted from among the entries taken from the nine-leaf index. This seems to indicate that the reviser or proof-reader, realizing that two additions were to be made under H, inadvertently put one in the place of the other and considered his duty done. And again, in attempting to improve the entries for Cologne, he inserted the two entries peculiar to the nine-leaf index but failed to correct from that index the entries directly above and below which are peculiar to the eight-leaf issue. The Speier edition adds two entries to the index, Dunstanus and Spira, and at the end of the text a supplement of three paragraphs. Otherwise as the colophon states it is close to the original.

At the end of his index, Peter Drach added the pious wish "Sit laus Deo" — suggestive also of a sigh of relief and expressing a sentiment that one feels moved to echo after collating the various editions of the chronicle with their progenitors. But, through collation such as this, much may be learned of the temperament of the men who operated these early presses. Some show themselves to have been painstaking; some both intelligent and conscientious; others lacking in skill or in patience.

Much also may be learned of the methods employed in following copy and in revising proof. Certain of these have been noted in the present paper. Others are revealed in the following tables, to which this is an introduction. And still others, no doubt, will come to light in the future. For the study cannot be considered in any sense complete until all recorded copies of the various editions have been collated — to see whether the copies described in the present survey are each typical of their edition; or whether, as in the case of the five or more issues of the Ther Hoernen, these editions also must be subdivided into variant issues.

NOTE ON THE TABLES

N.B. The placing of the 8-leaf and 9-leaf-index issues one after the other in the collation is without chronological significance.

The source of inherited features is indicated in the right-hand column of each collation.

For the benefit of the modern printer abbreviation marks are omitted. The spelling of each phrase quoted in the collation is that of the edition in which it first appeared. Subsequent changes in spelling, in later editions, are not noted providing that in wording the phrases are the same.

TABLE B. FASCICULUS TEMPORUM — COLOGNE SERIES

	1474. COLOGNE: ther HOERNEN		1476. WINTERS	[1478.] GOTZ	1479. QUENTELL
	8-Leaf-Index Indicated in other columns by: H74-8) or (8 — Harvard copy Sm. fol., 72 leaves; without page nos. and sigs.	9-Leaf-Index Indicated in other columns by: H74-9 or (9* — Annmary Brown copy Sm. fol., 74 leaves, the first blank (wanting); without page nos. and sigs.	Indicated in other columns by: Win76) or (W — Annmary Brown copy Fol., 74 leaves; the ninth and last two, blank (ninth and last wanting). Without page nos. and sigs.	Indicated in other columns by: G78) or (G — Annmary Brown copy Fol., 74 leaves, the ninth and last two, blank (the last two, wanting). Without page nos. and sigs.	Indicated in other columns by: Q79) or (Q79 — Harvard copy Fol., 72 leaves; the first blank. Without page nos. With sigs.: b-f in 10s; g-h in 8s; [j] in 6
Index:	*Index:* Fols. [ia-viiib] 3 cols, 48 ll.	*Index:* Fols. [iia-xbl] 3 cols, 44 ll	*Index:* Fols. [ia-viiib], 3 cols, 48 ll.[1]	*Index:* Fols. [ia-viiib], 3 cols, 48 ll.	*Index:* Fols. [64a-71a], 3 cols, 51 ll.[3]
VARIANT ENTRIES:					
Abdias ppha 12.	c)	m) .12	sic) .12 (9*	sic)	sic)
†Abdon iudex ix 8.	ix for xiiij	†. . . .	. . . . †(9	. . . .	. . . .
Achitob potifex .9	c)	c)	c)	c)	° reversed with .13
Adrian helize ipator .29	c)	c)	†m) .29.	m) .29.	†(W °c)
Adrian cronogphus 54.	m) 54.	c) .54	m) 54. (8	sic)	sic)
Agapes 33.	Agap.mart./	c) Agamen./	Agap.mart./ (8	sic)	sic)
Agar 5.	Agamenon/	c) Agap.p.scd./	Agamen./ (8	sic)	sic)
Alexi vir scus .35	c)	c)	c)	c)	°m) 35.

							†(G
†H74-9)* Alex.p.pmus	.29	· · · ·	†c)	sic)	†(9	sic)	sic)
†H74-9) Alex.p.scdus	.54	· · · ·	†c)	sic)	†(9	sic)	sic)
Alexader papa terci	56.	c)	c)	dot om)	c)	c)	°dot om.
Archesios phus	19.	c)	c)	†dot reapp)	c)	†dot reapp)	sic)
Auetin silui	.12	c)	c)	c)	c)	c)	°m) 12.
Azarias pontifex	51.	Azaias v.oz./	c) Azar.p. 11./	Azar.v.oz./	(8	sic)	sic)
†Win76)Babilonie.. oritur	13.	· · · ·	· · · ·	†c)		sic) †W)	sic)
Baleus rex assirior	6.	c)	c)	c)		dot om)	°dot reapp)

H74-9)* Appearing in this issue for the first time. (When no edition is cited, the entries are quoted from the 8-leaf-index issue.)

(9 A feature inherited from this issue,

‡ New matter inserted, a determining factor of inheritance,

† Other determining features, inherited from sources indicated.

sic) Entry identical with that described in column at the left, emphasizing inherited features. (Variant spelling is not regarded providing the entry itself is the same.

. . . . Entry omitted.

/ If at the beginning, the entry appears above the phrase quoted; if at the end, the entry is below the phrase.

° Features peculiar to Quentell's 1479 edition which are repeated in his edition of 1480.

c) correct.   C) complete.   m) misprinted.   reap) reappears.
om) omitted.

1. The Winters 1476 index follows that of the 1474 ther Hoernen edition, even to the numbers of the folios which correspond to the 1474 edition rather than to this. In its variations the index follows the 8-leaf-index issue in the more important features, though apparently both issues were consulted by Winters in setting the type for this edition. From [3a] onward, the references of the index may be found in the text by looking one page prior to that indicated in the index.

2. The Götz [1478] index follows the setting of the index in the Winters edition, and like the Winters edition has the reference numbers of the 1474 ther Hoernen edition. From [3a] onward, the references of the index may be found in the text by looking one page prior to that indicated in the index.

3. Since the text of the Quentell 1479 edition begins with signature "b," it seems evident that it was first intended to prefix the index, but that it was later decided to continue the index upon the unused leaves of folio "h," adding the six extra leaves needed to complete it. From [3a] onward, the references of the index may be found in the text by looking one page prior to that indicated in the index. (The blank leaf preceding the introduction is not included in the present folio count.)

TABLE B. FASCICULUS TEMPORUM — COLOGNE SERIES (CONTINUED)

Index (continued):		1474. COLOGNE; THER HOERNEN		1476. WINTERS	[1478.] GOTZ	1479. QUENTELL
		8-LEAF-INDEX	9-LEAF-INDEX			
Balthaz. rx babiloie	.16	c)	sic)	c)	c)	°w.n.) .19
†Benedcus sextus papa	.25	†w.n.) .25	c) .52	w.n.) .25 †(8	sic)	sic)
†Bizantiu ciuitas codit	14.	c)	sic)	c)	†m) .14	sic) †(G
Boheia vastatur	.63	c)	sic)	c)	c)	°m) 63.
†Cassiodor glos vir	.39	c)	sic)	c)	†m) 39.	sic) †(G
Cesarius dyaconus	32.	c)	sic)	c)	c)	°m) 23.
Cethura uxor abrahe	5.	c)	sic)	c)	c)	°w.n.) 4.
†Ciprian doctor glosus	.32	c)	sic)	†m) 32.	sic) †(W	sic)
Clemes papa qnt	.60	c)	sic)	c)	c)	dot om.)
†Colonia costruit	35.	†sic)	c) .24	35. †(8	sic)	sic)
‡H74-9) Colonia pficit.	.28	†	†c)	. . . . †(8	. . . .	. . . .
‡H74-9) Coloia ihitat	35.	†	†c)	. . . . †(8	. . . .	. . . .
†Colonie tepestas oritur	.40	†w.n.) .40	c) .49	w.n.) .40 †(8	sic)	sic)
†Conciliu cartaginen	36.	c)	sic)	†m) .36	sic) †(W	sic)
Cociliu latanense	.58	c)	sic)	c)	c)	°m) 58.
†Cocordi subdiaco & mar	.30	c)	sic)	†n.om.)	sic) †(W	sic)
†Constancius comes	.36	c)	sic)	†w.n.) .39	sic) †(W	sic)
†Costatinopolis capit	63.	†Costan.rcupat../	c)/Costan.rcupat	Costan.recup./ †(8	sic)	sic)
†Crisipp phus	19.	†at end of CO)	c) (in CR	at end of CO) †(8	sic)	sic)
†Crisogon	33.	†at end of CO)	c) (in CR	at end of CO) †(8	sic)	sic)
Dyoisi alexadrior eps	.32	c)	sic)	c)	c)	°m) 32.

Dyoisi p papa & mar. 32.	c)	sic)	c)	c)	°m) .32 †(G
†Domician frarer titi 28.	†m) 28.	c) .28	m) 28.	sic)	sic) †(G
‡H74–9) Eccia maior col. 58.	† . . .	‡Eccia . . .	. . . . †(8	. . .	. . .
Edgarus rex anglie 52.	c)	sic)	c) †(8	c)	°m) 52.
Edward rex anglie 54.	c)	sic)	c)	c)	°m) 54.
†Elburga filia edwardi 54.	c)	sic)	sic)	†m) 54.	sic) †(G
‡H74–9) Electores imper. 52.	. . . . .	†c)	c) †(9	sic)	sic) †(G
†Enoch iust fili iareth .3	c)	sic)	sic)	†m) 3.	sic)
Ethbinus britanicus 40.	c)	sic)	c)	c)	°m) 40.
†Festuitas oim scor tns 48.	†c)/Festu. . .	Festu. . ./	c)/Festu oim. . . †(8	sic)	sic)
†Fracia in merore 63.	†c)	w.n.) .62	c) †(8	sic)	°m) 63.
Gherard bituren eps 55.	c)	sic)	c)	c)	°w.n.) 75.
†Gherardus groet. 62.	c)	sic)	†m) .62	sic) †(W	sic)
Geruasius martir 27.	c)	sic)	c)	c)	°m) 27.
Gregori ix. papa 58.	c)	sic)	c)	c)	°m) 58.
Helias coloien abbas 53.	c)	sic)	c) †(8	c)	°w.n.) 83.
‡H74–9) Heraclides q 36.	†	‡c)	. . .	. . .	. . .
Heresis adamitar 62.	c)	m) .26	c)	c)	°m) 54.
Herliui abbas 54.	c)	sic)	c) †(9	c)	sic)
‡H74–9) Hester 18.	. . .	†c)	sic)	sic)	°m) 37.
Hilari eps arelaten 37.	c)	sic)	c)	c)	sic)
†Hildebert cenomanen 55.	†c)	w.n.) .57	c) †(8	sic)	sic)
Hirenea 33.	c)/Hireneus. . . 28	Hireneus. . 28/	/Hireneus (8	sic)	sic) (G
Historia libri iudicu .7	m) .7	sic)	c) 7.	m) .7	°m) 18.
Historia hester 18.	c)	sic)	c)	c)	°m) 27.
Jacobus mior aplus 27.	c)	sic)	c)	c)	

TABLE B. FASCICULUS TEMPORUM — COLOGNE SERIES (CONTINUED)

Index (continued):	1474. COLOGNE: THER HOERNEN		1476. WINTERS	[1478.] GOTZ	1479. QUENTELL
	8-LEAF-INDEX	9-LEAF-INDEX			
Inuetio sancti mich. .38	c)	sic)	m) 38.	sic) (W	sic)
†Job vir scus .17	†w.n.) .17	c) .7	w.n.) .17 †(8	sic)	sic)
Johanes filius iude 18.	c)	sic)	m) .18	sic) (W	°w.n.) .14
Johanes baptista nasc. .24	c)	sic)	c)	c)	°w.n.) .28
Johs anglicus nacone .49	c)	sic)	c)	c)	°m) 49.
Johs dyaconus 49.	c)	sic)	m) .49	sic) (W	sic)
‡Win76) Isis .6	. . . . .	. . . . .	‡c)	sic) †(W	sic)
Judei plures &c .37	c)	sic)	c)	c)	°m) 37.
Judeus quidam &c .40	/Judeus quidam 58.	sic)	Judeusquidam 58.1	sic) (W	sic)
‡H74–9) Judith 16.	. . . . .	‡c)	sic) †(9	sic)	sic)
Justina impatrix .35	c)	sic)	c)	c)	°m) 35.
Karol marcellus .45	c)	sic)	c)	c)	°m) 45.
Leodegai augustudu. .44	c)	sic)	c)	c)	°w.n.) .43
Lodowicus 3 impator 50.	Lowod. rex fr. 58./	sic)	m) .50	sic) (W	sic)
Lodowic olim rex fracie .60	c)	sic)	sic)	sic)	°/Londoaldus
Lucius scdus papa .56	c)	sic)	c)	c)	°w.n.) .57
Ludus scacor repitur 15.	c)	sic)	m) .15	sic) (W	sic)
Malchus martir 32.	c)	sic)	m) 23.	sic) (W	sic)
Manasses rex iuda 13.	c)/Manicheor	Manicheor.../	c)/(Manicheor (8	sic)	sic)
Maria dei gen. nascit .24	Maria pphetissa/	c)/Maria....	Maria.../ (8 †(8	sic)	sic)
‡H74–9) Martinus eps tur. .35	†	‡Martinus...35	. . . . .	. . . . .	. . . . .

‡H74-9) maternus eps col. .28	†	‡maternus. . .28	. . . . †(8	. . .	. . .
‡H74-9) maternus morit 29.	†	‡maternus. . .29	. . . . †(8	. . .	. . .
Milo de anglei dux .48	c)	sic)	c)	c)	°m) 48.
‡H74-9) moab filius loth 5.	†	‡c) (but) mortali-tas/	. . . . †(8	. . .	. . .
Mortalitas maxima .53	c)	sic)	c)	c)	°m) 53.
‡H74-9) Mundi etates .3	†	‡c)	. . . . †(8	. . .	. . .
‡H74-9) Oda duxissa aqtanie 44.	†	‡c)	. . . . †(8	. . .	. . .
†Onias magnus 20.	c)	sic)	†w.n.) 40.	sic) †(W	sic)
Onias pius .21	c) (but) Ordo. pmos./	sic)	m) 21.	sic) (W	sic)
†Ordo canoicus 54.	c) (but) Ordo cistel./	sic)	†w.n.) 55.	sic) †(W	sic)
Ordo cistercien .55	c)	(at begin. of OR	Ordo cistel./ (8	sic)	sic)
Othoniel iudex 7.	c)	sic)	c)	c)	°m) 7.
Otto tercius impator 52.	c)	sic)	c)	c)	°m) 25.
Papirius romanus .19	c)	sic)	c)	c)	°m) 19.
†Patricius eps egipti .34	c)	sic)	†w.n.) 35	sic) †(W	sic)
Paulinus episcopus 36.	c)	sic)	c)	c)	°w.n.) 26.
†Pax eccie reddita .34	c)	sic)	†m) 34.	sic) †(W	sic)
Pestilencia magna .61	c)	sic)	c)	c)	°m) 61.
Plotinus platonicus .	n.om.)	n.&dot om.)	n.om.) (8	sic)	°n. & dot om.)
Poncianus martir .30	c)/Pon. . . papa	Pon. . . papa/	/Pon. . . papa(8	sic) (W	sic)
Praxedis virgo .27	c)	sic)	m) 27.	sic) (W	sic)
‡H74-9) Prometheus fecit .6	†	‡c)	. . . . †(8	. . .	. . .
Prothasius martir .27	c)	sic)	m) 27.	sic) (W	sic)

TABLE B. FASCICULUS TEMPORUM — COLOGNE SERIES (CONTINUED)

Index (continued):	1474. COLOGNE: THER HOERNEN		1476. WINTERS	[1478.] GOTZ	1479. QUENTELL
	8-LEAF-INDEX	9-LEAF-INDEX			
†Prudecius poeta .36	c)	sic)	†w.n.) .37	sic) †(W	sic) †(W
†Puella huit & vulnea .64	c)	sic)	†. . . .	. . . . †(W	. . . . . †(W
Pueri de almania 57.	c)/Pueri sci mich.	Pueri sci mich./	/Pueri sancti (8	sic)	sic)
Quatuor coronati .33	c)	sic)	c)	dot om.)	c)
Quirinus martir 32.	c)	sic)	c)	c)	°m) .32
‡Win76) Rabanus .48	. . . .	. . . .	‡Rabanus .48	sic) †(W	sic)
Rhea virgo filia .13	c)	sic)	c)	c)	°m) 13.
Safrus rex assirior .7	c)	sic)	c)	c)	°w.n.) .37
Salmanazar rx assirior .13	c)	sic)	c)	c)	°m) 13.
Samuel iudex .9	c)	sic)	c)	c)	w.n.) 97.
Scisma xii ecclesie 52.	c)	sic)	m) .52	sic)	sic)
Scisma xvi eccie 54.	c)	sic)	m) .54	sic)	°w.n.) .14
Seno impator 37.	c)/Seno papa	Seno papa/	/Seno papa (8	sic)	sic)
†Serapia martir et vir. 29.	c)	sic)		†m) .29	sic) †(G
Sibilla samia .14	/Sibilla cumana	/Sib.delphica	/Sibilla cumana (8	sic)	sic)
Simon fili onie .20	c)	sic)	c)		m) .02
‡H74–9) Sinodi fut sex pricip. 43.	†. . . .	†c) (but)/Sindul-phus	. . . . . †(8	. . . . .	. . . . .
†Socrates phus 17.	c)	sic)	c)	†m) .17	sic) †(G
Stigmata xpi 61.	c)	sic)	c)	c)	° . . . .
Stulta martir .36	c)	sic)	c)	c)	°w.n.) .39

Tauri eps eboraceu 28.	c)	sic)	m) .28	sic)	sic) (W
†Theodericus rex fr. .48	†w.n.) .48	c) .44	w.n.) .48 †(8	sic)	sic)
†Theodora .33	†m) .33 (& abbr.	c) Theodora et 270 mres 33.	m) .33 (& abbr. †(8	sic)	sic)
Trifon puer .32	c)	sic)	c)	c)	°m) 32.
Tripho pditor .22	c)	sic)	c)	c)	°m) 22.
†Vacat impiu .58	c)	sic)	c)	†m) 58. (W	sic) †(G
Valerius graccus .25	c)	sic)	m) 25.	sic)	sic)
Varro doctissim .23	c)	sic)	m) 23.	sic) (W	sic)
Victor miles .30	c)	sic)	c)	c)	°m) 30.
†Visiones condali .56	c)	sic)	c)	†w.n.) .50 †(W	sic) †(G
Visio horredo 56.	c)	m) .56	c) (8	sic)	sic)
†Vitalis 33.	c)	sic)	†n.om.)	sic)	sic)
†Volfranus eps 45.	c)	sic)	c)	†dot om.)	sic) †(G
†Urbanus qrtus papa .59	c)	sic)	†w.n.) .53	sic) †(W	†w.n.) 61.
‡Q79) Xpo nato reges .24	. . .	. . .	. . .	. . . .	†°Xpo nato...
Yesabel uxor ahab 10.	c)	sic)	c)	†m) .6	°m) .10
†Ysaac moritur 6.	c)	sic)	c)	c)	sic)
Ysachar filius iacob .6	c)	sic)	c)	sic) (W	°m) 6. †(G
Ysaias mart. corotur .14	c)	sic)	m) 14.	sic)	sic)
Zacharias & eliza .24	c)	sic)	m) 24.	sic) (W	sic)
Zerses rex psar 7.	w.n.) 7. (for 17.	w.n.) .7	w.n.) 7. (8	sic)	sic)

TABLE B. FASCICULUS TEMPORUM—COLOGNE SERIES (CONTINUED)

	1474. COLOGNE: ther HOERNEN		1476. WINTERS	[1478.] GOTZ	1479. QUENTELL
	8-LEAF-INDEX	9-LEAF-INDEX			
Introduction: Fol. [1a-2a], 40 lines. Fasc, tpm...cronicas coplectens incipit feliciter, at end [4]		Fols. [1a-2a], 40 lines ..., at end, but loosely clamped; "copletens" lacks second "c"	Fols. [1a-1b], disregarding the blank leaf,* 58 lines. Fasc...feliciter at end [5]	Fols. [1a-1b], disregarding the blank leaf, 58 lines. Fasc...at end [6]	Fols. [1a-1b], disregarding the blank leaf,* 58 lines. Fasc...(increased)[7]
Text: Fols. [2b-64a.] Square diagrams for the six Biblical eras [4]		Fols. [2b-64a]. Square diagrams for the six Biblical eras [4]	Fols. [1b-63b] Square diagrams... [5]	Fols. [1b-63b] Square diagrams... [6]	Fols. [1b-63b] Square diagrams... [7]
3b¶ *Beneath Noe:* cha. sem. iaphet	sic)	sic)	3a** sic)	sic)	°(each in 2 circles)
4b *Last paragraph:* ...recognosceret.§	sic)	sic)	4a †(C)...fuerut	sic) †(W	sic)
5a *Continued paragraph:* § Inueiunt...fuerunt	sic)	sic)	5b sic)	sic)	
6a *On Jacob:* Natus e ioseph...	sic)	sic)	†Iste iacob...duos.	sic)	sic)
. . . . .				sic) †(W	sic)
Diagram for Levi: c) leui	"1" inverted	. . . . .	c)	sic)	sic)
6b Ysuar /Amram	sic)	sic)	6a sic)	Amram/	°/Amram (W

7a *Near Moises:*	• • • •	6b †Incepit ano mudi. 3688.	sic)	†(W	sic)	°†... scripta sunt. reg. prio ca. xxvi
With Eleazar:	• • • •	8b †fili aaron.	sic)	†(W	sic)	°C) but A.M. inverted; B.C. 1124 m) 114.
9a *On David:* Iste dauid... scpta sut.	sic)		sic)		sic)	
A.M. *and* B.C. *dates:* (reversed in position)	sic)		sic)		sic)	
10a *On Abya:* ...regu 14. et 2 palipomenon 13.	sic)	9b	sic)		sic)	°... et 2 paral 15.

* The blank leaf is the first leaf in the first quire of the introduction. But, as copies of the Chronicle have invariably been numbered in contemporary hand according to the actual printed leaves and without including this blank leaf in the count, it seemed necessary in order to avoid confusion to disregard the blank leaf in the present collation.

¶ The folios upon which the references may be found in the two issues of the ther Hoernen edition.

** The folios upon which the references may be found in the Winters, Götz, and Quentell editions.

§ Continuation sign, representing the symbol used in the text to denote a broken paragraph.

4. With the exception of the last line, the setting of the introduction in the two issues of the ther Hoernen edition seems to be identical, even to a broken "s" in "Psal-mos," [1 b,] lines 16-17. The text of the two issues seems also to be identical with the exception of the variations which are listed above, in the collation of the 9-leaf-index issue.

5. The introduction in the Winters edition follows that of the 1474 edition but, because the paper is larger on which the book is printed, the introduction here occupies only a page and a half. The text follows the introduction on [1b,] and the text of folio [2] is differently arranged than in the 1474 edition. But at [3a] and from that page onward, the text follows [3b] etc., page for page as in the 1474 edition. Folio [63b] in this edition, for instance, is equivalent to [64a] in the 1474 edition.

6. The introduction follows that of the Winters edition and occupies 22 lines on [1 b]; and the text begins on the same page. Like the Winters edition the second folio is differently spaced than the 1474 edition but from [3a] it follows [3b] onward as the text appears, page for page, in the 1474 edition.

7. The introduction follows the usual wording with the exception of the "incipit" sentence at the end in which has been inserted: admissus ab alma univisitate Colon. . . . The first registration mark, "b3," appears on the second printed leaf. The text follows the setting of the Winters edition, [63b] in this edition is equivalent to [64a] in the 1474 ther Hoernen edition.

TABLE B.   FASCICULUS TEMPORUM — COLOGNE SERIES (CONTINUED)

| 1474. COLOGNE: THER HOERNEN | | 1476. WINTERS | [1478.] GOTZ | 1479. QUENTELL |
8-LEAF-INDEX	9-LEAF-INDEX			
Text (continued):				
12a *In the chronology:*	· · · ·	11b ‡Victoria...no impune.	†(W	sic)
15a *Page reset, i.e.:* Second paragraph: (6 lines)	(9 lines)			
On Sedechias: (4 lines)	(6 lines)			
15b *On Ludus:* Ludus.. ad emendatione	sic)	15a sic)	sic)	‡°...ad mendatione quia...pcurabat.
16a *Page reset, i.e.:* On Cyrus: (9 lines)	(8 lines)	17b sic)	sic)	
18a *On Plato:* Plato...discipul ei	sic)		sic)	‡°...discipulus... famosissimi.
21b *Near Tiberius Graccus:* · · · ·	· · · ·	21a) ‡Proubiu...otiosus sum.	†(W	sic)
22a *First paragraph:* Scipio...vicior.	sic)	21b ‡...vitior. Iste ec... soceri sui.	†(W	sic)

Location				
23a Second paragraph: Bella ciuilia...qd cu adeptu§	†sic)		C)	C)
23b Fourth line:	‡§fuit nullo pacto re-tieri...labor tu &c.%	22b †C)...labor tu &c †(?g	C)	†(W
On Octavius: Iste oct....redegit§	sic)	†C)...redegit...suis largit.	sic)	‡°...redegit...dilect orib
24a Second paragraph: §Hic e ille...largit.	sic)		sic)	sic)
24b First paragraph: Roma...& 80 milia.	sic)	24a ‡...80 milia. Mud. describit...dic gregori	. . . .	...ad labore Filias§
Third paragraph: Impatores...ad labore ...imitabat.	sic) C)	sic)	. . . .	‡°Ultima cumei.. apollo (7 lines) / ‡°Celeberrimo...mirra (with cut)
In chronology:	. . . .	. . . .	sic)	§suas...imitabantur
Below...locis suis &c	. . . .	. . . .	sic)	sic)
25a (Fols. 25–26 lacking)	C) (For...imitabat. paragraph, see 24b)	24b sic) (see 24a)		
27b Below Epaforas & Sileas:	. . . .	27a ‡Marcus...causar &c.		
34b At side: c) Imperatores	"m" inverted			

% The Thacher-LC copy of the 9-leaf-index issue lacks this continued sentence.

TABLE B. FASCICULUS TEMPORUM — COLOGNE SERIES (CONTINUED)

| 1474. COLOGNE: THER HOERNEN | | 1476. WINTERS | [1478.] GOTZ | 1479. QUENTELL |
8-LEAF-INDEX	9-LEAF-INDEX			
Text (continued):				
35b *On Theodosius* (line 11): rati..huit i	ti..huit i			
40a *First paragraph* (line 4): ...& ob illa igra	...igrati			
45a *With diagrams for:* Philippus, Anastasi, Theodosi, Gregori II.	sic)	44b †sic)	.... (45b in duplicate)	Philippus.... †(W
53b *Last paragraph:* ...bona...dices.§	sic)	53a †...dicens.Nucq... ctepti§	sic) †(W	...bona§ †(W
54a *Last paragraph:* §Nucq...abundare	sic)	53b †§bili repete...abundare.	sic) †(W	§pposituraz...dicens ...abundare
58a *Gregory:* m) xi	sic)	57b †c) non(us)	c) †(W	c)
59a *On Saint Clara:* ...canonizat...1254.	sic)	58b sic)	sic)	°...Alexandro .1354.
60a *Last paragraph:* (with heading:) .1311.	sic)	59b †sic)	(Without date.)	°1311. †(W
Page reset, i.e.: (last line) huit vocabuln hoc	no...vobulu hoc			

61a *Page reset, i.e.:* (*last line*) imus.	sta maxim · sic)	61a sic)	sic)	°....
61b *Stigmata xpi*...	sic)	63b ‡...terra ortu...in Magutia	sic) †(W	sic)
64a *On printing:* Artifices...multiplicant i tra	sic)	‡....	.... †(W	....
Third paragraph: Puella noie...erat.		†....	sic) †(W	sic)
On Calixtus: ...uno elapso. Ipe... Katherina de senis 1461.	sic)	‡...uno elapso...predicator.	sic) †(W	sic)
On Pius: ...morit...augusti.	sic)	‡...augusti. Ipse...de Senis. 63b (*continued*)	sic)	sic)
64a *Colophon:* (5 lines, red.) Impressa est...	sic) (For full text see Annmary Brown Memorial Catalogue)	(7 lines, black.) Opusculu...(see AmBM Cat.)	.... (see below)	(7 lines, black.) Opusculum...(Text is followed in 1480 edition. See AmBM Cat.)
Device, red.	sic)	*Device, black.*	.... (see below)	°Beginning of the index. (See Index-table, above.)
64b *Blank*	sic)	64a *Blank*	†11 paragraphs added. *Colophon:* (6 lines, black.) Fasciculus... (see AmBM Cat.) *Device, black* (believed to have been engraved on metal).	

TABLE C. FASCICULUS TEMPORUM—LOUVAIN-VENICE SERIES*

Summary of the collation of the 8-leaf and 9-leaf-index issues of the 1474. Cologne: ther Hoernen edition with:

1476. LOUVAIN: VELDENER	1479. VENICE: WALCH
Annmary Brown Memorial copy Sm. fol. Without sigs. and leaf numbers. 72 ll.	Annmary Brown Memorial copy Sm. fol. With printed leaf numbers on rectos, excluding index 72 ll., the first blank (wanting)

Index:

Fol. [ia–viiib], 3 col., 48, 49 lines.

The Louvain index contains the "Abdon iudex" entry which appears in the 8-leaf issue but not in the 9-leaf; and like the 8-leaf, it gives the shortened form of the "Theodora" entry and omits the seventeen entries peculiar to the 9-leaf-index issue. In fact, in all of the determining points of variation between the two issues, it follows the 8-leaf with the exception of two minor variations which from their nature might well have been made by the editor of the Louvain edition without consulting another volume.

In the index, five errors and two minor variations of its own have been noted.

Fol. [iia–viiib], 3 col., 55 lines.

The 1479 edition follows the 8-leaf index in all respects excepting one correction which might have been made by Walch himself, and the insertion of entries for Pope Alexander I and Pope Alexander II which, although omitted in the 8-leaf index, appear in the 9-leaf. Here again, the editor or printer might well have noticed the omissions from among the several Alexanders, and have inserted the entries himself.

Since the five errors noted in the Louvain are not here repeated and one of the points corrected in the Louvain edition here gives the incorrect numbering of the 8-leaf issue, it seems that the Walch index must have been set direct from the 8-leaf-index issue.

The Walch index offers five new variations which, in turn, are repeated in Ratdolt's 1480 edition.

Introduction:

Fol. [1a–2a], 40 lines.

The text of the introduction follows that of the 1474 ther Hoernen edition, with variations in spelling.

Fasc . . . feliciter, at end.

Text:

Fol. [2b–64a]. Circular diagrams.

The text contains the continued half sentence, on 23a. (For discussion, see above on pages 418–419 of this volume.)

Fol. 64a contains the "Puella nomine styna" paragraph which appears in the 1474, ther Hoernen edition but is omitted in subsequent editions issued at Cologne.

The Louvain edition adds twenty paragraphs to the text and corrects two minor misprints.

Colophon dated: .M.cccc.lxxvi. qrto kaledas ianuarias. . . .

(For full colophon, see AmBM Cat.) With device.

Fol. 1a–2a, 49 lines and numerals. As the type is small, the text occupies only 16 lines on 2a, the remainder of which is blank.

The number 5199 in its second appearance is misprinted 5169, a misprint which is copied in Ratdolt's edition of the following year.

Fasc . . . feliciter, headline on 2b.

Fol. 2b–64a. Circular diagrams.

The text follows the usual reading, although in certain cases of ambiguity the wording is sometimes altered. Typographically the book is better than the 1474 edition, although historically not so interesting since it obviously is further from the form of the author's manuscript compilation.

In the first variation between the 8-leaf issue and the Louvain edition, the Walch follows the 8-leaf. Although it gives the substance of Louvain's first added paragraph, it omits the second. From that point on, however, it gives all of Louvain's added paragraphs and includes the continued half sentence on 23b. and the "Puella" paragraph.

Twenty-three minor variations are introduced by Walch and one new paragraph — all of which are repeated in the Ratdolt edition of 1480, this added paragraph being rewritten.

(For colophon, see AmBM Cat.) Without device.

---

* The table of collations, from which this summary was made, is on file at the Annmary Brown Memorial.

TABLE D.   SPEIER SERIES*

Summary of the collation of the

1474. COLOGNE: ther HOERNEN		1477. SPEIER: DRACH
8-Leaf-Index Issue	9-Leaf-Index Issue	Annmary Brown Memorial copy. Sm. fol. Without sigs. & leaf numbers. 74 ll., the first blank.

Index:

Fol. [11a–xa], 3 col., 50, 51 lines.

The appearance of the "Abdon iudex" entry, which is in the 8-leaf but not in the 9-leaf index, indicates that the 8-leaf index must have been consulted in setting up the Speier edition. This thesis is further substantiated by the fact that the Speier edition follows the reading of the 8-leaf index in two significant errors and in nineteen minor variations.

On the other hand, the Speier edition contains sixteen of the seventeen entries peculiar to the 9-leaf issue and not appearing in the 8-leaf; and it follows the 9-leaf in an important correction and in eight minor variations — six of which are corrections, and two of which (occasioned by the transposing of the dot accompanying the leaf number) are without significance. Of the sixteen entries taken from the 9-leaf issue, one in the Speier edition is out of alphabet; two are added at the end of sections; and one is inserted in the place which alphabetically belongs to the only entry not included from the seventeen peculiar to the 9-leaf issue.

All of which weighed together seems to indicate that copy was set first of all from the 8-leaf issue, and that subsequently additional entries from the 9-leaf issue were inserted, plus such corrections as the editor chanced to notice.

In itself, the Speier index adds two entries not found in other editions, and it has twenty-five minor variations in leaf numbers or in arrangement.

Introduction:

Fol. [1a–2a], 42 lines.   Fasc. . . feliciter, at beginning.

The text follows that of the 1474 edition though without regard to abbreviations; on the first two pages the words are spelled more fully and on the third page they are much more abbreviated than in the 1474 edition.

Text:

Fol. [2b–64b], square diagrams.

The text follows that of the 1474 edition, excepting that the paragraphs are frequently arranged differently upon the page and the spelling is variant throughout. With regard to the only pertinent variation between the texts of the 8-leaf and the 9-leaf issues of the 1474 edition, the continued sentence of which half is omitted in the 8-leaf issue appears in full in the Speier edition. The "Puella" paragraph appears on 64a.

At the end, the Speier edition adds three new paragraphs and a new colophon. (For the latter, see AmBM Cat). With device.

* The table of collations, from which this summary was made, is on file at the Annmary Brown Memorial.